Irma F'

W9-CNO-208

Building
Masterpiece
Miniatures

Building

Masterpiece

Miniatures

Joseph Daniele

Stackpole Books

BUILDING MASTERPIECE MINIATURES
Copyright © 1980 by Joseph Daniele
Published by
STACKPOLE BOOKS
Cameron and Kelker Streets
P.O. Box 1831
Harrisburg, Pa. 17105

First printing, January 1980
Second printing, October 1980

Published simultaneously in Don Mills, Ontario, Canada
by Thomas Nelson & Sons, Ltd.

Printed in the U.S.A.

Library of Congress Cataloging in Publication Data

Daniele, Joseph William.
  Building masterpiece miniatures.

  Includes index.
  1. Miniature craft. 2. Doll-houses. I. Title.
TT178.D36 1979   745.59   79-10631
ISBN 0-8117-0306-1

To the four women in my life:
My wife Jean
and my daughters Sharon, Lanore, and Daria.
Thank you
for allowing my visits
into that very special world
reserved for little girls.
Each in your own unique way
helped to make this book possible.

Contents

SECTION TWO

Display Cases and Miniature Shops

SECTION THREE

Miniature Houses

SECTION FOUR

Suppliers, Organizations, and Publications

Preface

From the same block of marble, one man creates artistry, while another makes cobblestones. Some people say the form is already in the stone; the worker merely releases this form with his tools. The eventual outcome lies within the intention, ability, and eyes of the artist. The creative result often reflects the prevailing times, available technology, and the character and purpose of the individual worker. It is within this realm that specific architectural characterization falls. In each era, treatment of the same basic building materials varies. What the artists of a particular era do with these same materials is what makes the construction style unique.

The muse or phantom that rules over originals and reproductions is the memory of people and time long passed. Many houses retain some of the spirit of the lives they once contained and develop personalities of their own.

Small cosmetic differences—a special treatment of glass and wood, a cascade of moldings—all blend to create singular individuality.

Most houses, full or miniature size, are made from the same basic building materials: timbers, shingles, bricks, stone, windows, doors, and moldings. What makes a house a unique type, whether Victorian, colonial, early American, or contemporary, is the way the basic materials are put together.

Colonial style is one of basic functionalism—plain with a minimum of intricate moldings or lathe turnings. This style is reflected in the millwork and furnishings in the homes. Batten doors, strap hinges, plain board casings, and simple cornices adorn most frontier colonial houses.

The early American house incorporates a partial return to classical Greek and Roman architecture. Perfect balance and form appear

Interior of miniature Victorian house (Courtesy H. L. Childs)

as symmetry; and built-up cyma-curve moldings, detail work, and crown molds grace windows, doors, and room interiors, as well as exteriors. Raised-panel wainscotting and doors express the growth of the craftsman's technology and expertise.

The Victorian style rivals the elaborate ornamentation of the baroque period. Massive scrolls, molds, reliefs, and intricate turnings were part of the Victorian house's exterior and interior furnishings. Stained and etched glass brought artistic expression and color to ordinary millwork and furniture. This was an era when form overshadowed function.

One of the chief aims of this book is to provide clear and precise diagrams for the reproduction of such architectural styles in miniature homes, rooms, and shops. This book provides readers with the basic construction concepts needed for making the designs found in the text. While we cannot all possess the eye or skill of a Michelangelo or Rodin, we can very often follow the line and designs laid out by past or present masters.

The original colonial, early American, Victorian, and contemporary construction design have been laid out by our predecessors, and this book has been developed around their concepts. Some minor adjustments have been made where feasible or expedient to the construction of miniatures. However, style and design have not been knowingly forsaken. The original flavor has been preserved wherever possible, and a concentrated effort has been made to retain the charm and grace that made these particular styles a pleasant part of our heritage and history.

Normal houses spring from brute strength and force; straining muscles deliver heavy hammer blows to drive framing timbers and long spikes into place. But force is the major enemy of miniature homes. Miniature work must flow together smoothly and gently, almost like a child's kiss or a butterfly's wing touching a leaf.

The reduction in the size of materials does not equally reduce the required skill or the degree of difficulty. In many cases, the smaller the work the more difficult it becomes. Miniaturists often find that fingers seem too large and thick. The thin wood splits under the slightest pressure. The average materials are too bulky for the small work. Eyesight becomes strained, and even special tools are too cumbersome to do the work. And so the problems go on. But once the particular furnishing, miniature room, or house is completed, the individual's satisfaction is beyond expression.

Seventeen-room miniature Victorian house (Courtesy H. L. Childs)

VICTORIAN
ROCOCO
CIRCA 1850-1880

Victorian Room (Courtesy Sonia Messer Imports)

The miniaturist's three greatest assets are desire, invention, and imagination. The recommended materials and procedures expressed in the following pages have been developed from exploration, rejection, experimentation, and eventual selection. These suggestions should be used merely as a guide; many readers will have their own discoveries or inventions that will work just as well or surpass those expressed here.

New enthusiasts should start off slowly, and not attempt to buy every tool or machine offered. However, what is purchased should be of good quality. Such starting tools will become the main items in all future miniature making.

Most of the following reproductions can be made with a minimum of hand tools, while some may require the basic machine tools common to every home workshop. It is best to feel one's way through several pieces. If you

then find that you have developed a new interest, add to the tool inventory as your progress and needs dictate.

Miniature making is now the third largest hobby in America and growing everyday. Many national and local organizations and clubs have been founded so that members can meet, correspond, and lend assistance to one another. Workshops, clinics, and meetings are held across the nation often with guest experts or company representatives who offer suggestions and possible construction advice.

The scope of miniature making is wide. Individual or group period pieces can be made; single room settings or a completely furnished house are all possible areas for development. The following drawings and instructions have been designed to fulfill these anticipated needs. This book covers a time period from the early 1700s to the present, with different styles and options included. Where regional styles are presented, typical sizes are given so that readers can transfer their own area concepts or forms into the miniatures.

As this book developed on the drawing board, I found that not every area could be covered in detail. To do so would require several volumes. Just to cover all the different types of door and window styles alone would be a massive undertaking. Compromise became the ultimate censor. Construction techniques and procedures are the same regardless of particular style, form, or size. Sample styles and general sizes are given in the drawings; readers can easily transfer such information to fit any type of unit they desire.

A governing factor in the ultimate content selection of this book was the avoidance of projects requiring special machinery. Ordinary tools, skills, materials, and fasteners are suggested and used as the criteria for all reproductions included in this text.

Readers should draw out scale plans for any special millwork such as windows, doors, trim, or wainscotting. Particular period styles can then be developed with the needed adjustments made, before the actual construction starts.

If several pieces of the same item are to be made, the time taken to construct a jig proves well worth the effort both in the ease of construction and the insurance of consistency. Some miniature experts feel that the real art of miniature making is in the construction of the jig. Once the correct jig is made, the pieces made from the jig will also be correct.

The first part of this book deals with general construction information. Tools, fasteners, stock, millwork, and procedures, which will be utilized in later construction plans, are covered here.

In construction there are several options open to miniature makers: (1) the outright purchase of completely finished windows, doors, or furnishings; (2) the purchase of precut, premilled stock for construction of windows,

doors, or furnishings in kit form; and (3) the construction of all millwork, moldings, furnishings, and shops from common everyday materials. This book was designed expressly for those working with kits or building from scratch. However, suppliers of finished products are also listed.

Section two of this book presents sample shadow boxes, single room settings, and cottage-industry shops of various time periods. Because some collectors want only a sample exhibit, shadow boxes, picture frame cases, and protective glass display areas are featured. For collectors who want to concentrate on larger, specialized projects, plans are provided for such projects as a general store, a carpenter's shop, an ice cream parlor. While all possible areas cannot be duplicated in detail, the basic information provided is applicable to any situation or building.

Section three concentrates on actual multiple room dwellings. Included is a house styled after Paul Revere's home, a saltbox house of the early American period, a Victorian house, and a contemporary miniature house offered in colonial or ranch styling. Detailed plans are provided with construction notes for the millwork in the style of a particular architectural period. Once again, the construction principles involved in this section are adaptable to any house, regardless of size, design, or intention.

Section four lists many commercial miniature supplies and companies, plus national organizations, magazines, and clubs. Many of these suppliers offer customers catalogs of their materials and a library of current miniature supplies, furnishings, and specialized items. These are an immense aid to the miniature maker and collector. Very few items are not made in miniature by someone, somewhere. Often the most difficult part is locating the source for particular articles. This section was designed to answer those needs.

With the miniature hobby growing so quickly, more and more local hobby and craft stores now carry a full line of miniature construction materials. If such retail outlets do not have the desired materials, then the reader has the option of ordering needed stock by mail from the companies listed.

Just as normal houses are not built in a week or a month, miniature pieces are not constructed overnight. However, when finished, miniatures have a special magic all their own. They have a way of becoming treasures, perhaps because they represent personal skill, dedication, and perseverance. Miniatures are a mixture of history and fantasy, and they have a special aura all their own. They take one back to childhood paths along memories' archives to revisit and own, "once upon a time."

I have a great many people and organizations to personally thank for their immense help in developing this book. Various historical associations provided the authentic photographs and models. National and regional miniature businesses provided photographs and information, and private miniature enthusiasts gave freely of their advice, consent, and encouragement. I have been blessed with the help of an excellent publishing editorial staff and an understanding wife. To one and all I owe my sincere gratitude and appreciation.

SECTION ONE

Miniature Construction

1. *Scale, Tools, and Materials*

SCALE

The most common scale used by miniaturists is the $1/12$th or one inch equals one foot reduction. Most premade furnishings, fixtures, and millwork are offered in this scale size. Working on this reduced scale requires a little more concentration and practice.

When measurements are even, such as 36 inches or 18 inches, the reduced scaling is relatively simple; 36 inches reduces to 3 inches, and 18 inches reduces to 1½ inches on the $1/12$th scale. However, not all measurements are even, and one inch does not divide readily into twelve equal parts.

Special miniature $1/12$th scales are available in many retail outlets and hobby shops. Architect scales are divided or scaled into a $1/12$th series designated as one inch on the rule. See figure 1–4. The architect scale has only one sample

inch divided into twelfths. The remainder of the scale is divided into full-inch markings, which equal one foot, and half-inch markings, which equal six inches.

Any measurement under one foot is taken from the sample fraction scale. Any measurement over one foot is taken from the nearest foot mark with the inches added on. Figure 1–3 shows an example of a full-size, blanket-chest plan being scaled down to the $1/12$th miniature size.

The first measurement (A) is a drawer that measures 8 inches full-scale. The corresponding $1/12$th measurement is found in the foot fraction division on the left-hand side of the scale. Quarter, half, and full inches are marked, and full inches are designated in multiples of three: 0, 3, 6, and 9. Figure 1–3, part A, shows the 8-inch measurement in miniature scale.

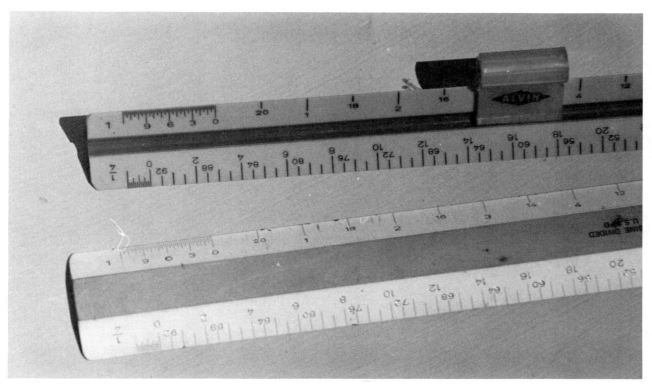

Fig. 1–1.   Architect scales showing ¹/₁₂-inch scale

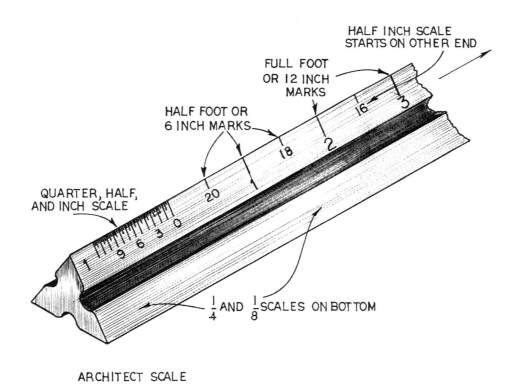

HALF INCH SCALE
STARTS ON OTHER END

FULL FOOT
OR 12 INCH
MARKS

HALF FOOT OR
6 INCH MARKS

QUARTER, HALF,
AND INCH SCALE

$\frac{1}{4}$ AND $\frac{1}{8}$ SCALES ON BOTTOM

ARCHITECT SCALE

Fig. 1–2.   Architect scale

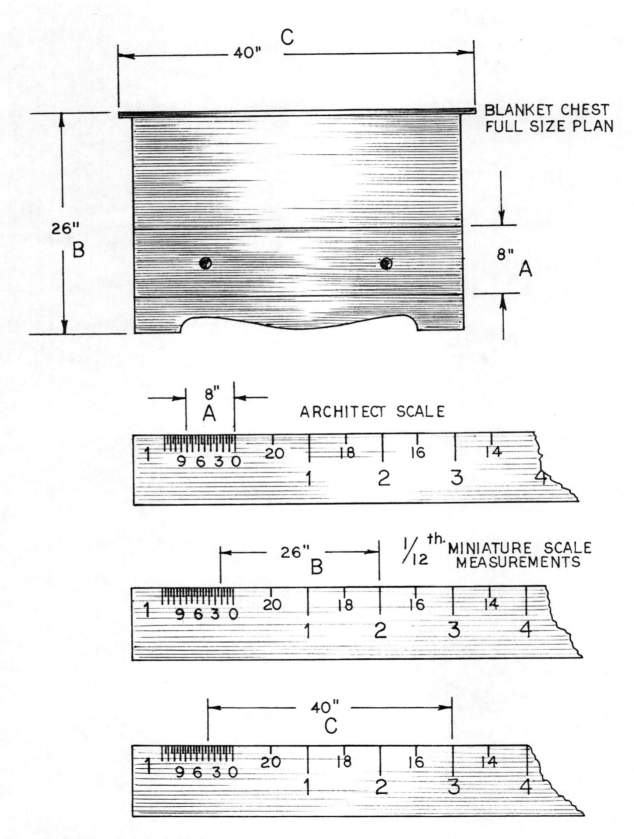

Fig. 1–3. *Reducing the scale of a blanket chest*

18

The second measurement (B) is the chest height of 26 inches. The two-foot (24 inches) mark is picked up on the architect scale, and two of the fraction inches are added to make up the total size: 24 inches + 2 inches = 26 inches. See part B in figure 1–5.

The third measurement (C) is the chest top of 40 inches. Again, the major part of the measurement is picked up at the three-foot mark (36 inches), and four of the fraction inches are added to make up the required size: 36 inches + 4 inches = 40 inches. See part C in figure 1–3.

By employing the 1/12th scale, any full-size plan, regardless of size, can be reduced easily for miniature making. There are many more period stylebooks available on full-size furniture than on a miniature size, and such plans

can be used to design and make the small furnishings. It is recommended in the beginning that the reader make scale drawings for his intended construction. In time, the miniaturist can reduce the size and draw the patterns directly on the wood stock.

The various scales on the architect ruler are an immense aid in dividing a given space into equal parts, such as the muntins of a window sash. Rather than measuring the space and dividing by the number of muntins desired, select any scale that is greater than the width of the space and place the scale on any angle to obtain the desired division.

In figure 1–4 a sample window requires three equal spaces. The 1/12th scale is selected, and the ruler is placed over the space at an angle

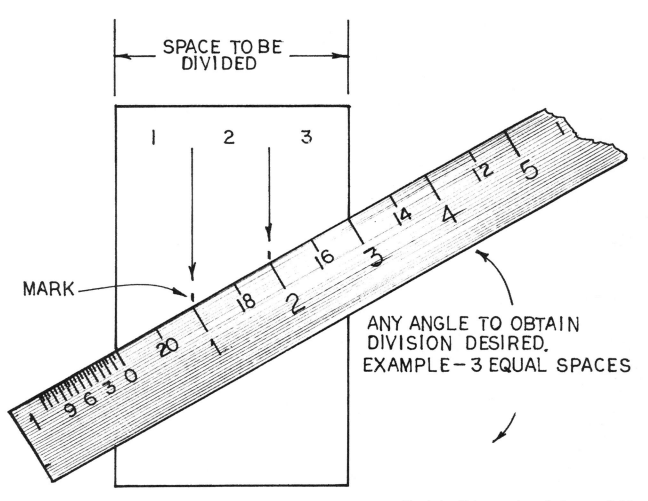

Fig. 1–4. *Using a scale to obtain space division*

MINIATURE HUTCH TABLE

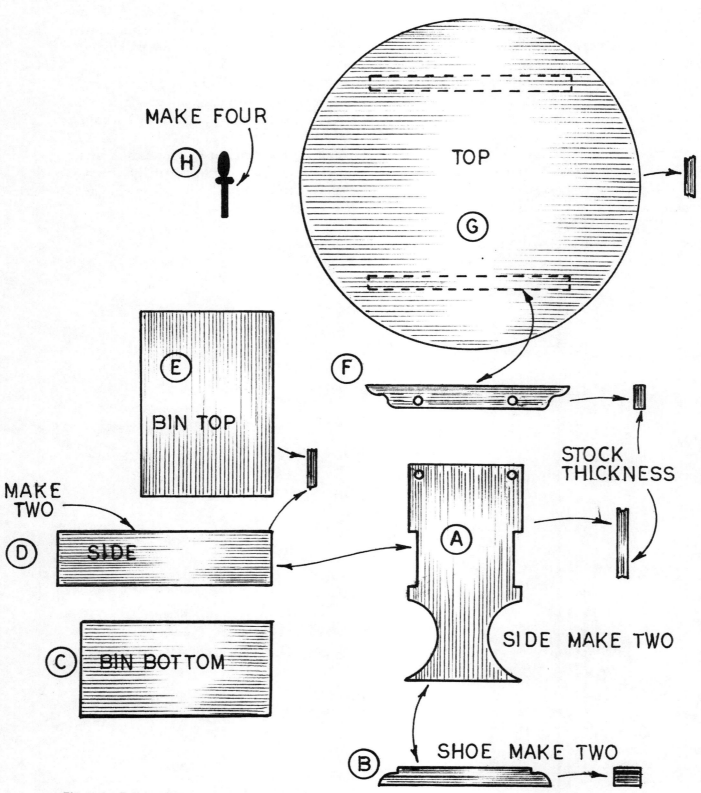

Fig. 1–5. *Patterns for miniature table and chair*

that offers the division required: 0 to 3. In this case, whole numbers are used with the zero on the left-hand side and the number three on the right-hand side. Marks are made on the full-inch markings at 1 and 2, and a line is drawn with a tri-square at these markings. The result is three (or any number) equal divisions without any complicated mathematics or any chance of error.

Actual Size Patterns

One of the best methods of constructing miniatures from actual size dimensions is to lay out actual size miniature patterns. Most of the reduction work, sample curves, scrolls, and turning profiles can be made on heavy gauge paper, where changes and corrections can be made with relative ease. The resulting patterns can then be stored, saved, and used again. Even more important, the pattern lets you see exactly what the miniature will look like before construction.

A small drawing board, a T square, a 45-degree or 30/60-degree angle, and a few French curves are all that are required. Tape a piece of drafting paper to the drawing board. With the T square, draw a horizontal line across the paper, and draw a vertical line with the T square and one of the angles. This creates a true right angle and a place from which to start drawing the patterns. After the various parts are drawn, use a divider to insure correct sizing by checking each part where it meets another.

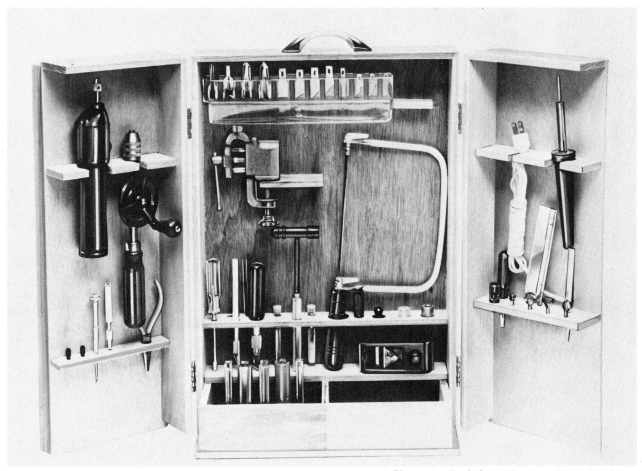

Fig. 1–6. Tool chest (Courtesy X-acto Tool Co.)

21

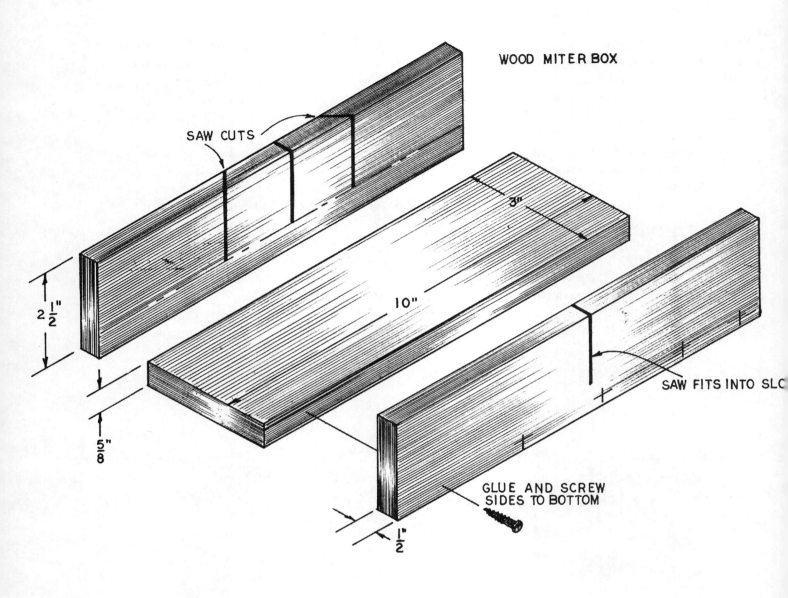

WOOD MITER BOX

SAW CUTS

3"

10"

2 1/2"

5/8"

1/2"

SAW FITS INTO SLO

GLUE AND SCREW
SIDES TO BOTTOM

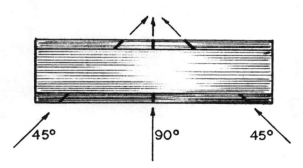

45°   90°   45°

Fig. 1–7. *Shopmade miter box*

The finished patterns can then be cut from the paper, or the patterns themselves can be traced directly onto the wood stock.

TOOL SELECTION

Beginning miniaturists should not invest too heavily in machine tools or expensive hand tools until they are certain such work offers the ultimate goal—a sense of achievement and satisfaction for the worker. Miniature making demands a certain discipline that not every craftsman is willing to give, and an expensive collection of specialized tools could become unused and wasted. The new miniaturist should start off with just the basic hand tools. Many of them are already on hand in the average household, and tools can be added to this inventory as the means and needs dictate.

Fig. 1–8.   Drill and bench mount

Primary Tools

1. Ruler of preferably the architect or miniature scale. Both of these rulers have a 1/12th divided scale.
2. Small miter box and razor saw. (Miter box can be shop made from scrap wood.)
3. Files: one 10-inch rat-tail or round, one 12-inch flat with cutting edges, one 10-inch knife file, and one 8-inch triangle file.
4. Set of X-acto knives.
5. Pair of long-nosed pliers with side cutters.
6. Hobby clamps: plastic, screw, or spring type. Several snap-type clothes pins.
7. Assorted drill bits (metal cutting): typical sizes are 1/32, 3/32, 1/16, and 1/8 inch. Hand (egg beater type) or finger drill.
8. Tweezers, heavy duty.
9. Small T square, 45-degree angle, and small drawing board.
10. Small tri-square or combination square.
11. Divider and compass.
12. Circle template.

Secondary Tool List

1. Bench or table vise, vacuum or clamp type.
2. Hammer, 10 ounce.
3. Jeweler's screwdriver set.
4. Coping and dovetail saws.
5. Magnifier, bench type.
6. Block plane.

Suggested Power Tools

1. Electric or battery drill 3/8-inch. (This can double as a small lathe.)
2. Electric saber saw.
3. Orbital sander.
4. Hobby-type electric jig or scroll saw, table-top model.
5. Moto grinder and assorted bits.
6. Miniature lathe: Dramel, Moto, Sears.
7. Table saw with planer blade.
8. Table-top band or jig saw.

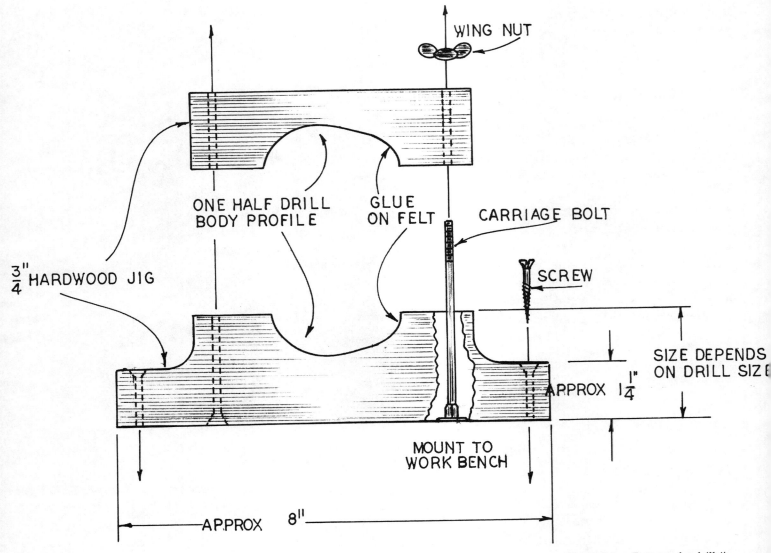

WING NUT

ONE HALF DRILL
BODY PROFILE

GLUE
ON FELT

CARRIAGE BOLT

SCREW

$\frac{3}{4}$" HARDWOOD JIG

SIZE DEPENDS
ON DRILL SIZE

APPROX $1\frac{1}{4}$"

MOUNT TO
WORK BENCH

APPROX ——— 8" ———

Fig. 1–9A.   Patterns for drill jig

Drill Lathe

The ordinary electric drill can be used as a type of lathe for certain work. The only requirement is that the electric drill has a trigger lock. The lock is a device for continuous operation of the drill. One of the main advantages of using a drill as a lathe is the common three-jaw chuck. With this chuck, any size dowel can be centered and held. A ⅛-inch to 1/16-inch dowel, often too small to insert evenly in a chuckless model or miniature lathe, can be turned in the drill chuck. Most of the design work on small dowels, such as chair legs, can be performed with files and sandpaper.

A jig or vise must be used to hold the drill to a work bench. The jig is made of ¾-inch hardwood or plywood with the bottom section screwed or clamped to a bench. The drill chuck should extend over the bench to allow free access for turnings.

Construction of a Drill Jig

Select two pieces of ¾-inch by 3-inch by 8-inch hardwood or plywood. With a jig or

24

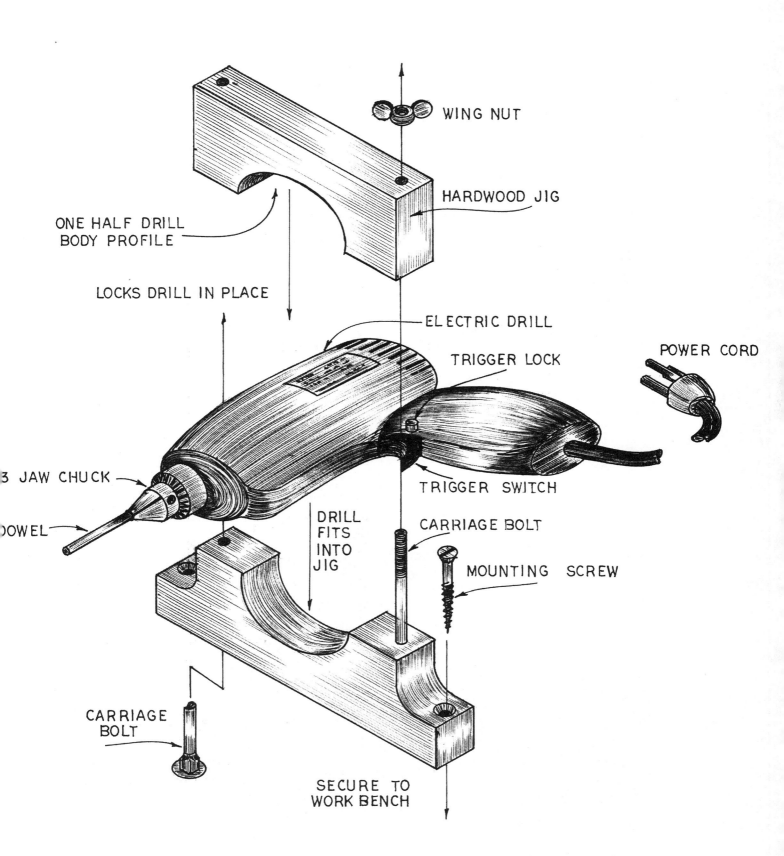

WING NUT

HARDWOOD JIG

ONE HALF DRILL
BODY PROFILE

LOCKS DRILL IN PLACE

ELECTRIC DRILL

TRIGGER LOCK

POWER CORD

3 JAW CHUCK

TRIGGER SWITCH

DOWEL

DRILL
FITS
INTO
JIG

CARRIAGE BOLT

MOUNTING SCREW

CARRIAGE
BOLT

SECURE TO
WORK BENCH

Fig. 1–9B.   Drill-jig assembly

25

Fig. 1–10.   Bedroom (Courtesy Realife Miniatures)

Fig. 1–11.   Library kit (Courtesy Realife Miniatures)

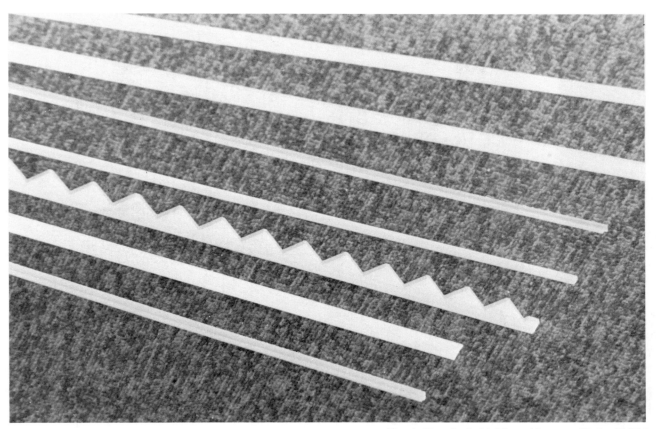

Fig. 1–12. *Scale Moldings (Courtesy H. L. Childs)*

saber saw, cut out one-half of the drill-body profile on each piece of stock where the two pieces will join together. Drill two counter-bore, screw-mount holes into the bottom piece. Drill ¼-inch holes through both jig pieces for the carriage bolts. Line the profile cuts with felt or canvas to prevent marring the drill. Insert two carriage bolts, ¼ inch in diameter and 5 inches long, into the lower jig block from the bottom up. Screw this block into the work bench. Insert the drill into the jig bottom and install the jig top over the carriage bolts. Tighten the blocks and drill together with wing nuts and large washers on the bolt tops.

Place the desired piece of dowel into the drill chuck, and plug in the drill. Lock the power switch on for full continuous operation.

Make the desired designs with files and sandpaper on the dowel. On very thin or small-diameter pieces of dowel, the fingers of the left hand should support the rotating work from underneath. After a little practice, very fine turnings can be achieved on this device. Small door knobs, drawer pulls, or trammel pins can also be made using this method. Some small metal turnings can also be made on this lathe-type device using files. Most hobby stores carry hardwood dowels as well as small brass or aluminum round stock.

MATERIALS

The materials for making miniatures are available from three sources. Furniture and house units can be purchased precut in kit form. Several large suppliers offer such kits for sale through hobby and craft outlets. In these kits, every piece of required stock has been cut

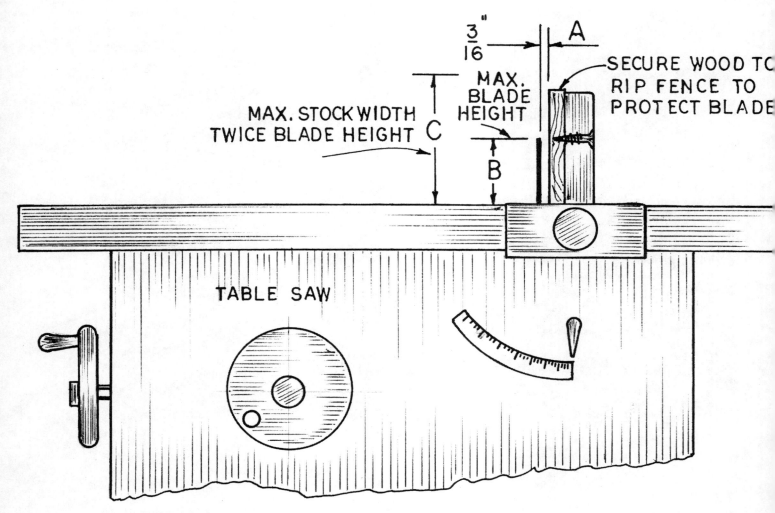

$\frac{3}{16}''$

MAX. BLADE HEIGHT

A

SECURE WOOD TO RIP FENCE TO PROTECT BLADE

MAX. STOCK WIDTH TWICE BLADE HEIGHT C

B

TABLE SAW

Fig. 1–13A. Set-up for table saw

and milled to fit together. All that remains is to finish fit all the pieces, then glue and assemble the selected item.

A second source is the several commercial companies, which offer scale-size lumberyard supplies. In effect, the miniaturist can find just about everything that the average contractor or "do-it-yourselfer" can find in normal lumberyards, but on a ¹/₁₂th scale. The miniature lumberyards carry flooring, clapboard, shingles, windows, doors and frames, moldings, and precut wood stock into various widths and thicknesses. Hobby or craft outlets also carry several assorted sizes of balsa and basswood, which can be utilized by the miniaturist. The soft balsa is not recommended for long-last-

ing miniatures. This soft wood is very fragile and will not, as a rule, endure normal handling except in sealed room settings. Basswood, however, is very compatible to miniature making. Basswood has a nondescript grain and cuts easily in either direction. Basswood sands and forms well, and accepts stains and finishes readily.

The third and one of the best and least expensive methods to obtain the miniature stock is to recut your own from normal lumberyard supplies. This type of operation requires the use of an average table saw. Any species of wood available can be cut to sizes suggested for each reproduction or for miniature house supplies.

Resawing Normal Stock

The procedure for resawing normal stock is a simple operation, and the total recut width size is limited to twice the total blade height of the particular table saw. Care should be taken in the selections of stock to be resawed. Obtain clear, knot-free boards, and select lumber without a pronounced grain. The reasons are obvious. Both the pronounced grain, which intensifies after staining, and the knots are out of scale for miniature furnishings and house construction.

To recut standard stock, rip the boards to a width just under twice the height of the maximum table-saw blade (B), and set the table saw's rip fence at the desired thickness from the saw blade (A). It is best to make the cut

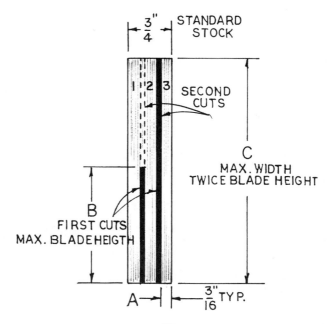

Fig. 1–13B.   Sample saw cuts

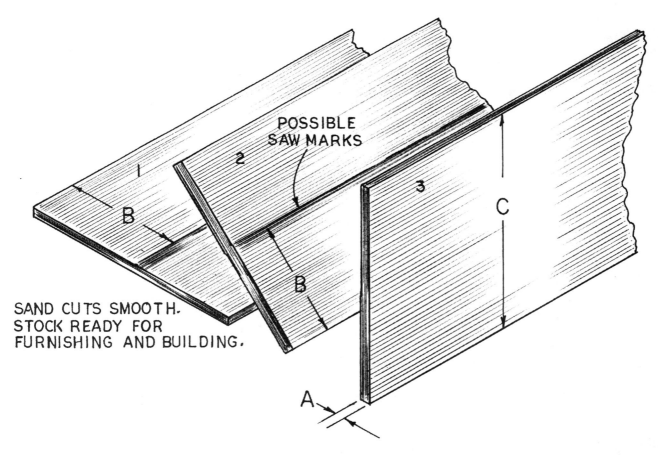

SAND CUTS SMOOTH.
STOCK READY FOR
FURNISHING AND BUILDING.

Fig. 1–14.   Resawed strips

Fig. 1–15.   *Furniture made from resawed stock*

thickness a little greater than the desired finished size, because sanding will be required to resmooth the saw-cut side. Rip the standard stock to the preset thickness.

The first cut should be slightly more than halfway through the stock width. See figure 1–13A. Reverse the board and rip the stock again. The two saw cuts will meet somewhere around the center of the board. A slight saw bead may form along this cut depending upon the uniformity of the board and method of rip feeding. Meeting beads and rough saw-cut marks can be sanded away to create a smooth surface.

A smoother cut can be obtained by using a planer-type blade on the table saw. Such a blade is recommended when ripping clapboards or trim, because saw-tooth marks are, as a rule, eliminated. Planer blades do not have a pronounced set and therefore require a slower feed speed. (The feed speed refers to the speed at which a board is pushed through the cutting surface of the moving blade.)

A large percentage of the required furniture stock does not demand excessive width, and very often the furnishing stock can be reripped with a single pass on the table saw. By employing the resaw or reripped method of obtaining stock, often three or more miniature-size strips of lumber can be obtained from a normal ¾-inch board. The number of finish pieces depends upon the type of saw blade used and the desired thickness of the finished stock.

After the stock has been resawed, lay the smooth side down on a work bench. If a pronounced saw bead remains on the resawed side, remove as much of this bead as possible with a block plane. Sand the entire rough surface with a belt or orbital sander. Sandpaper wrapped around a square piece of wood will also work very well. Sand in the direction of the grain only. After both sides of the wood stock are smooth, the lumber is ready for final cutting and forming.

2. *Flooring, Wainscotting, and Moldings*

FLOORING

The resawing method discussed in the previous chapter works very well for manufacturing hardwood flooring for miniature houses or room settings. The finished, resawed wood is glued over the basic plywood base with the smoothest side down. Use any good commercial white resin glue. For flooring, glue the wide strips directly to the plywood base. Edge match all the strips until the complete floor is covered. Small brads or bank pins can be used to hold the wood strips in place until the complete floor can be clamped under pressure. Allow the glue to set under this clamp pressure for the time suggested by the glue manufacturer. Remove the clamps. With a belt or orbital sander, smooth the entire floor surface. Mark off the desired random or even plank flooring widths on the sanded surface. Score the floor-

ing with a sharp chisel or knife to resemble individual boards. Staining and finishing the floor emphasizes the scorings, so the lines need not be deep. See figure 1–16.

After the flooring is scored lengthwise, mark the boards for the random end matches. Planks or boards seldom come in lengths exceeding sixteen feet, and most flooring is made up of shorter lengths: 4, 6, 8, 10, or 12-foot lengths are the average. Once the end matches are finished, a pegged effect can be achieved by marking the end matches with a blunted 4d finishing nail. Once again, staining will accent the scoring and pegging effects.

WAINSCOTTING

The same resawed method is used to create wood-paneled walls and wainscotting for

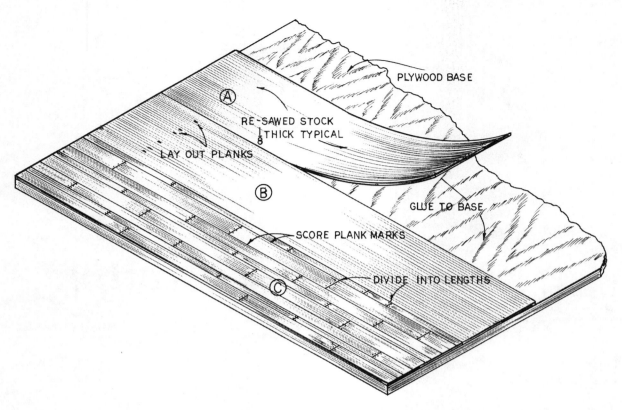

Fig. 1–16.   *Scale flooring made from resawed stock*

SCORE $\frac{1''}{8}$ PANELS INTO BOARDS

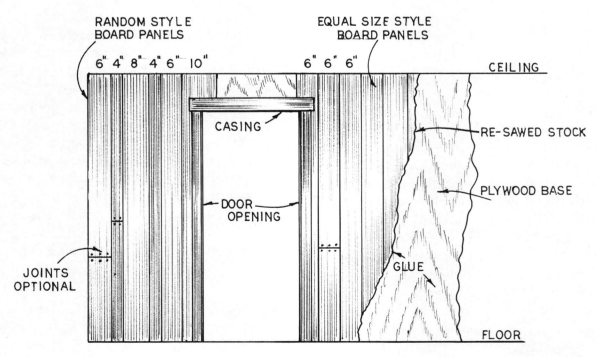

Fig. 1–17.   *Vertical resawed panels*

Fig. 1–18.   Sample wainscotting (Courtesy Sonia Messer Imports)

miniature rooms. The same fastening procedures are used as in the flooring process except the grain runs in a vertical position. Resawed panel stock can be scored into equal or random boards for full or half-wall wainscotting. Wainscotting is a wood covering placed on interior room walls. The wainscotting can be vertical or horizontal boards; raised panels with stiles and rails; simple chair rail and molding; or in the case of contemporary homes, plywood panels.

Board wainscotting

Full or partial wall coverings of vertical or horizontal boards are the easiest to construct. The general instructions offered for construction of plank flooring also apply to scale-model wainscotting. Strips of ⅛-inch by 2, 3, 4, or 5-inch stock are cut to cover the height of the whole wall or any part.

After the strips have been cut to size, dry fit the stock to the wall to be covered. Stock can be held in place temporarily with bank pins until

the whole wall is fitted. Remove the rough stock and sand the outer surface smooth. Score the sanded stock to resemble various width boards.

Very often late colonial or early American wainscotting featured equal width boards: 6, 8, or 10 inches wide. See figure 1–20. Random width boards were very popular in early colonial construction, and the strips can be scored into random planking if preferred. See figure 1–20.

The chair-rail wainscotting was often topped with a chair rail and a molding. The rail stock is ⅛-inch by ¼-inch wood strips fastened to the planks. The molding is ⅛-inch cove. Victorian kitchens often had chair-rail-height wainscotting made up of 2½, 3, or 4-inch matched boards. See figure 1–27 left.

Raised Panel Wainscotting

Early American and federal period raised-panel wainscotting is made from a series of rails, stiles, and panels in various sizes. The

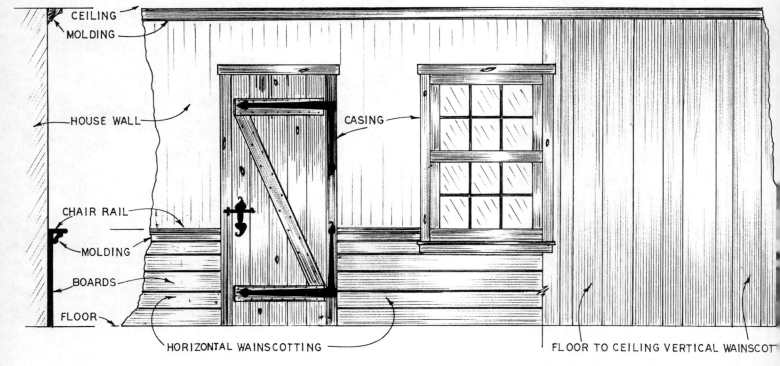

CEILING
MOLDING

HOUSE WALL

CASING

CHAIR RAIL

MOLDING

BOARDS

FLOOR

HORIZONTAL WAINSCOTTING

FLOOR TO CEILING VERTICAL WAINSCOT

Fig. 1–19. *Sample colonial wainscotting*

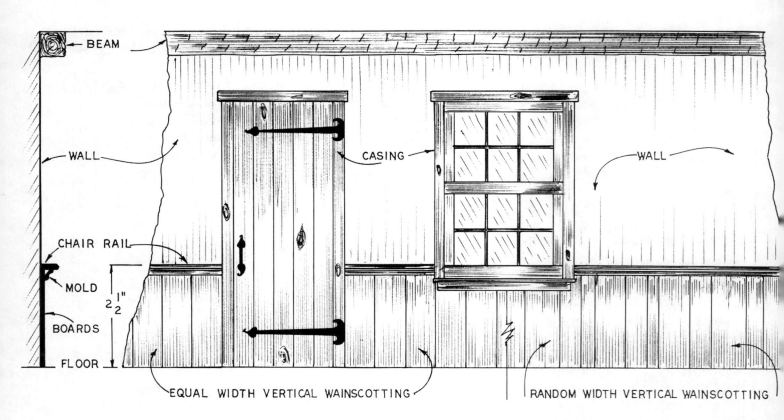

BEAM

WALL

CASING

WALL

CHAIR RAIL

MOLD

$2\frac{1}{2}"$

BOARDS

FLOOR

EQUAL WIDTH VERTICAL WAINSCOTTING

RANDOM WIDTH VERTICAL WAINSCOTTING

Fig. 1–20. *Plank wainscotting of chair-rail height*

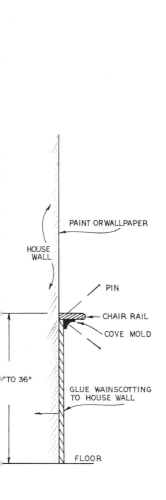

PAINT OR WALLPAPER

HOUSE WALL

PIN

CHAIR RAIL

COVE MOLD

"TO 36"

GLUE WAINSCOTTING TO HOUSE WALL

FLOOR

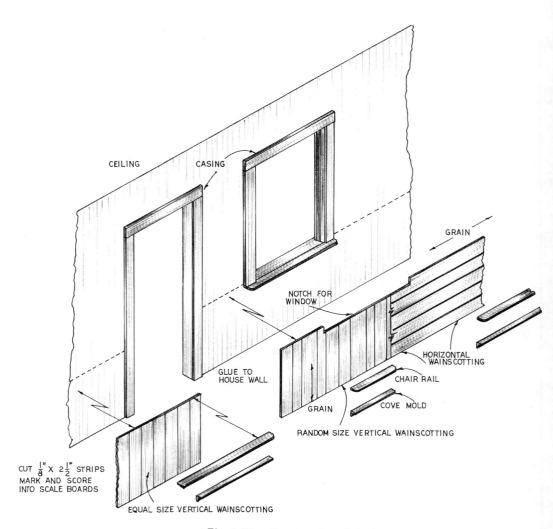

CEILING

CASING

GRAIN

NOTCH FOR WINDOW

HORIZONTAL WAINSCOTTING

GLUE TO HOUSE WALL

CHAIR RAIL

COVE MOLD

GRAIN

RANDOM SIZE VERTICAL WAINSCOTTING

CUT $\frac{1}{8}$" X $2\frac{1}{2}$" STRIPS MARK AND SCORE INTO SCALE BOARDS

EQUAL SIZE VERTICAL WAINSCOTTING

Fig. 1–21.   *Construction of plank wainscotting*

normal full-size wainscotting has the raised panels inserted into rabbets cut into the other framing members. When making a ¹/₁₂th scale reproduction, it is very difficult to match the tenon and rabbet construction. The rails, stiles, and panels are, therefore, added to existing wood backgrounds.

To construct raised-panel wainscotting, make a sketch and lay out the scale-sized wall(s) to be covered. Determine the best height for the chair rail. Remember in life-size buildings, a chair rail is used to prevent furniture from marking the walls. Most often the chair rail is the same height as the window sill; however, some window sills are lower than

feasible for chair-rail wainscotting. Chair-rail height varies in full-size buildings, but the most common height is between 30 and 32 inches (about 2½ inches on the ¹/₁₂th scale).

After determining the height, select the number of panels you desire. Square panels are to be avoided except in extreme circumstances. For the most successful look, the panel should be taller than it is wide. Width to height ratios of one to two, or one to three, are good examples to follow.

Because windows, doors, and other breaks in house walls create odd measurements, you may need several panels that are shorter or narrower than the rest of the panels. See figure

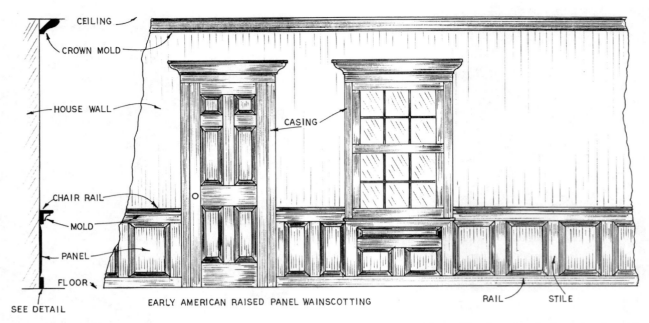

CEILING

CROWN MOLD

HOUSE WALL

CASING

CHAIR RAIL

MOLD

PANEL

FLOOR

SEE DETAIL

EARLY AMERICAN RAISED PANEL WAINSCOTTING

RAIL   STILE

Fig. 1–22.   Sample raised-panel wainscotting

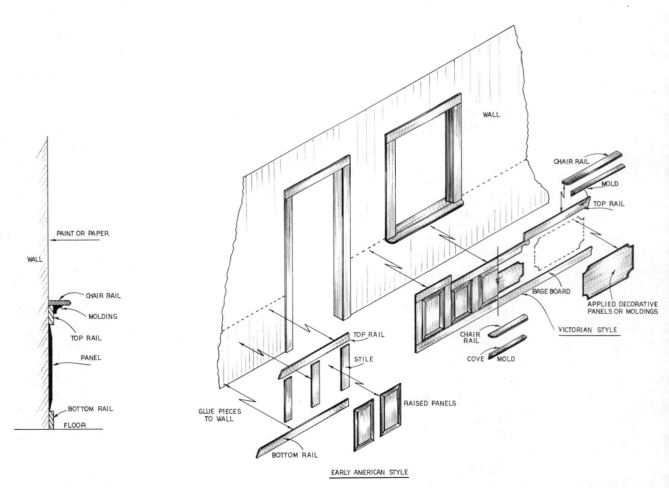

WALL

PAINT OR PAPER

WALL

CHAIR RAIL

MOLDING

TOP RAIL

PANEL

BOTTOM RAIL

FLOOR

CHAIR RAIL

MOLD

TOP RAIL

BASE BOARD

APPLIED DECORATIVE
PANELS OR MOLDINGS

VICTORIAN STYLE

CHAIR RAIL

COVE MOLD

RAISED PANELS

TOP RAIL

STILE

GLUE PIECES
TO WALL

BOTTOM RAIL

EARLY AMERICAN STYLE

Fig. 1–23.   Raised-panel construction

TYPICAL PANEL WAINSCOTTING FRAMING

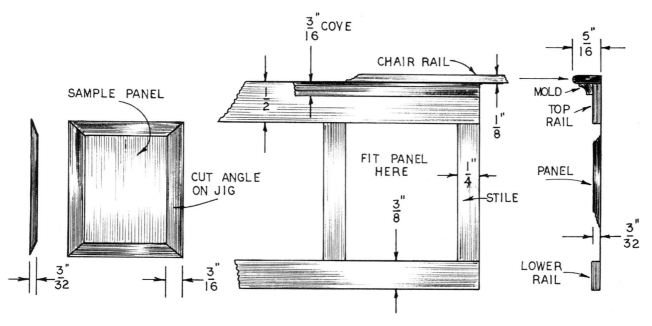

SAMPLE PANEL

CUT ANGLE
ON JIG

$\frac{3}{32}$"

$\frac{3}{16}$"

$\frac{3}{16}$" COVE

CHAIR RAIL

2"

$1\frac{1}{8}$"

FIT PANEL
HERE

$\frac{1}{4}$"

STILE

$\frac{3}{8}$"

$\frac{5}{16}$"

MOLD

TOP
RAIL

PANEL

$\frac{3}{32}$"

LOWER
RAIL

Fig. 1–24. *Sample sizes for raised-panel wainscotting*

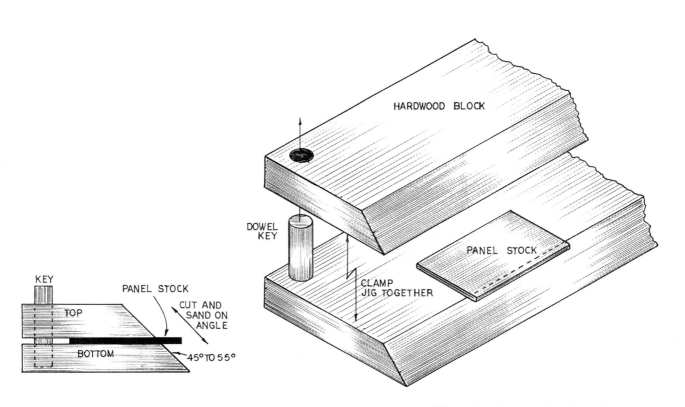

HARDWOOD BLOCK

DOWEL
KEY

CLAMP
JIG TOGETHER

PANEL STOCK

KEY

TOP

PANEL STOCK

CUT AND
SAND ON
ANGLE

BOTTOM

45° TO 55°

Fig. 1–25. *Construction of raised-panel jig*

37

Fig. 1–26. Panel-making jig

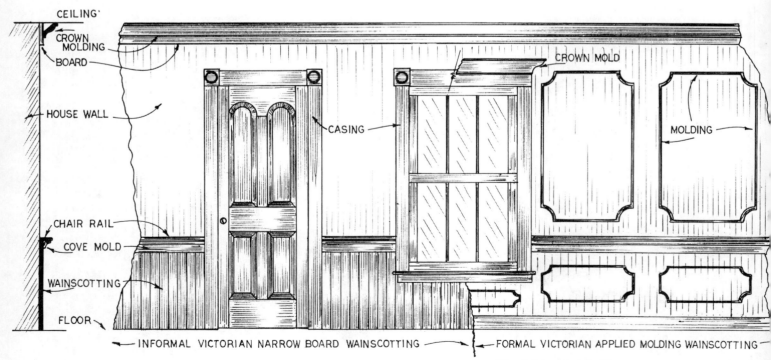

CEILING

CROWN
MOLDING

BOARD

HOUSE WALL

CHAIR RAIL

COVE MOLD

WAINSCOTTING

FLOOR

CROWN MOLD

CASING

MOLDING

← INFORMAL VICTORIAN NARROW BOARD WAINSCOTTING → ← FORMAL VICTORIAN APPLIED MOLDING WAINSCOTTING →

Fig. 1–27. Sample Victorian-style wainscotting

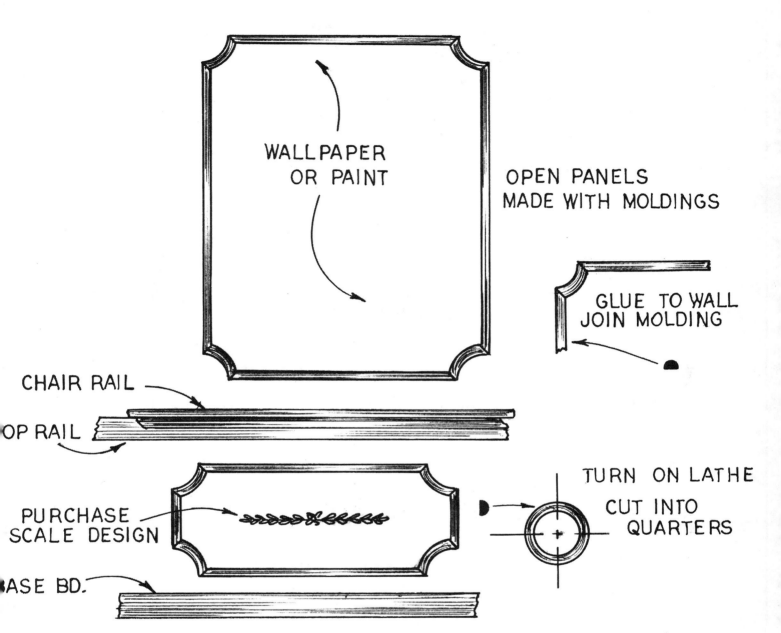

WALLPAPER OR PAINT

OPEN PANELS MADE WITH MOLDINGS

GLUE TO WALL JOIN MOLDING

CHAIR RAIL

OP RAIL

PURCHASE SCALE DESIGN

ASE BD.

TURN ON LATHE CUT INTO QUARTERS

Fig. 1–28A. Construction of formal Victorian-style panels

1–22 around the window. The odd-size panels should contain the same basic elements of the regular, raised-panel ratio if at all possible.

When the actual size paper pattern is made, corrections or adjustments can be easily made until an artistic pattern is developed. The eye is the final judge of how a wall should look, and the paper plan offers this judication without extensive work or error. Each wall to be covered should have a separate pattern.

After the paper pattern is made, cut $1/16$-inch

by 4-inch strips for the background covering. (This size is typical, and some retail outlets sell basswood in this thickness.) Try to lay out the background material so that the joints will be covered by a stile. Glue the wood with its grain running vertically to the miniature house wall.

Mark out the location of the rails and stiles. Cut $1/8$-inch by $1/4$-inch (or $5/16$-inch) stock for the rails and stiles. Cut these members to length and secure them to the background stock with glue. After the glue has dried, cut

ACTUAL SIZE SAMPLE PANELS

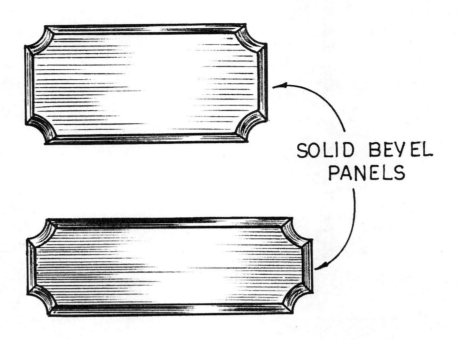

SOLID BEVEL
PANELS

UNDER WINDOW PANEL

Fig. 1–28B. Actual-size sample panels

the stock for the various panels from clear ⅛-inch-thick wood strips. Sand and shape the panel edges as shown in figure 1–24.

The best method for making the raised panel edges is to construct a jig, as shown in figure 1–25. Such a jig allows you to plan and sand the panel edges to a uniform size and angle. The cut panel stock is inserted into the jig mouth, and the extended edge of the panel is shaped with sandpaper on a wood block. The proposed panel is rotated in the jig until all four edges are finished.

Secure the finished panels to the back-ground stock with glue. Extra care should be taken to insure equal spacing within the proposed area and to keep all the panel heights the same.

Once the walls are covered and the glue has dried, finish the panel walls with a piece of chair-rail nosing made from ³/₁₆-inch by ¼-inch stock. See figure 1–24. Install a cove or bed molding under the nosing, if preferred. See detail in figure 1–24. Scale molding can be purchased, if desired, and a list of suppliers is given in the last section of this book.

If the entire wall from floor to ceiling is to be

covered, follow the same construction procedure. Most often fully wainscotted walls contain three or four panels for the given height.

Victorian Scalloped Panels

Some Victorian homes had formal sitting rooms decorated by scalloped or rounded wainscotting panels with matching wall panels or molded inserts. (See figure 1–27 right.) Panels can be applied directly to a painted or papered wall, or they can be applied to a wood background. The chair rail and molding are installed at the normal height. The smaller panels are applied below the chair rail in equal spaces. See figure 1–27.

The panels below the chair rail are solid wood, while those above the chair rail contain papered or painted inserts. The matching top wall panels can be wooden, flock papered, or painted a compatible color to the wall finish. The panel shapes can be made of simple moldings if preferred. The inverted quarter-round corners used here are difficult to purchase. Use a lathe to turn out rounds to match the molding. The finished turned rounds are then cut into quarters, and each section is applied to a corner. Matched moldings can then be applied between the quarter rounds to form the shape of the scalloped panels. See detail figure 1–28. Medallion inserts can be used in the panels if preferred.

Fig. 1–29. Miniature-size lumber supplies (Courtesy H. L. Childs)

41

COVE MOLDING

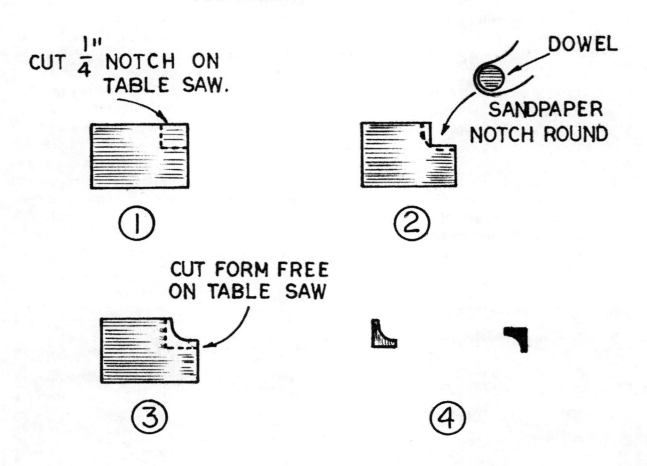

CUT $\frac{1}{4}$" NOTCH ON TABLE SAW.

①

DOWEL

SANDPAPER NOTCH ROUND

②

CUT FORM FREE ON TABLE SAW

③

④

CROWN MOLDING

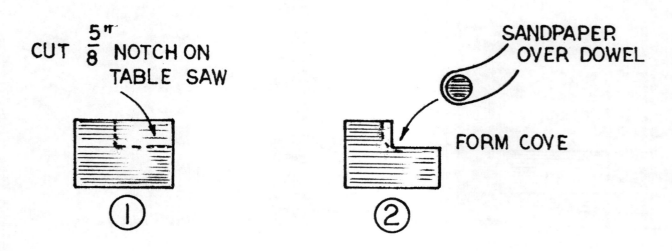

CUT $\frac{5}{8}$" NOTCH ON TABLE SAW

①

SANDPAPER OVER DOWEL

FORM COVE

②

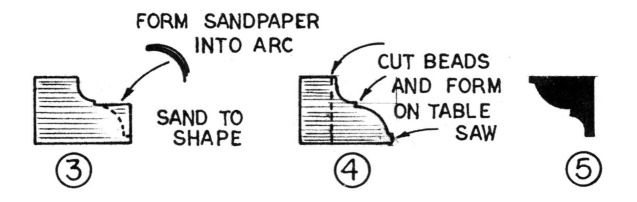

FORM SANDPAPER INTO ARC

SAND TO SHAPE

③

CUT BEADS AND FORM ON TABLE SAW

④

⑤

COMBINED MOLDINGS
FOR CORNICE AND TRIM

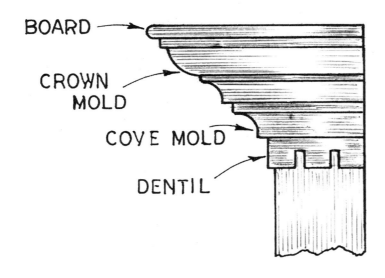

BOARD

CROWN MOLD

COVE MOLD

DENTIL

ACTUAL SIZE TEMPLATE

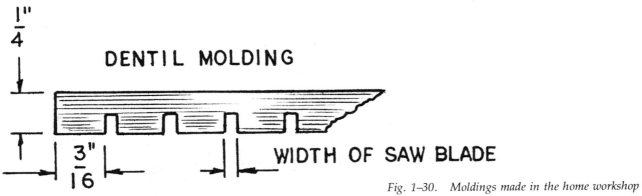

$\frac{1''}{4}$

DENTIL MOLDING

$\frac{3''}{16}$

WIDTH OF SAW BLADE

Fig. 1–30. Moldings made in the home workshop

MOLDINGS

Scale moldings are a little difficult to make in the home workshop. Most of the average router or shape cutters were designed for full-size stock and do not adapt very well for miniature molding work. Moldings expressly designed and scaled for miniature work can be purchased by the lineal inch. (See list of suppliers and figure 1–12.) Many hobby or craft stores carry a line of premade stock moldings. It is recommended that when moldings are required they be purchased. However, some standard cove or crown moldings can be made in the home shop.

Cove Moldings

1. Select clear stock for the moldings. Shorter lengths form better than long strips, so plan projected use and sizes before starting.

2. Cut a slight rabbet into the edge of a clear board. See figure 1–30.

3. With a small rat-tail file or sandpaper wrapped around a dowel or pencil, sand the rabbet into a quarter round. See figure 1–30.

4. Cut the finish-sanded cove from the board edge using a table saw.

Crown Moldings

Crown moldings are a combination of a convex and concave curve.

1. Select clear stock for moldings.

2. Cut a deep vertical rabbet into the edge of a clear board. With a rat-tail file or sandpaper wrapped around a dowel or pencil, create a cove or quarter round at the right angle of the rabbet. See figure 1–30.

3. After the finish cove is formed, score at the bottom of the vertical leg on a table saw, if desired.

4. Form sandpaper into a cove and sand the molding edge into a round. The round, or crown, will run in the opposite direction and blend into the quarter round. Once the finish crown mold is shaped, cut the form free from the board edge. See figure 1–30.

Crown and cove moldings are used as the head casing on windows and doors, around room and ceiling lines, under fireplace mantels, and as trim for some furniture pieces.

3. *Windows*

Several companies offer either window and door kits or premilled stock for construction of window and door jambs, sashes, and door panels. Many commercial outlets offer premade double hung or casement windows of various sizes and two, four, or six-panel doors. Such suppliers are listed in Section four, and many of these outlets offer catalogs for a nominal fee. As an alternative to buying, miniaturists can make their own millwork if they have access to a table saw. In this chapter, the steps in making several different styles of windows are discussed.

DOUBLE-HUNG WINDOWS AND SASH

The various parts of a window are the side jambs (the tracks the windows ride in), the head jamb (the top of the window frame), the exterior and interior casing (the trim in and outside the window frame), the sill, the sash (the panes of glass plus the framework), and the muntins (the strips dividing the small panes of glass).

The governing factor for deciding window jamb size is the thickness of the house wall. Very often the basic framing material is ½-inch plyscord. The jamb width should be slightly larger, or around $17/32$ of an inch.

Cut 24-inch or 26-inch strips of clear pine or basswood, $17/32$ inch wide by $3/16$ inch thick. Set up the table saw and rip fence to cut the sash dadoes as shown in figure 1–33. Each cut should be ⅛ inch deep. The top window sash fits into the dado cut, and the lower sash rides in the rabbet cut. After the interior casing is installed, it acts as a type of stop to contain the lower sash unit in place. (Note: The procedure can be reversed, if preferred, so that the exterior casing retains the top sash instead.)

Fig. 1–31. Sample windows and doors (Courtesy Houseworks Ltd.)

Double-Hung Frame

Four pieces comprise a window frame: two side jambs, one head jamb, and one window sill. See figure 1–32. The window sill is wider than the window jambs and exterior casing combined. If the casing is to be $3/16$ inch thick and the jamb material is $17/32$ inch wide, the sill material is around $23/32$ inch by $1/8$ inch. Cut clear wood strips 24 to 26 inches long for the sill material. The sill pieces should be cut from this stock as window frames are assembled.

Window Frame Assembly

Determine the desired width and height of the proposed window units. Let's take the example of a window whose outside dimensions minus the casing material are to be 3 inches by 4 inches. After studying figure 1–37, which illustrates the standard construction jig for window frames, construct a jig to accommodate this window size. Cut the side jamb stock into 4-inch lengths. The top of the side jambs must have a top rabbet cut in order to receive the head jamb, and a lower rabbet in order to receive the sill. Remember, the lower rabbet cut must be made on a 7 to 10-degree angle.

The two side jambs are mirror images; that is, one reflects or represents the other side exactly. Cut the stock to size for the side jambs and make the required rabbets. Insert the side

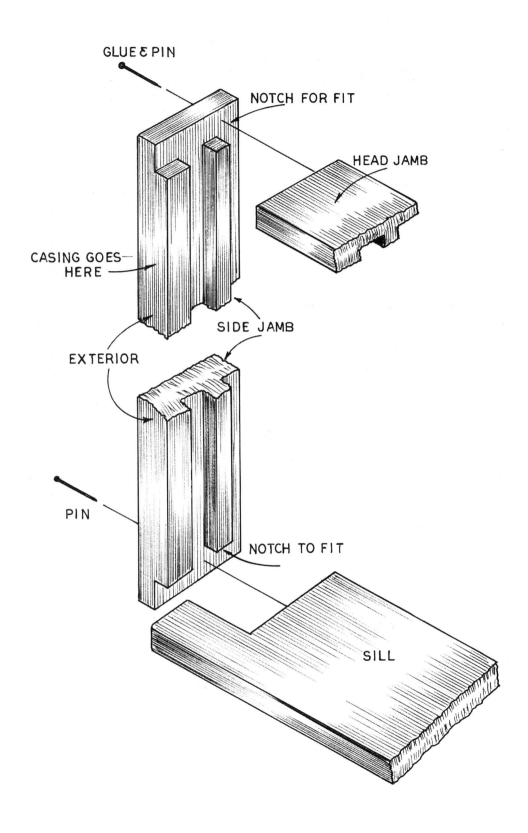

GLUE & PIN

NOTCH FOR FIT

HEAD JAMB

CASING GOES
HERE

SIDE JAMB

EXTERIOR

PIN

NOTCH TO FIT

SILL

Fig. 1–32. Sample window construction

47

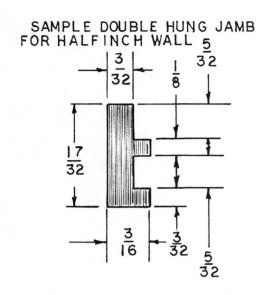

SAMPLE DOUBLE HUNG JAMB
FOR HALF INCH WALL

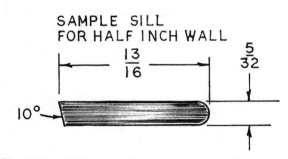

SAMPLE SILL
FOR HALF INCH WALL

Fig. 1–33.   Millwork made in the home workshop

Fig. 1–35.   Miniature-size windows and doors
(Courtesy H. L. Childs)

TOP VIEW

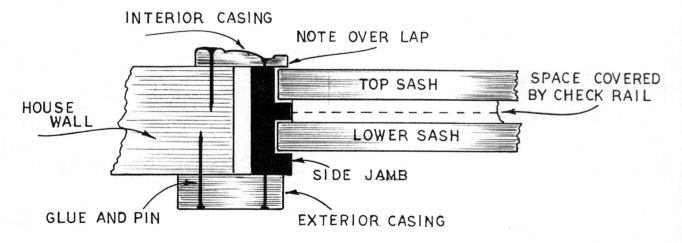

INTERIOR CASING

NOTE OVER LAP

TOP SASH

SPACE COVERED
BY CHECK RAIL

HOUSE
WALL

LOWER SASH

SIDE JAMB

GLUE AND PIN

EXTERIOR CASING

Fig. 1–34.   Sash location in a window unit, top view

48

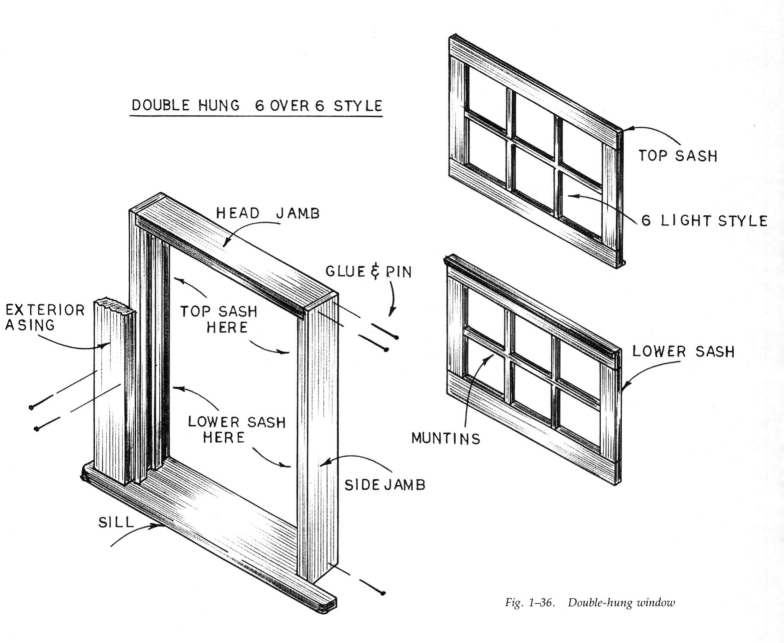

DOUBLE HUNG 6 OVER 6 STYLE

HEAD JAMB

GLUE & PIN

EXTERIOR
ASING

TOP SASH
HERE

LOWER SASH
HERE

SIDE JAMB

SILL

TOP SASH

6 LIGHT STYLE

LOWER SASH

MUNTINS

Fig. 1–36. Double-hung window

jambs into the jig. Cut the head jamb stock and install it between the two side jambs with glue and pins. Refer to figure 1–32. Cut the stock for the window sill. This sill must be notched to fit into the side jambs and extend over the exterior. Tack the sill temporarily in place. The sill must be removed later in order to install the top sash unit.

Cut the exterior casing material to size. Remember, the header casing extends over the two side casings. The lower end of the side casings are cut on the same angle as the sill (such as 10 degrees) to fit perfectly on the sill when it is installed. Glue and pin the exterior casing to the window frame. Install one or two temporary braces into the top window corners in order to hold the unit square until the window frame is installed in the house. Remove the unit from the jig.

When laying out a miniature house, keep the window dimensions to the same general overall size if possible. Bathroom and kitchen win-

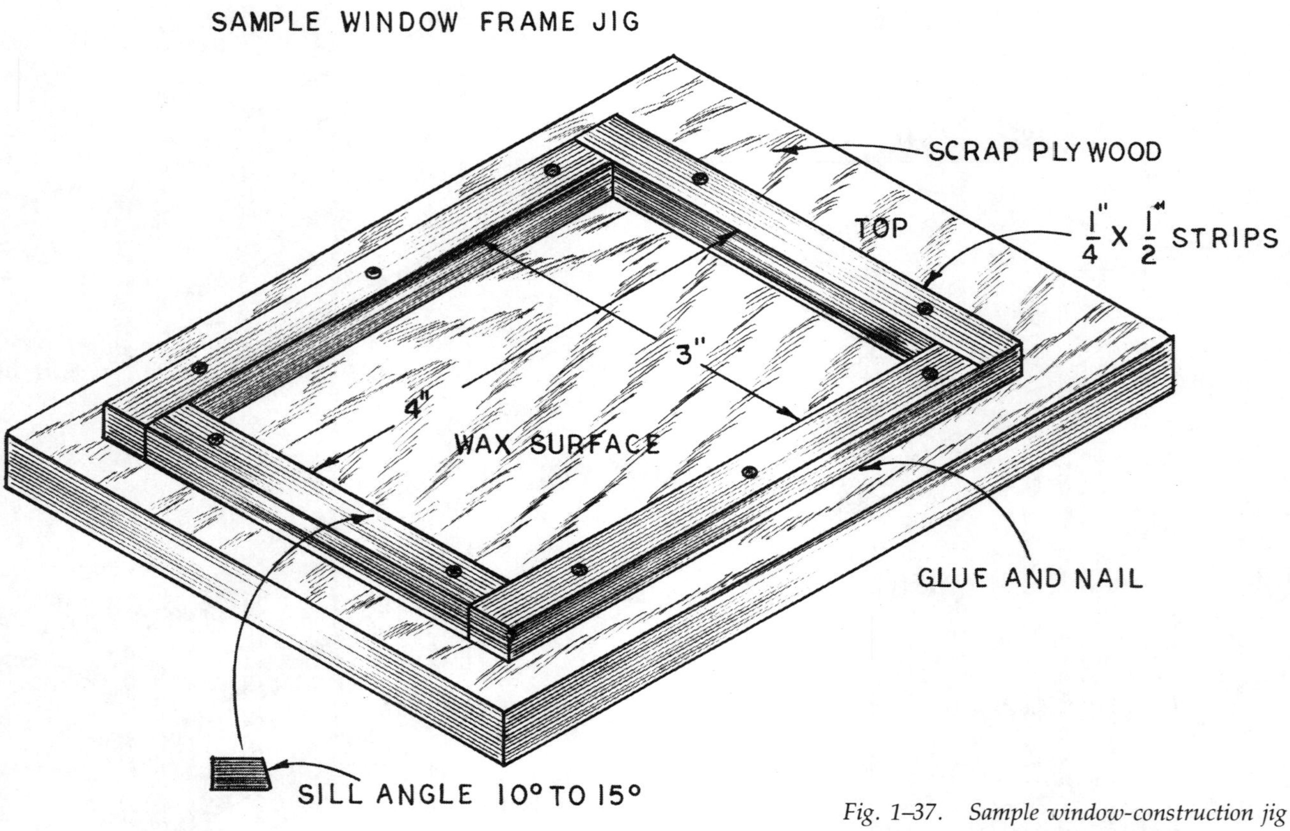

SAMPLE WINDOW FRAME JIG

SCRAP PLYWOOD

TOP

$\frac{1}{4}$" X $\frac{1}{2}$" STRIPS

3"

4"

WAX SURFACE

GLUE AND NAIL

SILL ANGLE 10° TO 15°

Fig. 1–37. Sample window-construction jig

dows, as a rule, are shorter than normal room windows, but try to restrict variations to a minimum. A different construction jig is needed for each different window size.

Double-Hung Sash Construction

Most double-hung window sash units overlap at the center of the window, and the bottom rail (near the sill) is most often one and one-half times the size of the center of top rails. Therefore, the top sash differs slightly from the lower or bottom sash. Perhaps one of the best methods for construction of sash units is to measure the inside clearance within the window frame rabbets and then add an extra $1/16$ inch to the width. This extra width allows the miniaturist to sand fit (to fit the pieces to size by sanding excess stock from the ends) each sash unit to a particular window frame.

Colonial or early American sash units often require small window panes called lights. Six panes over six panes and eight panes over eight panes are the most common types. The construction of the sash unit, regardless of style, remains the same. Only the size and number of muntins change.

A master sash jig should be made for sash construction so that all the units are the same size and dimensions. This jig eliminates the need to remeasure for each unit. Often the same jig used for making the window frames can be used for making the window sash units by adding filler strips to the sides and bottom to make up for the thickness of the jamb stock. See figure 1–38. After all the window frames have been constructed, add the filler strips to the jig. Carefully lay out the two sash units and any muntin divisions right on the jig itself.

Cut $1/8$-inch by $1/4$-inch clear wood strips for the stiles and rails, and $1/8$-inch by $3/8$-inch clear wood strips for the bottom rail. This bottom rail

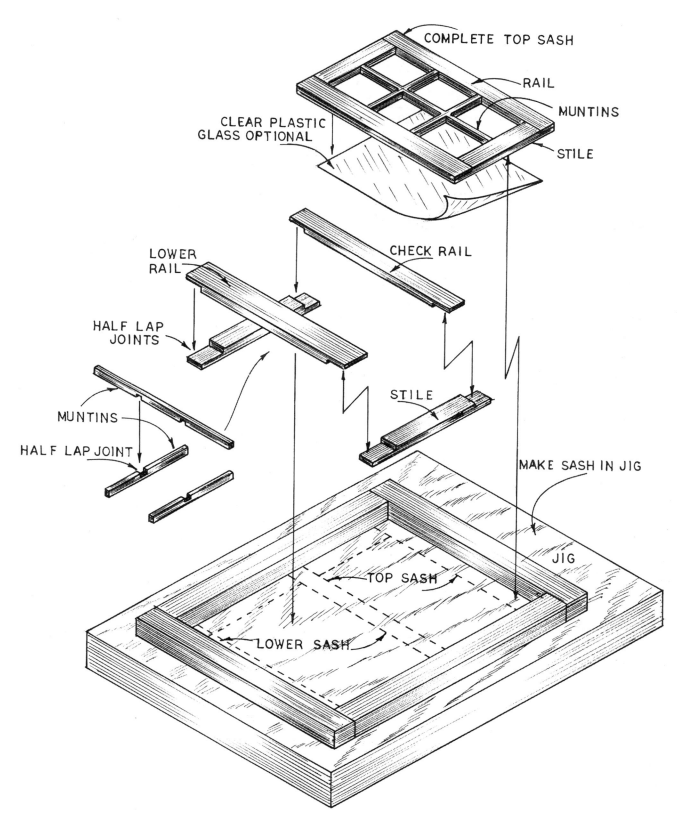

COMPLETE TOP SASH

RAIL

MUNTINS

STILE

CLEAR PLASTIC
GLASS OPTIONAL

CHECK RAIL

LOWER
RAIL

HALF LAP
JOINTS

STILE

MUNTINS

HALF LAP JOINT

MAKE SASH IN JIG

JIG

TOP SASH

LOWER SASH

Fig. 1–38. Sash construction

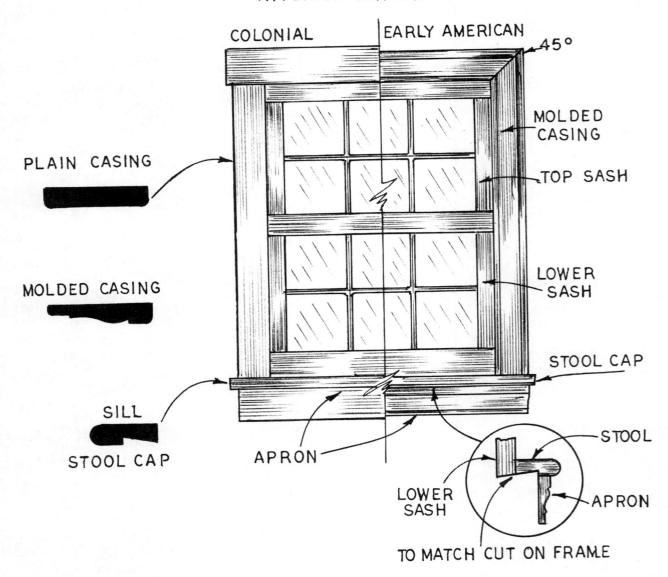

INTERIOR WINDOW TRIM

COLONIAL | EARLY AMERICAN

45°

PLAIN CASING

MOLDED CASING

SILL

STOOL CAP

MOLDED CASING

TOP SASH

LOWER SASH

STOOL CAP

APRON

STOOL

LOWER SASH

APRON

TO MATCH CUT ON FRAME

Fig. 1–39. Colonial and early American interior window trim

should have a 10-degree angle on the bottom to match the angle of the window sill. Cut ⅛-inch by ⅛-inch clear wood strips for the window muntins. All the top sash units should be made at one time; then make all the bottom units. In this way, a rhythm and procedure can be established, and the work will go smoother.

Sash Construction

The sash rails and stiles have half-lap joints. Cut the top and bottom rail stock to size and insert these into the sash jig. Cut the two side stiles to size and glue them between the two rails. Mark out and cut each horizontal muntin

52

to size and insert each one into the center of the sash frame where marked on the jig. Cut the vertical muntins and insert them on the marks. Mark out where the vertical and horizontal muntins intersect each other. With a mat knife or file, cut half-lap joints into the muntin parts. See figure 1–38.

Glue the half-lap joints and the muntin grid into the top sash unit. Check the construction for correct design, placement, and squareness. Allow the glued unit to dry for the suggested time. (The unit can be taken out of the jig for drying.) After the glue has set, the window sash can be pinned with bank pins if desired. Continue this process until all the top sash units have been completed. To be safe, make one or two extra units as possible replacements; breakage can occur during the final sanding or fitting.

When all the top sash units have been completed, repeat the operations for construction of the bottom units. Remember, the bottom rail will be wider and have an angle compatible to the sill angle. The various muntins are constructed and installed in the same manner as the top units.

Shaping

After all the window sash units are completed, sand the surfaces smooth to fit into the jamb dadoes and rabbets. Using a thin strip of sandpaper in a motion like a shoe-shine cloth, sand and shape the muntins smooth and round. See figures 1–38 and 1–39. If the window sash units and frames are to be painted, they should be painted now, before final assembly, to prevent any paint lock. Touching up can be done after installation.

Install the finished top sash into the window jamb dado by removing the pretacked sill. After the top sash is installed and works

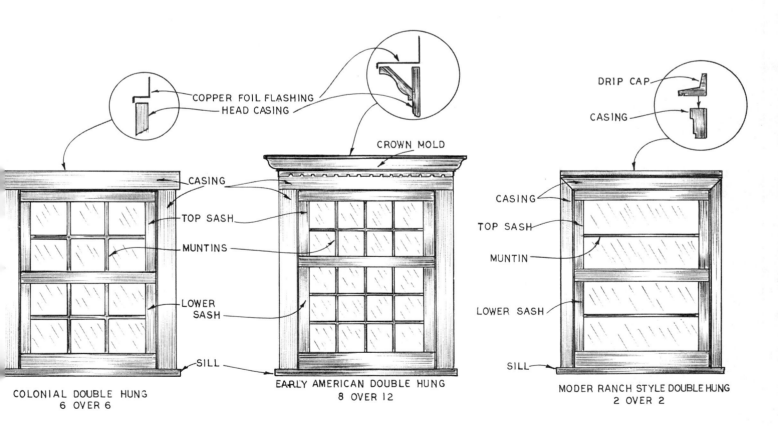

Fig. 1–40. Double-hung windows in colonial, early American, and ranch styles

53

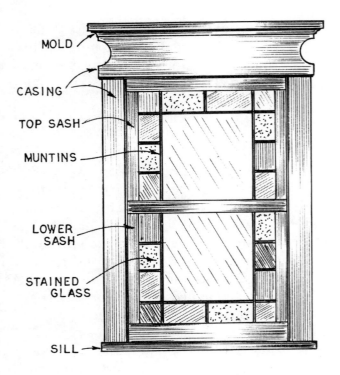

MOLD

CASING

TOP SASH

MUNTINS

LOWER SASH

STAINED GLASS

SILL

VICTORIAN STAINED GLASS WINDOW

Fig. 1–41. *Victorian-style stained-glass window*

smoothly, the sill can be permanently fastened to the jamb with glue and pins. The lower sash is contained in the rabbet track by the interior casing. Install the completed window unit and sash into the house wall. Secure the window frame to the house wall with glue and pins through the exterior casing. Install the lower sash into the track and install the interior casing with glue and pins to the inside of the house wall. See figure 1–34.

Interior Trim (casing)

The interior trim consists of side and header casings, stool cap (sill), and an apron. See figure 1–39. Interior casing can be made from ⅛-inch by ³/₁₆-inch clear wood strips or purchased as molded casing. See figure 1–12.

The stool cap can be made from ³/₁₆-inch by ³/₈-inch clear stock. Mark and cut the stool cap to fit against the lower sash unit when the

window is down. Mark and cut the stool cap to fit against the window and to extend out over the intended width of the side casings. The stool cap should be equal to, or extend just slightly beyond, the sides of the casings. Glue and pin the stool cap in place. Measure and mark the side casing pieces. Note that colonial-style casings have plain butt joints, while molded casings require a 45-degree miter joint. Refer to figure 1–39.

Cut the head casing to size. Butt or miter the joints, and install the side casings members with glue and pins. Remember, the casings must extend over the jamb material in order to keep the lower sash units in place. Install the head casing member with glue and pins. Pin the casings into the house wall.

Cut the apron stock from the same casing material and install the apron under the stool cap. The apron length is equal to the outside measurements of the side jamb casing. Stain, paint, and finish the interior trim to a color of your choice at this time.

VICTORIAN-STYLE WINDOWS

Very often Victorian windows have a one to three, or one to four width to height ratio. Decorative exterior casings is another major characteristic.

The construction of the frame and window sashes follow the procedures given for double-hung windows. The only differences are the overall size and the change in the light (windowpane) divisions. While some Victorian windows do have a six over six style, most Victorian sash units have only one or two vertical muntins. The muntin layout is placed on the construction jig and the same construction procedures are followed.

Head Casings

The large decorative head casing can be made in one of several ways. In a majority of

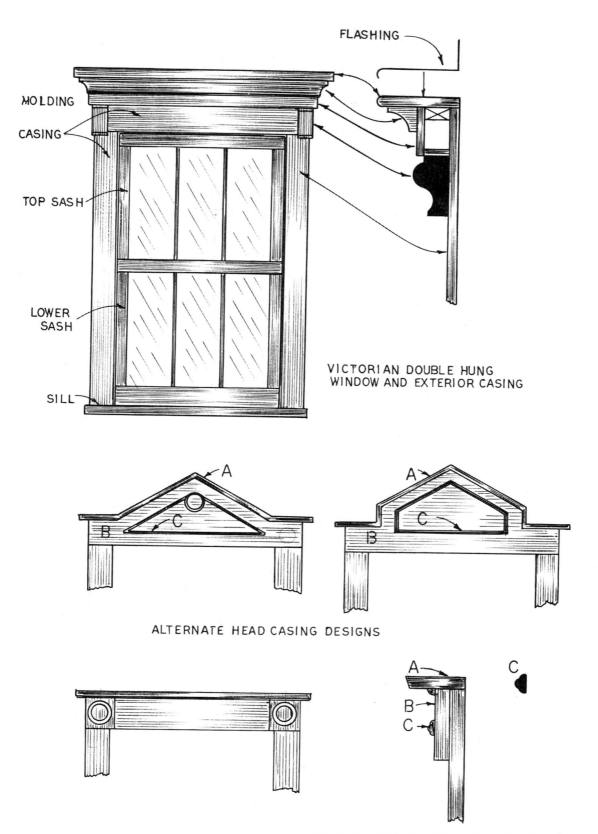

FLASHING

MOLDING

CASING

TOP SASH

LOWER SASH

SILL

VICTORIAN DOUBLE HUNG
WINDOW AND EXTERIOR CASING

A

C

B

A

C

B

ALTERNATE HEAD CASING DESIGNS

A

B

C

C

Fig. 1–42. Victorian-style window with alternate casing

55

the windows, the head casing extends out over the window frame and side casings. The decorative head is made up of several blocks overlapping each other. See detail figure 1–42 for various styles.

Start the exterior construction by installing the suggested plain flat casing. Cut out the ¼-inch by ⅝-inch support blocks. Secure the blocks to the corners of the flat head casing as suggested in figure 1–42 top. Install the soffit board on top of the blocks. Install the fascia board with glue and pins into the soffit board. Use a spacer or nailing block on the top edge for support.

Cut and install a cove or crown molding on the top of the fascia board. This molding has a 45-degree miter joint on the ends, and the molding sets at a right angle back to the house wall. Cut and install the cap into the molding and fascia boards. Cut and install copper flashing over the cap. (Copper flashing is made from copper foil available in hobby/craft stores.)

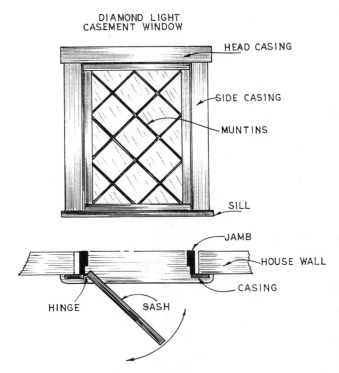

Fig. 1–44. *Single casement window*

Fig. 1–43. *San Francisco-style window*
(Courtesy Houseworks Ltd.)

The peaked head casings are made from a single head board cut to a desired shape. See part B in figure 1–42 lower. Most often the head board extends over the side casing. The cap board is installed on the top of the angle cuts to act as a type of roof. Copper flashing is installed over this cap. The decorative designs are made with flat, quarter, or half-round moldings, as shown in C.

The ring or bull's eye casing is the most common style of interior casing and has been used for some exterior finish as well. The head casing is installed flush with the side casings for interior finish and extends over the sides for exterior usage. Very often a small block is installed where the side and head casings meet. This block is a little thicker and slightly larger than the first casings. The rings for miniature homes are small metal snap rings glued to the block or head casing. For exterior work, use copper flashing over the head casing. See figure 1–42.

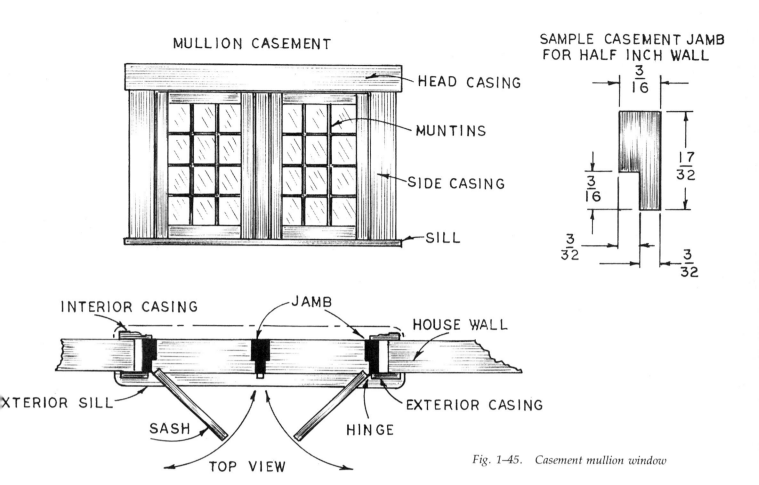

MULLION CASEMENT

HEAD CASING

MUNTINS

SIDE CASING

SILL

SAMPLE CASEMENT JAMB
FOR HALF INCH WALL

$\frac{3}{16}$

$\frac{17}{32}$

$\frac{3}{16}$

$\frac{3}{32}$

$\frac{3}{32}$

INTERIOR CASING

JAMB

HOUSE WALL

EXTERIOR SILL

SASH

HINGE

EXTERIOR CASING

TOP VIEW

Fig. 1–45. Casement mullion window

Victorian Stained-Glass Windows

The stained-glass window sash is made like any double-hung unit. The design should be laid out on paper with the suggested muntin detailing, as shown in figure 1–41. For a stained-glass window make the top and bottom sash units as suggested for colonial double-hung units. See figure 1–38 for reference. Install the desired muntins. Allow the sash and muntins to dry overnight. Sand and finish the sash units.

For the window panes, install a clear plastic pane into the full sash. Mark out the different glass areas and color each area with magic markers or commercial stained-glass paints. A more authentic window can be made by cutting small pieces of colored plastic into each muntin to make separate panels. Colored plastic can be purchased in hobby or craft stores, or cut from colored plastic report covers available in stationery stores.

A more authentic, leaded stained-glass window can be made by inserting a full plastic pane into the sash unit without any division muntins. Liquid solder, which is available in tubes, can be applied for a lead-like came string or bead. After the liquid solder has dried, color the panes with magic markers, transparency markers, or stained-glass paints. Individual, colored, plastic inserts can be used if preferred.

CASEMENT WINDOWS

Casement windows open and close much like a door. They are hinged on one side and usually open out to the exterior. As a rule, casement windows are smaller than double-hung units, but very often several mullions or window units are assembled together to make a double or multiple window fixture. Construction and framing materials are a little different from those used for double-hung windows.

The casement frame is made similar to a door frame, except only a single rabbet cut is required. The rabbet, located where the casement sets, faces the house exterior. Cut $3/16$-inch by $17/32$-inch strips of clear pine stock to the suggested shape and size shown in the detail in figure 1–44.

Make a jig for the desired size of the proposed casement unit. (See figure 1–37 on double-hung windows for suggested jig shape.) Cut the side jambs, the head jamb, and the sill jamb to size. Mark the side jambs for the rabbet cuts after the side and head/sill pieces are fitted together.

The exterior sill does not have an angle as in double-hung construction, but is installed straight, just like the head jamb. Assemble the desired frame rectangle for the casement frame with glue and pins. Cut the stock for the exterior sill, as shown in figure 1–44. This sill is cut on a 10-degree angle, so it will tilt down and away from the sash seat. Cut the stock for the exterior casing (trim). See figure 1–39 and figure 1–40 for suggested exterior casing. Make as many casement units as needed.

Mullions

Many times multiple casement units are desired. These are made by using a center mullion that contains a double rabbet cut, one on each edge. The double rabbet accommodates two sash units. See figure 1–45. However, the head and sill jambs are continuous and contain slots, or dadoes, to accept the mullion jambs. Two, three, or more multiple window units can be made in this manner.

In mullion casement construction, the window sash units can be hinged as shown in figure 1–45, or they can all be hinged from the same side, i.e., all right or left-hand swings. Sometimes in three or four unit construction, the center sash units are fixed, and do not move, while the outer units are hinged and operative.

Sash and Casing

The casement sash is made just like a single sash unit for double hung windows. See figure 1–39. Make a plywood jig with the sash size laid out. Mark out the desired muntin shape, as depicted in figures 1–44 and 1–45. Small square or diamond-shape muntins can be used. Cut the stiles and rails to size. Make half-lap joints on the corners. Glue the stiles and rails together in the construction jig. Cut the muntins to size and make half-lap joints where these pieces cross each other. Use figure 1–38 for reference.

Glue the muntins in place and allow the sash to dry. Remove the sash unit from the jig and sand smooth. Round and shape the muntins with a file and sandpaper. Sand fit the sash to the premade frame and attach the sash to the frame with small hinges. A pin-type hinge can be used, if desired. See the instructions on hinges in the hardware chapter.

After the window frame and sash unit is installed into the house wall, cut and shape the interior casing material. Interior casing is installed just like the casing for double hung windows, shown in figure 1–39.

4. *Doors and Jambs*

Life-size doors range from 6½ feet to 6⅔ feet in height. The width of doors varies more than the height. The majority of exterior doors are 3 feet wide, while room entrance doors average about 2½ feet in width. Closet doors are often only 2 feet wide. This same basic size holds true whether the door is early American, federal, colonial, Victorian, or modern in style. The major exception to these standard sizes is a double-door unit; the two-door unit may have a combined width of 4, 5, or 6 feet.

Miniature doors and door jambs can be made or purchased in the same general manner as windows. Door kits are available. Miniature lumber outlets provide materials to make your own doors on the ¹/₁₂th scale, or the doors can be purchased already made. See figure 1–12. The least expensive method is to make the doors and jambs in the home workshop from normal stock.

JAMB CONSTRUCTION

Before making the door, you should construct the door jamb. The jamb is the term for the pieces that form the side of the wall opening around the door. Two options are available for door jambs: a plain (smooth) board or rabbeted style. The plain jamb requires a door stop to prevent forcing the door beyond a closed point. The rabbet jamb has a built-in stop but requires special attention to prevent hinge bind.

Plain Jambs

To construct plain jambs, cut the side and head jamb stock to size, about ¹⁷/₃₂ inch by ³/₃₂ inch for a wall ½ inch thick. Glue and pin the side jambs into the head jamb. No sill, or threshold, is required for interior doors.

Fig. 1–46.   *Entrance hall (Courtesy Realife Miniatures)*

Fig. 1–47.   *Jamestown door (Courtesy Houseworks Ltd.)*

Next the casing, or door frame, is made from
1/8-inch by 5/16-inch clear wood strips. Usually
the head casing extends over the side casing in
the early colonial style. Glue the side and head
casings to the jamb frame on one side only.
Install the jamb unit plumb and level into a
precut opening in the house wall. Then glue
and pin the casing into the wall. Once the door
frame is secured in place, case the other side.

Rabbet Jambs

When making rabbeted jambs, follow the
general directions given for casement window
construction and refer to figure 1–44. The
thickness should be 3/16 inch with a width 1/32

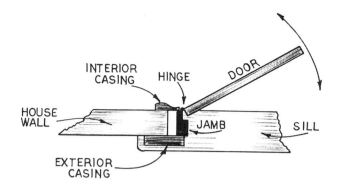

INTERIOR CASING HINGE DOOR

HOUSE WALL

EXTERIOR CASING

JAMB SILL

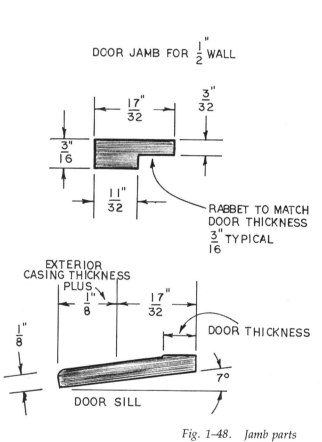

DOOR JAMB FOR $\frac{1}{2}$" WALL

$\frac{17"}{32}$ $\frac{3"}{32}$

$\frac{3"}{16}$

$\frac{11"}{32}$

RABBET TO MATCH DOOR THICKNESS $\frac{3"}{16}$ TYPICAL

EXTERIOR CASING THICKNESS PLUS $\frac{1"}{8}$ $\frac{17"}{32}$

DOOR THICKNESS

$\frac{1"}{8}$

DOOR SILL   7°

Fig. 1–48. Jamb parts

inch larger than the proposed wall thickness. For example, use a $^{17}/_{32}$-inch jamb width for a $\frac{1}{2}$-inch-thick wall.

DOOR CONSTRUCTION

One of the easiest doors to construct is the door made during the colonial period. Then the prevailing style was a plain single-board jamb, plain casings or door frame, and batten doors. A batten door is made of boards held together by pieces of wood nailed across the boards. The hardware for a colonial door was a simple wood handle, thumb latch or slide bolt, and strip/pintle hinges.

Batten Doors

To make the colonial batten door, cut $^3/_{16}$-inch stock from wood free of blemishes or pronounced grain. (Resawed stock can be used.) For an interior entrance door, the door's measurements should be $^3/_{16}$ inch by 2½ inches by 6½ inches. Sand the stock smooth. Then score vertical lines into the door at ½-inch to ⅔-inch intervals to resemble the batten

Fig. 1–49. Batten door from a miniature carpenter's shop

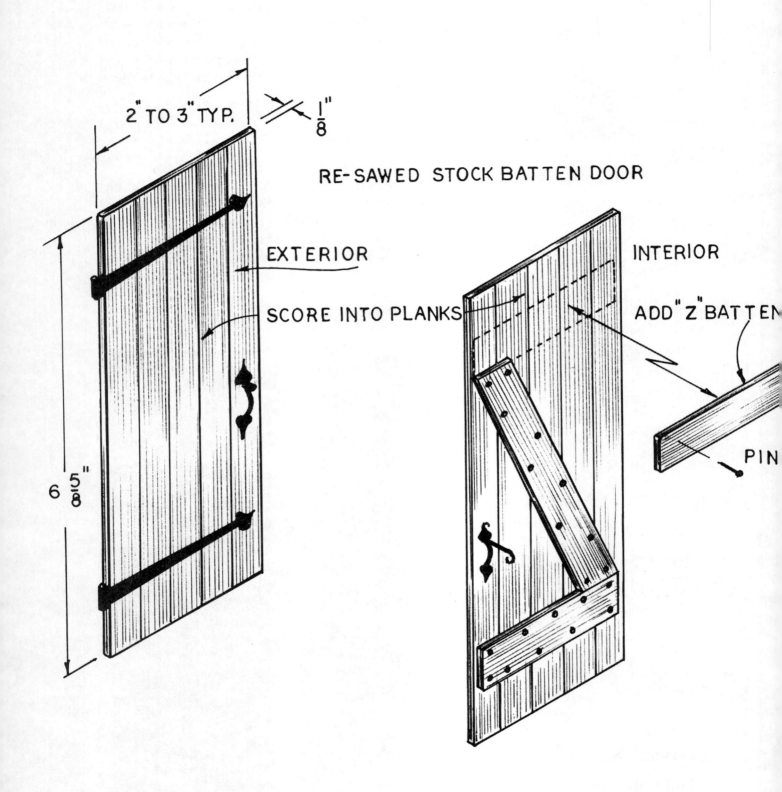

2" TO 3" TYP.   1/8"

RE-SAWED STOCK BATTEN DOOR

EXTERIOR

SCORE INTO PLANKS

6 5/8"

INTERIOR

ADD "Z" BATTEN

PIN

Fig. 1–50A. Batten door

62

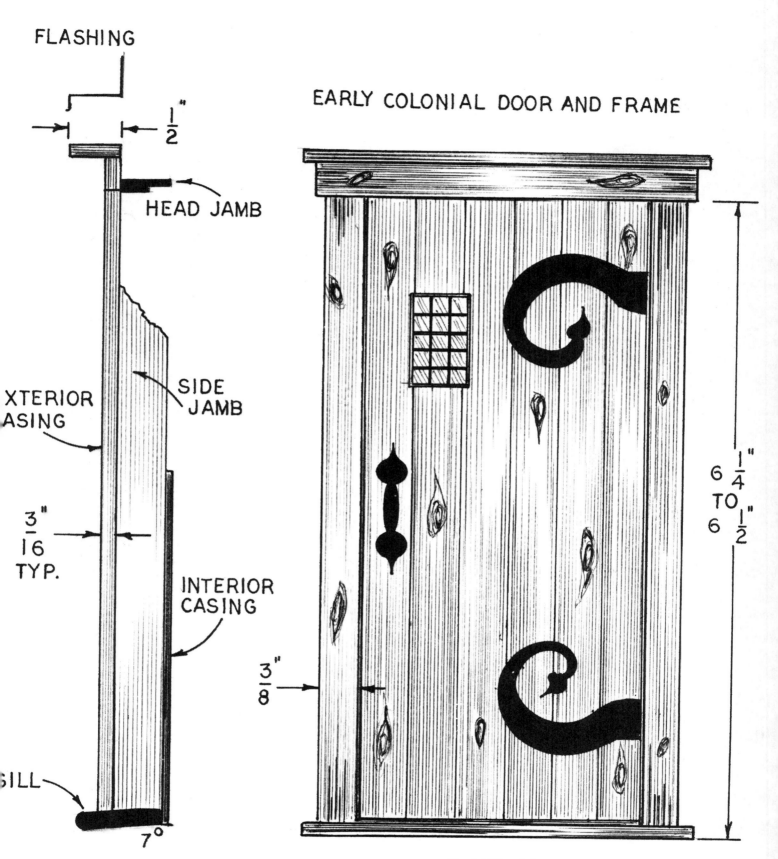

FLASHING

$\frac{1}{2}$"

HEAD JAMB

EXTERIOR CASING

SIDE JAMB

$\frac{3}{16}$" TYP.

INTERIOR CASING

$\frac{3}{8}$"

SILL

7°

EARLY COLONIAL DOOR AND FRAME

6 $\frac{1}{4}$" TO 6 $\frac{1}{2}$"

Fig. 1–50B. Colonial batten entrance door

63

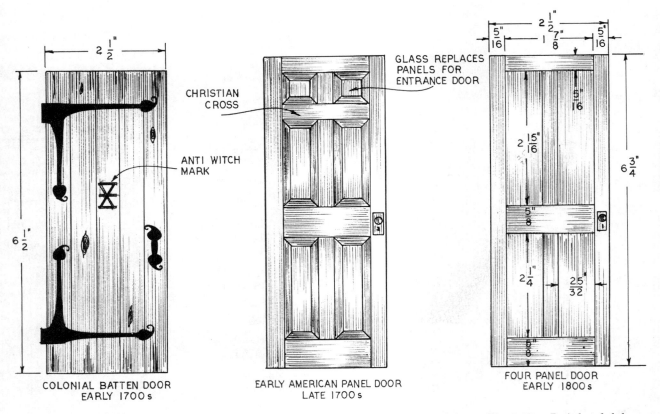

COLONIAL BATTEN DOOR
EARLY 1700s

EARLY AMERICAN PANEL DOOR
LATE 1700s

FOUR PANEL DOOR
EARLY 1800s

CHRISTIAN
CROSS

ANTI WITCH
MARK

GLASS REPLACES
PANELS FOR
ENTRANCE DOOR

Fig. 1–51.   Period-styled doors

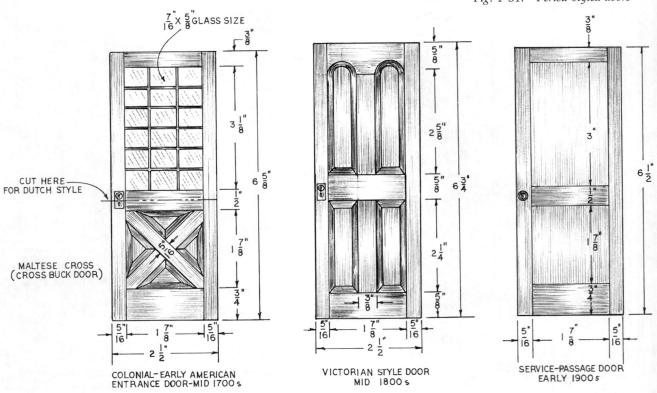

COLONIAL-EARLY AMERICAN
ENTRANCE DOOR-MID 1700s

VICTORIAN STYLE DOOR
MID 1800s

SERVICE-PASSAGE DOOR
EARLY 1900s

CUT HERE
FOR DUTCH STYLE

MALTESE CROSS
(CROSS BUCK DOOR)

Fig. 1–52.   Period-styled doors

SIX PANEL (CHRISTIAN ✝) DOOR

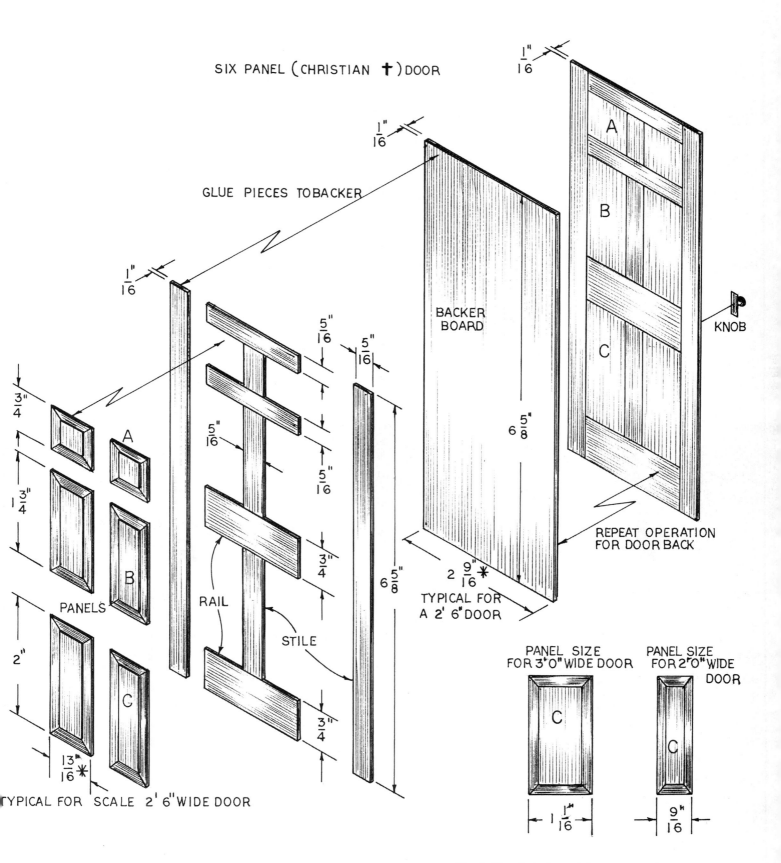

GLUE PIECES TO BACKER

1"/16

1"/16

BACKER BOARD

KNOB

A

B

C

REPEAT OPERATION FOR DOOR BACK

6 5/8"

2 9/16" ✳

TYPICAL FOR A 2' 6" DOOR

5"/16

5"/16

5"/16

3"/4

3"/4

5"/16

6 5/8"

RAIL

STILE

3"/4

1 3/4"

2"

3"/4

A

B

C

PANELS

13"/16 ✳

TYPICAL FOR SCALE 2' 6" WIDE DOOR

PANEL SIZE FOR 3' 0" WIDE DOOR

C

1 1/16"

PANEL SIZE FOR 2' 0" WIDE DOOR

C

9"/16

Fig. 1–53. Raised-panel door construction

65

Fig. 1–54. *Shopmade raised-panel doors*

ment may be required to insure proper action and fit.

Raised-Panel Doors

A raised-panel door is a series of rails, stiles, and inserted panels. The number of panels involved varied during different periods of furnishings. Six and four-panel doors were common in the early American, federal, and Victorian periods. Two-panel doors were common in the early 20th century and contemporary ranch houses use flush single plywood panel doors.

The following instructions are given for a standard six-panel door, but the construction is the same for other styles regardless of the number of panels used. The millwork (dadoes and rabbets) required for most raised-panel doors cannot be made in home workshops as a rule. To circumvent this restriction, shopmade doors are made up of various thicknesses of wood instead of inserted panels.

To construct a panel door, lay out the overall size on a piece of $1/16$-inch wood free of blemish. The rails, stiles, and panels are also cut from $1/16$-inch clear stock. Parts A, B, and C are then carefully glued to the main door body. See figure 1–53.

Next the panels are cut to fit the openings between the rails and stiles. A slight angle is sanded on the panels to create a bevel edge. A jig is used for the bevel operation to insure straight, even lines. The suggested jig is shown in figure 1–25. Complete one side of the raised-panel door and reverse the process on the other side. Sand the finished door smooth; the finished door will be $3/16$-inch thick.

Fix the completed door to a rabbeted jamb. The rabbet should be $3/32$-inch deep and $3/16$-inch wide, which is the same thickness as the raised-panel door. It is important to note that the jamb material is not strong enough to hold hinge pins or screws. Therefore the hinges should have fasteners long enough to penetrate the wall material beyond the jamb.

boards. Finally cut the $1/8$-inch by $1/4$-inch strips for the Z-batten, and glue the pieces forming the Z-batten to the rear of the door.

Note that the lower end of the Z-batten should be attached where the bottom hinge will be set. This, in effect, supports the weight of the door at the hinge point. Fit the finished door into the jamb, and attach the door to the frame with appropriate hinges. (See the metal hardware chapter in this section for an example of colonial-style hinges.) After the door is installed upon the hinges, some sanding adjust-

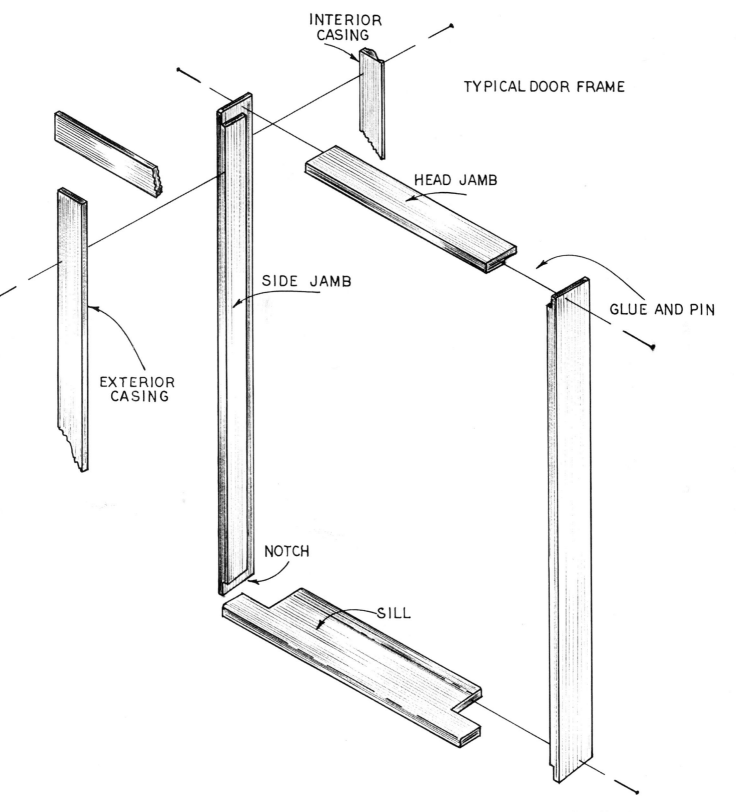

INTERIOR CASING

TYPICAL DOOR FRAME

HEAD JAMB

SIDE JAMB

GLUE AND PIN

EXTERIOR CASING

NOTCH

SILL

Fig. 1–55. *Exterior rabbeted jamb*

INTERIOR DOOR FRAME AND JAMB

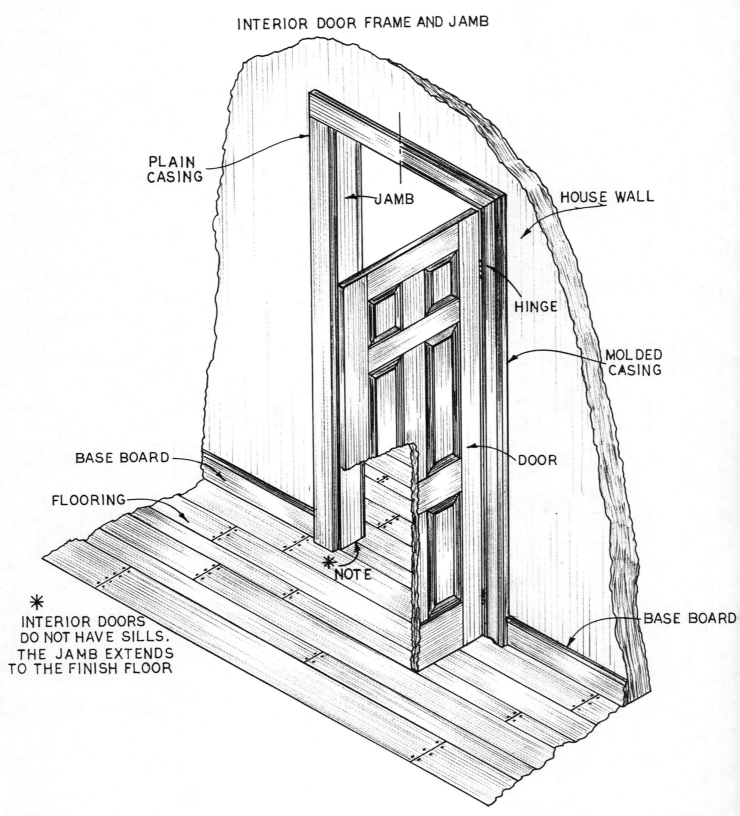

PLAIN CASING

JAMB

HOUSE WALL

HINGE

MOLDED CASING

BASE BOARD

FLOORING

DOOR

* NOTE

* INTERIOR DOORS
DO NOT HAVE SILLS.
THE JAMB EXTENDS
TO THE FINISH FLOOR

BASE BOARD

Fig. 1–56. Interior door construction

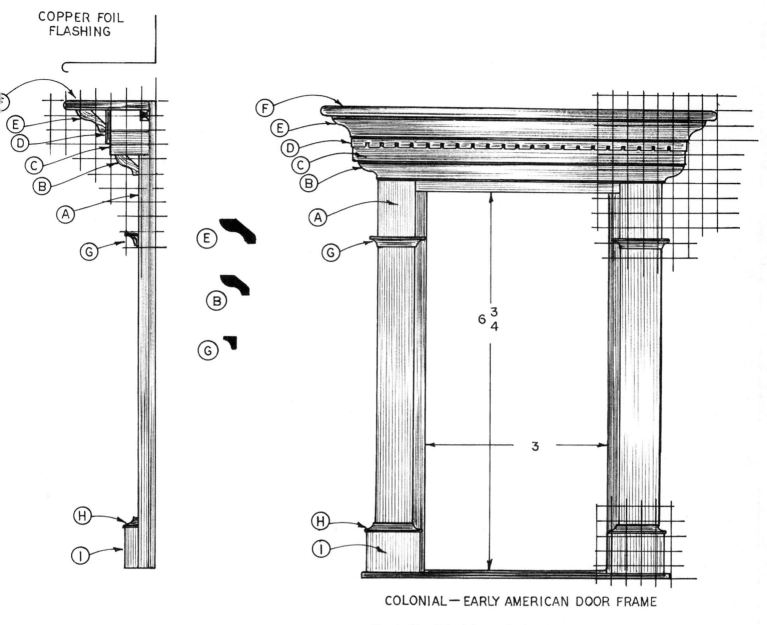

COPPER FOIL
FLASHING

E
D
C
B
A
G
B
G

F
E
D
C
B
A
G

$6\frac{3}{4}$

3

H
I

H
I

COLONIAL—EARLY AMERICAN DOOR FRAME

Fig. 1–57. Colonial or early American-style exterior frame

Each door should clear the floor by ¹/₁₆ inch. If a rug is to be used in the door area, a greater floor clearance must be allowed.

The four-panel Victorian door is made in the same manner as the six-panel door. The only exception is the crown or half-round in the top rail. A matching crown will be required in the top panels. See figure 1–52.

Figure 1–56 shows a typical interior door detail. The jamb is installed into a premade opening. The casing or trim is installed on both sides of the wall. The door in the selected style is then hung on the jamb. Note that most interior doors do not have a sill or threshold.

This particular style door frame is made from a series of built-up wood blocks and moldings. The basic casing (A) is a flat piece of stock. The built-on soffit board (B) is glued to A. The various moldings and head boards are glued on to create the crown, using parts B, D, E, and F.

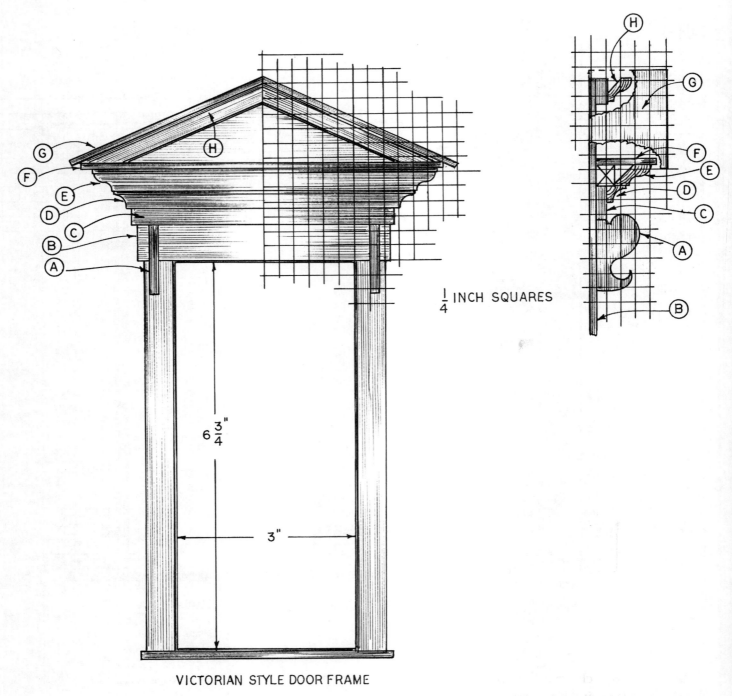

$\frac{1}{4}$ INCH SQUARES

VICTORIAN STYLE DOOR FRAME

Fig. 1–58. Victorian-style entrance

See detail figure 1–57. The frame foot-boards (I) are also glued to the frame and topped with a mold (H).

This door frame is made with plain wooden side casings. The decorative look-outs (A), head boards (F), built-out moldings (D, E, and H), and roof boards (G) are all added to the basic frame to create the continuous building out of the ornate head jamb.

5. *Staircase Construction*

The average stairway in miniature scale offers the worker some minor problems in construction. Most often the miniature house or room setting has an above average ceiling height in order to properly view interiors. This height can produce problems in stair construction, because each step may be higher than the acceptable standards for full-size houses. The result of high second or third floors could mean that a staircase could have more actual steps than found in normal houses or that the rule for standard rise height could be exceeded. Of the two options, extra steps seem the best solution even if more space is required in the stairwell opening.

CONSTRUCTION

The following instructions are given for normal full-size staircase construction, be-cause the scale and size remain faithful to the details in the rest of the miniature dwelling.

Measurements crucial to stair construction include the normal rise and run, which is the riser height and stair-tread size, of a proposed stairwell. As a general rule in full-size houses, the average rise should neither exceed 7¾ inches nor be less than 7¼ inches, and the tread width should neither exceed 12 inches nor be less than 8 inches. In miniature work, some minor adjustments can be made to these standard sizes if necessary. The height of the rise and the width of the tread determine the total length of the stair frame and opening.

Determining Size

To determine the space required for a stair-way opening or stairwell, measure the distance

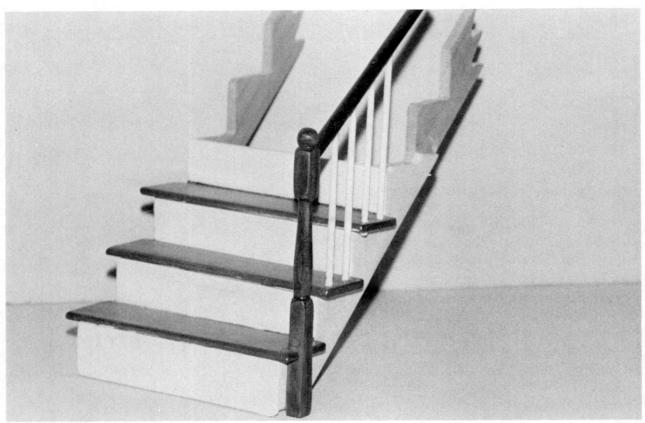

Fig. 1–59. Sample stairway construction

from the floor to the ceiling. For example, see figure 1–61. The size shown is 7½ inches, which has been reduced to the ¹/₁₂th scale from 7½ feet. Change this measurement to any convenient fraction: 7½ = ⁶⁰/₈. Note: each riser is ⅝-inch high. Divide ⅝ into ⁶⁰/₈ to get the answer: 12. This tells you that twelve risers are needed to make the stairs 7½ inches high. Twelve risers are needed but only eleven treads, because the twelfth tread is, of course, the floor of the next level.

To find the length of the stairwell, multiply the width of the tread in ¹/₁₂th scale times the number of stairs required. If the tread width is 9 inches in full-scale, it converts to ¾ inch in miniature. Figure this: ¾ x 11 = ³³/₄ or 8¼. This tells you that the stairwell should be 8¼-inches long, and you have determined above that it should be 7½-inches high.

The length and height of a staircase can be adjusted to fit any size room or ceiling height. See figure 1–61. Stairways can be broken with a landing, made in a curve or spiral, or curved in order to conserve space. However, the basic pitch, run, and rise remains the same for all types of construction. See figure 1–62.

Most often the stairwell ceiling will slant to match the pitch or slant of the stairs themselves. The minimum head room requirement is 6½ feet, or 6½ inches in the miniature scale. Normal handrail height is 30 inches, or 2½ inches in the ¹/₁₂th scale. See figure 1–61.

Stair Stringers

Stair stringers are the rough framing members that contain the cutouts for the rise and tread sizes. Normal-size stringers are laid out with a framing square. Perhaps the best method for miniature work is to make a jig of the desired run and rise. Figure 1–64 offers three common-size templates. Make a cardboard triangle of the desired run and rise. Mark the template riser height on one side (A) and mark the tread width on the other side (B). Draw a line between these two points and cut along this line. Invert this cardboard jig so that the cut line is even with the edge of the ³/₁₆-inch by ¾-inch wood strip, and mark out the proposed cuts. Remove the stock on the lines. Once one stringer is marked, tack it to another strip of wood and cut both stringers at one time. Remember, there will be one less tread than riser. For exposed stairs, cut the finished stringer-trim-board to match the stair cutout. Fit, glue, and pin the finished work to the stringer frame. See figure 1–59.

Line up, glue, and pin the finished stringers to the stairwell, or opening. Most homes with more than one level have all the stairs in the same location. For example, the cellar stairs are put under the first-floor stairs. The bottom of the first-floor stringers create the ceiling for the cellar stairs. Care must be taken to insure straight, level, and plumb placement of the stringers.

The stair risers can be made from clear pine strips. Cut ⅛-inch stock to the required width and length. Glue all the risers to the framing stringers at one time. Tight fits are required where the risers meet the side walls or trim work.

The stair treads are most often maple, or oak, but any hardwood will do. Cut ⅛-inch by ⅞-inch hardwood strips. The finished stair tread should extend ⅛ inch beyond the riser. Cut the strips down to required width and length. Glue the treads to the stringers and risers. Very often, the stair risers and trim are painted white and the treads are stained.

HANDRAILS, BALUSTERS, AND NEWEL POSTS

An exposed stairway, one not enclosed with a wall, has a starting newel post and balusters for the handrail. See figure 1–64 for suggested size and designs. The spacing on the balusters depends on the tread width. In the example offered in figure 1–64 where a 9-inch-scale tread is used, the baluster spacing averages 4¾ inches full-size, or ⅜ inches in scale.

Newel posts can have a side or top-rail mounting. With the side mount, the handrail attaches to the square top of the newel post. See A in figure 1–64. With a top mount, the rail is attached to the tenon of the newel. See B in figure 1–64. The balusters' tops fit into holes drilled into the bottom of the hand rail. The bottoms of the balusters fit into holes drilled into the treads.

Fig. 1–60. Staircase kit
(Courtesy Houseworks Ltd. and AMSI Miniatures)

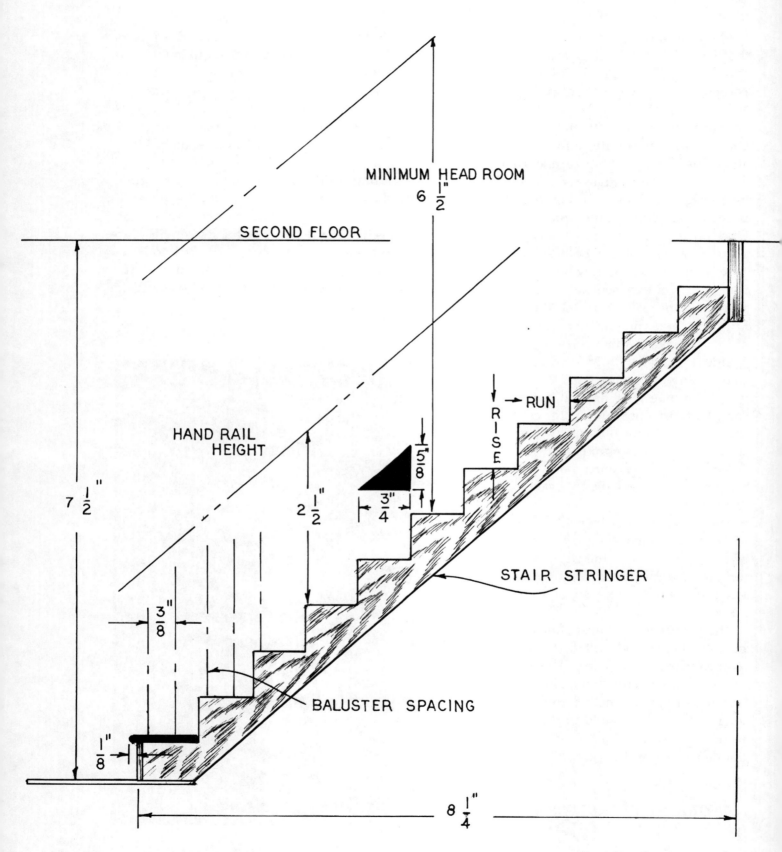

MINIMUM HEAD ROOM
6 1/2"

SECOND FLOOR

HAND RAIL
HEIGHT

RISE → RUN

2 1/2"

5/8"

3/4"

7 1/2"

STAIR STRINGER

3/8"

BALUSTER SPACING

1/8"

8 1/4"

Fig. 1–61. Sample stair stringer

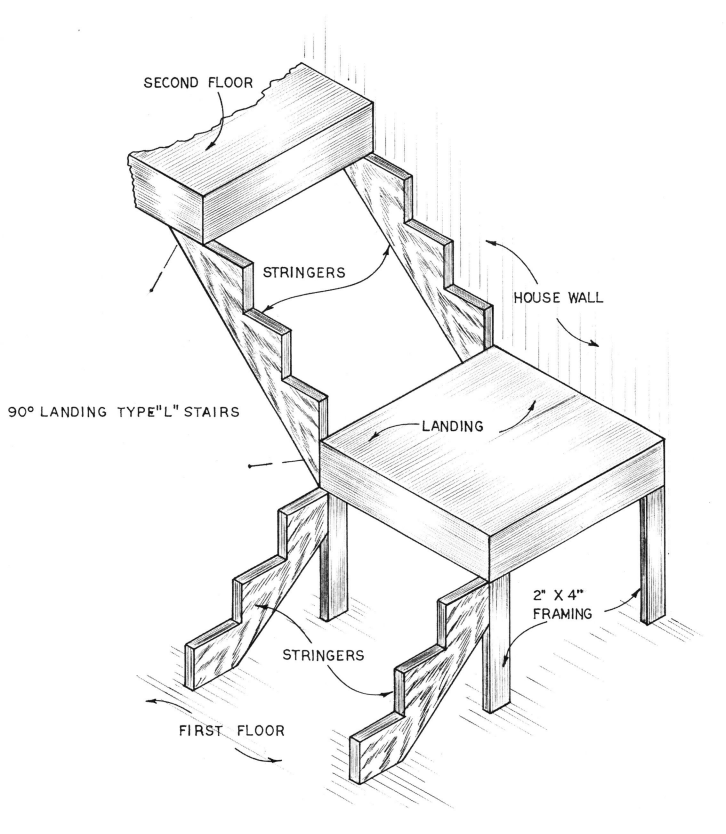

SECOND FLOOR

STRINGERS

HOUSE WALL

90° LANDING TYPE "L" STAIRS

LANDING

STRINGERS

2" X 4" FRAMING

FIRST FLOOR

Fig. 1–62. Stairway with landing

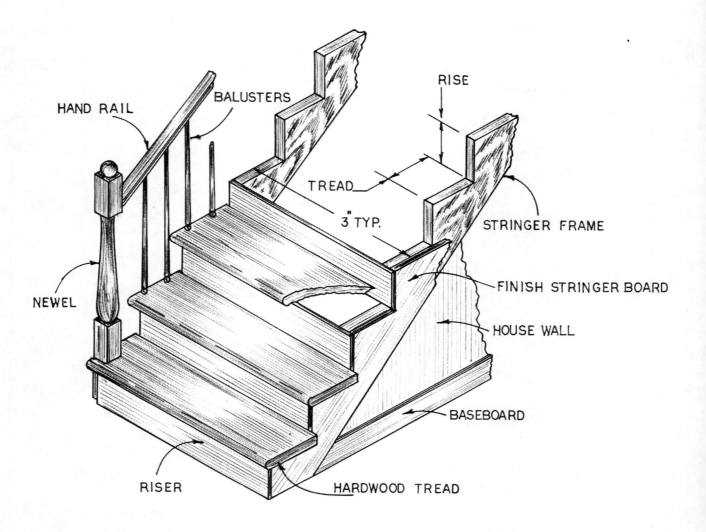

HAND RAIL

BALUSTERS

RISE

TREAD

3" TYP.

STRINGER FRAME

NEWEL

FINISH STRINGER BOARD

HOUSE WALL

BASEBOARD

RISER

HARDWOOD TREAD

SAMPLE EXPOSED STAIRWAY

Fig. 1–63. Sample construction

Handrails, balusters, and newel posts can be purchased from several suppliers listed in this book. The following instructions are given for normal home workshop construction.

Handrails

The molded handrail is very difficult to make except by hand-carving various short lengths. However, a flattened round glued to a thin flat strip makes an acceptable molded handrail. Perhaps one of the easiest rails to make is the plain round or oval handrail. See figure 1–64.

A length of hardwood dowel, ⅛ inch or ³/₁₆

inch in diameter, is sanded flat on one side. The flat surface provides an area for baluster holes, metal brackets, or wall attachments. The rails require mitered joints on any angles or turns. Mounting brackets are made from strips of sheet brass. The mount brackets are made to fit over an escutcheon pin. The pin is pushed into the house wall with the handrail fixed on top.

Balusters

The balusters can be turned on a lathe or drill-type lathe. Plain ¹/₁₆-inch-diameter

FULL SIZE STAIR PARTS PATTERNS
SCALE NEWEL POSTS

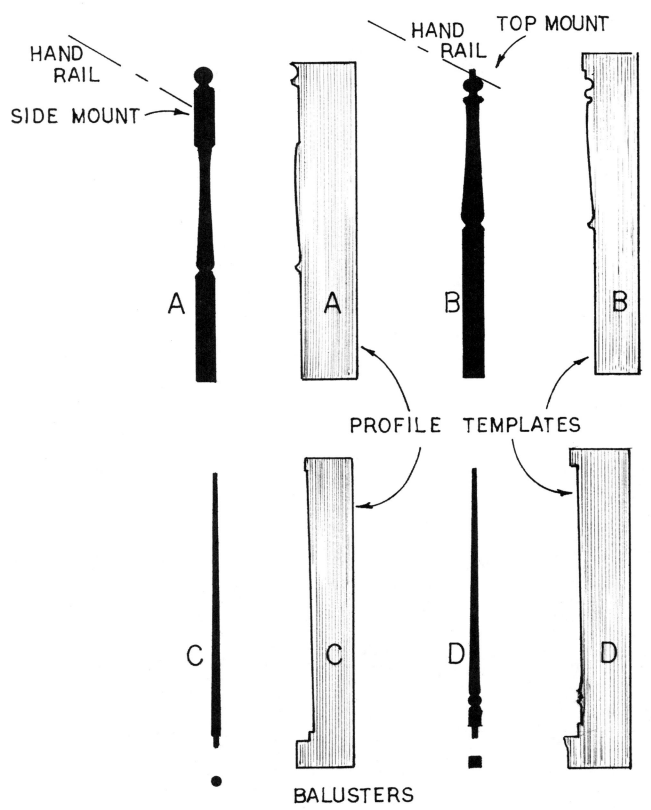

HAND RAIL

SIDE MOUNT

HAND RAIL

TOP MOUNT

A

A

B

B

PROFILE TEMPLATES

C

C

D

D

BALUSTERS

Fig. 1–64A. Newel and baluster profiles

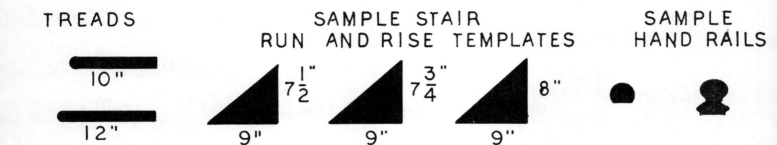

TREADS

10"

12"

SAMPLE STAIR
RUN AND RISE TEMPLATES

$7\frac{1}{2}$" 9"

$7\frac{3}{4}$" 9"

8" 9"

SAMPLE
HAND RAILS

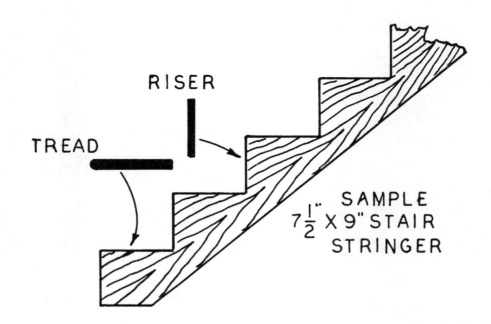

RISER

TREAD

SAMPLE
$7\frac{1}{2}$" X 9" STAIR
STRINGER

Fig. 1–64B.   Sample tread, rails, and pitch templates

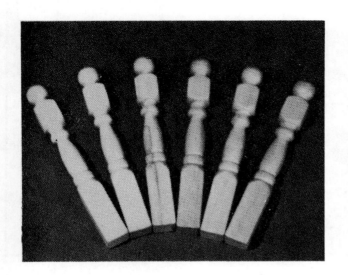

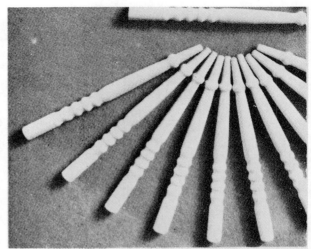

Fig. 1–65.   Miniature balusters and newel posts

rounds can be used if preferred. Hospital-size Q-tips make excellent balusters. If turned balusters are to be used, keep the design to a minimum. See figure 1–64 bottom. The miniature scale does not allow for excessive design depth. Figure 1–64 offers optional styles and profiles.

Newel Post

The newel post is the first solid member to hold the handrail in an open stairway. Most often the newel is a decorative member made from a turned-square of hardwood. Scale-sized newels are made from ¼-inch-square by 3-inch stock turned on a lathe or drill-type lathe. See figure 1–64 for profile and shape. The finished newel is mounted to the floor by a tenon on the post's bottom. The handrail is attached on the side with a drilled hole or on the top with a small tenon. See figure 1–64 top.

Make a newel post in a design of your choice.

As mentioned, the newel can be made on a lathe or in a mounted drill-press lathe. See figure 1–9, and the possible profile templates for newels and balusters in figure 1–64.

Insert the newel post next to the first stair tread. Mark out and notch the newel bottom so that the connecting handrail extends slightly over the tread edges. Mark out each tread for baluster holes. Each tread should have two balusters evenly spaced. Cut the handrail and fit it between the newel and the wall. The handrail should be 2½ inches above stair-tread height. See figure 1–63.

Temporarily install the handrail in place. Insert the premade balusters into the tread holes and mark the handrail where the baluster tops meet. Balusters must be plumb. Remove the handrail and drill the holes to accept the baluster tops. Glue the balusters into the handrail and stair treads. Glue the handrail to the newel post, and pin the other end into the wall.

6. *Fasteners, Finishes, and Hardware*

FASTENERS

The main fastening tool for miniaturists is glue. Most scale furniture stock is much too thin and fragile to allow nailing. However, bank, or sequin, pins can be used without splitting small pieces. Bank pins are very thin, ½-inch-long straight pins available in hobby or craft stores.

Several glues are available for miniature work. Any good white resin glue used for average full-size work will perform on miniatures. Elmer's, Sobo, Titebond, Franklin, and LePage glues work very well, and a small bottle lasts a long time for small work.

Excessive glue, the main enemy of miniaturists, has spoiled a great deal of fine work. Therefore, use caution when gluing stock together. All glues act as a wood sealer; the glue glazes, or fills, the wood pores wherever used.

Once the glue has dried, it is impossible for any stain to penetrate the wood in that area, and white spots appear. All traces of glue must be removed before staining. See figure 1–66, which is a Windsor chair fastened only with glue.

When gluing, wipe away any excess glue beads around the exposed area with a damp paper towel immediately after the joint is put together. After the joint has dried, a very thorough sanding is required to remove any trace left on the work. Visually inspect the whole general area of the joint carefully before staining to insure complete removal. Some spots appear clean only to show up after the stain is applied. If such spots show up while you are applying stain, sand the area immediately to remove the glue trace and restain.

Some manufacturers sell a prestained, colored glue. However, the precolored glue is available in only a few shades. The intended finishing stain could be several shades different from the colored glue, so the same exact care should be taken when using a precolored glue. Don't be lulled into a sense of false security or carelessness while using colored glue. Foresight is much better than hind work.

Readers can make their own colored glue by using normal universal color tints and white glue. The concentrated color is added to small amounts of standard white glue. The mixture is thicker than plain white glue; yet the adhesive power is retained.

Some craftsmen like to stain all of their miniature parts before assembly; thus any excessive glue glaze, as a rule, does not show as much. The only disadvantage to this process is that all the proposed parts must fit perfectly before assembly. Parts cannot be adjusted by sand-

Fig. 1–66.   Windsor chair

Fig. 1–67.   Miniature room (Courtesy Scientific Models, Inc.)

Fig. 1–68.   Miniature bedroom (Courtesy Sonia Messer Imports)

ing, because the color stain would be removed. Parts sanded can be restained sometimes, but often the resulting shade is not the same as the finish on the rest of the piece. The main word in using any or all glues is care. The time and care spent at this vital stage of the work prevents disappointment, redoing the piece, or rejection later of a worthwhile reproduction.

STAINING AND FINISHING

Several types of oil or water stains are available at craft and hobby stores in small amounts. Such stains are somewhat expensive in relation to the offered volume. Standard oil or water stain work as well with miniature furnishings as with full-size pieces. The standard stains can be purchased in pints and, in some cases, half-pint cans. The various color ranges and densities are almost limitless. If care is taken resealing the can, the contents last a very long time. Should stains dry or thicken, they can be cut with compatible thinners: turpentine for oil

stains, water for water stains. All of the miniature reproductions and parts of the houses in this book were finished with Minwax oil stain.

Staining wood is a fairly simple procedure. First carefully check to see if the furnishing is free of all defects, glue glaze, or filler residue. Apply the selected stain with a brush or by dipping the miniature into the stain can. Allow the stain time to penetrate: three minutes for softwoods, five minutes for hardwoods. Wipe the stained reproduction down with a cloth. Softwoods, such as pine, absorb stains quickly and should be wiped down soon after application. Hardwoods require a much longer set time and should be allowed to stand for several minutes before wiping. Allow the stain to dry overnight before applying the finish.

Finish Coats

A dull finish can be achieved by applying a coat of paste wax over the stain coat. Such a covering resembles the colonial-style, linseed oil finish. In most cases, however, a greater field of depth is desirable in the covering coat. All of the miniatures in this book, stained or painted, were finished with a lacquer-based product called Deft. This product and an acrylic finish called Wood Armour dries quickly, so that two to four coats can be applied in one day. A light sanding with #800 wet and dry finishing paper between every two coats produces an excellent semi-gloss finish. On the average, pine reproductions require about six coats of finish, while the hardwood reproductions have four coats. The Deft products are available in a spray can, which is useful for miniature work, or they can be purchased in pints or larger containers. This type of finish can be applied with a brush and does not leave marks. After the final coat has dried, apply a light coat of paste wax and buff to a deep gloss.

Several companies including Minwax produce a polyurethane covering. This finish can be obtained in a satin or high-gloss tone. Both finishes offer an excellent, highly durable finish and the only restriction is a twelve-hour waiting period between coats.

The Cunningham Company produces several craft products that work very well with

Fig. 1–69. Miniature furnishings (Courtesy Old Sturbridge Village, Sturbridge, MA)

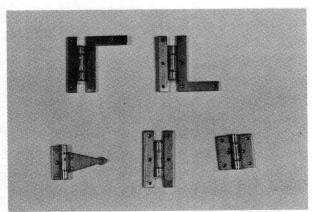

Fig. 1–70. Sample cabinet hinges
(Courtesy Northeastern Scale Models, Inc.)

miniatures. A six-pack set of acrylic colors is available in different tones and supplies a wide range of colors for furnishings. This company also produces several shades of stains and finish coverings under trade names. Regency is a satin finish and Coat Royale is a high gloss finish. Acrylic-based materials have the advantage of needing only a plain soap and water cleanup.

It is important to know the base of any finish material used. Oil stains or oil paints require turpentine or paint thinner for cleaning or thinning. Deft, which has a lacquer base, requires a lacquer thinner. Water-based stains, paints, or acrylic finishes clean with plain water. Remember, lacquer-based materials cannot be applied over oil-based paints, but can be applied over thoroughly dried oil stains.

Painting

At times some furnishings require painting and antiquing. While craft paints work very well, the painted furniture in this book was covered with standard latex wallpaints. In order to allow the wood's grain to show through the finish, the latex paint must be thinned or cut with water. The reproduction is painted and wiped down to a desired density. If the paint dries and is too thick or dense, sanding will cut the painted finish and bring back the wood grain. After the paint has dried, antique the surface by applying a glaze coat, which is half flat-black paint and half thinner. Wipe the glaze coat immediately to achieve the desired streaks and depth. Allow the glaze to dry and cover the reproductions with several coats of Deft or similar finish. Finish off with paste wax.

HARDWARE

Hardware is, perhaps, the most difficult area in miniature making. Good quality hinges, pulls, and handles are often scarce, somewhat expensive, and difficult to apply. One of the main problems is the scale involved. A normal cabinet hinge measures around 3 inches. When reduced to a 1/12th scale, the hinge size becomes 1/4-inch. Securing such a hinge with nails or screws becomes almost impossible. Therefore, many hinges are glued in place, but become less functional. To compensate, hinges, while still small, are often produced oversize. Extreme care must be taken in selecting and employing such hardware so as not to distract from the finished product. Hinges should be concealed if at all possible or placed in the back of furnishings where they will not show.

An alternative to exposed hinges for flush colonial doors or other types of furnishings is a hinge or swing pin. The hinge pin can be made from a brad, bank pin, large paper clip, or stiff wire. This particular type of hinge will work only on flush or full-lap doors. Such an operation will not work as inset or offset doors. Shopmade colonial-style strap hinges offer a means to hinge some offset cabinet doors, except that such hardware was used mainly on cottage-type or early period furniture and is not compatible with early American or federal period pieces. Instruction for making this type of hinge hardware is offered in the chapter on metalwork.

Door or drawer pulls do not create a major

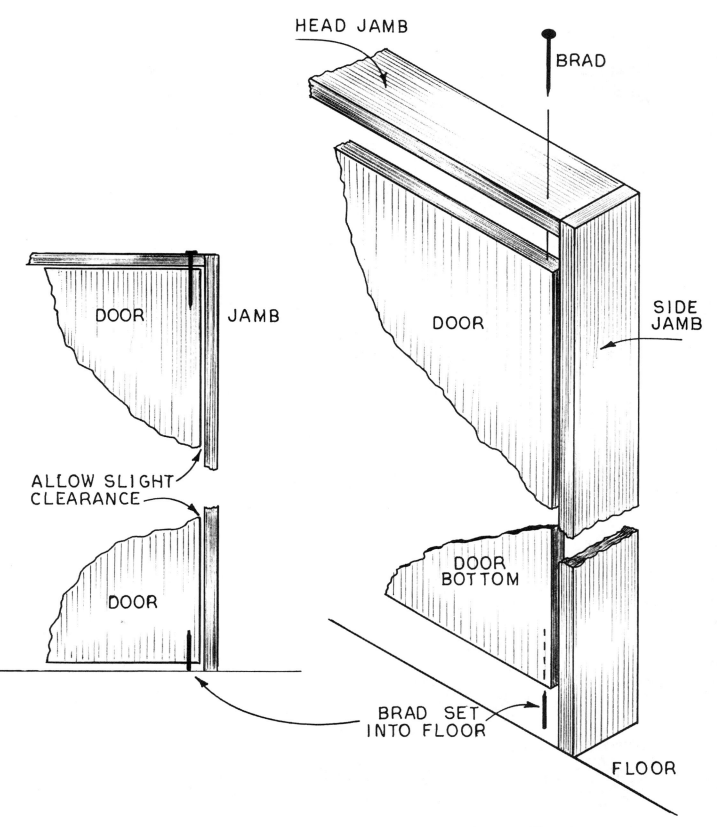

HEAD JAMB

BRAD

JAMB

DOOR

ALLOW SLIGHT
CLEARANCE

DOOR

DOOR

SIDE
JAMB

DOOR
BOTTOM

BRAD SET
INTO FLOOR

FLOOR

Fig. 1–71. Hinge-pin construction

85

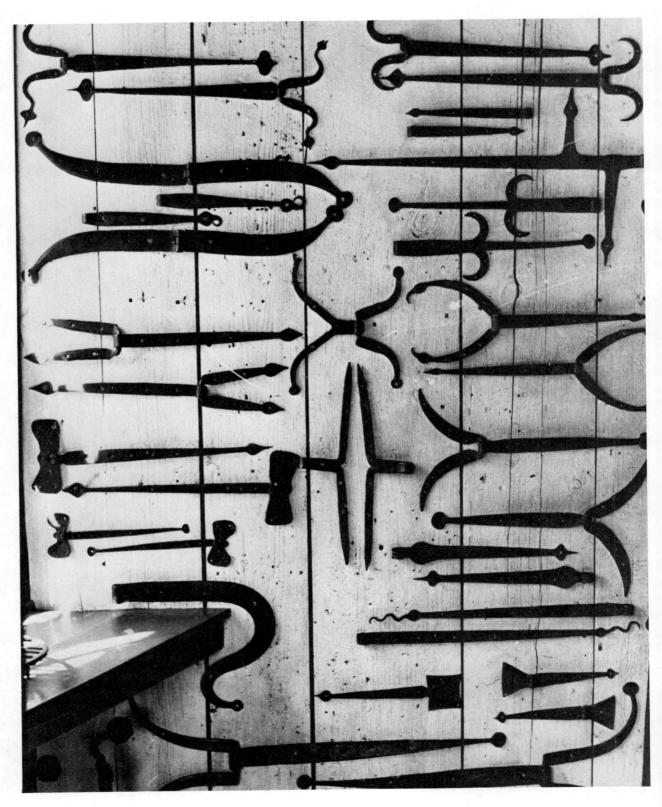

Fig. 1–72. Sample colonial and early American cabinet hardware (Courtesy Old Sturbridge Village, Sturbridge, MA)

Fig. 1–73. *Maple leaf bail drawer pulls (Courtesy Scientific Models, Inc.)*

problem in miniature work, depending again on the period style desired. Maple-leaf-bail, knob, or strap-type pulls can be purchased in perfect scale. At times exposed escutcheon heads make suitable pulls, or wooden or brass knob-type pulls can be made on a lathe or drill-press. Instruction for making this type of pull is offered in the chapter on metalwork.

Survey local craft and hobby outlets for hardware. If such hardware is not available, see the list of suppliers at the back of this book for suggestions and locations.

7. *Electrical Work*

Lighting is an important part of miniature homes and room settings, just as it is in full-size dwellings. Simulated soft tones, accented highlights, flickering fireplaces, or bright, golden sunlight can be achieved through the use of artificial lighting. The construction and final achievement of such illuminative effects requires a good deal more than just installing some wire or an electrical bulb here and there. Miniature wiring requires careful preconstruction planning coupled with a working knowledge of available electrical values, fixtures, hardware, bulbs, and special effects.

ELECTRICAL TERMS

In order to understand electrical wiring, the miniaturist should be familiar with electrical terms and concepts.

A.C. or Alternating Current: A.C. current is a flow of electricity that reverses direction at a given cycle. Most common in the United States is 60 cycles per second, which is sometimes called Hertz.

D.C. or Direct Current: D.C. current is a flow of electricity that moves in one direction only, such as battery-fed circuits in flashlights and automobiles.

Transformer: A transformer is a small apparatus that reduces normal wall-outlet voltage of 115 volts down to 6, 10, or 12 volts. Almost every home has a transformer somewhere for the operation of the doorbell chimes or the furnace thermostat.

Wire Gauge: Gauge refers to the size (thickness or diameter) of the electrical feed-conductor wire and the larger the gauge number, the smaller the wire size. For example, normal full-size houses, 120-volt wire often is 12 or 14-gauge wire, while low-voltage, miniature wire sizes are 28, 30, or 32-gauge. A 32-gauge wire is 1/32 of an inch in diameter.

Series Circuit: The most common example of a series circuit is Christmas-tree-light sets. The electrical feed wire runs to the first light and then goes to each light in turn. The return wire exits from the last light on the string back to the plug. If one light goes out, the circuit breaks, and all lights go out. Figure 1–82 is a series circuit. The main advantage of such a circuit is that the line voltage is divided by the number of lights in the string. Normal full-size strings could have twenty lights on a series circuit. The 120-volt string is thus divided by the number of lights. (120 ÷ 20 = 6 volts each.) The amount of illumination is somewhat reduced along with the voltage, but the life of the bulb is increased.

Parallel Circuit: This is the normal type of wiring used in full-size homes. The voltage is

Fig. 1–74. Victorian-style chandelier
(Courtesy It's a Small World)

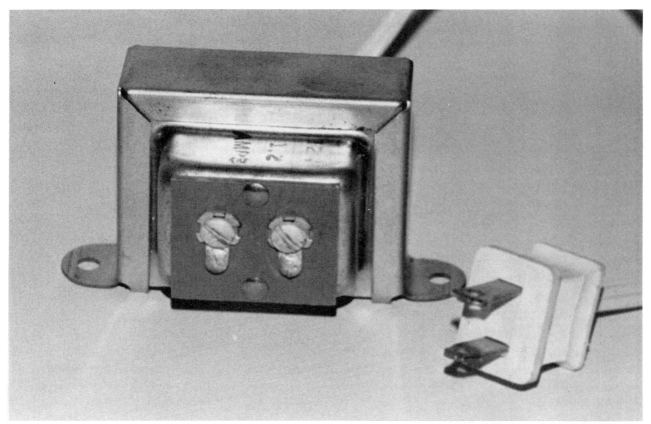

Fig. 1–75. Twelve-volt transformer

89

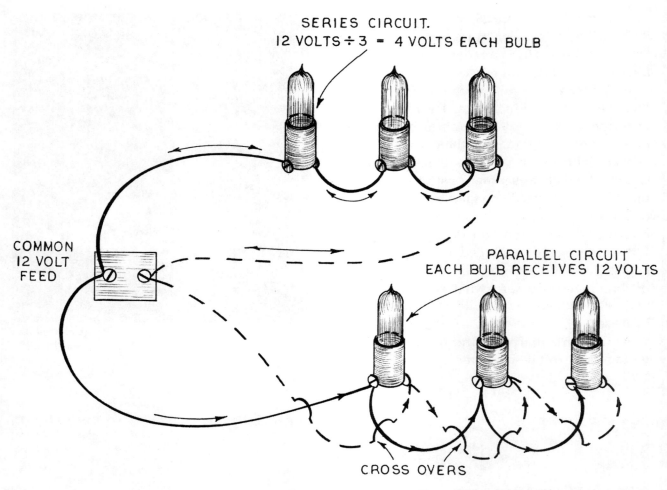

SERIES CIRCUIT.
12 VOLTS ÷ 3 = 4 VOLTS EACH BULB

COMMON
12 VOLT
FEED

PARALLEL CIRCUIT
EACH BULB RECEIVES 12 VOLTS

CROSS OVERS

Fig. 1–76. Parallel and series circuits together

the same at the end of the circuit as at the beginning. Two wires (live and neutral) are connected to the first light and in turn to several other lights without a major voltage drop or decrease. Unlike the prior example of a series-circuit string, three lights wired in parallel to a 12-volt circuit would each have 12 volts. Figure 1–83 is an example of a parallel circuit. Series and parallel circuits can be used together if worked off a common feed line. A series circuit cannot be used to feed a parallel circuit, because the series circuit makes the parallel section into part of the series; thus it reduces the line voltage by the number of lights on the line.

Switch: A switch is a device that interrupts and controls the flow of electricity. The most common are the on/off switches.

Dimmer Switch: The dimmer switch turns power on or off, and through built-in resistors, it offers control of the line voltage from very low to full power. Such a switch can be used to control interior lighting from mere candle power to full illumination.

Splice: A splice occurs when two or more wires are connected together. To make a two-wire pigtail splice, remove one inch of plastic insulation from each wire. Twist the two wires together. Trim the splice neatly to ½ inch. It is recommended that splices be soldered. Install wire nuts, silicone sealer, or plastic electrical tape on the splice to reinsulate it.

Volts: Volts measure the amount of push that moves electricity along a conductor. Volts can be equated to pressure in a water system, and they are the force that moves the volume. In an average wall outlet, the voltage is 120 volts. In a miniature house, the average voltage force is 12 volts. The difference between the two voltage systems is something like the difference between a hand pump and city water pressure. Several other factors are involved, but the push or voltage is one important part to be considered.

Ampere: Ampere or amp is the electrical term for volume: amount, bulk, strength, quantity. Using the water system example again, compare a garden hose to a large fire hose. While a garden hose, like a small wire, can only support a limited number of gallons per minute regardless of pressure, the large fire hose, like a large wire, can handle a huge cascade. Similarly the large wire can support high amps, and the small wire can take only low amps.

Capacity: Another factor involved with volts and amps is the conductor capacity or the amount of push and pressure a given wire will carry. If the number of gallons per minute that a fire hose supplied was forced through a garden hose, the garden hose would burst. The same is true of conductor wires. If too much voltage and amperes are forced through a small wire, the result is a break or a short circuit. All three factors are contingent upon each other. The force, or voltage, and the volume, or amperage, must rely upon the size or capacity of the conducting wire.

Milliamperes: Miniature systems use such small bulbs that they are computed in milliamperes. One thousand milliamperes equals 1 ampere. For example, the flourettes shown in figure 1–83 consume 80 milliamperes or .08 amperes. It would take slightly more than twelve such bulbs to equal one ampere. In comparison, normal household wall outlets have 15 amperes. Normal kitchen wiring has 20 amperes.

PIGTAIL SPLICE

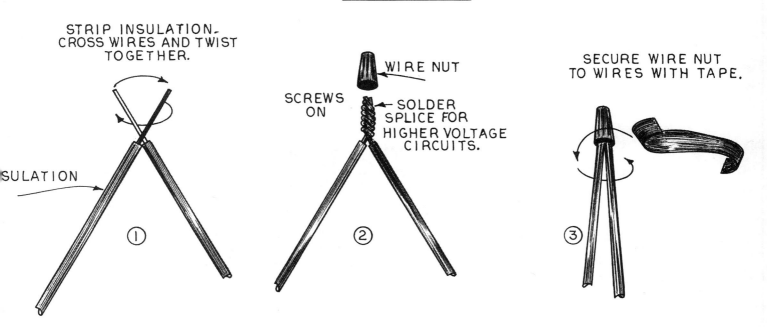

STRIP INSULATION.
CROSS WIRES AND TWIST TOGETHER.

SULATION

①

SCREWS ON

WIRE NUT

SOLDER SPLICE FOR HIGHER VOLTAGE CIRCUITS.

②

SECURE WIRE NUT TO WIRES WITH TAPE.

③

Fig. 1–77. Pigtail splice

Fig. 1–78. In-line fuse

Watts: Watts measure power, or the rate in which electrical energy is delivered and consumed by devices such as bulbs. Watts are a combination of amperes and volts. To return to the water concept, a watt is the volume multiplied by line pressure; this produces total gallons per minute. The formula for finding the number of watts is amperes multiplied by volts. In a miniature house, a single flourette bulb rated at 80 milliamperes, or .08 amperes on a 12-volt circuit consumes .096 watts: .08 x 12 = .096.

The following formulas are useful in finding reverse qualities if needed: Amperes x volts = watts; Watts ÷ volts = amperes; Watts ÷ amperes = volts.

Fuse: A fuse is a devise that contains a thin strip of soft metal. The metal melts when

Fig. 1–79. Snap-in fuse

92

overloaded, and thereby breaks the circuit. This is the equivalent of a one-time shut-off switch.

Without a fuse, excess demand could mean a fire, equipment breakdown, or burnt-out wires. The fuse is a prerated, safety device. Even so, the miniaturist must design the total electrical system to conform to the equipment limits. If, for example, a 1.2 amp, 12-volt transformer is used as a power supply, the total consumption must not exceed this rated capacity of 14.4 watts.

The best method to protect the miniature house or room setting from an electrical overload is to place an in-line or snap-in fuse on the secondary (low-voltage) side of the transformer. A one-ampere fuse, which is set into lower than the maximum output of the transformer. A one ampere fuse, which is set into the low-voltage side of a 1.2 amp transformer, will protect the miniature house from overloading. If more than one amp of power is drawn, the fuse wire will melt and shut down the system. Of course, the best method to prevent overload is to carefully compute all electrical equipment for total requirements and keep such demands under the maximum limit of the transformer. If more power is needed, a second or even third transformer can be added to large miniature homes.

MINIATURE LIGHTING

Miniature houses most often use a low voltage circuit system for all lighting. One of the reasons for a low-voltage circuit system is the fact that electrical fixtures and bulbs have been reduced in scale and cannot accommodate higher voltages. Another reason is that the smaller gauge wire required can be hidden within thin walls, floors, or moldings. The possible fire hazards of normal everyday household electrical service is reduced along with the reduction of line voltage. A 12-volt system eliminates many of the shock possibilities except where normal 120-volt household current

Fig. 1–80. Lamp fixture with plug

is used to feed the reduction transformer. Many miniature single room settings, however, use a combination of both a 120-volt system for background or general lighting, and a 12-volt system for specific fixture lighting.

The first step in wiring a miniature house is to decide what type of lighting you desire: general, specific, or both. General lighting is used mostly to illuminate the interiors of the houses, so that the furnishings and details can be seen. Specific lighting includes table lamps, ceiling fixtures, or fireplace effects.

A floor-plan sketch should be laid out before construction so that each fixture or bulb can be placed in particular rooms or places. Along with placement of sockets for fixtures, the proposed path for the circuit-feed wires should be planned. Wires can travel through floors, walls, moldings, or ceilings; therefore, feed holes have to be drilled during the various stages of construction. In some cases, wire feeds may be installed during construction, but the connections cannot be made until after the house is finished. See figure 1–84.

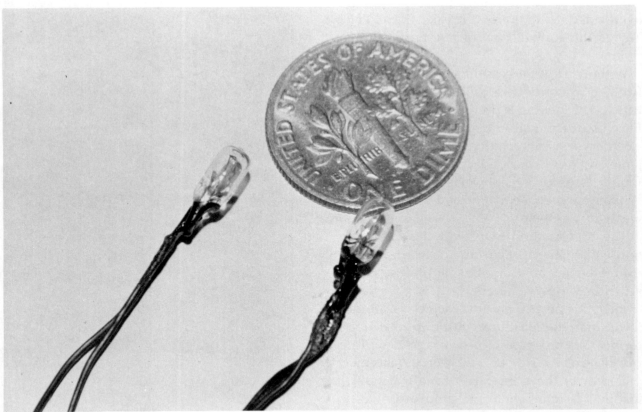

Fig. 1–81.   Grain of Wheat bulb

A suitable space must be found for the low-voltage transformer. All the low-voltage feed wires and the main 110-volt transformer feed line must run together and meet. Transformers can be installed in the attic, a closet, under stairwells, or within false walls. Perhaps the safest placement of a transformer is outside the miniature house itself. With this type of arrangement, only the low-voltage wires enter the house, and this reduces the chance of fire. See the plans for an exterior power-pack transformer later in this chapter. See figure 1–87.

The selected transformer space must have adequate ventilation, because some heat develops from the unit itself depending upon its electrical load. Easy accessability should be another criteria for space selection. Should a malfunction develop with the wires, fuse, or transformer, replacement will be necessary. The transformer can be located within one space,

with the main feed terminal block or distribution panel in another space some distance away. The two low-voltage wires from the transformer can be run to another floor or section of the house to feed a central terminal block, which in turn feeds several different circuits.

Specific Lighting

Several different types of low-voltage lights and fixtures are available through local or mail-order miniature suppliers. Each one serves a purpose and care should be taken in their selection.

Bedroom ceiling fixtures, chandeliers, table lamps, or wall fixtures can be purchased premade or in kit form. (See list of suppliers in Section four.) Each fixture contains a two-wire lead and bulb(s) ready to be connected to a

12-volt system. Many contain the Grain of Wheat bulb, which often has a 10,000-hour life.

If such fixtures are to be used, placement should be planned in advance so that the circuit-feed wires can be concealed. Some miniaturists have gone so far as to plan where a table lamp will rest. They have fed the wires up through a drilled table leg so that the connection could be made under the table top. It is obvious that such placement requires careful planning, because the table and its lamp once installed cannot be easily moved.

For lamps or fixtures, the rough wiring is concealed within drilled holes in room partitions, ceilings, moldings, or floors. When the miniature house is completed, a splice is made between the fixture feed wires and the circuit feed wires. The splice is soldered and insulated and pushed back into concealment as the fixture is fastened to the wall or ceiling. Individual fixtures or lamps can be operated off a switch, if desired.

Special lights installed in a fireplace can give an illusion of the red glow of a log fire. The

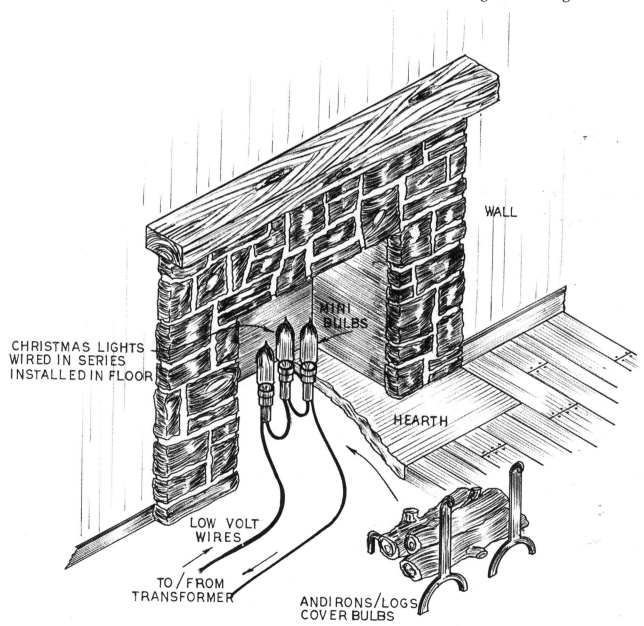

Fig. 1–82. Normal miniature bulb from Christmas tree light string used for firelight

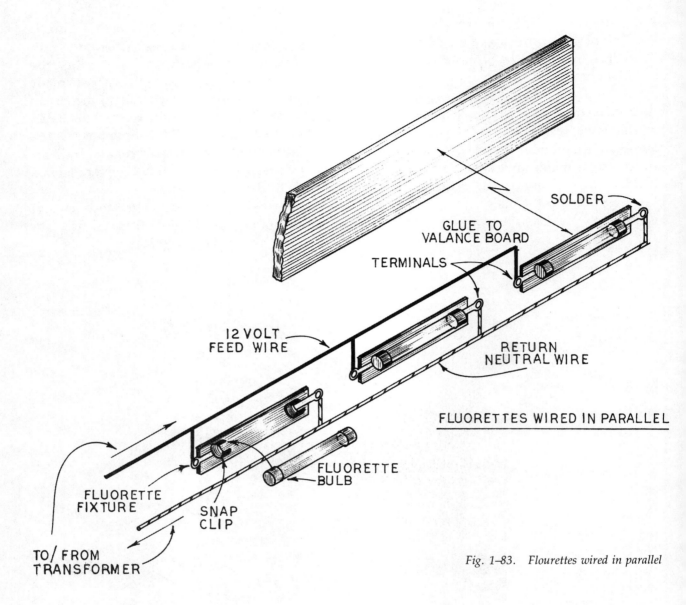

SOLDER

GLUE TO
VALANCE BOARD

TERMINALS

12 VOLT
FEED WIRE

RETURN
NEUTRAL WIRE

FLUORETTES WIRED IN PARALLEL

FLUORETTE
BULB

FLUORETTE
FIXTURE

SNAP
CLIP

TO/FROM
TRANSFORMER

Fig. 1–83. Flourettes wired in parallel

lights are inserted into the hearth floor or rear fireplace wall, where they can be concealed with andirons and miniature logs. One method that has worked well for fireplace effects is to insert three light sockets cut from a regular mini-light Christmas tree string. The normal voltage of such lights can be determined by dividing the number of lights on the original string into 120 household voltage. Example: A string has 20 lights, so divide 120 by 20. You will determine that each light uses 6.0 volts.

If a 12-volt power system is used in the miniature house, it would burn out the mini lights quickly. Therefore, such lights must be wired in "series" of two or three units, which means that each light will get one-third of 12 volts, or 4 volts each. Such a circuit, while a little dimmer, increases the overall life of the bulb.

Typical fireplace lighting includes one red and two amber lights. One or two of these bulbs can be the blinking type if preferred. With two bulbs blinking out of synchronization and one constant bulb, the effect is one of a crackling, burning fire. Some miniaturists have used individual 40-watt flicker candelabra lights for fireplaces. However, flicker bulbs are rather large and require full 110-line voltage.

Many hobby and craft outlets carry a com-

96

mercial fireplace flicker unit. It operates from a normal 12-volt transformer, has solid-state construction, and changes lights and shadows to offer realistic firelight. See the list of suppliers in Section four.

General Lighting

The interiors of most miniature houses are dark. To enhance ordinary viewing of furniture and details, a type of valance general lighting is employed using a small 12-volt flourette bulb, which comes complete with a snap-in socket and wiring terminals.

A strip of wood, or valance, is installed at the top of the open section of the house. Several fluorette fixtures are installed on the strip in a string. When lit, the light from the fluorettes flows and reflects off the ceiling to give a soft, subtle tone to interior rooms. Such general lighting does not distract from the specific lighting of lamps, fireplaces, and chandeliers.

To wire fluorettes, glue or screw the snap-in sockets to the walls, ceiling, or valance strip. After the glue has set, run 32-gauge wire to the terminals as shown in figure 1–83 and solder the joints. The fluorettes are wired in parallel, because each fixture requires 12 volts for effective brightness. Several fluorettes can be used in such a manner. Each fluorette consumes 80 milliamperes; therefore, consideration must be given to the total number of bulbs used and the total transformer output available for operation. Amperes and transformer ratings have been discussed earlier in this chapter.

Single-Room Settings

Many single-room settings employ 110-volt lights for general or daylight, and 12 volts for specific fixture lighting. Such construction becomes rather simple because 110 volts must be used to supply the transformer. The 110-volt feed line is used for the larger general bulbs and then is used to supply the reduction transformer. See figure 1–85. Ample space must be provided for the 110-volt bulbs and sockets plus the transformer. Each bulb, regardless of wattage or size, gives off heat when in use, and adequate ventilation must be provided for such an operation.

Well-made, single-room settings can simulate daylight or nighttime lighting. In such a system, it is recommended that two switches be used; one heavy-duty switch to control the 115-volt line and another to control the specific low-voltage lighting. Observers can then choose their own lighting effects. A 115-volt dimmer switch may be used to control the gen-

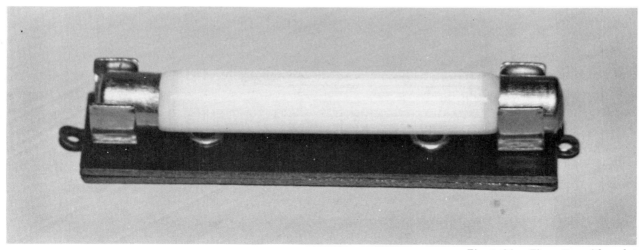

Fig. 1–84. Flourettes with socket

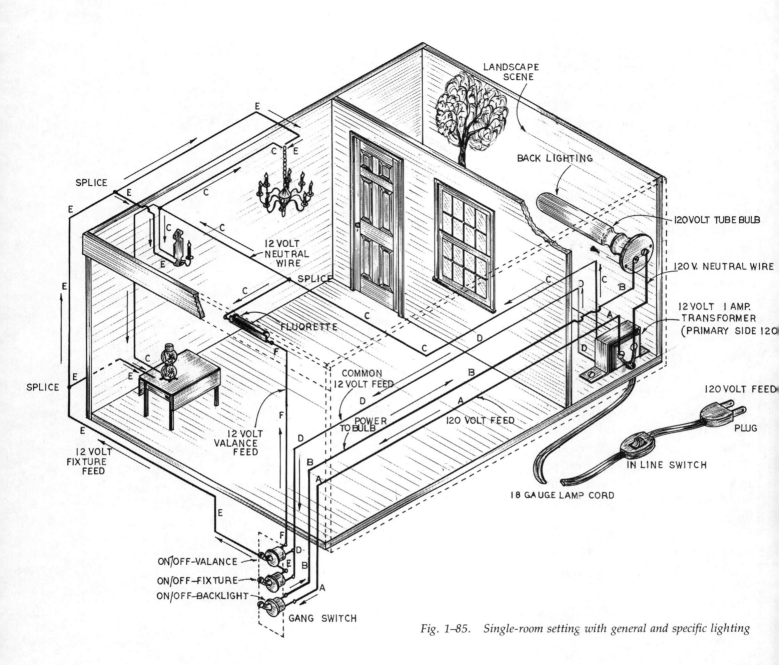

LANDSCAPE SCENE

BACK LIGHTING

120 VOLT TUBE BULB

120 V. NEUTRAL WIRE

12 VOLT 1 AMP. TRANSFORMER (PRIMARY SIDE 120)

120 VOLT FEED

PLUG

IN LINE SWITCH

18 GAUGE LAMP CORD

SPLICE

12 VOLT NEUTRAL WIRE

SPLICE

FLUORETTE

SPLICE

COMMON 12 VOLT FEED

POWER TO BULB

120 VOLT FEED

12 VOLT VALANCE FEED

12 VOLT FIXTURE FEED

ON/OFF-VALANCE

ON/OFF-FIXTURE

ON/OFF-BACKLIGHT

GANG SWITCH

Fig. 1–85. Single-room setting with general and specific lighting

eral lighting in order to simulate high noon, late afternoon, dusk, twilight, or evening. The transformer feed cannot be connected to such a dimmer switch, because the dimmer switch would reduce voltage to the reduction unit.

In figure 1–85 the transformer and 120-volt bulb is installed behind the miniature back wall. Notice that the normal 120-volt feed wires are connected to both the transformer and the light bulb on the *primary* side only. This circuit, A and B, can be operated from a front end

switch if preferred. The low-voltage, miniature circuit operates from the secondary terminals of the transformer, lines D and C. Line D runs to front switches in order to feed lines E and F.

In this type of construction, the rear back light can be turned on and off from the front. The soft balance lighting in circuit F is controlled by a front switch as are the specific lamp lights in circuit E. All the lighting circuits can therefore be used individually or in unison.

Figure 1–85 shows how a double box, or

room within a box, is used for room settings. Windows and doors look out onto landscaped scenes, some complete with miniature trees or shrubs. The daylight, 120-volt bulb illuminates the landscape and floods light through the windows. By switching off the larger bulb, darkness descends and small 12-volt specific lamps can be turned on. Soft, low-voltage general lighting can be used on the front by installing two or three fluorettes behind the molded frame.

TRANSFORMERS

As mentioned earlier in this chapter, the reduction transformer is an electrical device that takes 120-volt household current and reduces it to low-voltage amounts. The actual voltage depends on the reduction value of the transformer. Most miniaturists use a 12-volt circuit, and the transformer selected most often has a 12-volt circuit.

In addition to the voltage reduction, the am-

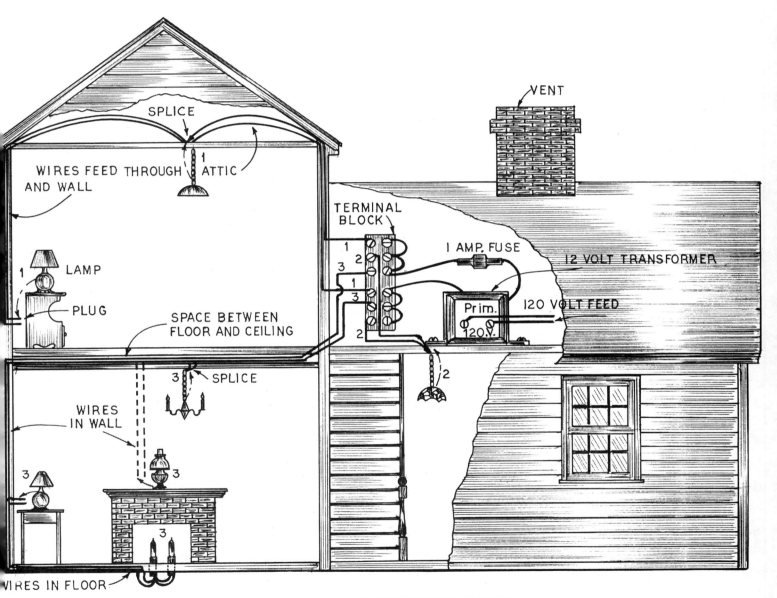

THREE CIRCUIT LOW VOLTAGE SYSTEM

Fig. 1–86. Low-voltage multiple circuit

pere value must be considered. While many household circuits are designed for 15 or 20 amperes, which is the capacity of the average fuse or circuit breaker in the fuse box, the miniature house uses only .75, 1.2, or 1.5 ampere ratings, depending upon the number and size of the lights involved.

It is very important to select a transformer large enough to accommodate the lighting circuits planned with little extra reserve for possible additions. For this reason, normal household doorbell transformers are inadequate for anything more than one or two miniature lamps. Overdrawing amperes from an undersize transformer can cause excessive heat, resulting in a possible fire hazard, short circuits, shocks, and equipment failure.

The best miniature transformer must maintain a constant voltage rating in order to protect the life of small bulbs. Some transformers can vary as much as four to six volts. Thus a miniature bulb designed for 12 volts may, in fact, receive 16 volts and this reduces the bulb life. Since some of these miniature bulbs cannot be replaced without excessive work, every effort should be taken to protect their estimated life.

Most transformers have two short primary supply wires marked "PRI." One wire is black and the other white. The 120-volt feed wire, the wire that supplies the power from the house wall outlet, is spliced to these transformer wires. This is the electrical supply side. Other transformers have a built-in prewired 115-volt supply cord. The advantage of this type of transformer is that it illuminates the splices and prevents possible wiring mistakes. The secondary (low voltage) side of the transformer may have two wires or two screw-type terminals. This is the reduction side of the transformer.

Warning: The transformer must be connected properly. If the 120-volt wire is mistakenly tied to the secondary side of the transformer, the transformer could produce in reverse. This would increase the exit voltage. Exit current could reach 1200 volts for a short period of time before the transformer burns itself out. Serious injury under certain circumstances could result from such a mistake. If the primary and secondary sides of the transformer are not clearly marked, have the original supplier check and mark the two sides. If there is any doubt about which side is primary and which side is secondary, *do not use the transformer.*

Wiring a Transformer

To wire a miniature transformer, strip ¾ inch of insulation from the primary white and black wires. Do not cut through the wire itself. Strip the same amount of insulation from the two-wire, 18-gauge supply cord. Supply lines can be extension cords, or lamp cord. Tightly twist one supply wire onto the black transformer wire and twist the other supply wire to the white transformer wire. Solder these pigtail splices. Trim neatly and install a wire nut on each splice. Stripped or bare wire should not extend below the wire nut. Insulate each wire nut with plastic electrical tape. When the supply cord is plugged into a wall outlet, the transformer becomes live and produces 12 volts on the secondary side. A switch can be installed in the supply line or at the miniature house or room to control the circuit, if desired.

If the transformer has secondary wires, strip away ¾ inch of insulation from each low-voltage feed wire. Strip the same amount of insulation from the low-voltage supply-circuit wires. Splice one circuit wire to one transformer secondary wire with a pigtail splice. Repeat the operation for the other circuit wire. Solder the two splices and trim neatly. Install small wire nuts and cover with electrical tape.

If the transformer secondary side has terminals, loosen the two screws with a screw driver. Wrap one low-voltage wire on each terminal and tighten the terminal screws in place. Such screws have right-handed threads and will tighten clockwise. The terminal eye, or open end, should be on the right-hand side of the terminal so tightening the screw will wrap the eye around the shaft.

Several low-voltage circuit feeds can be attached to terminal screws or the secondary wire splices. The transformer secondary supply wires can supply two or three circuits all with the same voltage as long as the total ampere rating is not exceeded.

If a multiple-unit, circuit-feed-wire operation is desired, have the transformer's secondary feed run to a terminal block, which in turn can accept several different low-voltage circuits. Another possibility is a series or master switch operation, so that individual rooms or individual specific lights can be turned on or off.

Figure 1–86 shows a multiple-unit, low-voltage circuit system. The main 12-volt supply

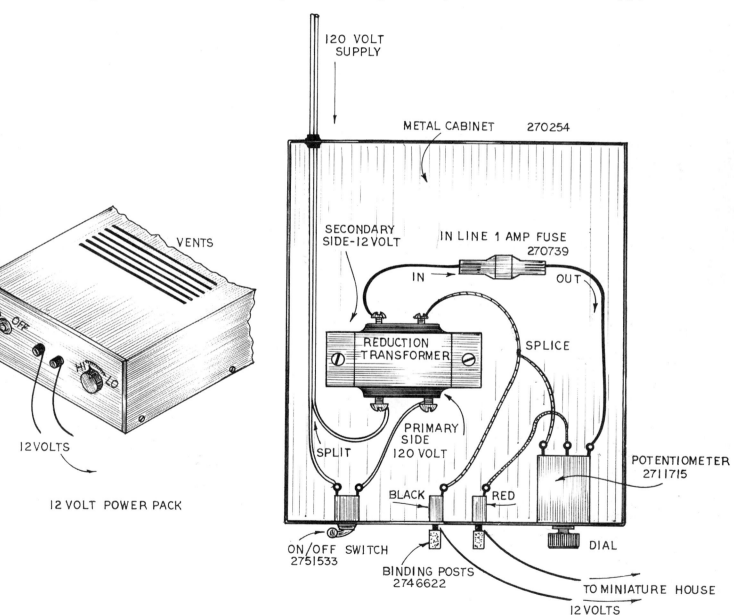

Fig. 1–87. *Drawing for power pack*

101

Fig. 1–88. Federal-period room setting with overhead chandelier (Courtesy Sonia Messer Imports)

lines are fed to a terminal block. In turn, the terminal block distributes power to the various circuits. Circuit 1 illuminates the upstairs overhead light and the table lamp. Circuit 2 powers the hall light plus any other fixtures in this area. Circuit 3 feeds the living room chandelier, table lamp, and fireplace. Care must be taken so that the total amperage of the circuits does not exceed the rated ampere output of the transformer.

Low-Voltage Power-Pack Transformers

A power-pack transformer source can be made to supply low-voltage power for miniature homes. The advantage of this type of op-

eration is that the transformer is contained outside of the house itself, and the secondary voltage line can be controlled. It operates much like a dimmer switch in full-size houses.

Power-pack containers can also become master switch panels, controlling individual rooms or specific lights with individual switches. The container can be built into the miniature house or into a base support table made for the miniature house.

Figure 1–87 offers the plans and parts required to build a 12-volt power-pack. The transformers, switches, parts, and container are available through normal electrical, hobby, or radio supply outlets. See list of suppliers for names and locations. All of the parts used in figure 1–87 are available through Radio Shack, Inc. Their stock numbers are included.

Construction

Material List

Part	Amount
Reduction transformer, 12 volt, 1.2 amp.	1
Binding posts	2
Fuse stand and 1 amp. fuse, in-line	1
Potentiameter, 10,000 ohms	1
Single pole, single throw toggle switch	1
Vented metal cabinet	1

1. Mark out and drill the required exits on the metal cabinet for the potentiameter control, the binding posts, and the on/off switch. Note that the size of the required holes will vary depending upon the parts manufacturer, so purchase the various equipment before starting work. Drill the 120-volt supply-cord hole, fuse, and transformer-mounting screw holes. See figure 1–87 for suggested locations.

2. Secure the transformer and fuse stand to the metal cabinet with machine screws. Run the entrance of the 120-volt supply cord into the cabinet through a rubber grommet. Strip ½ inch of insulation from the ends of the supply cord and wrap one wire around one terminal on the *primary* side of the transformer. (Note: Some transformers do not have a screw terminal on the primary side. Instead they have short lengths of wire. Such pigtail wires must be spliced to the supply cord wires. Insulate the splices very carefully.) Run the other sup-

ply feed wire to the on/off switch. See detail in figure 1–87. Secure the wire to one terminal on the switch. Run a short piece of 18-gauge supply wire from the other switch terminal to the remaining terminal on the transformer. The on/off switch now controls the transformer.

3. To construct the secondary side, run a single strand of 28 to 32-gauge wire from one secondary transformer terminal to one side of the fuse stand or in-line fuse. Continue this strand of wire from the other side of the fuse block to the left-hand terminal side of the potentiameter. Run another strand of single low-voltage wire from the remaining secondary transformer terminal to the right-hand terminal on the potentiameter. In the center of this wire, make a T splice and run the spliced wire leg to the black binding post. Run another single strand of low-voltage wire from the center potentiameter terminal to the red binding post.

The miniature low-voltage circuits operate from the two binding posts, and the on/off switch controls the transformer and in turn the low-voltage supply. The dimmer knob on the potentiameter allows low-voltage control from very low to 12-volt maximum. Terminal blocks or multiple circuits can be attached to this power-pack, if preferred. Such blocks could feed several low-voltage circuits. If a terminal block is used, it would receive the wires intended for the binding posts.

8. *Fireplaces*

There are as many styles for fireplaces as there are for doors or windows. Each time period has had a particular exterior style, but the basic construction measurements and components have remained about the same. It is the use of finish trim and the type of materials that have been dictated by style.

BASIC CONSTRUCTION

Every fireplace has depth, an actual firebox, a face area or masonry front, and a mantel or finished trim. The firebox depth is usually two feet in life-size or two inches in miniature size. The width of the firebox is slightly larger than the frontal opening. Except for some colonial styles, the common frontal opening is 3 feet wide by 2½ feet high, which is 3 inches by 2½ inches on the ¹/₁₂th scale. Therefore, the width of the interior firebox can average 3½ inches to 4 inches wide.

Form the firebox from a single U-shaped box frame as shown in figure 1–91. The interior of this box is coated with textural material and scored into brick. Seldom is the firebox interior a bright brick color, for the constant fire blackens the whole interior.

Fireplace Front

In many cases, the fireplace front is flush with, or extends slightly beyond, the house wall. See figure 1–91. The ultimate width and height of the face is determined by individual choice and style selection. Figures 1–97 and 1–102 offer an average colonial or contemporary-style fireplace front with simple moldings and mantel caps. However, federal, Victo-

Fig. 1–89. *Federal-period room with fireplace (Courtesy Sonia Messer Imports)*

Fig. 1–90. *Early American music room (Courtesy Scientific Models, Inc.)*

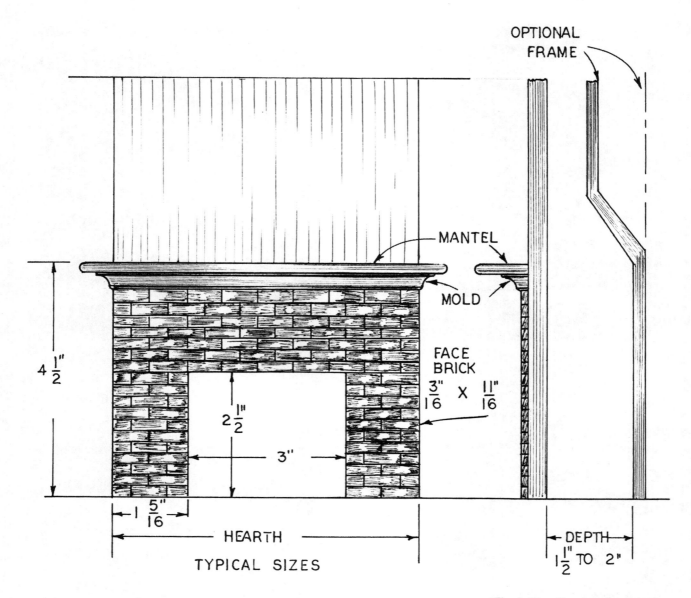

OPTIONAL FRAME

MANTEL

MOLD

FACE BRICK $\frac{3"}{16}$ X $\frac{11"}{16}$

$4\frac{1}{2}$"

$2\frac{1}{2}$"

3"

$1\frac{5}{16}$"

HEARTH

TYPICAL SIZES

DEPTH $1\frac{1}{2}$" TO 2"

Fig. 1–91. *Common fireplace sizes*

rian, and some contemporary styles have a narrow masonry front blanketed by decorative woodwork, as shown in figures 1–100 and 1–101.

Plans must be made for the fireplace placement when laying out the house floor plan. A firebox floor and a hearth are required for each fireplace. The area for the hearth and firebox floor should be marked out on the floor, and allowances for the area should be made when applying the finished flooring. The cut-out places on the floor act as a guide for the placement of the firebox floor and hearth. Normally the hearth is 2 feet wide, which is 2 inches on the miniature scale, and as long as the masonry front of the finished fireplace.

The firebox area should be given a brick texture. Follow the following construction techniques for making face brick. Although the firebox area is always brick, the hearth area can be brick, tile, or flagstone. See detail 5 in figure 1–96.

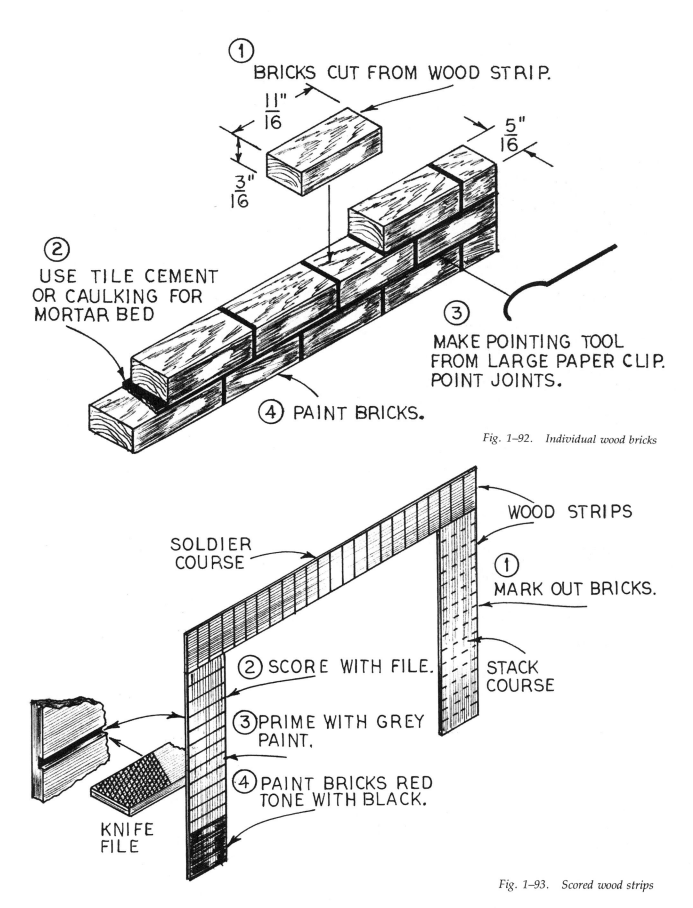

① BRICKS CUT FROM WOOD STRIP.

$\frac{11"}{16}$

$\frac{5"}{16}$

$\frac{3"}{16}$

② USE TILE CEMENT OR CAULKING FOR MORTAR BED

③ MAKE POINTING TOOL FROM LARGE PAPER CLIP. POINT JOINTS.

④ PAINT BRICKS.

Fig. 1–92. Individual wood bricks

WOOD STRIPS

SOLDIER COURSE

① MARK OUT BRICKS.

② SCORE WITH FILE.

STACK COURSE

③ PRIME WITH GREY PAINT.

④ PAINT BRICKS RED TONE WITH BLACK.

KNIFE FILE

Fig. 1–93. Scored wood strips

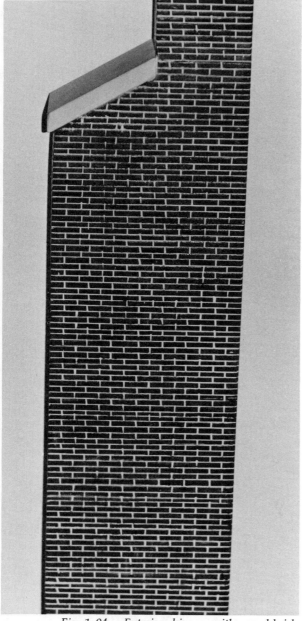

Fig. 1–94. Exterior chimney with scored bricks

Brickwork

Masonry brickwork can be achieved with three different methods.

1. Individual bricks: Several companies offer scale-size wood bricks for sale or wood strips can be cut into bricks in the home workshop. The average size of a common brick is 2 inches by 4 inches by 8 inches. See figure 1–92.

2. Wood faces: Soldier or stacked brick faces can be made from wood strips with saw cuts filed to resemble mortar joints. See figure 1–93. After scoring, the wood is primed with a grey paint to look like the mortar. After the prime coat is dried, paint each brick red and tone with flat black paint. Such an operation becomes very tedious for half-lapped or normal-bond brickwork. The same type of wood strips can be used for marble fireplace faces. Cut the strips to size. Cover the strips with marble-style contact paper, color pictures, or paint. Normal hobby stores or hardware stores sell these materials.

3. Textured brick: Determine the size of the frontal area you desire. Outline this area with thin, wooden guide strips. See figure 1–96. Apply a thin coat of texture material within this designated area and within the firebox. The masonry texture can be obtained from normal drywall joint cement, hydrocal model maker's texture (found in train hobby stores), or plaster of paris.

Allow the first thin coat of texture to dry. Mark the brick mortar lines on the guide strips. (Normal brick measures $3/16$ inch by $11/16$ inch on a miniature scale.) Apply a second coat of textural material to the fireplace areas. Mark out or score the mortar joints, to create scale bricks, and cut in the half-laps or bond marks. See 3 in figure 1–96.

Allow the second coat of texture to dry thoroughly. Sand the bricks to remove any rough edges. Paint each individual brick a flat dull red, but leave the mortar joints the color of the original texture material. (Most often this color is off-white, grey, or tan.) While the red coat of paint is still moist, shade each brick with flat black paint. See 4 in figure 1–96. Allow the paint to dry and install any trim or woodwork.

Stonework

Stone facing is made from the same texture material. See figure 1–97. Apply the second coat of texture as outlined for brick work. While

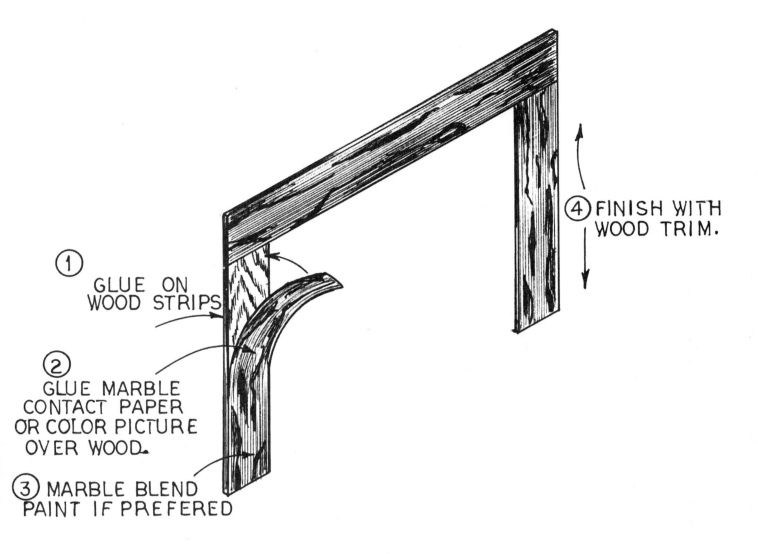

① GLUE ON WOOD STRIPS

② GLUE MARBLE CONTACT PAPER OR COLOR PICTURE OVER WOOD.

③ MARBLE BLEND PAINT IF PREFERED

④ FINISH WITH WOOD TRIM.

Fig. 1–95. Marble-faced masonry

the material is still moist, mark the mortar joints thereby creating individual stones.

Most masonry stonework contains pieces of assorted shapes and sizes. Full-lengthwise mortar joints are unique and not commonly used. The vertical joints need not be straight as in bricks. Irregular shapes become the norm and not the exception. When the texture has dried, paint the stonework a medium grey and leave the mortar joints the color of the original textural material. While the grey paint is still wet, tone and blend in flat black shades to achieve a stone effect.

Wood-Encased Fireplace Fronts: Federal and Victorian Periods

The federal and Victorian periods had several hundred different styles of fireplace fronts. The actual masonry material could be glass, polished stone, marble, tile, or face brick. (See the chapter on the Victorian house in section three.) The firebox construction for this style of fireplace is the same as for any other. The masonry face, as a rule, is much smaller than other period fireplaces, and is usually one brick on each side in a stack position (no half-joints)

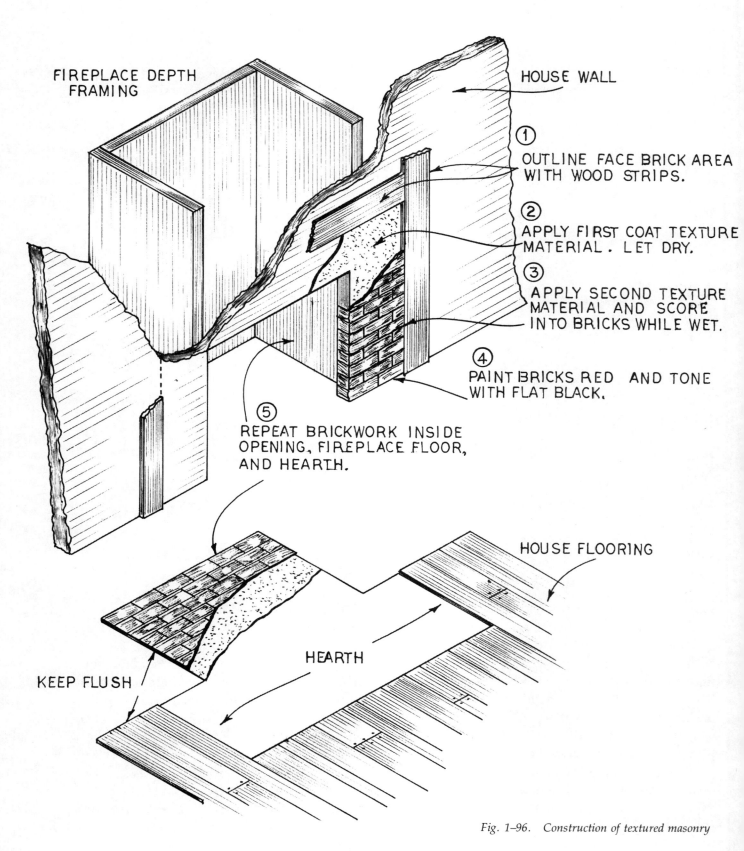

FIREPLACE DEPTH FRAMING

HOUSE WALL

① OUTLINE FACE BRICK AREA WITH WOOD STRIPS.

② APPLY FIRST COAT TEXTURE MATERIAL. LET DRY.

③ APPLY SECOND TEXTURE MATERIAL AND SCORE INTO BRICKS WHILE WET.

④ PAINT BRICKS RED AND TONE WITH FLAT BLACK.

⑤ REPEAT BRICKWORK INSIDE OPENING, FIREPLACE FLOOR, AND HEARTH.

HOUSE FLOORING

KEEP FLUSH

HEARTH

Fig. 1–96. Construction of textured masonry

110

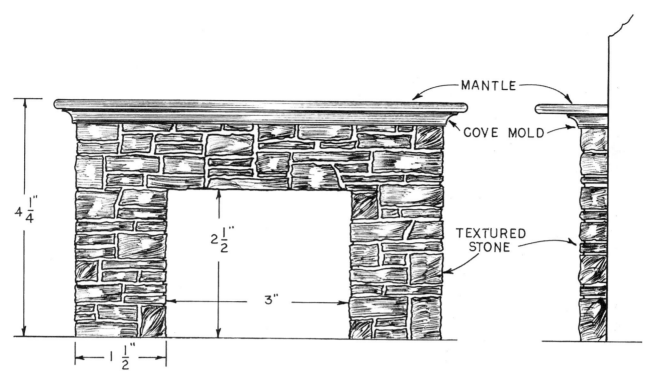

MANTLE

COVE MOLD

TEXTURED STONE

$4\frac{1}{4}''$

$2\frac{1}{2}''$

$3''$

$1\frac{1}{2}''$

Fig. 1–97.   Textured stone fireplace

Fig. 1–98.   Stone fireplace

Fig. 1–99. Victorian-style fireplace

and one brick in the soldier position for the top row.

Mark this area around the firebox for the proposed face. If scale-size tile is to be used, the size of the tile will determine the ultimate exposed area. For tile work, glue the tiles to the fireplace front and allow the glue to dry. The tile joints can be grouted (filled) with tile grout or plaster of paris. See figure 1–101.

If bricks are to be used, they can be made by using the texture method, the wood-strip method shown in figure 1–93, or by gluing individual wood bricks as shown in figure 1–92. If marble or glass facing is to be used, the marble consists of three pieces: the two sides and one header. Scale-size simulated marble or glass can be achieved by gluing contact paper to wood strips or by painting these strips with marble composition paint available in most hardware or hobby stores. See figure 1–95.

The enclosed wooden trim and frame and mantel is made of several blocks of wood and

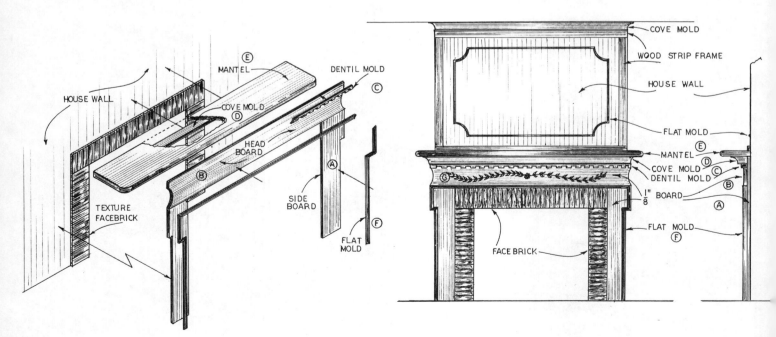

Fig. 1–100. Mantel construction

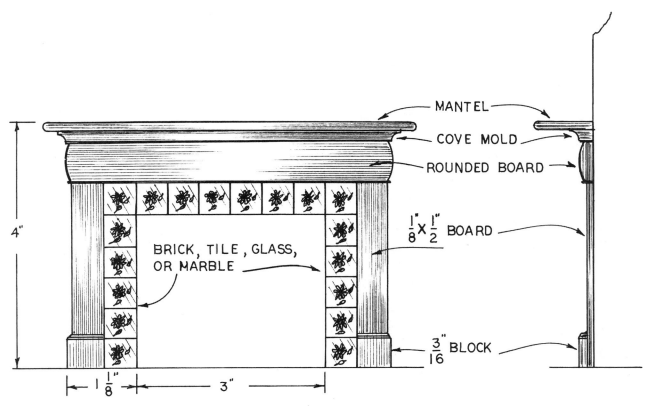

MANTEL

COVE MOLD

ROUNDED BOARD

$\frac{1}{8}" \times \frac{1}{2}"$ BOARD

BRICK, TILE, GLASS, OR MARBLE

$\frac{3}{16}"$ BLOCK

4"

$1\frac{1}{8}"$

3"

Fig. 1–101. Tile-faced fireplace

various moldings. See figure 1–100. Cut ⅛-inch by ½-inch smooth wood strips for the side pieces (A). Glue these strips to the fireplace wall next to the masonry material.

Cut, form, and shape the head trim (B). Glue the head trim to the wall over the finished masonry. Cut the dentil trim (C) if used, and apply this mold to the top of the head trim. Cut and fit the cove molding (D) and apply it over the dentil mold. Miter the cove molding ends so that this molding returns back to the house wall.

Cut the mantel (E) to suggested size and shape. Install the finished mantel over the cove molding and to the house wall. Apply the flat moldings (F), if desired. Carvings (G) can be purchased or made from jewelry findings and attached to the head strip if desired. Most often the woodwork of fireplaces in this period was painted pure white.

Colonial Walk-in Fireplace

The huge central fireplaces common to colonial farmhouses are much larger than other period fixtures. While the other fireplaces just supplied heat, the colonial fireplace was an oven, stove, central heater, and a gathering place for the whole family.

To perform all these functions, the colonial fireplace often had beehive ovens or bake ovens built into the large walls. An interior seat or shelf was often added to walls, or a space was allowed for the placement of a wood settee.

The wrought-iron crane was attached to one side wall, and the huge, solid beam mantel was pierced with pegs to hold the various tools and utensils used in the kitchen.

As mentioned, the central colonial fireplace is much larger than other fireplaces. A height of 5 to 6 feet, a similar size width, and a 3 to

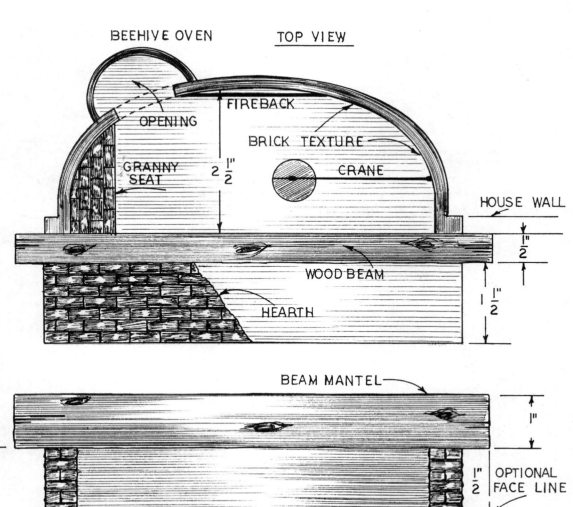

BEEHIVE OVEN   TOP VIEW

FIREBACK

OPENING

BRICK TEXTURE

GRANNY SEAT

$2\frac{1}{2}''$

CRANE

HOUSE WALL

$\frac{1}{2}''$

$1\frac{1}{2}''$

WOOD BEAM

HEARTH

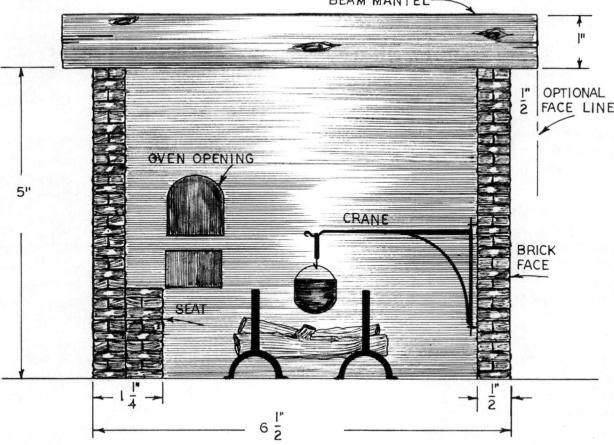

BEAM MANTEL

$1''$

OPTIONAL FACE LINE

$1\frac{1}{2}''$

OVEN OPENING

5"

CRANE

BRICK FACE

SEAT

$1\frac{1}{4}''$

$\frac{1}{2}''$

$6\frac{1}{2}''$

Fig. 1–102. *Colonial-style fireplace construction*

4-foot depth is not uncommon. Little if any facebrick area is employed.

Mark out and cut the house wall where the fireplace will go. Build a curved box around the back of this cut-out area. See figure 1–102, top view. If a beehive or roasting oven is to be used, cut the opening into the fireback framing. Build a frame for the oven and coat the inside area with textural material, like stucco.

Attach the oven fixture to the firewall framing. Build the granny seat or roasting shelf, if preferred, into the firebox side wall. See figure 1–102 bottom. Run ground strips for the exterior face area and cover the complete side of the firebox and exposed face area with textural material. Follow the general directions given in figure 1–96 for this operation. Paint the bricks a suitable color. Remember the interior firebox should be very dark to simulate a constant fire. Finally, install a scale-size beam mantel over the face area.

9. *Metalwork*

The common ironwork found in period miniature houses represents a large problem for hobbyists. The base material does not work as easily as wood, nor does it accept convenient fastening as a rule. Very often metal requires heating in order to construct curves or bends, and many wood craftsmen shy away from metal unncessarily.

AVAILABLE SUPPLIES

Anything made out of metal is a potential supply. Coffee cans are perfect sources of tin plate. Copper foil supplies sheet copper and flashing materials. Miniature railroad or model-aircraft hobby stores often carry a full line of brass, aluminum, or bronze tubing in rounds and sheet stock.

Large paper clips can be used for scale size ½-inch or ¾-inch rounds. Welding or brazing

Fig. 1–103. Miniature serpentine-style wrought-iron hinges

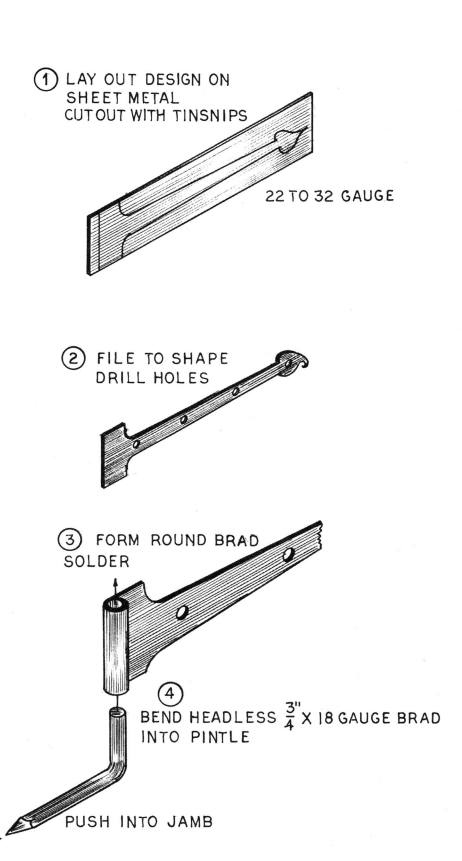

① LAY OUT DESIGN ON
SHEET METAL
CUT OUT WITH TINSNIPS

22 TO 32 GAUGE

② FILE TO SHAPE
DRILL HOLES

③ FORM ROUND BRAD
SOLDER

④
BEND HEADLESS $\frac{3}{4}$" X 18 GAUGE BRAD
INTO PINTLE

PUSH INTO JAMB

Fig. 1–104.   Strap-hinge construction

117

STRAP HINGE TEMPLATES

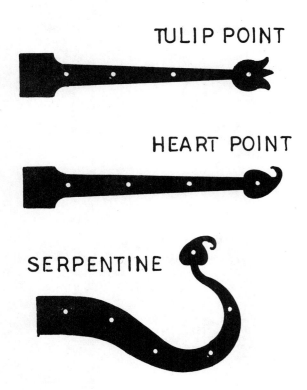

TULIP POINT

HEART POINT

SERPENTINE

ST. STEPHEN'S HINGE

RAM'S HEAD

PINTLE

Fig. 1–105.   Patterns for colonial-style hinges

rods can offer a wide variety of round stock in brass, copper-colored, or steel metal. Copper or aluminum flashing found in normal lumberyards can supply sheet metal for hinges, and copper pipe caps can be transformed into assorted pots and pans. Copper or bronze window screening can be worked into fireplace screens, and many hardware outlets offer short lengths of steel or brass rounds and flats. The possibilities are almost endless if you allow your imagination to wander.

HARDWARE

One of the most artistic hardware periods was the colonial era. Large strap hinges, or serpentine hinges, were featured on batten doors. (See figure 1–103.) Symbolism played a great part in the final design as hinges and handles became anti-witch agents, but the hinge design used in these periods was always functional. The long hinges helped hold green lumber in place yet offer strength and serviceability.

In miniature work, the most difficult part of a strap hinge is fastening it to the door jamb. To help solve this problem area, the old-time pintle pin was employed. (See figure 1–104.)

Suggested Tool Inventory

Hacksaw.

Soldering iron.

50/50 acid core solder. (Resin core solder is needed for electrical work.)

Straight tin snips.

Bench or drill vise.

Long-nose pliers.

Assorted files. (Round, triangle, flat, half-round, knife.)

Steel wool.

Emery paper.

Hinge Construction

1. Lay out the proposed design on 20 to 28-gauge sheet copper, which is normal house flashing. Cut out the rough shape with tin snips. File the rough-cut hinge to a finish design. See 1 in figure 1–104. Drill mounting holes where desired.

2. With long-nose pliers, turn the butt end of the hinge into a round that will fit around a small brad shank. See detail 2 in figure 1–104. Solder this formed round.

3. Cut the head from a ¾-inch brad and bend the shank into a right angle for the pintle pin. See Detail 3. Attach the finished hinges to the selected door. Fit the door to the premade jamb and mark the pintle placement. Push the sharp end of the pintle pin into the door jamb and hang the hinge rounds over the upright ends.

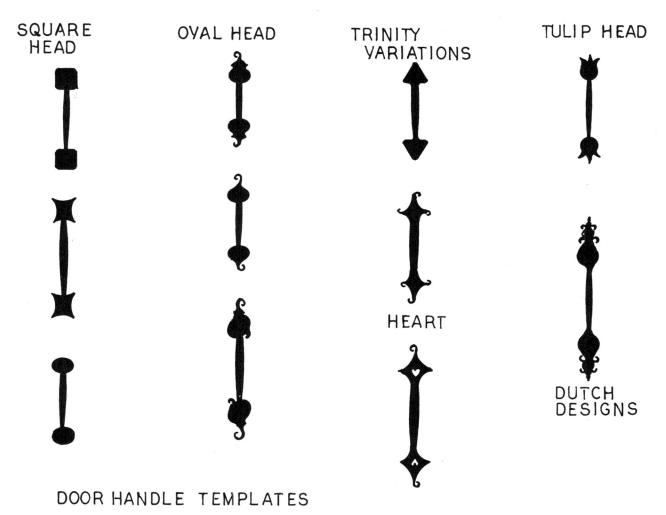

SQUARE HEAD

OVAL HEAD

TRINITY VARIATIONS

TULIP HEAD

HEART

DUTCH DESIGNS

DOOR HANDLE TEMPLATES

Fig. 1–106. Patterns for door handles

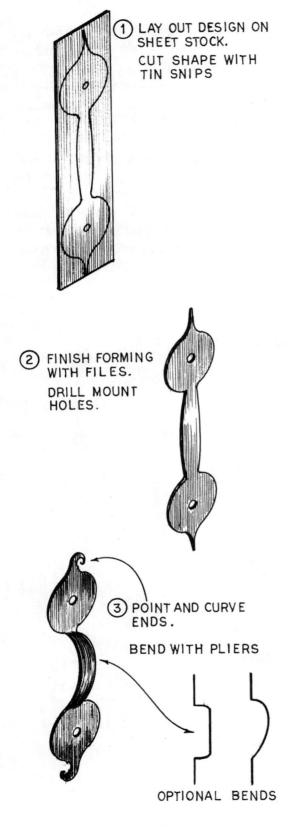

① LAY OUT DESIGN ON SHEET STOCK.
CUT SHAPE WITH TIN SNIPS

② FINISH FORMING WITH FILES.
DRILL MOUNT HOLES.

③ POINT AND CURVE ENDS.

BEND WITH PLIERS

OPTIONAL BENDS

Fig. 1–107. Handle construction

Handle Construction

Miniature colonial or early American-style door pulls and latches can be made from the same sheet of copper stock.

1. Lay out the shape on the metal stock. Remember the layout will be longer than the proposed finished length in order to allow for the various bends. See 1 in figure 1–107.

2. Rough cut the shape with tin ships. File-form the finished design. Drill mounting holes where suggested. Bend to handle shape with long-nose pliers. See 2 and 3 in figure 1–107.

Thumb-Latch Construction

1. Lay out the various suggested designs on sheet stock. Rough cut the pieces with tin snips. File each piece to finished shape and design. See top of figure 1–108. Drill mounting holes as suggested.

2. Drill and file the latch slot to final shape and size. Bend the premade thumb latch into a right angle as shown in detail at top of figure 1–108. Insert the thumb latch into the handle slot. Drill a small hole into the latch where it clears the handle. See detail in figure 1–108. Insert a small pin into this hole. The pin retains the latch in the handle. A relief must be cut into the wood of the door, where the latch and pin fit, in order to insure a free and easy up and down movement.

3. Install the finished handle and latch through the predrilled hole and the relief in the door. Drill a small hole into the drop latch. Mount the drop latch so that it rests on top of the thumb piece. Make a latch guide. Install the guide around the drop latch. The latch must work freely up and down within the guide.

4. Fit the door into the jamb. Make the latch strike as suggested in figure 1–108. Close the door, and mark where the drop latch hits the jamb. Install the latch strike to the door jamb at this point. When the door is closed, the drop latch will ride up the stopped section of the strike and drop into the slot, locking the door.

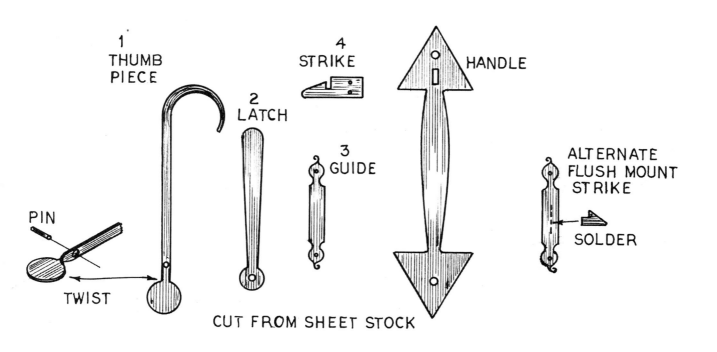

1
THUMB
PIECE

2
LATCH

3
GUIDE

4
STRIKE

HANDLE

ALTERNATE
FLUSH MOUNT
STRIKE

SOLDER

PIN

TWIST

CUT FROM SHEET STOCK

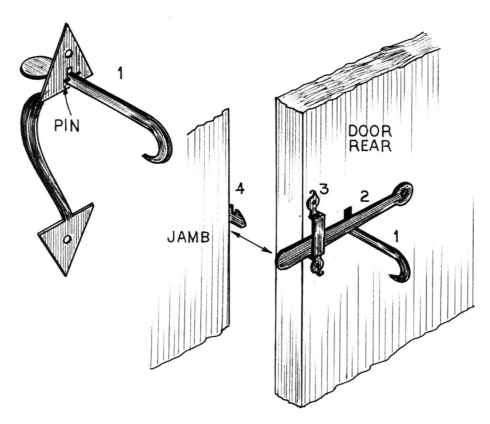

PIN

1

JAMB

4

DOOR
REAR

3   2

1

Fig. 1–108.   Thumb-latch construction

121

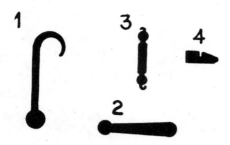

Fig. 1–109. Full-size patterns for thumb-latch parts

METAL HOUSEHOLD ITEMS

The miniaturist can purchase the various metal household items from any one of several excellent suppliers if preferred. However, a craftsman who has made the miniature house or room setting and the period furnishings is often reluctant to purchase premade items. It seems to distract from the satisfaction and sense of accomplishment gained from previous

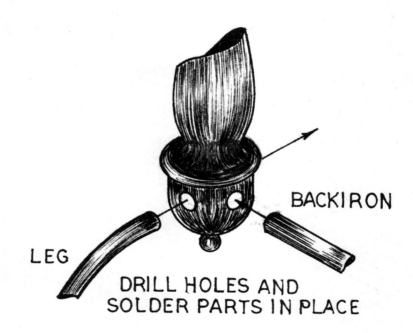

BACKIRON

LEG

DRILL HOLES AND
SOLDER PARTS IN PLACE

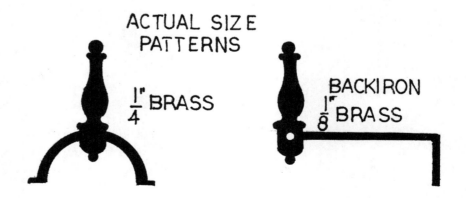

ACTUAL SIZE
PATTERNS

$\frac{1}{4}$" BRASS

BACKIRON
$\frac{1}{8}$" BRASS

Fig. 1–110. Turned andirons

WROUGHT ANDIRONS
ACTUAL SIZE PATTERNS

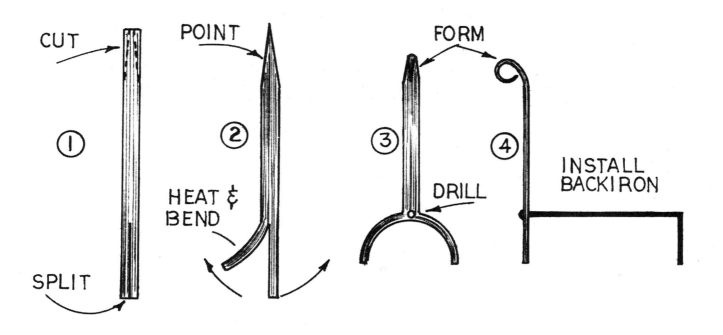

CUT

SPLIT

①

POINT

HEAT &
BEND

②

FORM

DRILL

③

FORM

INSTALL
BACKIRON

④

Fig. 1–111.   *Construction of wrought-iron andirons*

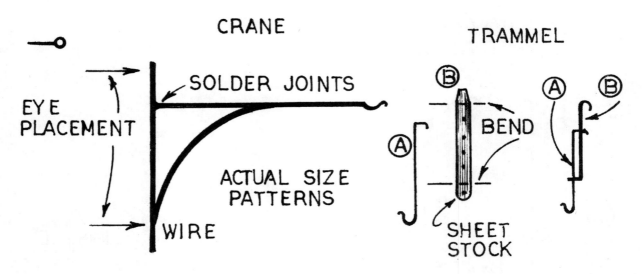

CRANE   TRAMMEL

Fig. 1–112. Patterns for crane and trammel

labor. The following instructions and drawings were developed to help miniaturists pursue the same individualism in the metalworking field.

Brass-Turned Andirons

Brass-turned andirons can be made from pieces of ¼-inch-diameter and ⅛-inch-diameter rounds. See figure 1–110. Ideas and styles can be obtained from historical books and visits to restoration settlements.

1. Lay out design and sizes on paper.

2. Chuck up a piece of ¼-inch-diameter round in a lathe or drill lathe. Cut in the proposed shape with files and emery paper.

3. Drill a ⅛-inch-diameter hole into the bottom of the upright irons. See detail figure 1–110 top. Bend a piece of ⅛-inch-diameter round to the suggested leg shape. Insert the legs through the hole and solder them in place. Clean off any excess solder.

4. Drill a ⅛-inch-diameter blind hole into the back of the upright irons on the same level as the legs. Bend a section of ⅛-inch round stock to the suggested back-iron shape. See detail in figure 1–110. Solder the back iron to the upright irons.

Wrought-Iron Andirons

The large hardware sections of hobby outlets carry various sizes of metal flats and rounds as stock items. A piece of ⅛-inch thick by ¼-inch wide flat stock can be worked into shapes that resemble wrought-iron andirons.

1. Lay out the suggested design on a piece of ⅛-inch by ¼-inch flat mild steel. See figure 1–111. Cut the steel to a rough shape with a hacksaw. Split the stock on the bottom as suggested for the legs.

2. Heat the flat stock and form the leg curves. (A butane torch or electric hot plate can be used to heat the stock.) File the upright irons to a finished shape. Heat the iron tops and form the scroll if desired with long-nose pliers.

3. Form the back irons from a ⅛-inch-diameter steel round or a heavy-duty coat hanger. Drill a countersunk mount hole into the upright iron as suggested. Insert the back iron into the hole and peen over the end in the countersunk hole. This joint can be soldered from the back if preferred.

Fireplace Crane and Firetools

Many period fireplaces require a crane. The scale-size crane is made from flattened,

WROUGHT IRON FIRETOOLS
ACTUAL SIZE TEMPLATES

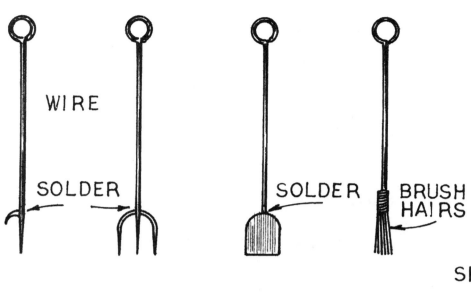

WIRE

SOLDER

SOLDER

BRUSH HAIRS

SHOVEL PARTS
SHEET STOCK

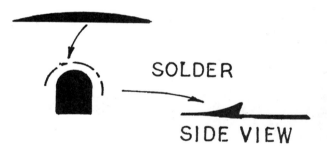

SOLDER

SIDE VIEW

HANDLE DESIGNS

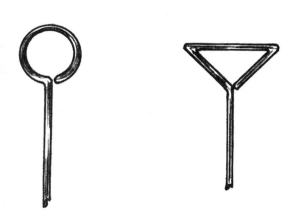

FLATTEN TOP.
FORM ROUND.
INSERT RING.

Fig. 1–113. Colonial firetools

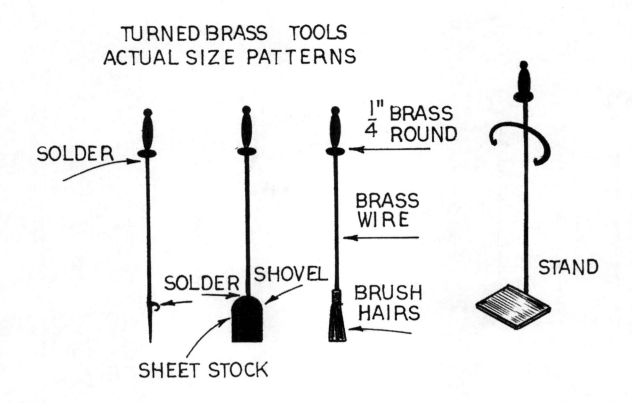

TURNED BRASS TOOLS
ACTUAL SIZE PATTERNS

SOLDER

SOLDER   SHOVEL

1/4" BRASS ROUND

BRASS WIRE

BRUSH HAIRS

STAND

SHEET STOCK

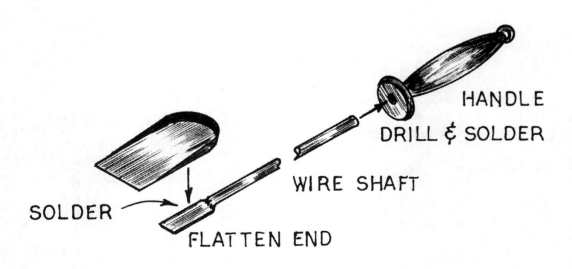

SOLDER

FLATTEN END

WIRE SHAFT

HANDLE
DRILL & SOLDER

Fig. 1–114.   Patterns for federal-style firetools

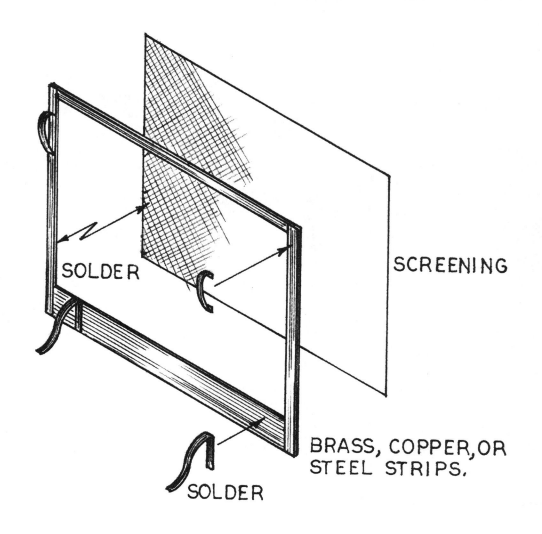

SOLDER

SCREENING

SOLDER

BRASS, COPPER, OR
STEEL STRIPS.

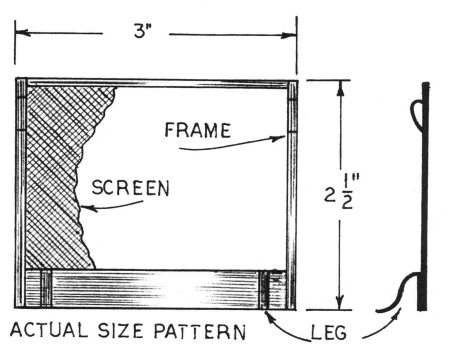

3"

FRAME

SCREEN

$2\frac{1}{2}$"

ACTUAL SIZE PATTERN

LEG

127

Fig. 1–115. Patterns for simple firescreen

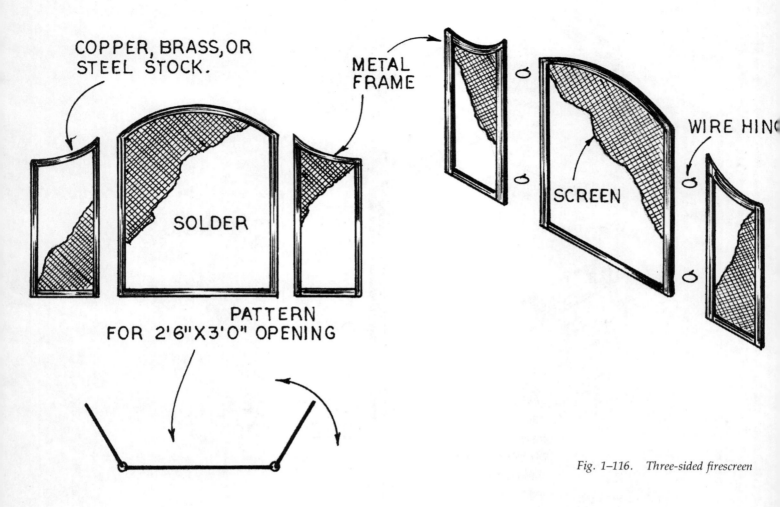

COPPER, BRASS, OR STEEL STOCK.

METAL FRAME

SOLDER

PATTERN FOR 2'6"X3'0" OPENING

WIRE HINGE

SCREEN

Fig. 1–116.   Three-sided firescreen

heavy-duty coat hangers or 1/16-inch rounds flattened on four sides.

1. Lay out the crane design on paper.

2. Flatten the metal and cut the stock to suggested size. With a file, taper A and form the end loop or hook. Bend C into a long curve.

3. Tack the stock to a piece of scrap wood in the desired form, and solder the parts together. The crane is mounted into two eyes set into the fireside wall. See detail in figure 1–112. Form the mount eyes and mark their position on the firewall. Install the eyes and insert the top of B into the top eye. Raise the crane up until the bottom of B drops into the lower eye. Please note that the top of B is twice as long as the lower tenon.

Trammel Hook

Pots were hung from the crane with hooks or trammels. For a trammel, cut sheet stock to the suggested size. See detail in figure 1–112 right.

1. Punch the small holes where marked. Form a section of paper clip into a hook.

2. Bend the sheet metal trammel as shown. Insert the hook into the mount holes. Hang the finished trammel over the crane end.

3. The trammel and crane should be painted flat black.

Firetools

Firetools can be made from coat-hanger

TRIVETS

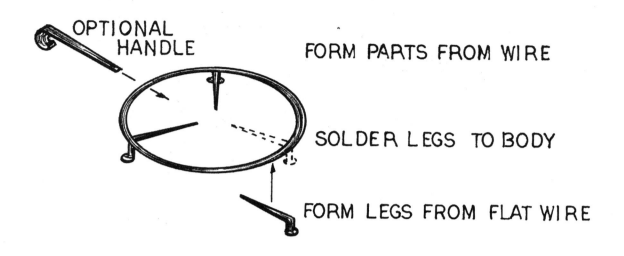

OPTIONAL HANDLE

FORM PARTS FROM WIRE

SOLDER LEGS TO BODY

FORM LEGS FROM FLAT WIRE

ACTUAL SIZE TRIVET PATTERNS

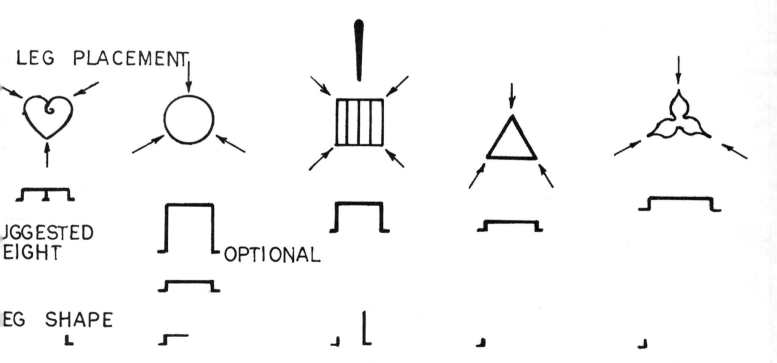

LEG PLACEMENT

SUGGESTED HEIGHT

OPTIONAL

LEG SHAPE

Fig. 1–117. Patterns for assorted trivets

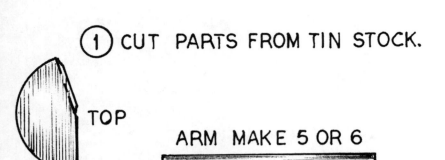

① CUT PARTS FROM TIN STOCK.

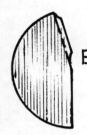

TOP

ARM MAKE 5 OR 6

TURN CANDLES.

BOTTOM

② FORM CONES. SOLDER SEAMS.

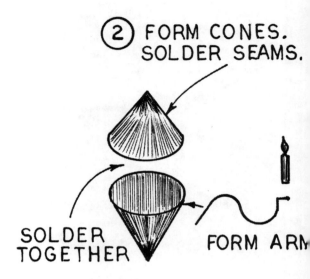

SOLDER TOGETHER

FORM ARM

③ MAKE WOOD JIG. MARK ARM LOCATION. 5 ARMS = 72°, 6 ARMS = 60°

72°

SOLDER ARMS TO BOTTOM CONE.

④ SOLDER ON CHAIN.

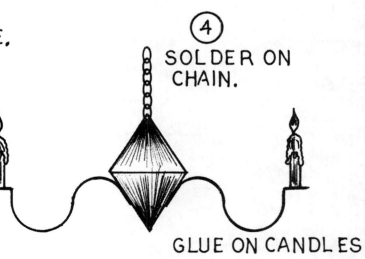

GLUE ON CANDLES

Fig. 1–118. Pattern for tin chandelier

ACTUAL SIZE PATTERNS

ARM <u>MAKE 5 OR 6</u>

CONE MAKE 2

CANDLE

ARM
SHAPE

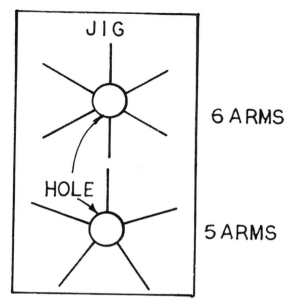

JIG

6 ARMS

HOLE

5 ARMS

Fig. 1-118. Pattern for tin chandelier (cont.)

wire, brazing or welding rods, or any stiff wire. Two different styles are offered: one for the colonial period in wrought-iron and the other as turned brass for the federal and Victorian periods.

For wrought-iron colonial firetools, cut heavy-duty, coat-hanger wire to suggested size as shown in figure 1–113 top. Form the handles with long-nose pliers. For the poker, form a point at the free end and solder on a small spur near the pointed bottom. For a shovel, cut a tin plate from a coffee can lid in a small shovel form. Bend into shape with pliers. Solder the shovel to a wire handle. See detail in figure 1–113. For the brush, glue hairs from an artist brush to a wire handle bottom. Wrap the hair tops to the handle with fine thread.

For turned brass firetools, use a lathe or drill-type lathe to turn small pieces of 3/16-inch brass rounds into handles. See figure 1–114 bottom. Drill a 1/16-inch-diameter hole in the finished handle ends before removing the stock from the lathe. Solder lengths of 1/16-inch brass rods into the handle holes. Make a shovel blade from sheet brass stock and form with pliers. Solder the blade to the bottom of one piece. Solder a small spur to another tool for

the poker. Wrap sable hairs from an artist brush to the third handle for a hearth brush.

Fire Screen

Scale-size fire screens can be made with 1/16-inch malleable copper or bronze wire and normal window screening. (Do not use aluminum screening because it can not be soldered.) Cut the wire and bend it to the suggested shape as shown in figure 1–115. Cut bronze window screening to suggested pattern. Wrap the ragged ends around the wire frame. Spot solder the screening to the wire from behind.

Trivets

Colonial-style trivets can be made from heavy-duty, jumbo paper clips. Form the clip wire into suggested shapes. Make three legs for each trivet from small pieces of the same wire. Carefully solder the legs to the trivet form. Handles can be made from excess wire and soldered to the trivet body.

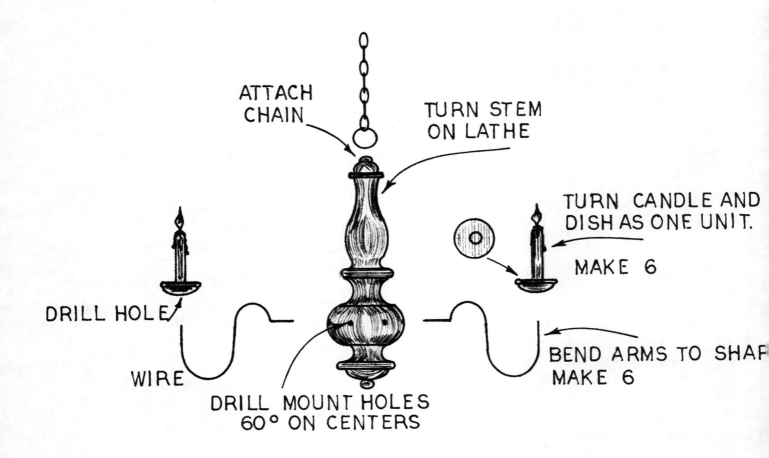

ATTACH CHAIN

TURN STEM ON LATHE

TURN CANDLE AND DISH AS ONE UNIT.

MAKE 6

DRILL HOLE

BEND ARMS TO SHAP MAKE 6

WIRE

DRILL MOUNT HOLES 60° ON CENTERS

ACTUAL SIZE PATTERNS

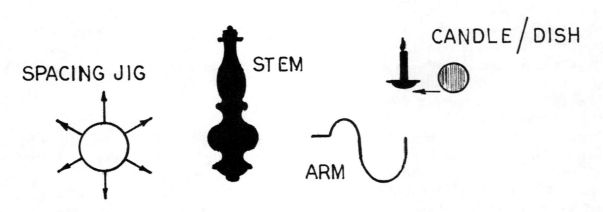

SPACING JIG

STEM

CANDLE/DISH

ARM

Fig. 1–119. *Pattern for federal-period chandelier*

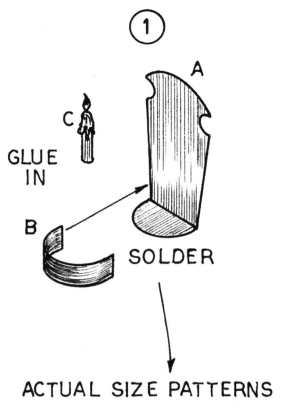

① GLUE IN

C

A

B

SOLDER

ACTUAL SIZE PATTERNS

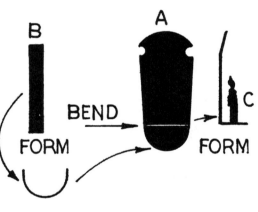

B

A

BEND

FORM

FORM

C

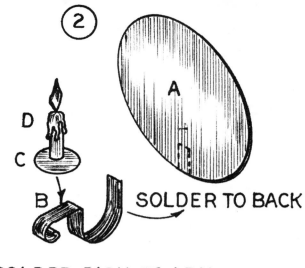

② D

C

B

SOLDER TO BACK

SOLDER DISH TO ARM
GLUE ON CANDLE

ACTUAL SIZE PATTERNS

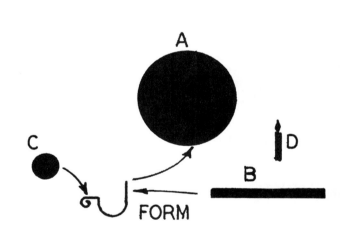

A

C

D

B

FORM

TABLE SCONCE ③

C CHIMNEY
$1\frac{1}{4}$" DOWEL B

HANDLE

C

A

A HEXAGON

BEND UP AND IN
BETWEEN POINTS.
FORMS STAR.

ACTUAL SIZE PATTERNS

A

C

B

Fig. 1–120. Patterns for candle sconces

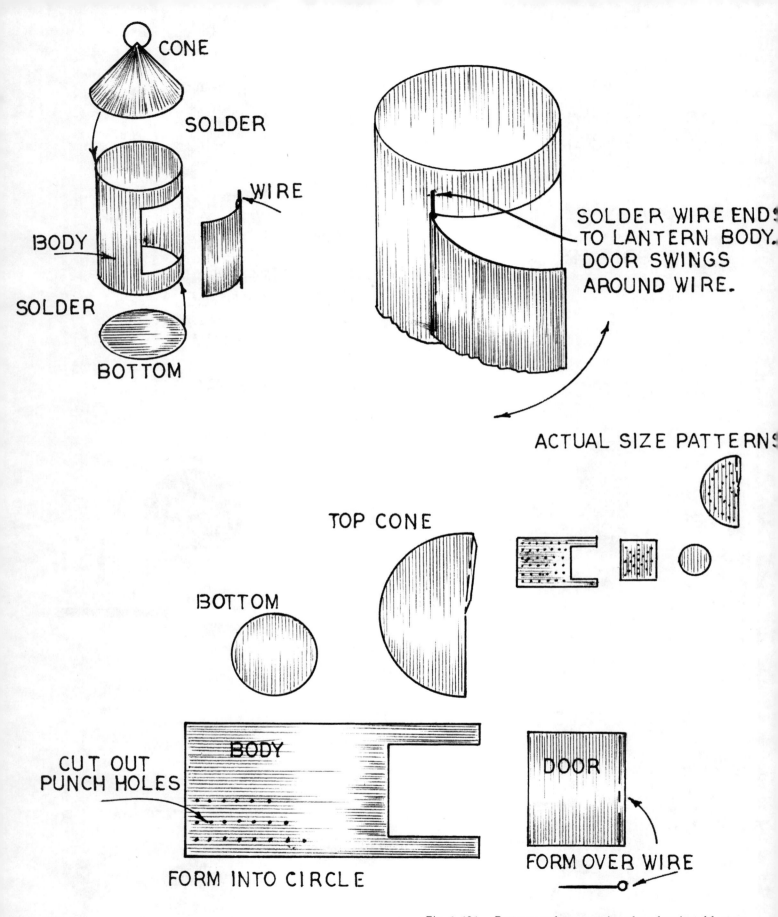

CONE

SOLDER

WIRE

BODY

SOLDER

BOTTOM

SOLDER WIRE ENDS TO LANTERN BODY. DOOR SWINGS AROUND WIRE.

ACTUAL SIZE PATTERNS

TOP CONE

BOTTOM

CUT OUT PUNCH HOLES

BODY

FORM INTO CIRCLE

DOOR

FORM OVER WIRE

Fig. 1–121.   Patterns and construction plans for pierced lantern

134

ACTUAL SIZE REFLECTOR OVEN PATTERNS

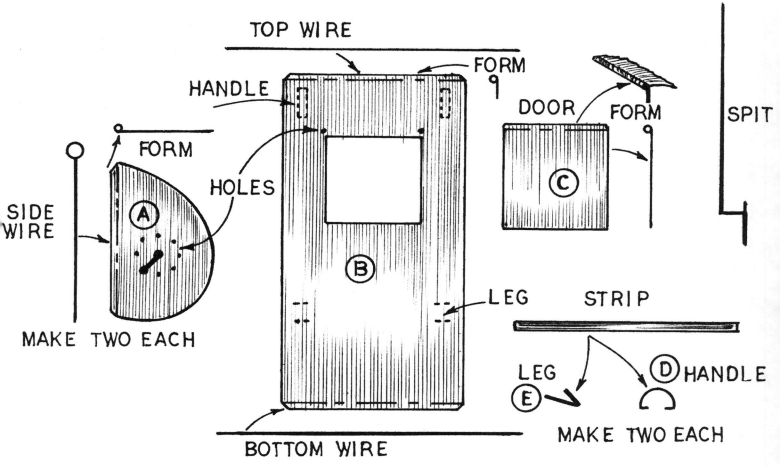

Fig. 1–122.   *Patterns for oven*

SHEET-METAL WORK

Perfectly scaled tin plate can be obtained from coffee can lids. The average top will supply stock for several reproductions.

Chandelier: Tin or Wood

A tin chandelier is made of two cones and five or six candle arms.

1. Cut the tin plate to suggested pattern shape and size. Form two cones. Fit the cones together and adjust if necessary. Fill the bottom cone with solder to add weight to the fix-ture. Solder the two cones together. Cut the stock for the candle arms and form them into the suggested shape. See figure 1–118.

2. Drill a countersunk hole into a block of scrap wood to act as a jig. Mark out five or six equal spaces around this hole for candle arm placement. Drop the cone into the drilled hole and proceed to solder the candle arms to the cone bottom. See detail figure 1–118 bottom.

3. On a lathe or drill-type lathe, turn minia-ture candles from $1/16$-inch wooden dowels. Paint the finished candles white.

4. Glue the candles to the chandelier arms.

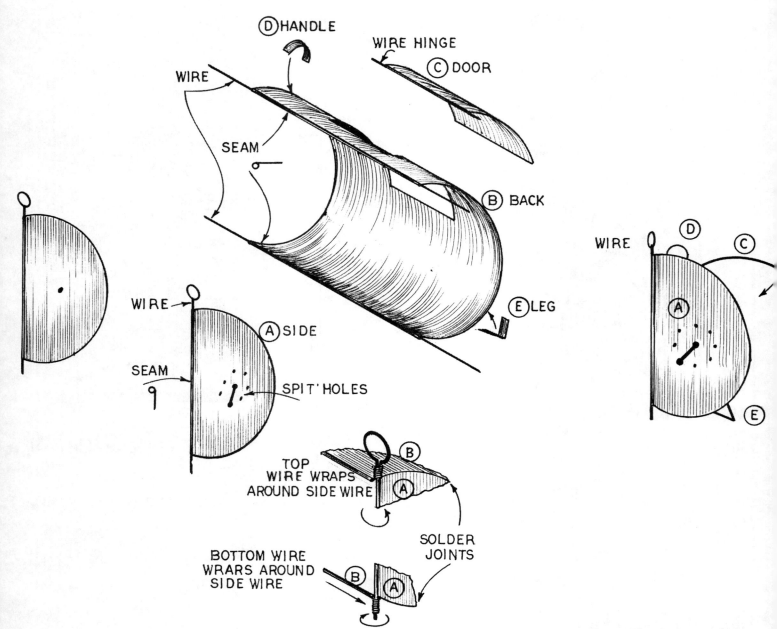

WIRE HINGE

(D)HANDLE

(C) DOOR

WIRE

SEAM

(B) BACK

WIRE

(D)

(C)

(A)

WIRE

(A)SIDE

SEAM

9

SPIT HOLES

(E)LEG

(E)

TOP
WIRE WRAPS
AROUND SIDE WIRE

(B)

(A)

SOLDER
JOINTS

BOTTOM WIRE
WRAPS AROUND
SIDE WIRE

(B)

(A)

Fig. 1–123. Oven construction

Solder a small length of jewelry chain to the top cone. Hang the fixture from an eye made from a pin.

To make a wooden chandelier, follow these steps:

1. Turn a ⅜-inch dowel to the suggested design as shown in figure 1–119 on a lathe or drill-type lathe. Mark the wood base for five or six candle arms. See detail figure 1–119 bottom.

2. Drill ¹/₃₂-inch-diameter holes into the base on the marks. Form the candle arms from jumbo paper clips. Insert the candle arms into the holes in the chandelier base. Turn candles and candle dishes as one piece on a lathe or drill-type lathe from ¼-inch-diameter dowels. See figure 1–119 bottom.

3. Drill a ¹/₃₂-inch-diameter hole in the bottom center of each dish/candle. Attach the can-

dle and dish piece to each arm. Paint the candle dishes and the chandelier base to a color of your choice. Paint the candles white and the arms flat black.

Wall Sconces

Scale-size wall sconces can also be made from the same coffee can lid.

1. Lay out the suggested design on paper or directly on the tin. See figure 1–120.

2. Cut out the rough design and file to achieve the suggested shape. Make the bends using long-nose pliers, and solder the parts together. Turn a scale candle from a 1/16-inch dowel. Paint the candle white.

3. Glue the dowel candle to the sconce.

Pierced Lantern

On the average, scale-size pierced lanterns are too small to be made from a clear-cut punched design. A general random piercing is used instead.

1. Lay out the tin plate to a size and shape suggested in patterns given in figure 1–121.

2. While the stock is still flat, punch random pin holes with a very fine awl or nail point. Shape the lamp body into a cylinder and solder the joint. Form the cone for the top. Adjust the cone if necessary and solder it to the lamp body.

3. Form the lamp door. Form the hinge pin from straight pins or a small paper clip. Bend the door edge loosely around this pin. Insert the pin top and bottom into predrilled holes in the lamp body. Solder the pin to the body. The door should work smoothly around this hinge pin.

4. From scrap stock, make a scroll catch like a clock spring. Solder the catch to the lamp body so that the scroll end holds the door closed. Insert a small snap ring through the lamp cone for hanging.

ACTUAL SIZE PATTERNS

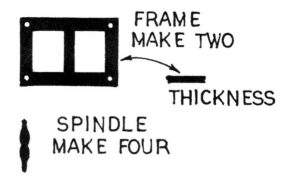

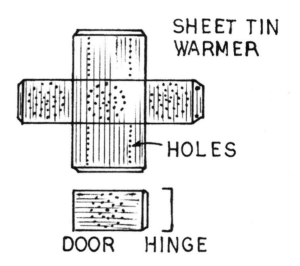

Fig. 1–124. Patterns for footwarmer

Reflector Oven

The reflector oven was placed in front of fireplaces to catch the radiating heat. Roast meals or fowl were cooked in this appliance.

1. Lay out the suggested shapes and sizes as shown in figure 1–122 on tin plate stock. Because of the size, two or more coffee can tops may be required. Punch the skewer holes into one side piece. Bend the ends of the side pieces (A) to accept the side wires. See detail. Form the side wires. Insert them into the side hems and close the hems over the wires.

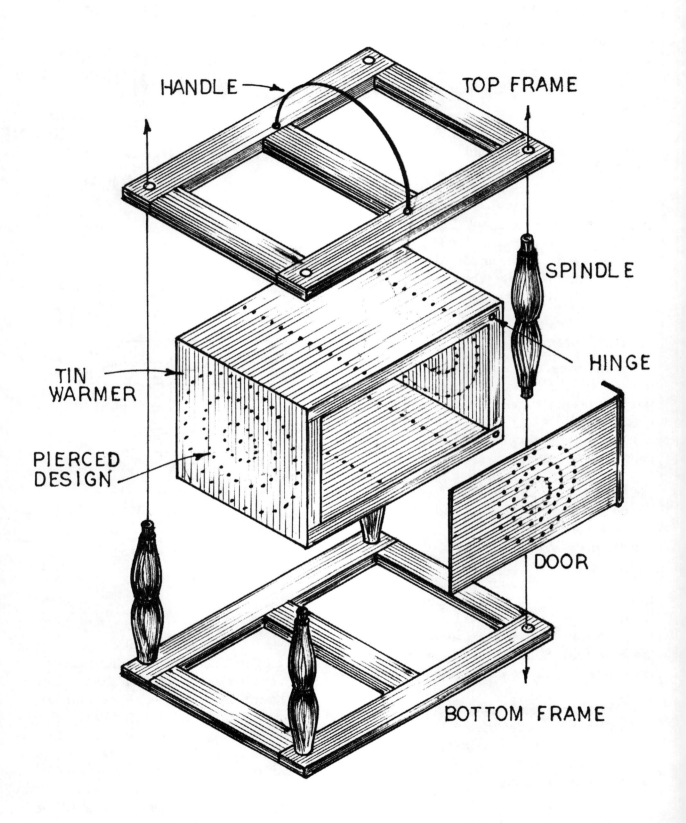

HANDLE

TOP FRAME

SPINDLE

HINGE

TIN WARMER

PIERCED DESIGN

DOOR

BOTTOM FRAME

Fig. 1–125. Footwarmer construction

2. Make a small hem on the top and bottom of the oven back (B). Wrap these hems over a length of paper clip wire. See detail figure 1–123. Solder the back piece to the two sides. Wrap the back piece's top and bottom wires around the extended wires in the side pieces, thereby locking the two pieces together. Trim off any excess. See detail figure 1–123 bottom. Make the oven door.

3. Install a paper clip wire as a door hinge into the top of the door hem. Close the hem over the wire. Install the wire ends into pre-drilled holes in the oven body. Solder the wire ends to the body. The oven door should work freely around this wire to open and close.

4. Make the two handles and legs. See detail figure 1–123. Solder the handles to the oven top and the legs to the oven bottom. See location in figure 1–122.

5. Make a spit from a jumbo paper clip. Install the spit into the oven through the spit holes.

Footwarmer

1. Lay out and cut the stock for the wood frames. See patterns in figure 1–124.

2. On a lathe, turn four spindles for the corners complete with tenons on each end. Glue

Fig. 1–126. *Miniature colonial kitchen*

the two frames together. Drill mortise holes for the spindle tenons into each corner. Glue the spindles into the holes on the bottom frame.

3. Lay out the stock for the tin warmer. Pierce the design as suggested in figure 1–124 into the tin plate. Form a small tin box. This tin box must fit between the four spindles glued into the bottom frame. Make a small door for the tin warmer. Hinge the door with a hinge pin made from a paper clip. Install the finished tin box into the bottom frame between spindles.

4. Glue the top frame to the tenons on the four spindles. This locks the tin box into the interior of the frames. Install a small bail handle on the center frame's top.

Display Cases and Miniature Shops

10. *Display Cases and Shadow Boxes*

An old proverb states that the longest journey starts with a single step. The same concepts holds true for miniature makers and collectors. The largest collection started somewhere, sometime, with a single piece. Such a single piece could be a vacation souvenir, an item appreciated and purchased for its exquisite workmanship, or a gift. The miniature seed thus planted very often bears the fruit of continued long-term commitment.

The proper setting creates a focal point for miniatures. Just as a picture frame draws attention to the art it surrounds, a miniature house or display area creates the proper atmosphere to complete the scene. And, regardless of the size of the collection, the fragile and delicate nature of miniatures demands some type of protection: protection from possible accident, from improper handling, and from the wear, tear, and moisture content of the environment.

This section was designed to give readers a wide choice of possible display areas. For the small collector, a simple glass case or shadow box may serve the purpose. The intermediate collector may desire a full room or more to display and contain his pieces. The specialized collector may want a specific shop building to create a realistic setting. To answer these needs this section explains how to build display areas from shadow boxes to individual period shops and stores.

Several specific examples of each category are shown in order to present the building techniques needed for construction. The general concepts shown can be adjusted and transferred to almost any room, style, or intention. Miniaturists are not restricted to the rooms shown; they can adopt the general principles to suit their own particular desires.

The last part of this section offers many

Fig. 2–1. *Shadow-box room display (Courtesy It's a Small World)*

Fig. 2–2. *Shadow-box display of a Victorian-style bedroom (Courtesy Sonia Messer Imports)*

Fig. 2–3. *Miniature country kitchen (Courtesy Scientific Models, Inc.)*

different single-room period shops and businesses. Again, the reader is not restricted to the shops illustrated. Any cottage industry or shop of the period can be adapted from these patterns. The millinery shop can easily become an apothecary, and the carpenter's shop can become a silversmith's or tinker's workroom. The collector of brass miniatures may want a whitesmith's shop as a display case, while the general collector, who loves everything small, may find his needs satisfied with the general store as a setting.

The sizes given are purposely general. There is no hard and fast rule to overall size except the reader's desire. Many times the given sizes were developed from actual structures found in different historical settlements, but the reader is not restricted to such criteria. The following pieces can be enlarged or reduced in overall size as desired.

SMALL GLASS-FRONT DISPLAY CASE

This case was designed to contain and display a few choice pieces. Several options are available in the construction. The rear wall of this piece may be made plain, or it can contain a false window or door, or it can be painted or papered to simulate a sample wall section. The unit base can be plain wood, or it can be scored or covered to resemble flooring.

Construction

Material List

	Part	Amount	Size	Materials
A	Bottom	1	8″ x 12″ x ¾″	
B	Top	1	8″ x 12″ x ¾″	
C	Back	1	8″ x 9″ x ¾″	
D	Wing	1	3″ x 9″ x ¾″	
E	Wing	1	3″ x 9″ x ¾″	
F	Front	2	3½″ x 9½″ x ⅛″	Glass
		2	4½″ x 9½″ x ⅛″	or
		1	8″ x 9½″ x ⅛″	Plastic

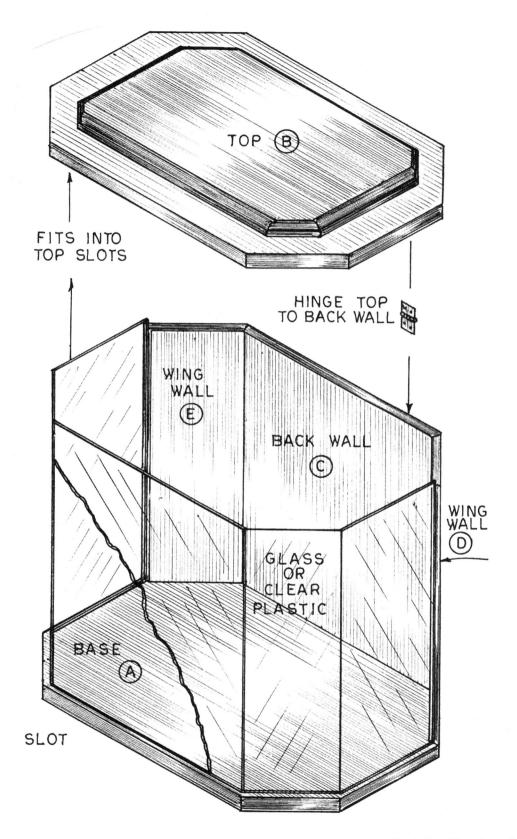

FITS INTO
TOP SLOTS

TOP Ⓑ

HINGE TOP
TO BACK WALL

WING
WALL
Ⓔ

BACK WALL
Ⓒ

WING
WALL
Ⓓ

GLASS
OR
CLEAR
PLASTIC

BASE
Ⓐ

SLOT

Fig. 2–4. Glass-front display case

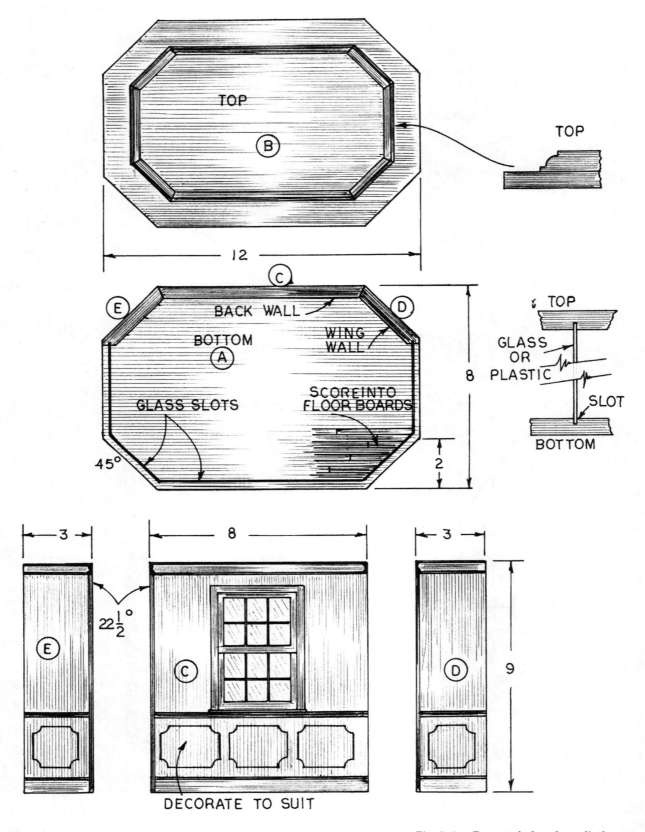

TOP

TOP

(B)

12

(C)

(E) BACK WALL (D)

BOTTOM
(A)

WING
WALL

GLASS SLOTS

SCORE INTO
FLOOR BOARDS

45°

8

2

TOP

GLASS
OR
PLASTIC

SLOT

BOTTOM

3

8

3

22½°

(E)

(C)

(D)

9

DECORATE TO SUIT

Fig. 2–5. Decorated glass-front display case

1. Lay out and cut the stock for A and B to suggested shape and size. See figure 2–4. Mark out the glass window slots on both pieces and cut a ⅛-inch-wide by ¼-inch-deep dado into each piece with a router. Score A into sample floor boards or cover it with appropriate flooring material.

2. Lay out and cut the material for the back and wing walls: C, D, and E. Make the required angle cuts so D and E fit to D. Cut a glass slot into the exposed edges of D and E. See detail figure 2–4. Decorate these back walls to suit your needs. If windows are used, you may wish to cut out a full-color scenic print and glue it to the back of the window sash. Or, paint the rear viewing area flat black. Install C, D, and E to A with small nails from the bottom up. Stain and finish all wood parts at this time.

3. Cut the single strength glass or clear plastic to suggested size. Insert the wing windows into the slots on D, E, and A. The glass or plastic may be glued in place if preferred. Cut and fit the front window sections. Drop this section into the slot in A and glue the edges to the wing window pieces.

4. Cut and fit the top (B) in place. Attach the top to C with small butt hinges. When the top is closed, the top edges of the glass or plastic will fit into the premade slots, locking the whole case together.

CARRIAGE CLOCK DISPLAY CASE

The original case was designed to contain a mantel or carriage clock. However, the case itself is a perfect container for federal, Victorian, or formal miniature settings. The sides and back of the case can be made to resemble a sample section of a period room. Many miniaturists seek old clock cases at tag sales or auctions to serve as display cases. This project is offered as an alternative. Instead of searching for a case, you can make the case expressly for miniature containment.

Fig. 2–6. Clock display (Courtesy It's a Small World)

Construction

Material List

Part	Amount	Size	Materials
A Side	2	5" x 9½" x ¾"	
B Ends	2	5" x 8" x ¾"	
C Back	1	8¾" x 8¾" x ¼"	Plywood
D Base	2	6½" x 12" x ¾"	
E Molding	1	36 linear inches	2½-inch crown molding
F Center	1	2½" x 6" x ¾"	
G Door	4	9½" x 1" x ¾"	
H Glass	1	9" x 9" x ⅛"	

1. Cut the stock for A, B, and C. Cut a ¼-inch by ¼-inch rabbet into the rear edges of A and B. Nail A into B. Nail C into the rabbets on A and B. Parts A, B, and C can be decorated to suit a particular need if so desired. Flooring, ceiling, wall materials, and false windows and doors can be used if preferred. Finish the interior of the case at this time.

2. Cut the stock of D. With a hand router, cut a molded edge on both parts. See detail figure 2–7. Glue and screw D to B. Cut the crown molding to form the top; see detail figure 2–7. Install F to the center of D top and

147

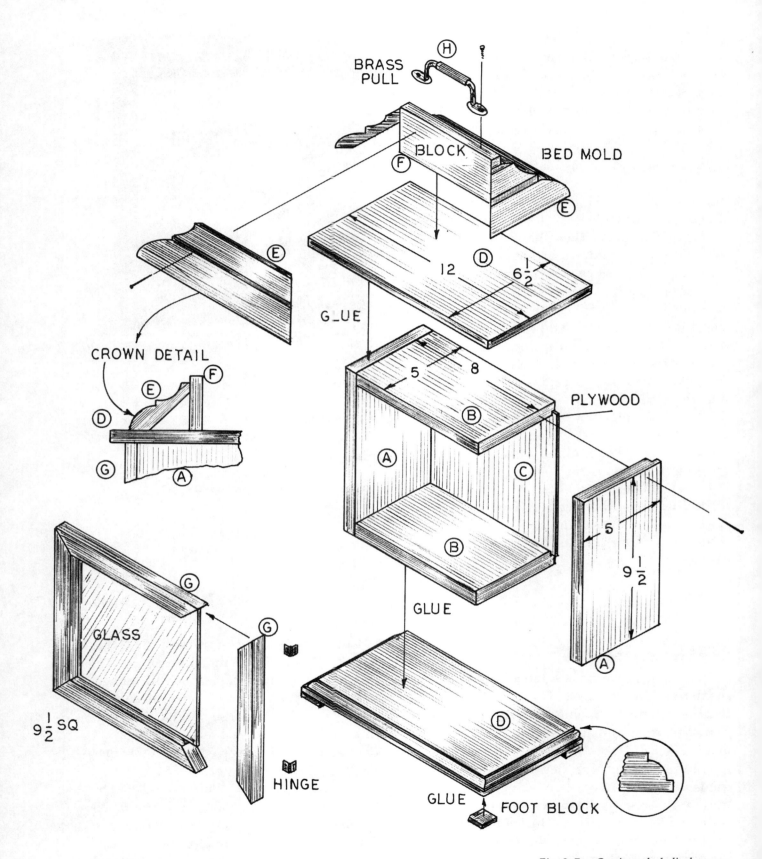

BRASS PULL

H

BLOCK

BED MOLD

F

E

E

GLUE

12

D

6½

CROWN DETAIL

E

F

D

5

8

B

A

C

PLYWOOD

G

A

B

5

9½

A

GLASS

G

G

GLUE

D

9½ SQ

HINGE

GLUE

FOOT BLOCK

Fig. 2–7. Carriage clock display case

Fig. 2–8. Shadow box (Courtesy Sonia Messer Imports)

secure the molding to F and D. The metal bail handle is optional. Secure four-foot blocks to the bottom of the lower D.

3. Cut the stock for G, the door. Cut a ⅛-inch by ⅛-inch dado into the edges of all four parts. Using a 45-degree miter cut, make a door to fit the case opening. Nail the door bottom to the two side pieces. Drop the precut glass into the dadoes and nail the top (C) to the door unit. Attach the door to the case with small butt hinges. Stain and finish the case exterior. Install miniatures into display case. Note: F can contain recessed lighting, if preferred. See Section one on wiring and lighting.

SHADOW BOX

Many miniaturists have made interesting display cases from favorite or antique picture frames mounted over a shallow box. Most often this type of shadow box is employed to show only a sample of a theme, such as a corner of a gardener's shed or potting shed.

The overall size is important only in regard to the intended purpose. For example, if the shadow box is designed to resemble a sample wall section, the frame should be restricted in height. Rarely are ceilings less than seven feet or more than twelve feet in height (seven to twelve inches in scale).

The construction of the shadow box can include a false window, door, or wainscotting on the back wall. See figure 2–10. Sometimes large-frame shadow boxes have been divided with horizontal and/or vertical strips in order to display several miniature samples. Such construction somewhat resembles a two or three-story house with appropriate samples on each level.

Fig. 2–9. Potting shed

Construction

Two options are available for possible construction. One is to use an existing picture frame and build the shadow box to match it in size and style. The other option is to build the shadow box and make a picture-frame-type door to cover it. In the first option, the frame itself governs the overall size of the box. In the later option, the constructed box determines the size of the frame.

1. Cut the stock for the box. The height, width, and length should be compatible with intended usages. See figure 2–10. Cut a ¼-inch by ¼-inch rabbet on the back edges of each box piece in order to receive the back. Construct a simple box with miter joint corners.

2. Cut the stock for the back piece from ¼-inch plywood or hardboard. Install doors, windows, or trim, if desired. Nail this back into the rabbets on the box proper.

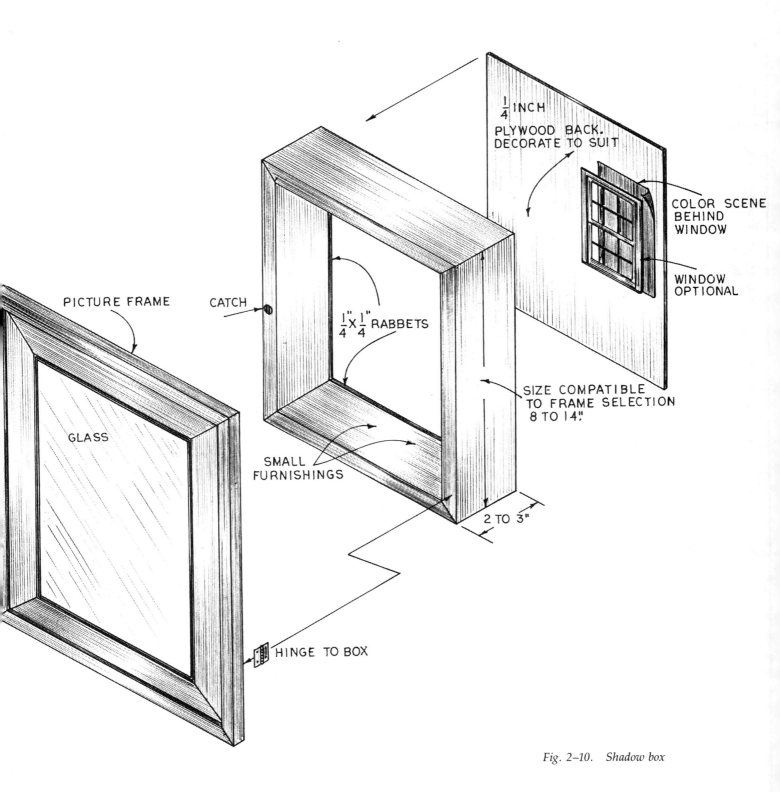

PICTURE FRAME

CATCH

$\frac{1}{4}$ INCH
PLYWOOD BACK.
DECORATE TO SUIT

COLOR SCENE
BEHIND
WINDOW

WINDOW
OPTIONAL

$\frac{1}{4}"$ X $\frac{1}{4}"$ RABBETS

GLASS

SIZE COMPATIBLE
TO FRAME SELECTION
8 TO 14"

SMALL
FURNISHINGS

2 TO 3"

HINGE TO BOX

Fig. 2–10. Shadow box

3. Using shopmade, commercial, or picture frame molding, construct a frame to cover the box. The frame should have a ⅛-inch rabbet or dado in order to receive single strength, non-reflective glass. Attach the frame to the box with small butt hinges. Install a small catch and pull.

4. The interior of the box can be decorated

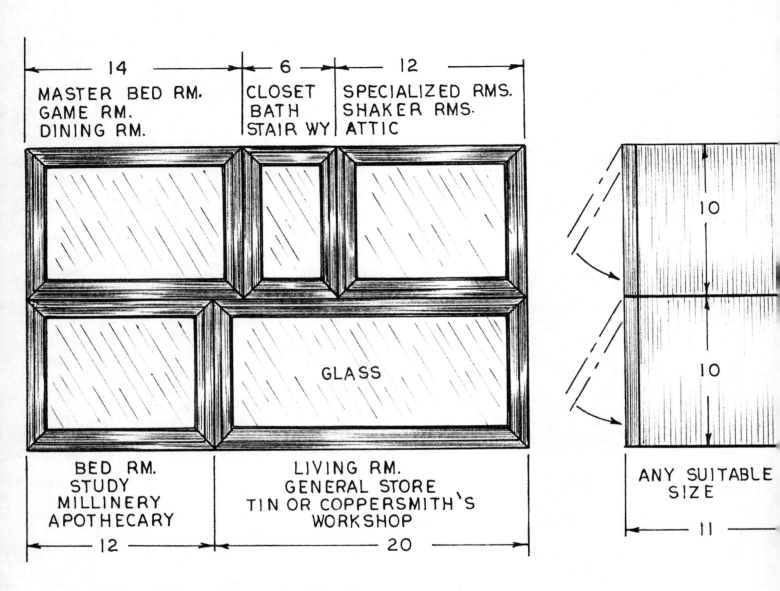

14

MASTER BED RM.
GAME RM.
DINING RM.

6

CLOSET
BATH
STAIR WY

12

SPECIALIZED RMS.
SHAKER RMS.
ATTIC

GLASS

BED RM.
STUDY
MILLINERY
APOTHECARY

12

LIVING RM.
GENERAL STORE
TIN OR COPPERSMITH'S
WORKSHOP

20

SINGLE ROOM MODULAR STACK

10

10

ANY SUITABLE
SIZE

11

Fig. 2–11. Stacking shadow boxes

now. Sample plank flooring, ceiling and wall materials, curtains, paint, paper, and trim can be installed at this time. Stain or paint the shadow box exterior. Install the miniature furnishings and attach to a wall.

The shadow box section of the gardener's shed contains a window with an exterior garden scene behind it. The walls have vertical siding with several racks attached. The floor is wide planks. An overhead exposed beam and a small potting table and stool complete the major pieces. Assorted garden tools, pots,

plants, herbs, scale, and watering can complete the total unit. See figure 2–9.

SAMPLE ROOM SECTION

While the previous shadow box frame offers only a small sample or section of a particular setting, the single-room display case affords miniaturists a protective device for a full room regardless of size. Often times, one-room collections lead to other acquisitions and many collectors stack or add rooms as their collec-

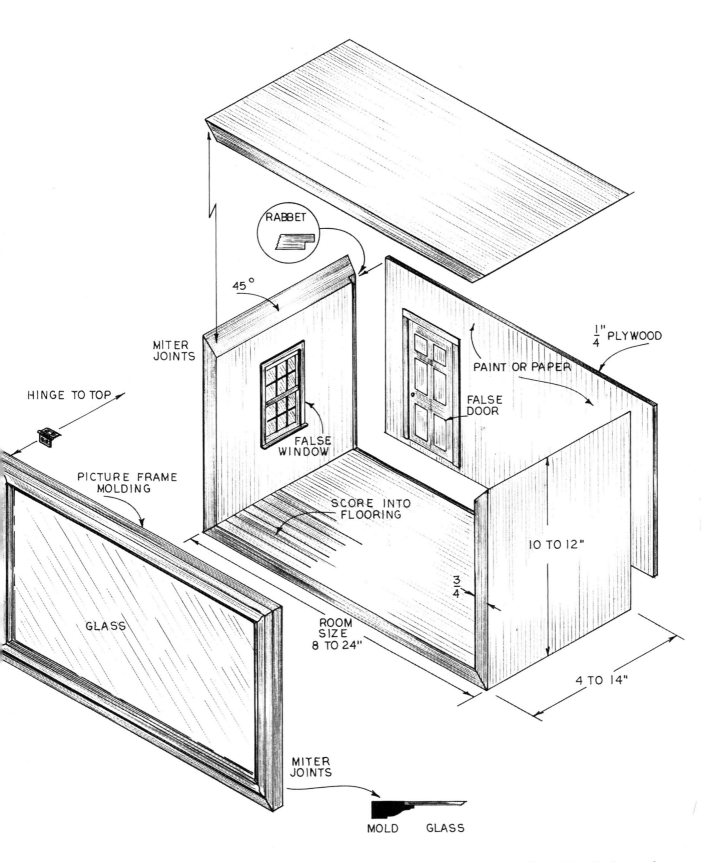

RABBET

45°

MITER
JOINTS

HINGE TO TOP

PICTURE FRAME
MOLDING

GLASS

$\frac{1}{4}$" PLYWOOD

PAINT OR PAPER

FALSE
DOOR

FALSE
WINDOW

SCORE INTO
FLOORING

ROOM
SIZE
8 TO 24"

10 TO 12"

$\frac{3}{4}$

4 TO 14"

MITER
JOINTS

MOLD   GLASS

Fig. 2–12.   Single-room box

153

tions increase. Figure 2–11 shows possible modular stacking with general sizes given for various rooms. The function of the cases is still to protect the contents and develop scene totality, but by stacking, several different themes, rooms, or time periods can be used together.

Construction

1. Determine the size of the room desired. Select clear stock for the sides. Any type of wood will work. See figure 2–12. Cut the stock for the sides and cut a ¼-inch by ¼-inch rabbet on the rear edges in order to receive the back piece. Construct a box from this stock using miter joints on the corners.

2. Install false windows, doors, trim, or moldings as desired. The wall pieces may be papered, painted, or stained. The bottom piece should be scored to resemble flooring and the top piece should be treated as a ceiling. Assemble the box. Cut the stock for the rear wall. Install any millwork desired and secure the back piece into the premade rabbets.

3. Make a picture-type frame for the door. Shopmade molding, standard lumber molds, or commercial picture frame stock can be used. Install single strength non-reflective glass in the door frame. Attach the door to the room box with small hinges. As a rule, single or multiple-room boxes are placed on a special shelf or bookcase because of their increase in size. These rooms can be wired for lights. See Section one on electrical wiring.

COMBINATION SINGLE-ROOM DISPLAY CASE

When a complex miniature room setting or when a third dimension is desirable, one large double-walled box can be the answer. In essence, this display case not only contains the room setting but it also allows for "depth-of-field" side effects such as exterior window scenes, open hall or stairways, indirect lighting, and room for electrical parts.

Construction

1. Lay out the proposed floor plan on paper. See figure 2–14 for a sample. Lay out the interior walls complete with window or door openings. Transfer the plan's dimensions to the actual wood as the work progresses.

2. Lay out the floor piece. Cut a ¼-inch by ¼-inch rabbet on the rear edge. Lay down the floor boards, or score the bottom stock to resemble random-width flooring. If a fireplace is to be used, make the masonry hearth at this time. Stain and finish the floor piece.

3. Lay out the stock for the wide walls. The side wall pieces have a ¼-inch by ¼-inch rabbet on the rear edges in order to receive the back. Any electrical paths should be plotted and made at this time. Nail the side wall to the floor stock.

4. Lay out the interior walls. Install any windows and doors into these walls. Paint any millwork at this time. Install stairways and the fireplaces. Such fixtures should be finished before installation. Cut any electrical paths and install rough wiring. All wire feeds will exit at the rear. See figure 2–14. Install the finished interior walls at this time.

5. Lay out and cut the stock for the ceiling piece. Cut a ¼-inch by ¼-inch rabbet on the rear edge. Very often several electrical paths must be laid out for overhead fixtures with exits at the rear. Drill or rout these paths before installation of this piece, because such electrical paths often require a routed groove. The ceiling board can be so ploughed, the wires inserted, and a thin covering glued over the work area. Paint the exposed ceiling area in a color of your choice. Install any overhead light fixtures at this time and secure the ceiling board to the side pieces.

6. Lay out the rear panel. A piece of ¼-inch plywood is suggested. Cut a few air vents into an area that will not be seen from any interior

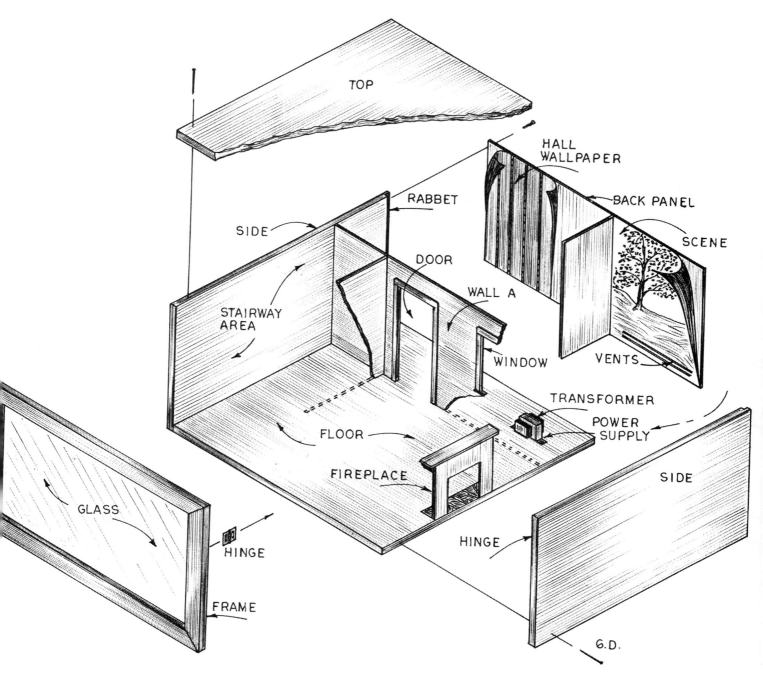

TOP

HALL WALLPAPER

BACK PANEL

RABBET

SCENE

SIDE

DOOR

WALL A

STAIRWAY AREA

WINDOW

VENTS

TRANSFORMER

POWER SUPPLY

FLOOR

FIREPLACE

SIDE

GLASS

HINGE

HINGE

FRAME

G.D.

Fig. 2–13.   Display-case assembly

windows. The light bulbs and/or transformer will be stored in this area and will give off some heat, so the vents allow air circulation. See figure 2–14. Decorate this panel. For example, figure 2–13 shows that the left-hand side is decorated as a hallway, while the right-hand side has a colored exterior scene to be seen

through the window. Any electrical connections should be made in the storage space at this time.

Install a low-voltage transformer and wire any low-voltage circuits. Install the 110-volt line feed wire to the transformer. If a daylight bulb is to be used, install the wires and socket.

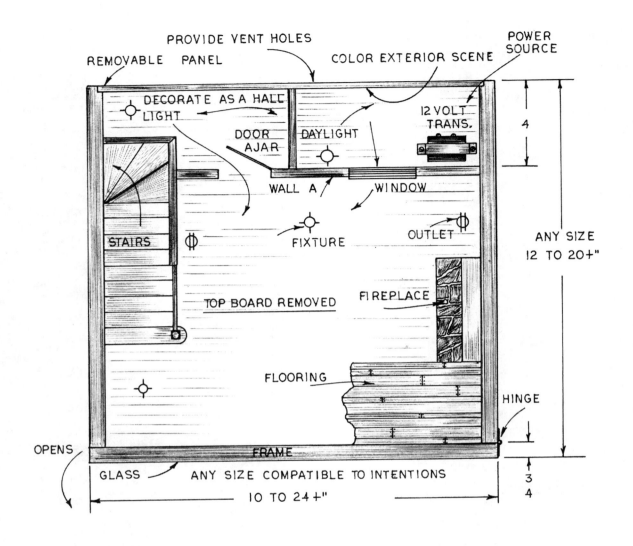

PROVIDE VENT HOLES

REMOVABLE PANEL

COLOR EXTERIOR SCENE

POWER SOURCE

DECORATE AS A HALL LIGHT

DOOR AJAR

DAYLIGHT

12 VOLT TRANS.

4

STAIRS

WALL A

WINDOW

ANY SIZE 12 TO 20+"

FIXTURE

OUTLET

TOP BOARD REMOVED

FIREPLACE

FLOORING

HINGE

OPENS

FRAME

GLASS

ANY SIZE COMPATIBLE TO INTENTIONS

10 TO 24+"

3 4

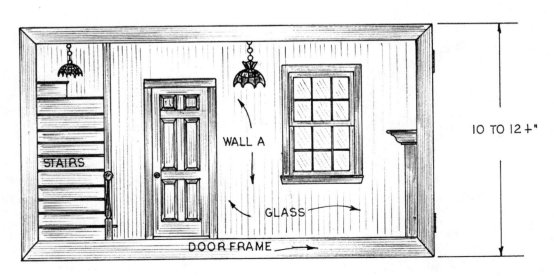

WALL A

STAIRS

GLASS

DOOR FRAME

10 TO 12+"

Fig. 2–14. Front view and floor plan of single-room settings

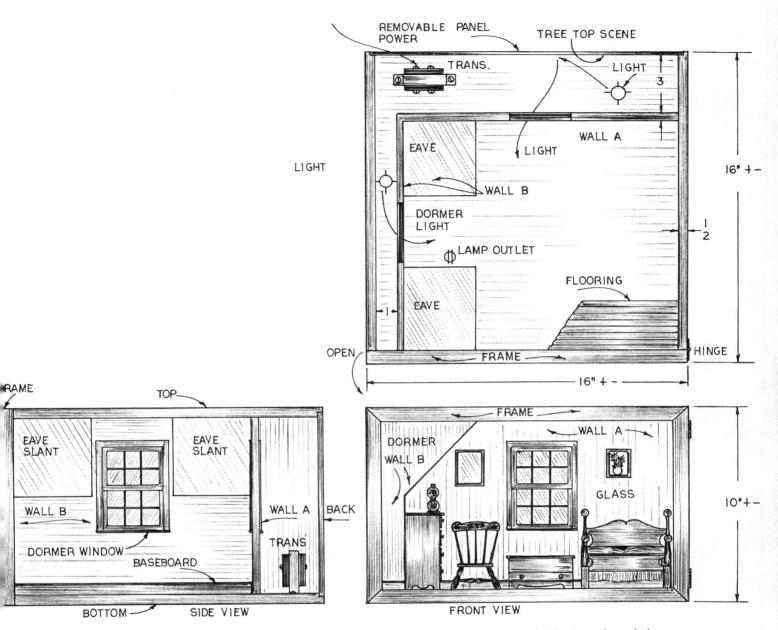

Fig. 2–15. Floor plan, front and side views of eave bedroom

If one or more switches are to be used, install them. Very often such switches are placed on the box exterior. See the chaper on electricity in Section one for wiring techniques. Attach the back piece to the basic box with screws. You may need access to the storage area from time to time, so a removable panel is necessary.

7. Make a door frame for the front of the case. See figure 2–10 for suggestions. Plain or molded stock, commercial molds, or picture-frame stock can be used for the frame. Install single strength, non-reflective glass to the frame. Attach the frame door to the case with small butt hinges. Install a catch and pull.

8. Stain or paint the case exterior. Finish with several coats of lacquer or similar covering.

Install miniature furnishings. Several of

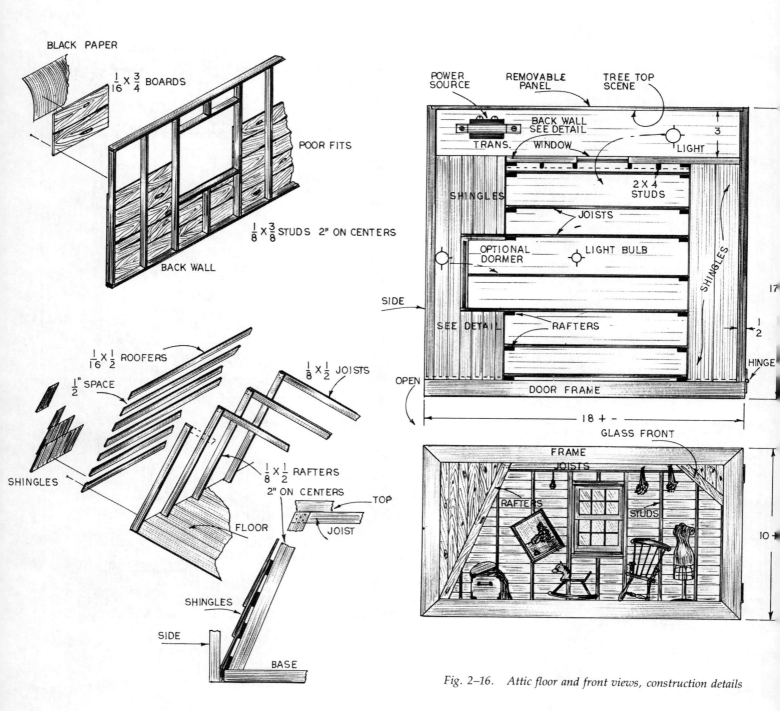

BLACK PAPER

$\frac{1}{16} \times \frac{3}{4}$ BOARDS

POOR FITS

$\frac{1}{8} \times \frac{3}{8}$ STUDS 2" ON CENTERS

BACK WALL

POWER SOURCE

REMOVABLE PANEL

TREE TOP SCENE

BACK WALL SEE DETAIL

TRANS.

WINDOW

LIGHT

3

SHINGLES

2 X 4 STUDS

JOISTS

OPTIONAL DORMER

LIGHT BULB

SHINGLES

17

SIDE

SEE DETAIL

RAFTERS

1 2

OPEN

HINGE

DOOR FRAME

18 + -

GLASS FRONT

FRAME

JOISTS

RAFTERS

STUDS

10

$\frac{1}{16} \times \frac{1}{2}$ ROOFERS

$\frac{1}{2}$" SPACE

$\frac{1}{8} \times \frac{1}{2}$ JOISTS

SHINGLES

$\frac{1}{8} \times \frac{1}{2}$ RAFTERS

2" ON CENTERS

TOP

JOIST

FLOOR

SHINGLES

SIDE

BASE

Fig. 2–16.   *Attic floor and front views, construction details*

these display cases can be stacked, if so desired. Because of their size, stacked cases require a special shelf or location.

SECOND-STORY BEDROOM

This display case is a variation of the sample or single room enclosure. It offers the concept of dual lighting and nonsymmetrical construction and suggests the many possible variations available to miniaturists. Display areas or sample rooms can contain slanted roofs and ceilings, partial hallways, off-center viewpoints, or any conceivable combination. Single rooms are not confined to perfect squares or rectangles; the ultimate shape and style are restricted only by the builder's imagination.

The basic construction follows the steps and methods given for the previous project. Wall A is the rear wall of the bedroom and is complete with a window that offers a second-story view. Wall B is built partly as a dormer with a window and partly as a slanted ceiling to simulate the roof pitch of a bedroom under the eaves.

Both of these window areas contain a small light bulb controlled by an exterior switch. These lights can simulate exterior daylight; and when they are controlled by a dimmer switch, they can duplicate almost any specific time of the day or evening. The transformer supplies low voltage for ceiling lights or miniature lamps. Note that all measurements are given with a plus or minus, so the size of the finished case depends on your own specifications.

SAMPLE ATTIC

Almost every American house contains a visual record of past and present generations in the form of an attic. All sorts of items are stored in attics, because someday they may prove useful, or someday someone will fix the broken whatever, or they are cherished reminders of past childhood and too memorable to be thrown out. The miniature attic offers a wide open area for collection. Almost anything, whole or broken, can be collected and displayed in the attic setting.

This project is offered in order to show the possibilities in such areas. Sample basements, closets, tool sheds, storage rooms, or garages make excellent miniature settings. A special treatment can be given such settings, and the following drawings are suggestions for the exposed framing, sheathing, and cobwebs commonly found in such areas.

Construction

The basic case or room box is made by the methods already outlined in the preceding drawings. The flooring in this case should be semi-rough wide boards with exposed nailing. The walls display the exposed miniature 2-inch by 4-inch boards and the sheathing of the back side. See detail in figure 2–16, left top. It is suggested that the sheathing boards have splits and poor fits in order to show the black construction paper simulating tar paper or building felt underneath the boards. An attic window is suggested in this back wall.

The left-hand side wall and the right-hand top wall simulate rafter eaves and pitch. Such rafter construction has 1/8-inch by 1/2-inch scale timbers exposed, and 1/16-inch by 1/2-inch roofers (boards) are secured to the back of these rafters with a 1/2-inch space in between each board. See detail in figure 2–16, left bottom. Cedar shingles are secured to the roofer boards, making a miniature roof as seen from the inside. A dormer and window can be installed in this sample roof section as suggested in figure 2–16. Because of the reverse detailing, the sample roof sections should be measured, made, and then installed in the box. The ceiling joists are scale-size 2-inch by 6-inch boards which are exposed with a rough board covering on the top edge.

Both windows on the dormer and side wall should have colored, rooftop, back-up scenes, and the two areas can be equipped with lights. A transformer can supply low voltage to overhead exposed bulbs. A possible variation to this scene is on a set of stairs exiting to the floor level.

The measurements are offered only as a suggestion, because the size is up to the builder.

11. *Colonial Carpenter's Shop*

The carpenter's shop was developed from existing examples found in Colonial Williamsburg and Old Sturbridge Village. It is a simple single-room building containing all the tools and basic machines for a one or two-man business. An exterior ladder allows access to the loft where lumber is stored to season.

BUILDING THE SHOP

While the plan given is for a carpenter's shop, the same building can easily be made to house any type of colonial business. A tinker's, coppersmith's, whitesmith's, or clockmaker's shop would work very well not only in the building itself but with the interior work benches as well.

Included in this chapter are plans for two work benches, one complete with a vise, a wood lathe, and actual-size patterns for carpenter's tools.

Construction

Material List

Part	Amount	Size	Material
Floor	1	11½" x 15" x ½"	Plywood
Front wall	1	9" x 16" x ½"	Plywood
Rear wall	1	9" x 16" x ½"	
Side walls	2	15" x 12" x ½"	
Roof	2	8" x 16" x ½"	
Ceiling	1	11½" x 15" x ⅜"	
Side window	1	3" x 3½"	casement unit
Front window	1	4½" x 6"	fixed unit
Door	1	3" x 6½"	exterior door and jamb
Shingles	Approx. 700	¾" x ½" x ¹/₁₆"	cedar
Clapboard		Approx. 91 linear feet x ½" x ¹/₁₆"	
Trim		Approx. 11 linear inches x ³/₁₆" x ¾"	clear stock

Fig. 2–17. *Carpenter's shop*

1. Study the drawings carefully. The four walls can be made of plywood covered by vertical siding, or the side pieces can be solid stock scored to resemble interior vertical boards. See figure 2–23.

2. Lay out and cut the stock to suggested size and shape. Cut the rough openings for the windows, doors, and loft hatch where indicated in the drawings. Score all the interior walls into scale-size random vertical boards, or glue on actual scale boards to the plywood base. When the interior walls are finished, install the windows and door frames. Install the finished interior door and window casing, or trim. Construct the basic floor board. Glue hardwood strips to the plywood base. See Section one for construction details.

3. Screw the finished sides to the floor piece. Secure the back wall piece to the floor and sides with screws. Note that the front wall of the shop opens as a large door to allow access to the interior. Install the corner boards to all corners. Hinge the front wall to one side with a small butt or continuous hinge. Note that the front opens just under the cornice or fascia trim in the front. See note on side elevation in figure 2–22.

4. Install the ceiling board. Secure this

Fig. 2–18.   *Miniature carpenter's shop*

Fig. 2–19.   *Miniature carpenter's shop interior*

162

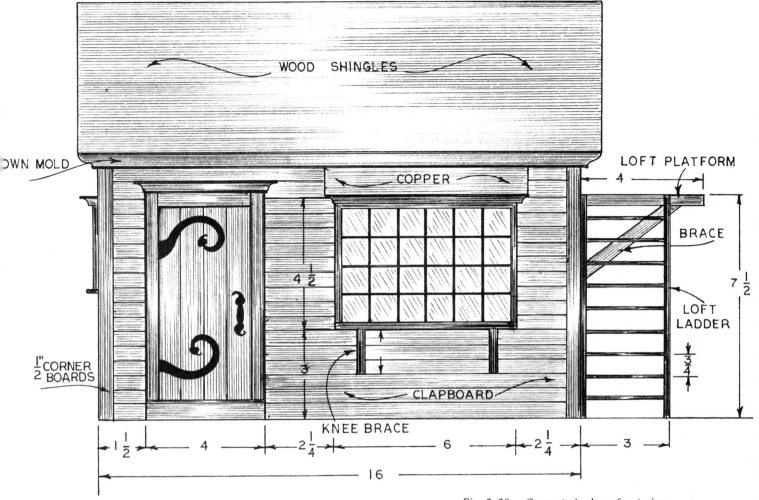

WOOD SHINGLES

OWN MOLD

COPPER

LOFT PLATFORM

4

BRACE

7 1/2

LOFT LADDER

3/4

4 1/2

3

1" CORNER
2 BOARDS

CLAPBOARD

KNEE BRACE

1 1/2   4   2 1/4   6   2 1/4   3

16

Fig. 2–20. Carpenter's shop, front view

member by nailing the sides and rear walls into it. Cut and install the roof boards. Nail the roof boards into the side rake angles and into the top of the rear wall. Install the 3/16-inch by 3/4-inch fascia and soffit trim. Glue and pin a scale-size crown molding to the fascia board and to the side rake trim. This molding must be installed on a plane that will allow the following roof shingles to rest upon the top edge of the molding. See Section one for details. The front wall operates just under the front fascia assembly.

5. Make a loft landing and knee braces (decorative reinforcement braces) from scrap lumber. See figure 2–23. Install the landing as

suggested. Install the loft door and trim as suggested. Rip-cut clear cedar or basswood into 1/16-inch strips for the exterior clapboard. (Commercially made scale clapboard may be used.) Attach the scale-size clapboards to the plywood walls with a 1/2-inch weather exposure. Spread glue on the back of each clapboard, and attach the top edge of each clapboard to the wall with pins or staples. The next clapboard will cover the staple or pins. Make a ladder to reach from just above ground level to the landing. Install the ladder to the side wall with small nails. Paint the whole exterior white or another suitable color.

6. Make the scale-size wood shingles from

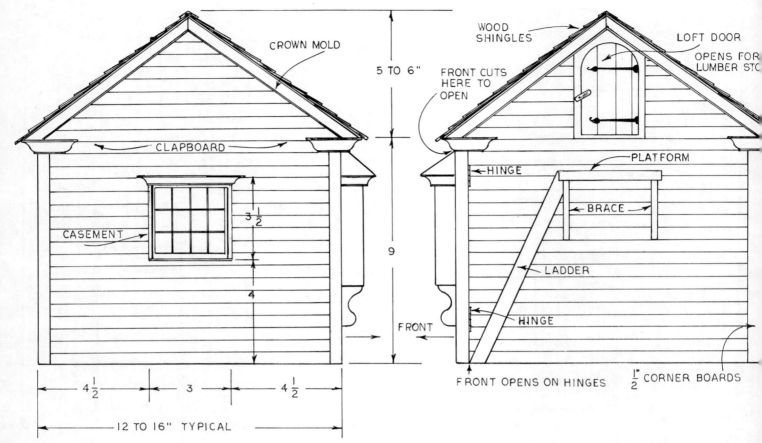

CROWN MOLD

5 TO 6"

CLAPBOARD

3 ½

CASEMENT

4

9

4 ½ — 3 — 4 ½

12 TO 16" TYPICAL

WOOD SHINGLES

LOFT DOOR

OPENS FOR LUMBER STO

FRONT CUTS HERE TO OPEN

PLATFORM

HINGE

BRACE

LADDER

HINGE

FRONT

FRONT OPENS ON HINGES   ½" CORNER BOARDS

Fig. 2–21. Carpenter's shop, side views

clear cedar. See Section one for details. (Commercial shingles may be used.) Scale-size slate can be substituted for the wood shingles. Attach the selected shingles to the roof boards leaving ¾ of an inch exposed to weather. It is suggested that the shingles be nailed or stapled above the weather exposure line so that succeeding shingles will cover the fasteners.

7. Stain and finish the interior walls and floor. Paint the ceiling white. Install any desired lights into the building. The attic or loft can conceal a transformer, if so desired. Cut and make a scale-size lumber stack and install in the loft.

INTERIOR MACHINES AND TOOLS

Large-Wheel Wood Lathe

1. Study the plans before starting work. Cut

the stock for parts A, B, C, D, and E from ¼-inch-thick clear hardwood. Cut a mortise into A, B, and C. Cut a matching tenon on D and E. Glue C to A and B. Glue E and D to A and B. This makes the lathe body. Make the tail stock (F). Drill and thread a hole as suggested in figure 2–25 into the tail stock. Cut a slot in the bottom as F clears the bottom of E. A wedge holds F in place. See figure 2–26. Make a dead center from a ⅛-inch-diameter machine screw with the head removed. Point the end of this center and screw into the threaded hole in F.

2. Make the live center as shown in figures 2–25 and 2–26. This center is turned from metal while the pulley is turned from hardwood. Drill a hole into A as suggested in figure 2–25 and push the metal live center through this hole. Glue the wood pulley to the end of this center where it exits outside A.

3. Drill a series of ¹⁄₁₆-inch-diameter holes,

¼ inch apart, into the the top edge of the front part E. These holes hold the tool-post-holder dowels. See figure 2–26. Insert the tool post into one of the holes.

4. Construct the wheel horse or housing as shown in figure 2–25. Part H has a tenon that fits a mortise in G. Parts J are braces that are pinned to G and H. Drill ⅛-inch-diameter holes in the centers of H as suggested for the wheel axle. Make a wheel as shown in figure 2–25. The large wheel is best made on a wood lathe from a single block of hardwood. Using the lathe, turn a hardwood block to the overall circumference of the large wheel. Mark out the wheel rim and hub size and cut away the stock from in between these two circles. Remove the block from the lathe but do not remove it from the face plate. While the wheel rim and hub are still attached to the roughly turned stock, drill the spoke holes. Glue the spokes (L) into the wheel rim and hub.

5. When the glue has dried, remount the

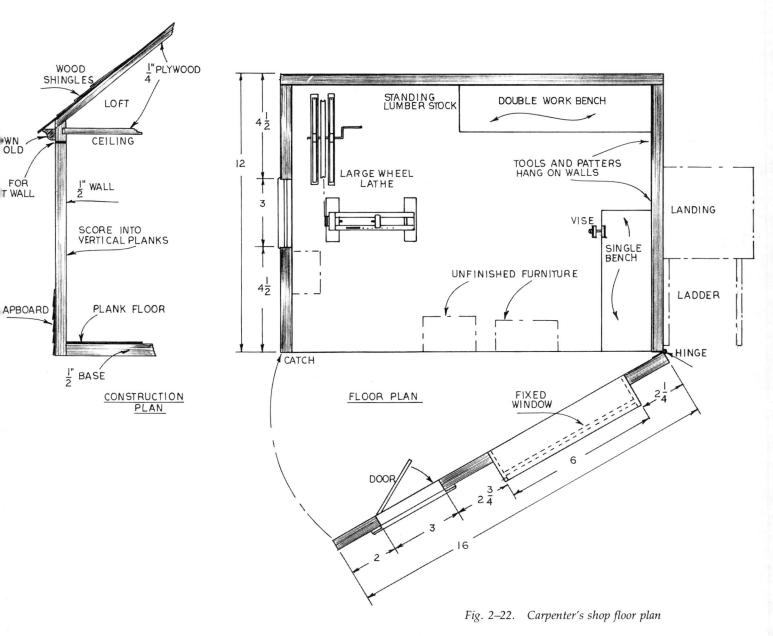

Fig. 2–22. *Carpenter's shop floor plan*

165

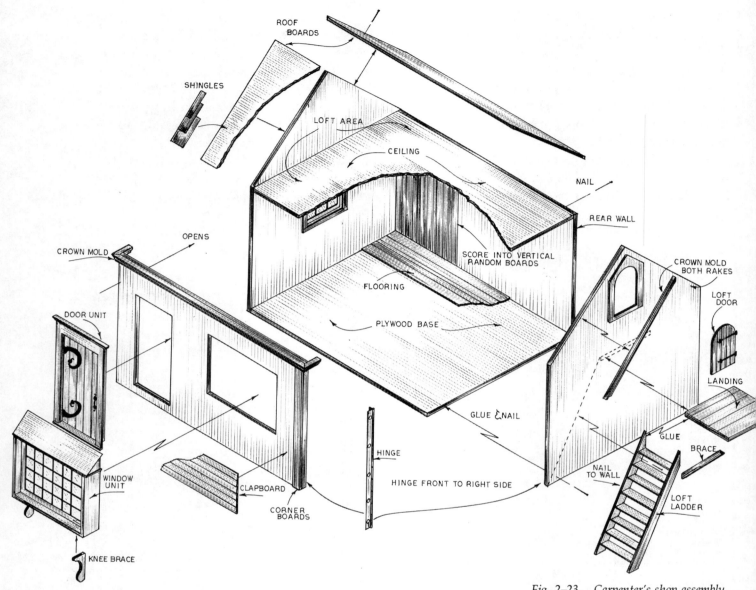

SHINGLES

ROOF BOARDS

LOFT AREA

CEILING

NAIL

REAR WALL

SCORE INTO VERTICAL RANDOM BOARDS

CROWN MOLD

OPENS

CROWN MOLD BOTH RAKES

LOFT DOOR

DOOR UNIT

FLOORING

PLYWOOD BASE

LANDING

GLUE & NAIL

GLUE

WINDOW UNIT

HINGE

BRACE

CLAPBOARD

HINGE FRONT TO RIGHT SIDE

NAIL TO WALL

CORNER BOARDS

LOFT LADDER

KNEE BRACE

Fig. 2–23. Carpenter's shop assembly

assembly on the wood lathe and finish forming, grooving, and sanding the wheel. Cut the suggested groove into the wheel rim. Cut the wheel rim, hub, and spoke assembly free from the main turning block. Drill a ⅛-inch axle hole into the center of the hub. Make the wheel axle from a ⅛-inch-diameter rod. The axle will have a half circle and handle on the exterior. Insert the axle through one wheel horse, glue it to the wheel hub, and push through the twin wheel horse. The wheel must revolve freely

between the two horses. Attach a rubber band around the wheel rim in the premade groove. Secure the wheel horses to the shop floor. See figure 2–26.

7. Secure the model lathe in front of the wheel so that the pulley wheel on the live center lines up with the large wheel groove. Attach a rubber band (or cord) from the wheel to the lathe pulley. When the large wheel is turned via the hand axle, the pulley rotates. The ratio is better than 5 to 1; therefore, the

pulley will turn five times for every turn of the large wheel. The faster the main wheel is turned, the faster the pulley will turn. A scale turning can be mounted between the live and dead centers for realism. Lathe chisels can be made and laid upon the lathe bed.

Workbench and Vise

The general design of this workbench lends itself to almost any type shop. The same bench will serve as a carpenter's, blacksmith's, tinker's, or coppersmith's work center.

Construction

Material List

Part		Amount	Size
A	Legs	4	¼" x ¼" x 2⅜"
B	Top Stretcher	2	¼" x ⅛" x 5½"
C	Lower Stretcher	2	¼" x ⅛" x 2"
D	Side Stretchers	4	¼" x ⅛" x 2"
E	Shelf	1	1/16" x 2¼" x 6"
F	Top	1	⅛" x 2¼" x 6"

1. Cut the selected stock to suggested shape and size. Cut notches into A for the let-in stretchers as shown in figure 2–28. Glue B, C, and D to A. Keep the unit square while the glue is setting.

2. Cut the stock for the bottom (E). Notch E for the legs (A). Part E can be scored to resemble planks, if preferred. Glue E to C and D. Cut the stock for the top (F). Score this piece into planks. Glue F to B and D.

Carpenter's Vise

The vise must be made from hardwood be-

Fig. 2–24. Miniature large-wheel wood lathe

167

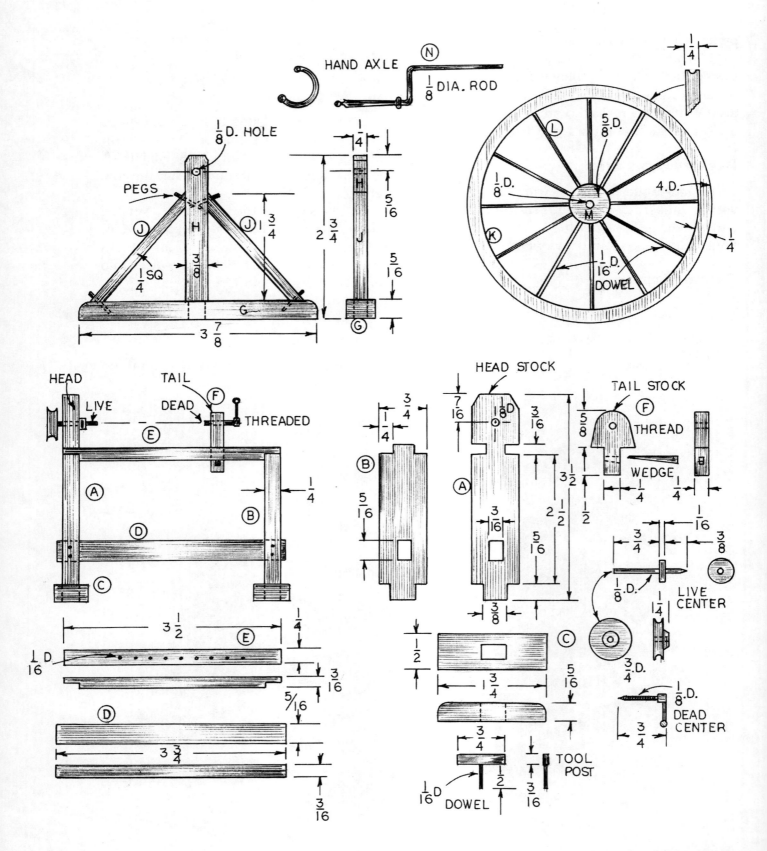

HAND AXLE $\frac{1}{8}$ DIA. ROD

$\frac{1}{8}$ D. HOLE

PEGS

$\frac{1}{4}$ SQ

$\frac{3}{8}$

$2\frac{3}{4}$

$3\frac{7}{8}$

$\frac{1}{4}$

$\frac{5}{16}$

$\frac{5}{16}$

$1\frac{3}{4}$

$\frac{5}{8}$ D.

$\frac{1}{8}$ D.

4. D.

$\frac{1}{4}$

$\frac{1}{16}$ D. DOWEL

HEAD
LIVE
TAIL
DEAD
THREADED

$\frac{1}{4}$

HEAD STOCK

$\frac{3}{4}$

$\frac{1}{4}$

$\frac{5}{16}$

$\frac{7}{16}$

$\frac{1}{8}$ D

$\frac{3}{16}$

$3\frac{1}{2}$

$2\frac{1}{2}$

$\frac{5}{16}$

$\frac{3}{16}$

$\frac{3}{8}$

$\frac{3}{16}$

TAIL STOCK

THREAD

$\frac{5}{8}$

WEDGE

$\frac{1}{2}$

$\frac{1}{4}$

$\frac{1}{4}$

$\frac{1}{16}$

$\frac{3}{4}$

$\frac{3}{8}$

$\frac{1}{8}$ D.

$\frac{1}{4}$

LIVE CENTER

$\frac{3}{4}$ D.

$\frac{1}{8}$ D. DEAD CENTER

$\frac{3}{4}$

$3\frac{1}{2}$

$\frac{1}{4}$

$\frac{1}{16}$ D

$\frac{3}{16}$

$\frac{5}{16}$

$3\frac{3}{4}$

$\frac{3}{16}$

$\frac{1}{2}$

$1\frac{3}{4}$

$\frac{5}{16}$

$\frac{3}{4}$

$\frac{1}{16}$ D DOWEL

$\frac{1}{2}$

$\frac{3}{16}$

TOOL POST

Fig. 2–25. Wood-lathe parts

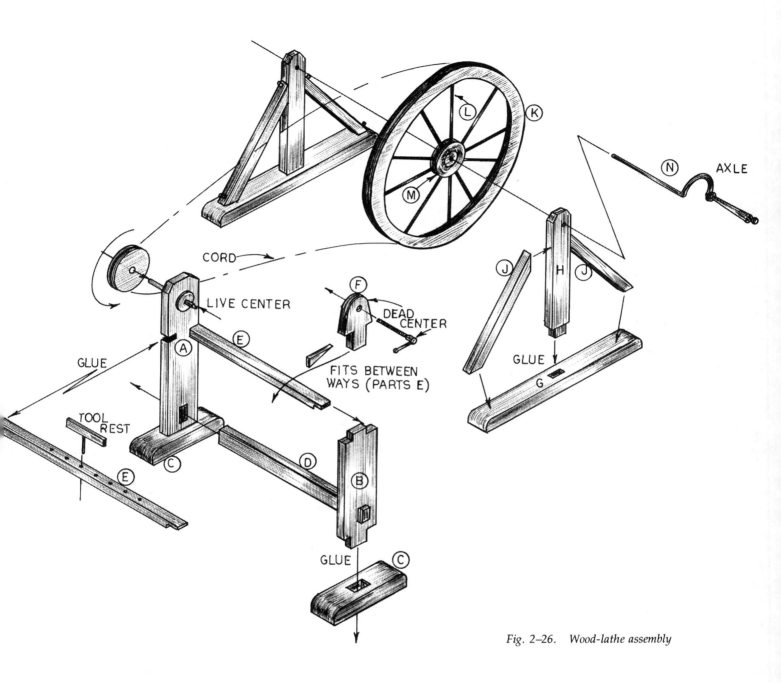

LIVE CENTER

GLUE

TOOL REST

CORD

FITS BETWEEN
WAYS (PARTS E)

DEAD
CENTER

GLUE

AXLE

GLUE

GLUE

Fig. 2–26. *Wood-lathe assembly*

cause of interior threading. Oak, maple, or birch are recommended.

1. Lay out and cut the stock for two matching vise faces. See top of figure 2–28. Drill a ⅛-inch-diameter hole in the lower end of the faces. Drill a ⅛-inch-diameter hole in the top of the front piece, and a ³/₃₂-inch-diameter matching hole in the same location of the back piece.

2. With a ⅛-inch national-course tap, cut threads into this ³/₃₂-inch hole in the back piece. Thread a section of ⅛-inch-diameter rod or turn down a machine screw and make a vise handle on the end. See figure 2–28. Screw this piece into the threaded hole in the vise back. This screw must move freely through the front piece. The screw action through the back will move the vise face in and out.

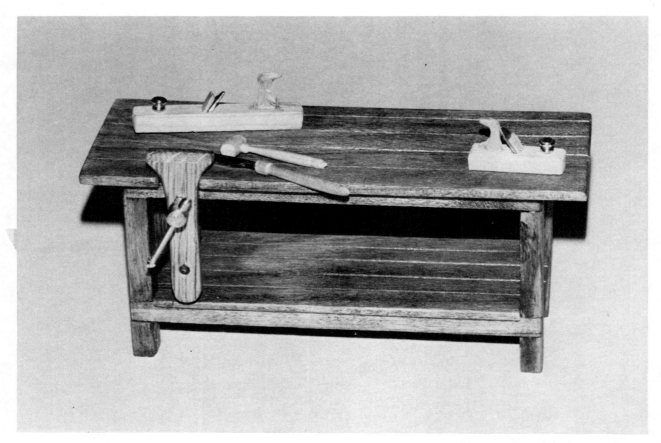

Fig. 2–27.   Miniature bench and vise

3. Glue a ⅛-inch-diameter dowel guide into the lower hole on the face piece. This guide must move freely through the hole in the rear piece. This guide will insure the in and out action of the front face.

4. Notch F of the work bench to receive the rear vise piece. See figure 2–29. Glue and pin the vise back piece into this notch.

Workbench With Drawers

This general purpose workbench will serve any shop. It can be made as a single or double unit. See figure 2–31.

Construction

Material List

Part	Amount	Size
A Leg frame	6	¼" x ¼" x 2⅜"
	3	¼" x ¼" x 1¾"
	3	³/₁₆" x ¼" x 8"
B Stretchers	1	¼" x ³/₁₆" x 8"
C Cleats	4	⅛" x ³/₃₂" x 2"
D Shelf	2	⅛" x 2" x 4"
E Drawers	4	½" x 1⅝" x 2" (typical)
F Drawer divider	2	⅛" x ⅜" x ½"
G Drawer divider	2	⅛" x ⅜" x 2"
H Top	1	⅛" x 2⅜" x 8½"

1. Lay out and cut the stock for the leg frames (A). See figure 2–32. Notch the legs for the top and bottom frame stretchers. Cut a mortise hole into the lower stretchers to receive B. Glue the leg frames together. Cut a tenon into B to fit the mortise on the leg frames. Glue B in place.

2. Cut the drawer cleats (C) to size. Glue and pin the cleats to the leg frames. See figure 2–32. Cut the stock for D. Glue D to the cleats (C). Cut the drawer dividers (F and G). Glue the dividers to D.

3. Make four drawer units (E). Fit the draw-

170

ers into the space between the dividers. Cut the stock for the top (H). Score the top to resemble planks. Glue H to the leg frames.

MINIATURE TOOLS

The colonial carpenter's shop, like any other work area, had an abundance of hand tools. Very often these tools hung on the walls surrounding the bench areas. The following tool selection is only a sample. Readers can study antique tool collections and use them as models for their miniature reproductions.

Saws

Make two handles of the suggested size and shape. Drill a $1/32$-inch-diameter hole into each handle as shown. Cut the center stretcher and make a $1/32$-inch tenon on each end. The tenons will fit the holes in each handle. Cut a slot in the bottom of each handle, and insert a piece of coping saw blade into this slot. These slots may be backed with small turned handles, if preferred. Tie a piece of twine around the top of the handles. Insert a piece of $1/32$-inch dowel into the center of this loop and twist the twine

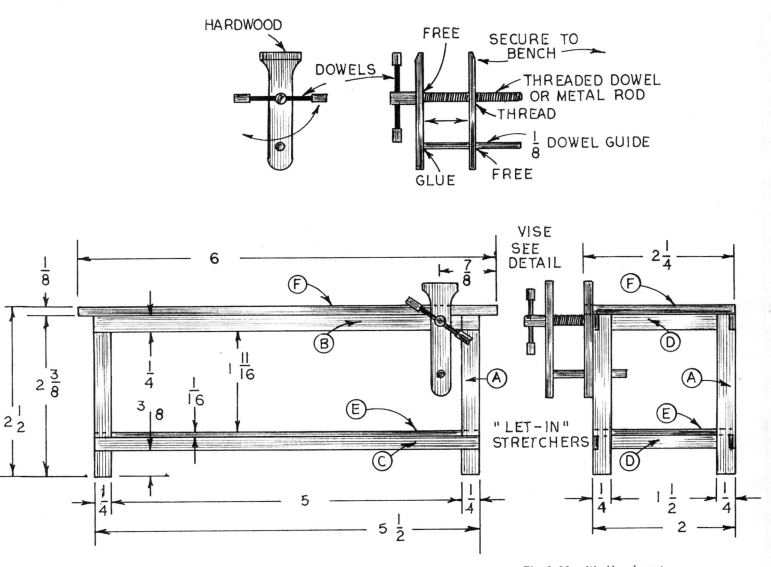

Fig. 2–28. Workbench parts

171

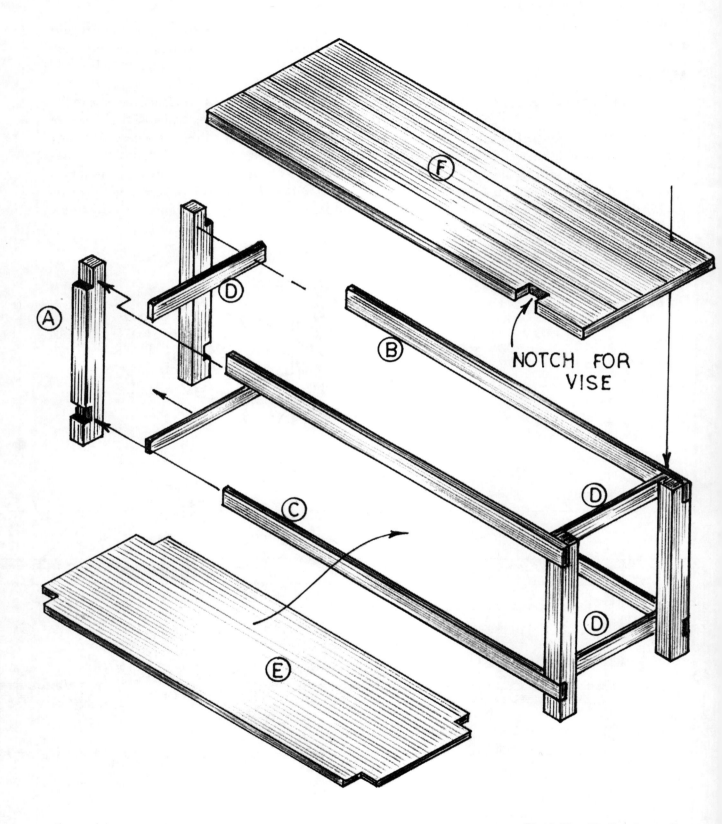

NOTCH FOR VISE

Fig. 2–29. Workbench assembly

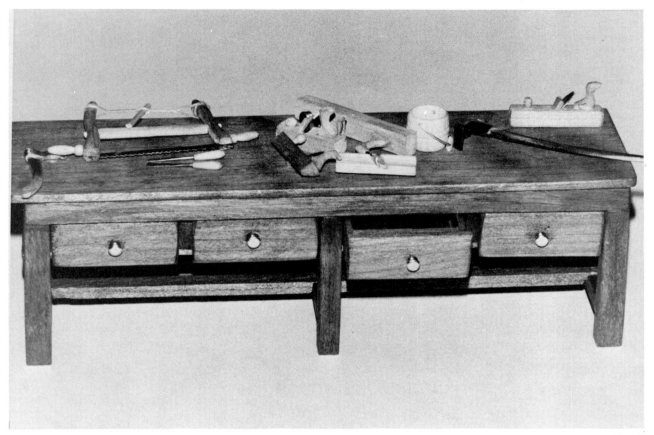

Fig. 2–30. *Miniature workbench*

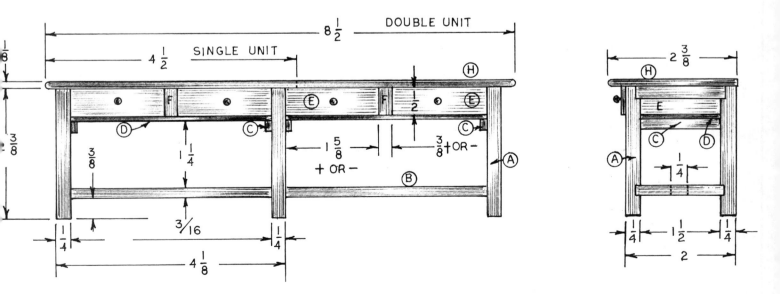

Fig. 2–31. *Double workbench parts*

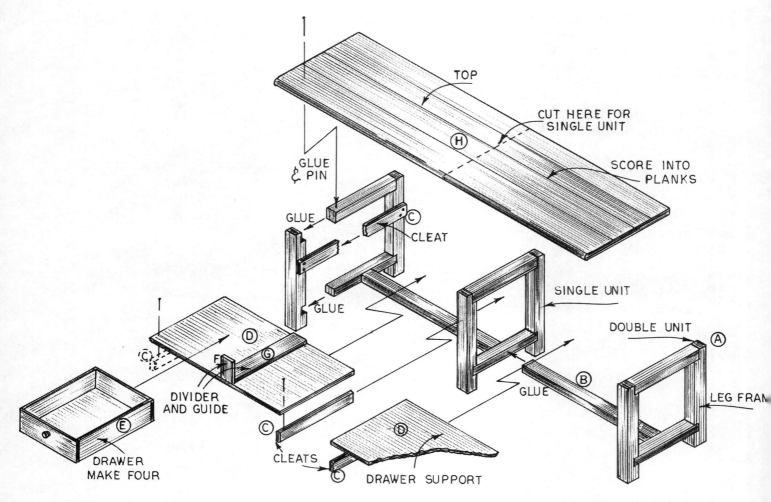

TOP

CUT HERE FOR
SINGLE UNIT

GLUE
PIN

SCORE INTO
PLANKS

GLUE

CLEAT

H

GLUE

SINGLE UNIT

DOUBLE UNIT

D

C

F

G

A

B

DIVIDER
AND GUIDE

GLUE

LEG FRAM

E

C

DRAWER
MAKE FOUR

CLEATS

C

D

DRAWER SUPPORT

Fig. 2–32. Double workbench assembly

taut. The twisted twine puts tension on the blade by drawing the handles in at the top.

The blades of these hand saws are made from flexible hacksaw blades with 32 teeth per inch. Such blades can be cut and shaped with tin snips. Cut the wooden handles in the shape suggested. Cut a slot into the handle end and glue the blade into the slot. Craft cement or Krazy Glue is recommended.

Lathe Chisels

The lathe chisel handles are made from turned 1/8-inch-diameter dowel. The steel chisel part is made from a brad. Drill a small hole, the same size as the brad, into the end of each chisel handle. Hold the brad with a pair of pliers and beat the brad shaft flat. File the tip of the flattened brad into a chisel shape. Cut the head from the brad and glue the shaft into the hole in the wooden handle. Make chisels of several different shapes and lay the chisels on the lathe bed or in a rack above the lathe.

Plumb

Make a U-shaped frame from 1/32-inch by 1/2-inch clear stock. Turn a brass plumb bob from a rod. Glue a thread to the bob top and insert the thread end to the frame top.

Level

Make a metal loop and glue it to a small block

174

of clear wood. See figure 2–34. Drill a ¹/₃₂-inch hole in the center of the metal loop. Turn out a small brass bob. Glue a thread to the bob top and place the thread through the hole in the metal loop. The wood base may be graduated, if preferred.

Hand Chisels

The hand chisels are made the same way as the lathe tools, but these chisels have shorter handles and are usually smaller. Make several of these chisels. Lay them on the work benches or hang them in a split rack near the work areas.

Hammers

The hammer handles are turned from ⅛-inch hardwood dowels. The claw hammer head is formed from a piece of ⅛-inch metal round. (The shaft of a 16d common nail will work.) Turn the head to suggested shape. Split one end of the turned head with a fine hacksaw and form the claws with pliers. The final shaping can be achieved with a file. Drill a small hole in the center of the head and glue the finished handle into this hole.

Hand Drill

The hand drill, or auger, is formed from sheet metal stock. Cut a thin pointed strip of metal and wrap it around a ¹/₁₆-inch dowel to create a screwlike twist. For the wooden top, wrap the thick end of the metal twist around this handle. Make several different sizes.

Planes

The hand plane is made from a block of hardwood. At a 15-degree angle, drill a hole

into this block as shown in figure 2–34. Enlarge this hole into a slot. Make a plane iron from sheet metal. Insert the iron into the slot and lock in place with a hardwood wedge. Form two handles for the larger planes and a single handle for the shorter planes. Glue the handles to the plane block as shown in figure 2–34. Make planes of several different sizes for the workbenches.

Two-Man Saw

The two-man saw is made by turning two handles from ⅛-inch dowels. Cut a slot in the bottom of the turned handles. Glue a section of hacksaw blade into these slots.

Ax

Form the ax handle from ¹/₁₆-inch-thick stock. Form the ax head from sheet metal. Wrap the metal around the premade handle and solder the points or face together. Form the blade with a file. Several different sizes and lengths of axes should be made. A clearing or smoothing ax can be made in the same manner.

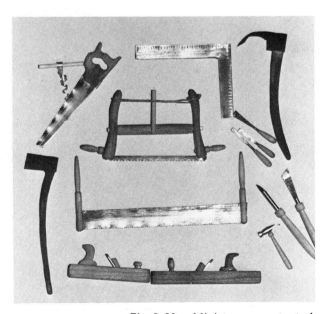

Fig. 2–33. *Miniature carpenter tools*

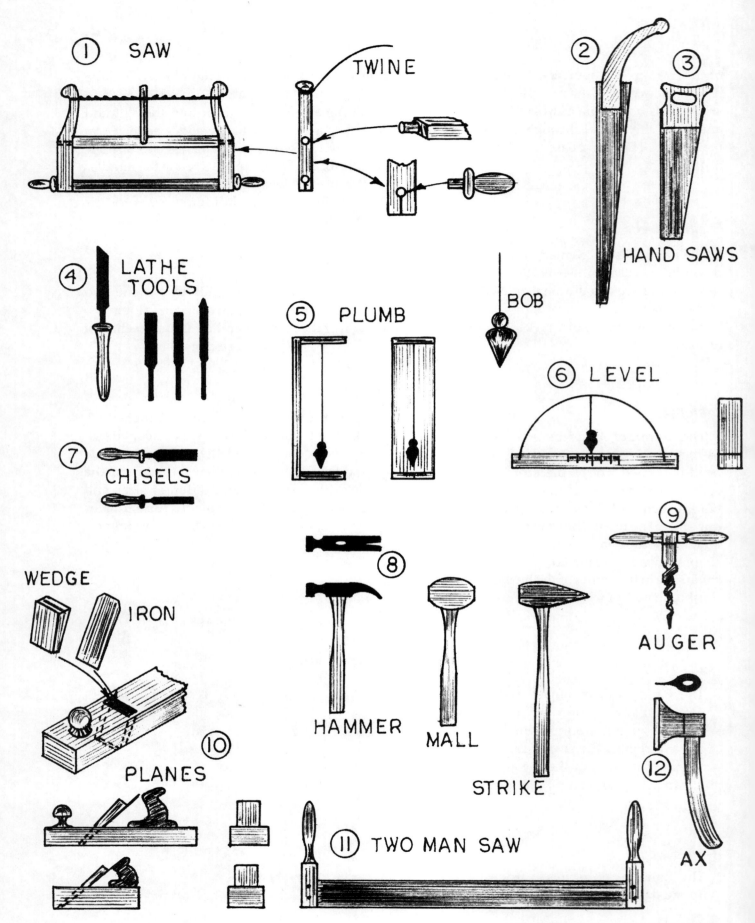

Fig. 2–34.   *Patterns for carpenter tools*

12. *Blacksmith Shop*

In Old Sturbridge Village, an early American blacksmith's shop is in operation. A constant fire heats metal to a deep red glow. Heavy blows shape the hot metal between the anvil face and the descending hammer to produce graceful metalware from a steel rod. From such a fiery birth sprang the trivets, fireplace cranes, tools, and hardware needed by a growing young America.

The following miniature shop is a composite developed from several blacksmith shops. The basic shape is the same as the building designed for the carpenter's shop with one addition—the large doors on the right-hand side. Because the blacksmith often worked on horses and wagons, which were too large to fit through the front entrance, large doors were needed.

The miniature building front operates as a large door to expose the interior. The front can be a right or left-handed operation. The construction procedures will be the same as outlined for the carpenter's shop. A possible variation to the basic design is a brick front as shown in figure 2–47. The shop exterior, window schedule, entrance, cornice trim, roof, and overall size is identical to the carpenter's shop drawings except for the large side doors. Because of these side doors, the optional loft and ladder should be on the opposite side wall.

INTERIOR STRUCTURES

The central point of the blacksmith's shop was the large forge and hand bellows. See figure 2–37. Figure 2–40 offers a typical forge design. While the drawing suggests stonework, any masonry material can be used.

Fig. 2–35.   *Early American blacksmith's shop (Courtesy Sturbridge Village, Sturbridge, MA)*

Fig. 2–36.   *Interior of the blacksmith's shop (Courtesy Sturbridge Village, Sturbridge, MA)*

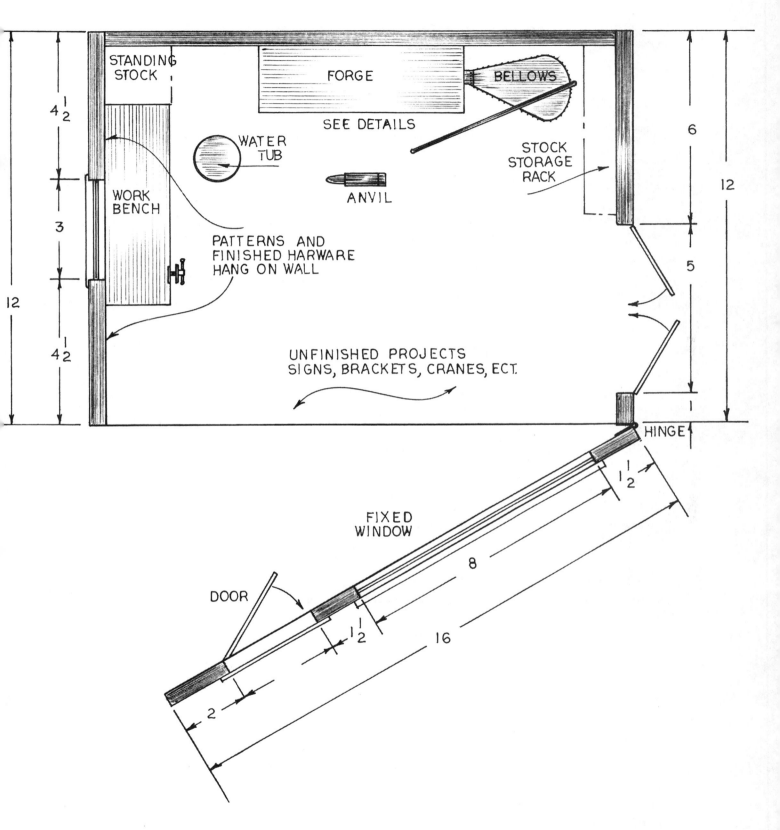

Fig. 2–37. Blacksmith's shop floor plan

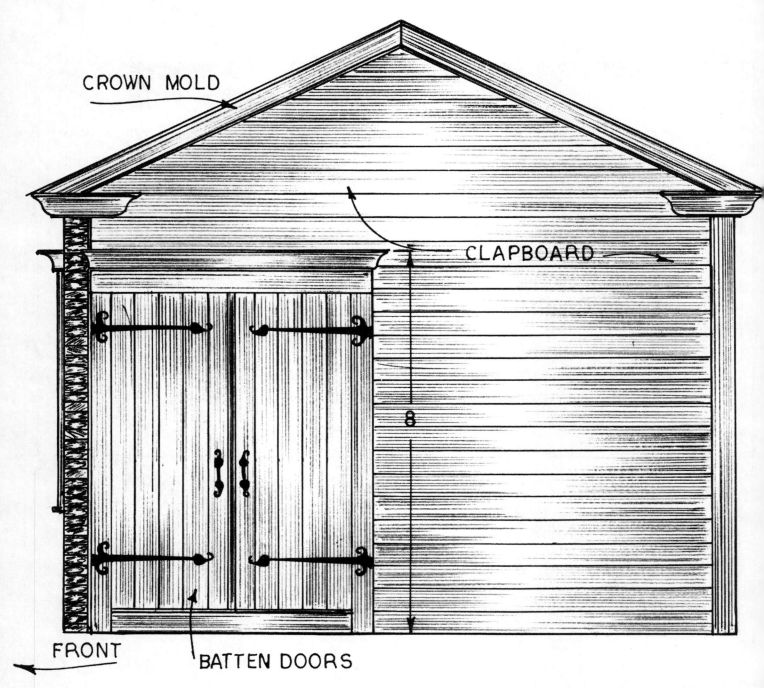

CROWN MOLD

CLAPBOARD

8

FRONT

BATTEN DOORS

Fig. 2–38. Blacksmith's shop, side view with large double doors

Forge

1. From ⅜-inch clear stock or plywood, construct a frame as suggested in figure 2–40. Apply a coat of drywall cement, plaster of paris, or commercial masonry to the frame and allow this coating to dry. Apply a second heavy coat of the same material. While the second coat is still wet, score the surface to resemble random-size stone or brick. Allow the second coat to cure. See Section one for masonry detailing.

2. Paint the individual stones a medium to

light grey. While this paint coat is still wet, blend in a flat black or dark grey paint to create tone and shading. The mortar joints are left the color of the base coating.

3. Form a copper hood as shown in figure 2–40. Copper foil can be purchased in most hobby or miniature outlets or copper flashing is available from lumberyards. Glue or pin the hood in place on the forge. An exposed chimney should be constructed above the roof line. Construct this chimney the same way as the forge.

Floor Bellows

The forge fire was fed by the bellows. See figure 2–41. When the wooden pole overhead was pulled down, it raised the lower bellows plate, which forced air into the charcoal fire. Gravity or a heavy rock made the plate return to the floor, and this movement gave the bellows a new breath.

1. Note that the bottom plate (B) is larger than the top plate (A). Lay out and cut A and B from 1/8-inch clear stock. Drill a 3/16-inch-diameter hole into A, as shown. Pin a flap of simulated leather material over this hole, so that one end is free. This permits the bellows to breathe. Hollow out a groove in the ends of A and B. See detail in figure 2–42. Cut 5/8 inch to 3/4 inch back from the front point of B. Install a small hinge on this cut. This will allow B to move up and down. Glue the small point of B

Fig. 2–39. Miniature forge and bellows

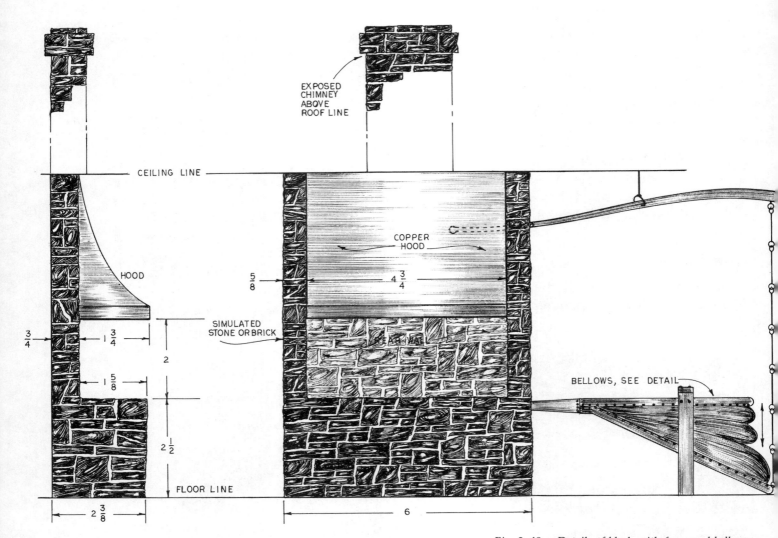

EXPOSED CHIMNEY ABOVE ROOF LINE

CEILING LINE

COPPER HOOD

HOOD

SIMULATED STONE OR BRICK

$\frac{5}{8}$

$4\frac{3}{4}$

$\frac{3}{4}$

$1\frac{3}{4}$

2

$1\frac{5}{8}$

$2\frac{1}{2}$

BELLOWS, SEE DETAIL

FLOOR LINE

$2\frac{3}{8}$

6

Fig. 2–40.   Details of blacksmith forge and bellows

to the point of A. These two parts now make a solid block with the interior groove creating a channel for the air. Part B must be able to move freely on the hinge.

2. Set A at the desired height. Allow B to rest on the floor and make a paper pattern to fit around the circumference of both parts for the bellows. Cut a piece of glove leather or plastic to the pattern size. Glue and pin this material, which is the lung, the edges of A and B. Trim the front points into a round. Form a metal tube from copper foil. See figure 2–42. This tube should enter the forge through a hole and point directly at the proposed fire.

3. The bellows horse should be constructed next. The floor horse or stand is made from $\frac{3}{8}$-inch-square stock. Cut the stock to the suggested shape and size for D and E. Part E glues to the D parts. Construct two metal brackets (F), and pin A to E. This makes A stationary and level. Part B must move freely between the two horses. Install the forge horses and bellows to the shop floor with glue and nails.

4. Form an iron chain from wire from a paper clip. See figure 2–41. Cut an overhead hand pole from $\frac{3}{16}$-inch stock. Attach this pole to the shop ceiling with an iron hinge pin.

Attach the iron chain to the pole end and B. A forward handle can also be attached to the pole front.

Many retail hobby outlets sell a flickering fireplace light to resemble a miniature fire. Wire the fire pit to receive such a light. Pieces of Grape Nuts cereal can be painted flat black to resemble charcoal and placed over and around the flickering bulb.

Anvil

Figure 2–44 offers a pattern for the blacksmith's anvil. From a block of hardwood, rough cut the anvil to the suggested shape and size. Finish form the anvil with files and sandpaper, and paint it black or dark grey to resemble metal. Mount the finished anvil on a simulated section of tree trunk. Attach the trunk bottom to the shop floor in front of the forge.

TOOLS

It is suggested that the reader search resource books for possible tool ideas. Patterns are offered in figure 2–44 for some of the more common blacksmith tools.

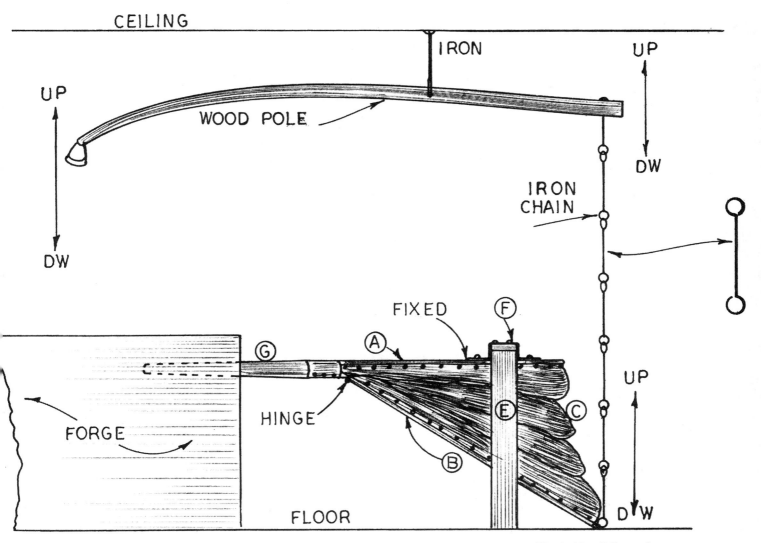

Fig. 2–41. Bellows plan

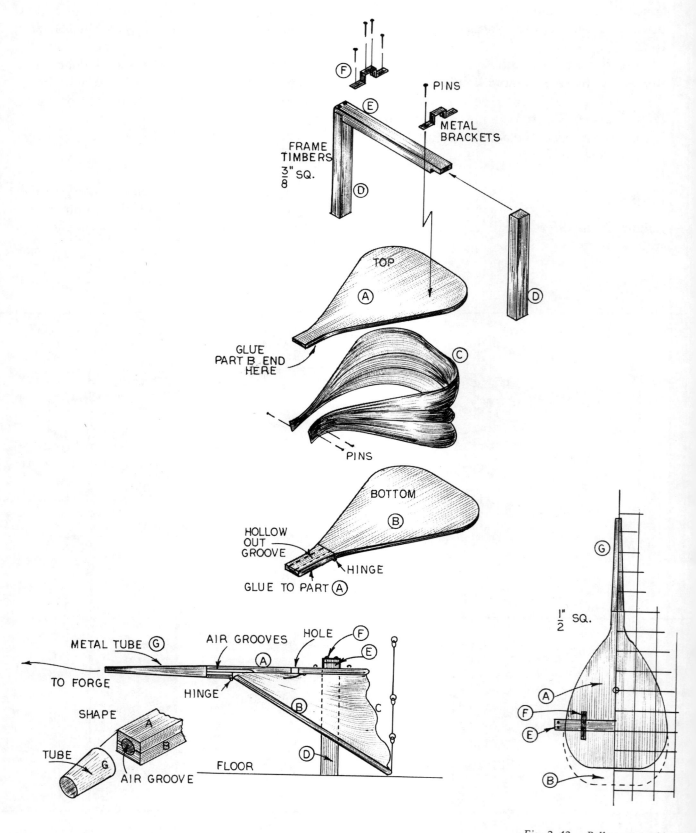

PINS

F

PINS

METAL
BRACKETS

E

FRAME
TIMBERS
$\frac{3}{8}$" SQ.

D

TOP

A

D

GLUE
PART B END
HERE

C

PINS

BOTTOM

B

HOLLOW
OUT
GROOVE

HINGE

GLUE TO PART A

METAL TUBE G

AIR GROOVES

HOLE

F

E

A

TO FORGE

HINGE

B

C

SHAPE

A

B

D

TUBE

G

FLOOR

AIR GROOVE

G

$\frac{1}{2}$" SQ.

A

F

E

B

Fig. 2–42. Bellows assembly

Fig. 2–43. Miniature anvil

Blacksmith or Machinist Vise

This vise is cut from a metal block. Aluminum, brass, or mild steel is suggested.

1. Lay out the patterns on the selected stock. Cut out the shape as close as possible with a hacksaw. File into finished shape. The back and face plates should be mirror twins. Mark the two plates for the suggested holes.

2. Drill a ⅛-inch-diameter hole into the front plate as shown in figure 2–44. Drill a matching ³⁄₃₂-inch-diameter hole into the back plate. Thread this hole for the ⅛-inch-diameter rod. The threaded rod can be made from a machine screw with the head removed. Form a handle from ¹⁄₁₆ inch (or smaller) rod. Thread the rod into the back plate. The rod must move freely in the face plate. Drill matching ¹⁄₁₆-inch holes into the bottom of both plates for the vise guide. See figure 2–44.

3. Solder a ¹⁄₁₆-inch rod into the hole in the face plate. This rod must move freely in the hole in the back plate. Attach the vise to a work bench. (The carpenter shop benches also work very well for the blacksmith shop. See figures 2–27 and 2–30.)

Tongs

Each blacksmith had several dozen tongs of various lengths and with various head shapes. Use heavy-gauge wire for the tongs. Flatten the wire and file smooth. Using pliers, shape the tong handles and head from two pieces of wire. Cross one handle over the other and drill a ¹⁄₆₄-inch-diameter hole through both pieces. This hole is for the hinge pin or rivet. On miniature tongs, use a bank pin for a rivet. Add a touch of solder to the pin end; the solder will secure the pin to the handle hole.

Hammers

The hammer, punch, mall, and strike heads are made from round metal stock formed on a lathe or drill. Drill a ¹⁄₁₆-inch hole in the center of the finish heads. Form a handle from ⅛-inch dowel. Glue the handle into the head hole.

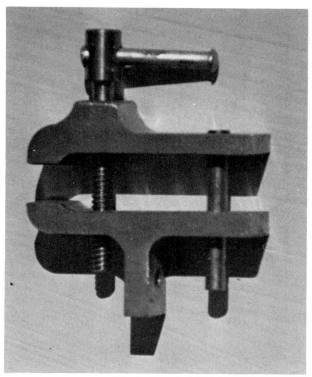

Fig. 2–45. Miniature blacksmith vise

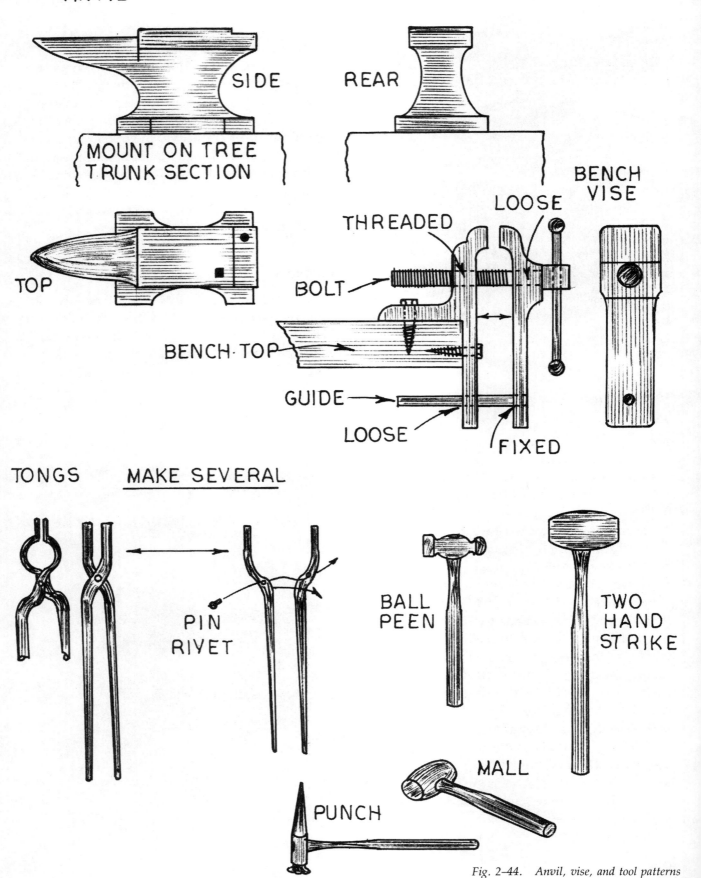

ANVIL

SIDE   REAR   BENCH
                                      VISE

MOUNT ON TREE
TRUNK SECTION

TOP   THREADED   LOOSE

BOLT

BENCH·TOP

GUIDE

LOOSE   FIXED

TONGS   MAKE SEVERAL

PIN
RIVET   BALL   TWO
                      PEEN   HAND
                                  STRIKE

                      MALL

PUNCH

Fig. 2–44.   *Anvil, vise, and tool patterns*

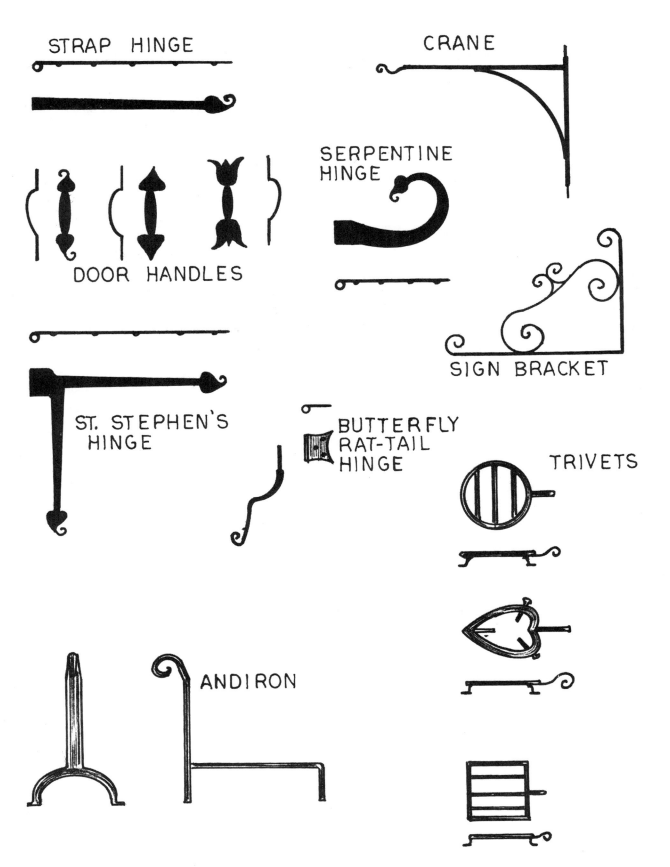

STRAP HINGE

CRANE

SERPENTINE HINGE

DOOR HANDLES

SIGN BRACKET

ST. STEPHEN'S HINGE

BUTTERFLY RAT-TAIL HINGE

TRIVETS

ANDIRON

Fig. 2-46.   Patterns for blacksmith's products

187

Make several hammers for the anvil and workbenches.

In most blacksmith shops, the anvil base had a leather strap nailed to the circumference, forming loops. The smith kept his hammers in these loops close to the anvil.

Smithy Products

Early American smith products, which have already been reduced to miniature size, offer some full-size patterns for blacksmith products. The hardware is made from scrap sheet metal. Trace the patterns to the sheet metal. Cut as close as possible with tin snips. Finish form the hardware with files. Paint the finished pieces flat black.

The andirons are made from heavy-gauge sheet metal or light-gauge wire stock. Transfer the patterns to the stock and cut to shape. Finish forming with files. The joints are soldered together.

The trivets can be made from paper clip wire. The joints are soldered. Forming is completed with pliers. Paint the trivets black when finished.

Research books or restoration settlements can supply other possible blacksmith ideas and products. It is suggested that the finished products be hung on the blacksmith shop walls as examples of the smith's work.

13. *Early American Brick-Front Shops*

The brick-front shop building is reminiscent of Colonial Williamsburg. Skilled craftsmen were readily available in the South, and brick construction was prevalent. Brick lends permanence and strength to a structure. Figure 2–47 shows a typical shop with a brick front. If the reader so desires, the shop's entire exterior can be simulated brick. This particular business shop can be used as an apothecary, a bakery, or a candy, silversmith's, dressmaker's, or clockmaker's shop. The dimensions given are general. The overall sizes can easily be longer, wider, and higher.

Because the rear of most shops is used for displaying goods on the walls or counters, the complete front wall of this building is made to open as a large door to expose the interior. See the hinge notation on the right-hand side of the drawing. Break the front wall just below the cornice work. Such a break line will not interfere with the artistic design of the building.

Construction

Material List (for given dimensions)

Part	Amount	Size
Front wall	1	9" x 16" x ½"
Rear wall	1	9" x 16" x ½"
Side walls	2	13" x 14" x ½"
Floor	1	13" x 15" x ½"
Ceiling	1	13" x 15" x ½"
Roof boards	2	8" x 16" x ⅜"
Corner boards	6	⅛" x ½" x 9"
Clapboard		1040" x ¹⁄₁₆" x ¾"
Crown molding		70" x ⅝"
Shingles	Approx. 500	¹⁄₁₆" x ¾" x 1½"

Typical Millwork

Part	Amount	Size
Double-hung windows, six over six	2	3" x 5½"
Fixed unit, small pane	1	8" x 5½"
Exterior door, glass optional	1	3" x 6½"

Part	Brand Name	Model
Double-hung window	Houseworks	5000
Fixed window	Houseworks	5007
Double-hung window	Carlson	CM 41
Double-hung window	X-acto	41210

The building itself is constructed using the same methods outlined for the carpenter's and blacksmith's shops. See figures 2–23 and 2–37. The basic walls can be ½-inch or ⅜-inch plywood or solid clear stock. This early American period interior can be painted, papered, or paneled. The floor is scored into planks or hardwood strip flooring can be glued over the base. See the chapter on flooring in Section one for details.

The exterior clapboards, corner boards, shingles, and cornice work have been discussed in the notes on the carpentry shop, but see the chapter on miniature construction in Section three for more detail.

Brick Front

The brick front can be achieved by three different methods.

1. The first method is to score solid wood. Mark out the plywood or solid wood wall for scale-size bricks. The horizontal lines for brick height should be placed every 3/16 inch. With a back or dovetail saw, cut a 1/32-inch saw kerf on each horizontal line. Next, mark out the brick length lines; each brick should be about ⅝ inch long. Remember that every other line of bricks is placed in a staggered (half bond) pattern. With a sharpened screwdriver or small wood chisel, cut these vertical lines to the same depth as the horizontal lines. This method creates recess or rake joints.

Paint the entire wall a light grey. After the grey paint has dried, paint each individual brick red. While the red paint is still wet, blend in a flat black paint for contrast and shading.

2. The second method is to make the ma-

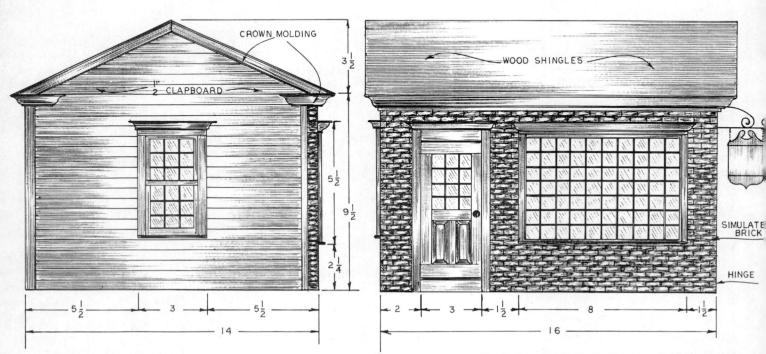

Fig. 2–47. Typical early American brick-front shop

Fig. 2–48. Millinery shop (Courtesy Colonial Williamsburg, Williamsburg, VA)

sonry texture. Apply a thin coat of dry-wall cement, plaster of paris, or commercial stone texture to the front wall. Allow this coat to dry. Apply a second, heavy coat on the wall and while the texture is still soft, score into bricks. Allow this coat to dry. Paint the individual bricks the same way as outlined in method one.

3. Finally, actual scale-size bricks can be applied. Some commercial companies sell scale-size bricks in a half or full width. This brick veneer front can be made from such material. The bricks are secured with an adhesive

and some mortar joints must be filled in and pointed. It is suggested that manufacturer's directions be followed for such an operation.

Masonry supplies can be ordered from a number of suppliers. Houseworks Ltd. sells miniature clay bricks (model 8201); Holgate and Reynolds sells embossed masonry (model 1010); and J. Hermes Company sells brick-printed paper (models 630, 502, or 475). For more information, see the list of suppliers in Section four.

191

Fig. 2–49.   Typical colonial women's wear (Courtesy Index of American Design)

Fig. 2–50. *Typical early American dress (Courtesy Index of American Design)*

193

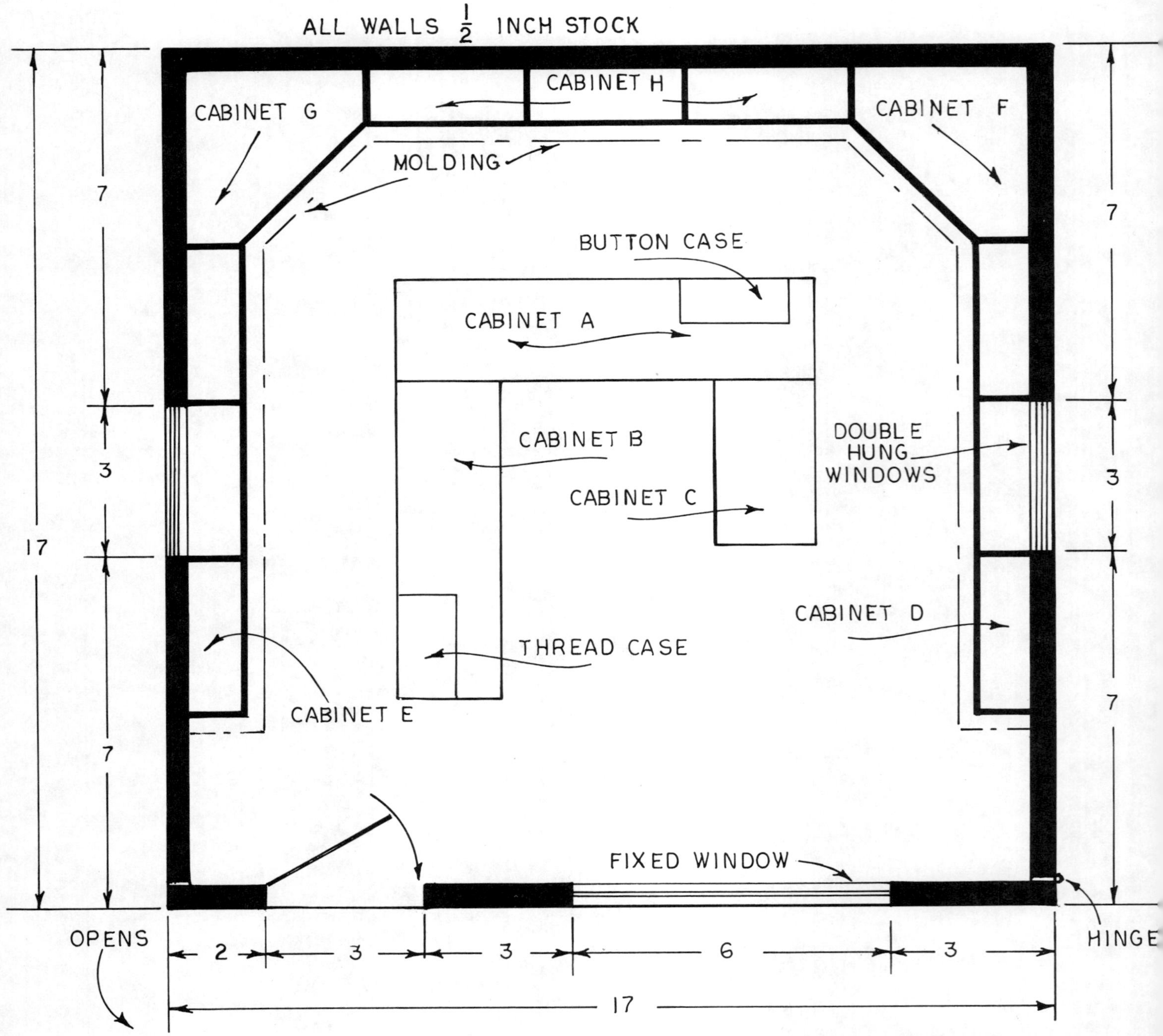

ALL WALLS $\frac{1}{2}$ INCH STOCK

CABINET G

CABINET H

CABINET F

MOLDING

BUTTON CASE

CABINET A

CABINET B

DOUBLE HUNG WINDOWS

CABINET C

CABINET D

THREAD CASE

CABINET E

FIXED WINDOW

7   3   7   17

7   3   7

OPENS

2   3   3   6   3

17

HINGE

Fig. 2–51. Millinery shop floor plan

MILLINERY SHOP, EARLY AMERICAN, CIRCA 1800

In early America, the millinery shop was the center of fashion. Gowns and dresses were sold along with bolted material, buttons, accessories, threads, and ribbons. Most of the beautiful women's wear of this period came from such shops, which were often operated by a talented seamstress.

The following drawings give the basic floor plan and the interior furnishings for such a

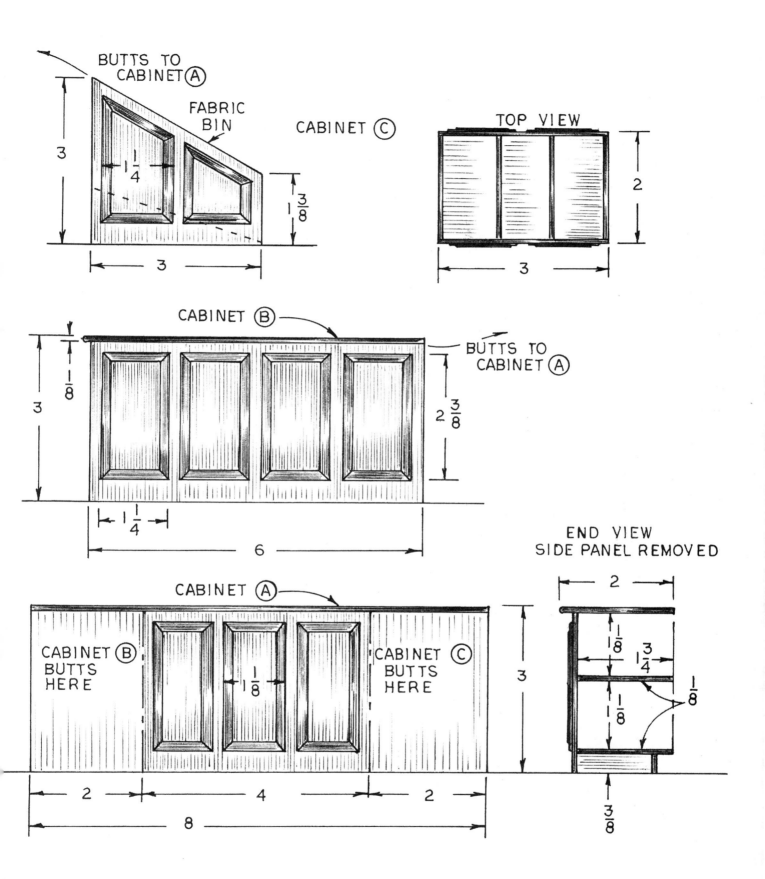

BUTTS TO CABINET (A)

FABRIC BIN

CABINET (C)

3

1 1/4

1 3/8

3

TOP VIEW

2

3

CABINET (B)

BUTTS TO CABINET (A)

1/8

3

2 3/8

1 1/4

6

END VIEW
SIDE PANEL REMOVED

CABINET (A)

CABINET (B)
BUTTS HERE

1/8

CABINET (C)
BUTTS HERE

2

2

4

2

8

3

1/8

1 3/4

1 1/8

1/8

3/8

Fig. 2–52. Millinery shop counter details

195

single-room business. If desired, the collector can stock his shelves with miniature bolts of material, scale-size buttons, ribbon and thread samples, and fully finished gowns.

Construction

Figure 2–51 offers a floor plan for a typical millinery shop. This building is slightly larger than the other previous shops. However, the exterior construction is similar to the methods already outlined for the carpenter's or blacksmith's brick-front shops. See figures 2–20 and 2–37. To construct the actual building, follow the directions given for the carpenter's shop or the sample early American building. This building also has the front wall opening as a large door for interior exposure. The front contains an entrance door and fixed window. In the center of each side is a double-hung window measuring 3 inches by 5 inches.

The interior should be painted or papered. A Wedgwood-blue color scheme is suggested. The interior side and rear walls have floor-to-ceiling cabinets and material racks. Center counters and cases complete the interior.

Center Counters and Cabinets

Cabinets B and C butt on to cabinet A to form a U-shape. These cabinets are made from 1/8-inch stock. Pine, cherry, or basswood is suggested.

1. Lay out and cut the stock for cabinet A. Make the base from 1/8-inch by 3/8-inch stock laid on edge creating a toe space. See figure 2–52. Cover the base with a 1/8-inch by 1¾-inch strip for the bottom shelf. Glue a 2⅞-inch by 8-inch strip of stock to the base unit front and 1⅞-inch by 2⅞-inch strips to the sides of the base unit. Install the center shelf by fastening it to the sides and front strips. Secure the top to the cabinet by gluing it to the front and sides.

2. Make cabinet B the same way as cabinet A. Glue the finished cabinet B to A as suggested in figure 2–52. Make the fabric bin,

cabinet C, following the dimensions given. The fabric bin is made like a box with a slanted floor and two or three dividers. Bolted material is stacked into the bins for display. The rear bolts are higher than the front bolts because of the inclined base. Secure cabinet C to cabinet A.

3. Cut raised panels of 1/16-inch solid stock or create raised-panel effects from scale moldings and attach the panels to the cabinet fronts as suggested in figure 2–52. Several retail firms sell ready-made raised panels. For example, Northeastern Scale Models makes a raised panel (model DPA-32-6), as does Carlson's Miniatures (model CM 83) and AMSI Miniatures (model GBP 103). See the list of suppliers in Section four.

4. Sand the center-counter assembly smooth. This counter can be painted or stained. Install the counter unit to the shop floor.

Button or Thread Case

All the stock for these cases is 3/32-inch pine, basswood, or hardwood of your choice. Cut the stock to suggested shape and size. Glue the sides, back, and front to the bottom piece and each other. Glue the top plate to the side pieces on the top flats provided. Make a door frame from 3/32-inch by 3/16-inch stock. See figure 2–53.

Glue a thin plastic sheet to the rear side of this door. Attach the door to the top plate with small miniature hinges. Glue bright felt or satin to the case interior. Make two or three of these cases. Place scale-size buttons in one case and thread or ribbons in the others.

Wall Cabinets

The wall cabinets are joined in the rear with angled display cabinets. The wall cabinets are made separately and then installed. These wall cabinets have doors on the bottom sections and shelves or bolt racks for fabric on the upper sections. Note that cabinets D and E are con-

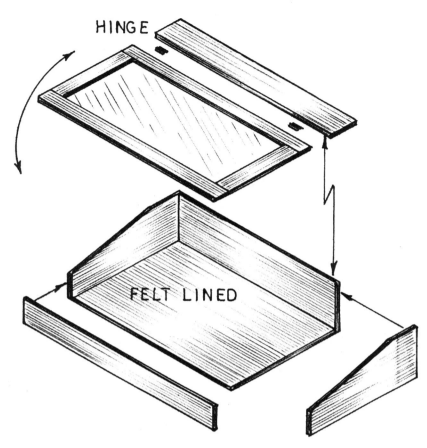

HINGE

FELT LINED

BUTTON/THREAD BOX CASE

ALL STOCK $\frac{3}{32}$" THICK

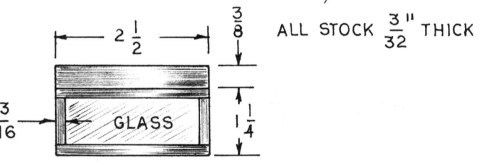

2 $\frac{1}{2}$

$\frac{3}{8}$

$\frac{3}{16}$

GLASS

1 $\frac{1}{4}$

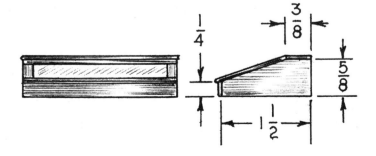

$\frac{1}{4}$

$\frac{3}{8}$

$\frac{5}{8}$

1 $\frac{1}{2}$

Fig. 2–53.   *Button case details*

197

structed around the double-hung windows on each building side. Study figures 2–54 and 2–55 before starting construction. All cabinet stock is ⅛-inch thick. Pine, basswood, or hardwood is suggested.

Cabinets D and E

1. Lay out and cut the stock for the vertical side pieces and the floor piece. Four vertical sides are required for each cabinet. The floor piece of the same width should be continuous. Measure and mark out clearance on the bottom strip for the window and trim area. A ceiling piece to match the bottom piece can be used.

2. Glue and pin the vertical sides to the bottom piece. Glue the shelving in between the vertical side pieces. See figure 2–54 for suggested spacing. Make and install the counter top. This top should be a continuous piece that is installed just below the window sill or apron. The window size will determine the ultimate height of this counter. The area under the counter top will be enclosed by doors.

3. Make and glue in place the required rails and stiles for the door openings. Make and install the top fascia arch. See cabinet H for sample grid design. The fascia arch piece secures to the vertical side pieces. Secure a crown molding to the top of the fascia piece. Glue ¼-inch-wide stiles to the vertical side edges from the counter top to the bottom of the fascia piece. If the racks for fabric bolts are to be used, see the detail in figure 2–55.

4. Make raised-panel doors to cover the openings. See figure 2–54 for suggested size. See Section one for door construction details. These doors can be made operable with hinges or they can be glued over the opening and not used.

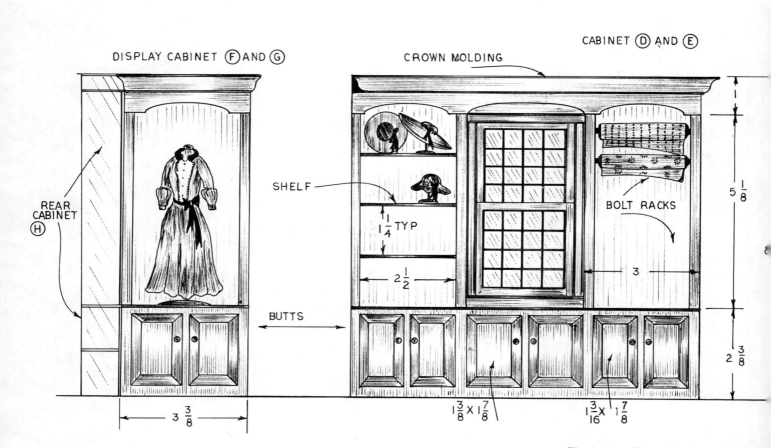

Fig. 2–54. Side wall cabinet detail

198

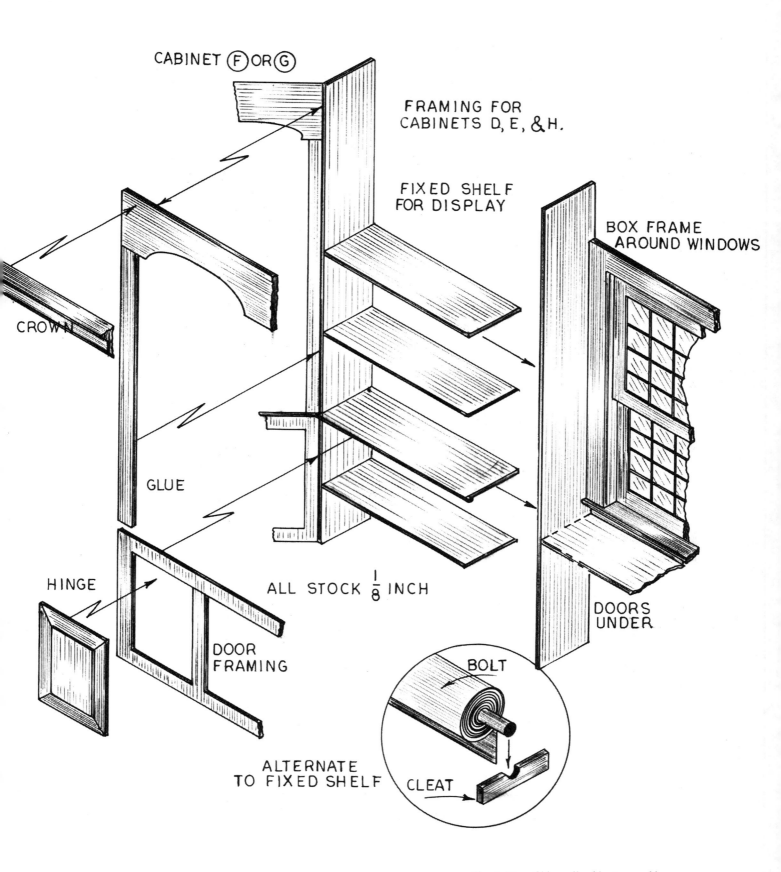

CABINET (F) OR (G)

FRAMING FOR
CABINETS D, E, &H.

FIXED SHELF
FOR DISPLAY

BOX FRAME
AROUND WINDOWS

CROWN

GLUE

HINGE

ALL STOCK $\frac{1}{8}$ INCH

DOOR
FRAMING

DOORS
UNDER

BOLT

CLEAT

ALTERNATE
TO FIXED SHELF

Fig. 2–55. Side wall cabinet assembly

199

Cabinet H

Cabinet H is a continuous piece across the back wall. Construct cabinet H following the directions given for units D and E. See figures 2–54 and 2–55. This cabinet contains all shelving between the vertical side pieces, because the rear wall does not contain a window. The vertical stiles, counter top, molding, and fascia arch should match the size and height of the side cabinet pieces.

Sand, paint, stain, and finish the cabinet assemblies. Do the finishing now, because when the cabinets are set against the building walls, the small spaces and parts are difficult to reach. Place the finished side and rear cabinets into the building and secure in place. The installation should create an equal space in each rear corner where cabinets F and G belong.

Cabinets F and G

The display cabinets should be made and mated to the rear and side cabinets at this time. If any adjustment is required, do it while these units are under construction. As construction proceeds, take the final measurements from the actual space rather than from the drawings.

1. Cut the ⅛-inch stock for the counter's top shelf. This material will be installed at the same height as the counter tops in cabinets D, E, and

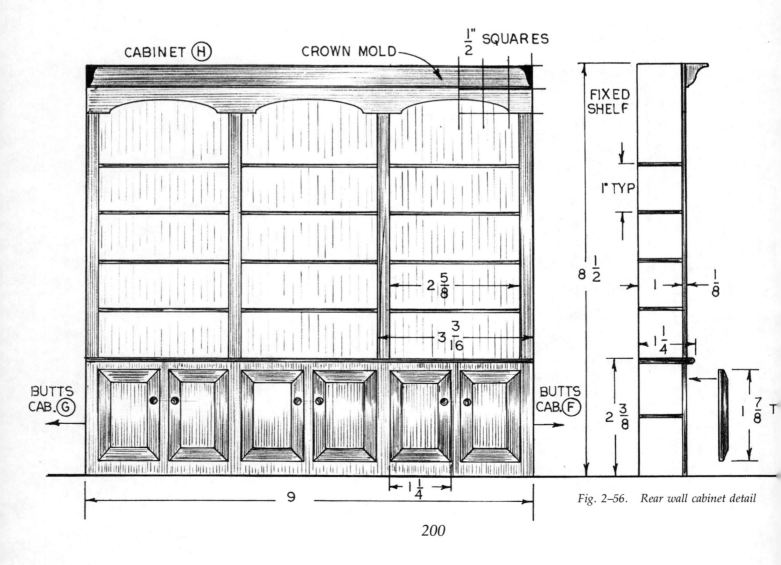

Fig. 2–56. Rear wall cabinet detail

200

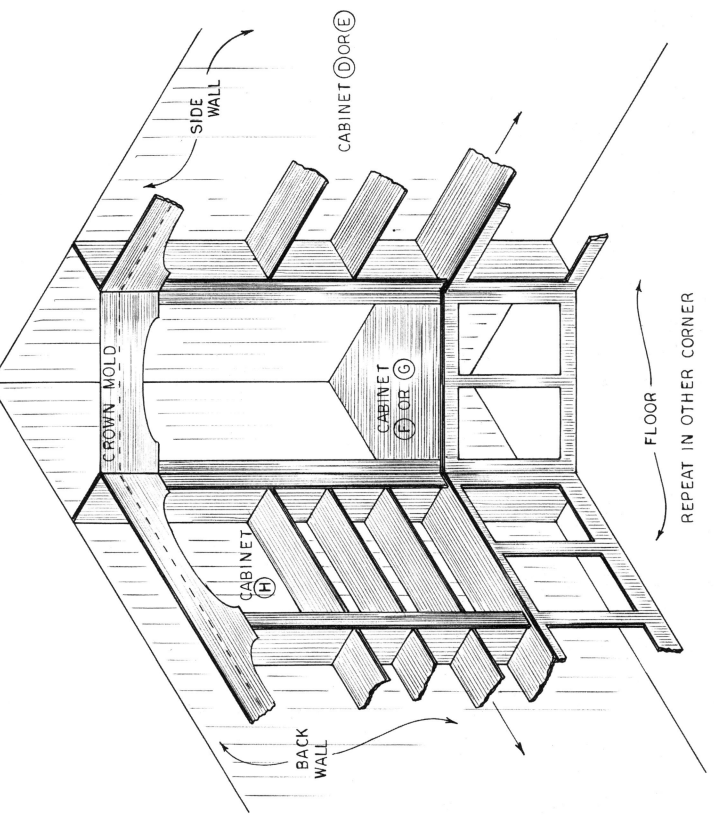

SIDE WALL

CABINET ⓓ OR ⓔ

CROWN MOLD

CABINET ⓕ OR ⓖ

CABINET ⓗ

BACK WALL

FLOOR

REPEAT IN OTHER CORNER

Fig. 2-57. Corner cabinet assembly

H. Mark the floor for this size angle. Glue the counter top between the vertical sides of D and H, and E and H. See figure 2–57.

2. Cut and install the door rails and stiles on the same angle. Glue these parts to the floor marks and under the counter top. Make raised-panel doors, false or real, to cover the openings.

3. Lay out and cut the fascia arch. Install this arch between the vertical sides of cabinets D and H, and E and H. Install a crown mold at the top of the fascia arch. You may wish to mount lights on the back of this fascia arch to illuminate the display case. Sand the corner cabinets smooth. Paint or stain these units to match the other cabinets.

14. *Ice Cream Parlor*

Almost every neighborhood once had an ice cream parlor and sweet shop. The cool, rich interior with its lazy overhead fans and the sweet smell of chocolate has created fond childhood memories. The marble counter had a wide display of penny candy and gum or jaw-breaker penny machines. Gourmet bonbons and specialties were available, and ices, phosphates, and frozen desserts were artistically made by the owner, who topped them all with a long-stemmed, bright red cherry.

The miniature sweet shop has been developed from several Victorian-style buildings. Its ornate storefront has decorative lookouts, a built-up crown cornice, and etched-glass windows and doors. Two options are given for this miniature reproduction: the ice cream parlor as a one-story single-room business or the same shop as a three-story building with two apartments over the ground-floor business.

Illustrations and directions are provided for the needed interior furnishings, including counters, fountains, storage cabinets, tables, and chairs. Everything can be made from normal stock found in any lumberyard or hardware outlet.

Once again, the storefront is constructed as a large door to allow for interior exposure. The building has plate-glass windows, which are fixed, and two entrance doors. The dimensions offered can be altered; the interior furnishings and placement can be changed to suit individual preferences. For the basic building, ½-inch plywood is recommended.

Construction

Materials List

Part	Amount	Size	Materials
Front wall	1	13" x 20" x ½"	
Rear wall	1	12" x 20" x ½"	
Side walls	2	12" x 21" x ½"	
Floor	1	21" x 19" x ½"	
Roof	1	23" x 19" x ½"	
Cornice		22" x ¾" x 1¼"	
lookouts	8	¼" x ⅝"	
crown molding		55" x ⅝"	
cove molding		22" x ¼"	
Corners	6	3/16" x ½" x 12"	
Exterior casing		75" x 3/16" x ⅜"	flat casing
Interior casing		75" x 3/16" x ⅜"	molded casing
Baseboard		80" x ⅛" x ½"	molded base
Ceiling molding		84" x ⅝"	crown molding
Clapboards		1500" x ⅛" x ¾"	
Windows	3	5" x 6"	single-strength glass
Entrance doors	2	3" x 6½"	

Note that jambs are required for windows and doors.

1. Review figures 2–59 and 2–60 to gain a concept of the building before starting to work. Select ½-inch or ⅜-inch plywood for the main wall parts, because they will be covered both inside and outside. If the building is to be wired, lay out the electrical paths and install feed wires during the various stages of construction. The transformer should be outside the building.

Fig. 2–58. Miniature ice cream parlor, design circa 1890

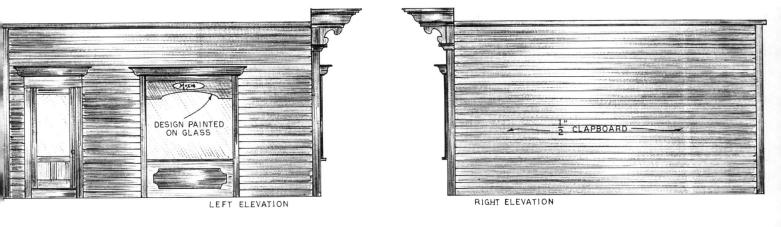

LEFT ELEVATION

RIGHT ELEVATION

½" CLAPBOARD

DESIGN PAINTED
ON GLASS

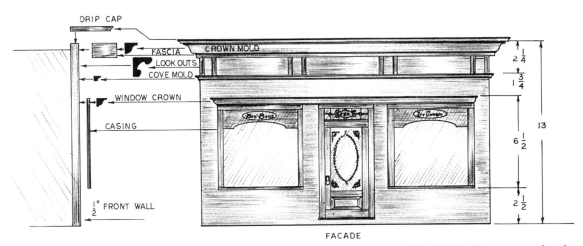

DRIP CAP

FASCIA

LOOK OUTS

COVE MOLD

CROWN MOLD

WINDOW CROWN

CASING

1½" FRONT WALL

FACADE

$2\frac{1}{4}$

$1\frac{3}{4}$

$6\frac{1}{2}$

13

$2\frac{1}{2}$

Fig. 2–59. Ice cream parlor elevations

2. Lay out and cut the plywood for the floor, front, back, and side walls. Lay out and cut the rough openings for the windows and doors. Slice the front wall lengthwise just above the window crown molding line; see drawing notes. The top section of this wall will be secured to the building, while the bottom section will be hinged to open. See figure 2–60. Cut and install the window and door jambs and exterior casing.

Nail the side wall pieces to the floor piece. Nail the rear wall to the floor and to the side walls. Nail the top of the front wall to the two side walls at the correct height.

3. Cut and install the exterior corner boards. Cut and install the clapboard with a ½-inch weather exposure to the sides and rear walls.

This clapboard should be glued and fastened at the top edge of each board. The succeeding clapboard covers the fastener heads. Sand the exterior surface smooth.

4. Cover the exposed edges of the front plywood with solid 1/16-inch wood strips. Sand the plywood front smooth. Install the fascia block, decorative eave brackets, lookouts, and moldings to the front wall. Cut and install the door and window crown molding. Hinge the lower wall front to the building with an exterior butt or continuous hinge. Paint the entire exterior white. The doors can be white or bright red.

5. For the interior, cut the single-strength glass for the openings. Paint the suggested design on the glass interior. Install the glass into

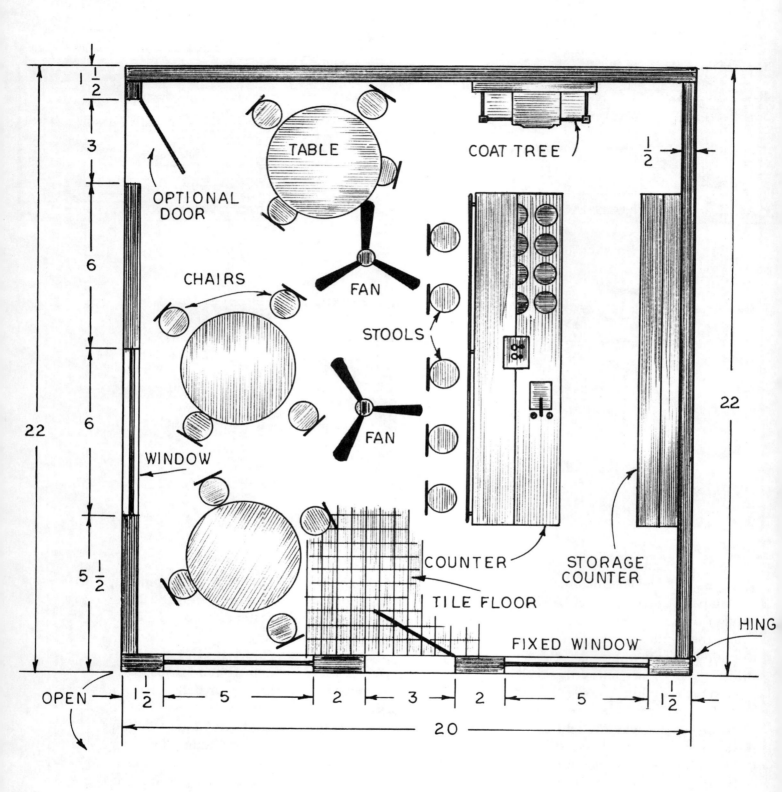

Fig. 2–60. *Ice cream parlor floor plan*

206

the frames and secure in place with the interior casing. Install the two entrance doors and interior casing. Paper or paint the building interior. (Most ice cream parlors had bright, decorative wallpaper.) Glue red felt squares or tiles to the shop floor. Install the baseboard on all four walls. Install the ceiling crown molding at the top of the walls. Paint the interior moldings before installation. After the interior trim is installed, the final painting can be completed.

6. Lay out and cut the ceiling/roof stock. If desired, install decorative medallions to the ceilings. Ceiling medallions can be ordered from Houseworks Ltd. (models 7022, 7023, and 7024) and The Peddler's Shop (models H3340 or H102).

7. Paint the ceiling part of this board white. Nail the ceiling/roof board to the rear and side walls. This roof board should overhang the sides and rear walls by approximately ½ inch. Paint the exterior roof surface flat black.

Fig. 2–61. Miniature Victorian-style coat stand

VICTORIAN-STYLE COAT TREE

This reproduction is a combined coat tree and umbrella stand. It can be used in a private home or in any business building.

Construction

Material List

Part	Amount	Size
A	2	³/₁₆″ x ¼″ x 6⅝″
B	1	³/₃₂″ x ½″ x 3″
C	1	³/₃₂″ x ¼″ x 3″
D	2	³/₃₂″ x ³/₁₆″ x 2¼″
E	1	³/₃₂″ x 2⅝″ x 3″
F	2	¼″ x ¼″ x 2½″
G	1	³/₃₂″ x ½″ x 3″
H	2	³/₃₂″ x ⅜″ x 1¹/₁₆″
I	2	³/₃₂″ x ¼″ x 1¹/₁₆″
J	1	³/₃₂″ x ¼″ x 3″
K	1	³/₃₂″ x 1¹/₁₆″ x 3¼″
L	1	³/₃₂″ x 1½″ x 1¾″
M Brass hooks	4	
N Stained-glass windows	3	
O Mirror	1	

Note that parts A are ³/₁₆-inch thick while all the other stock is ³/₃₂-inch thick. Parts A have a rabbet cut in back for the mirror. See detail in figure 2–62.

1. Lay out and cut the stock for A, B, C, D, and E. Cut the required glass rabbet in the backs of parts A. Glue A to B, C, and E. See figure 2–63 for spacing. Glue D to C and E. Sand entire back assembly smooth.

2. Lathe turn F to suggested shape and size. Glue G and J to F. After the glue has dried, glue this assembly to H and I. Glue H and I to the A as shown in figure 2–63. Keep this assembly square with the back assembly.

3. Fit and glue K and L in place. Cut the crown molding (P) and glue to B. Sand the entire reproduction smooth. Stain to a color of your choice. Finish with lacquer or similar covering.

4. Cut plastic strips to fit over the top and side openings. Mark out the plastic windows for the Tiffany design. See figure 2–62. Use India ink to draw in the lead divisions, and

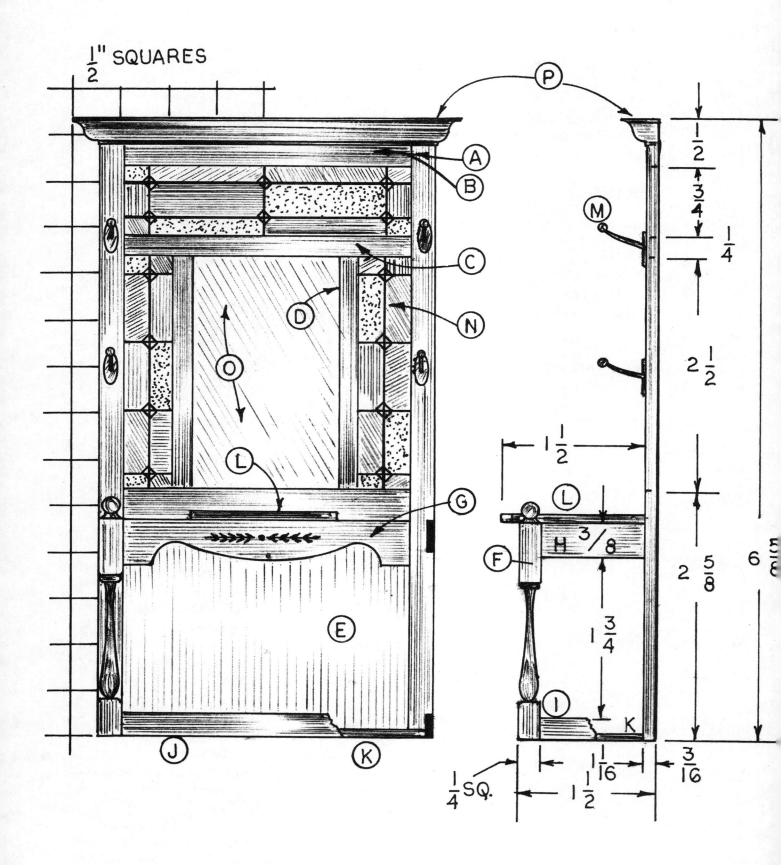

$\frac{1}{2}$" SQUARES

Fig. 2–62.   Coat tree detail

208

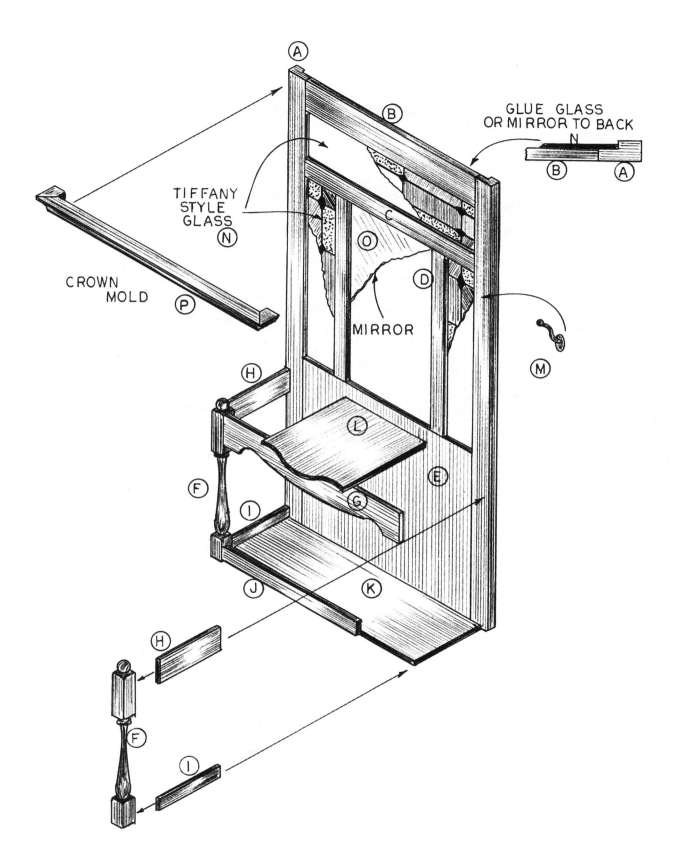

GLUE GLASS
OR MIRROR TO BACK

TIFFANY
STYLE
GLASS

CROWN
MOLD

MIRROR

Fig. 2–63.   Coat tree assembly

Fig. 2–64. Miniature ice cream store cabinet

paint in the suggested design with typical stained-glass colors. Or, you can purchase stained-glass kits, such as model SG 715 from AMSI Miniatures. Install a piece of single-strength mirror behind the back assembly in the premade rabbets. This mirror should cover the Tiffany-style glass. Glue the mirror in place with Krazy Glue.

5. Install the coat hooks (M). These hooks can be purchased or made from brass pins.

GLASS STORAGE CABINET

Every ice cream parlor had a cabinet that held the glassware for sundaes, soda phosphates, and banana boats. This miniature reproduction of a cabinet was developed from several prototypes. It follows the same basic Victorian style as the other furnishings.

Construction

Material List

Part	Amount	Size
A	2	$3/16'' \times 1\,3/8'' \times 8''$
	2	$3/16'' \times 1\,3/8'' \times 7\,7/8''$
B	1	$3/16'' \times 1\,3/8'' \times 11\,5/8''$
C	1	$3/16'' \times 1\,1/4'' \times 13''$
D	1	$3/16'' \times 2\,7/8'' \times 11\,5/8''$
E	1	$1/8'' \times 5/8'' \times 4''$
F	1	$1/8'' \times 3/4'' \times 12''$
G Crown molding	1	15 linear inches
H	1	$1/8'' \times 3/8'' \times 12''$
I	1	$1/8'' \times 1/4'' \times 12''$
J	7	$1/8'' \times 1/4'' \times 2\,1/4''$
K	1	$1/8'' \times 1\,5/8'' \times 12\,1/2''$
L	4	$1/8'' \times 1/4'' \times 4\,1/4''$
M mirror	1	$3/32'' \times 5'' \times 12''$
N	6	$1/8'' \times 5/8'' \times 3\,1/2''$
O doors	6	$1/8'' \times 1\,5/8'' \times 2\,1/4''$
P Stained-glass strip	1	

This cabinet has a mirror back. Therefore,

210

the center vertical uprights are smaller in over-all width than the end pieces. It is suggested the end verticals be made of 3/16-inch stock with rabbets cut into the rear edges.

1. Cut the stock for A. The center parts (A) will be 1/16 inch less in width to allow for the mirror. Cut out B. Glue and pin A to B. Lay out and cut C. Cut a rabbet in the lower back edge. Glue the tops of A to C. Cut out D and glue it between the two end pieces of A and to the center piece A.

2. Lay out and cut the fascia (F). Glue this fascia to A as suggested in figure 2–65. Cut the shelves (E and N). Glue these pieces to A.

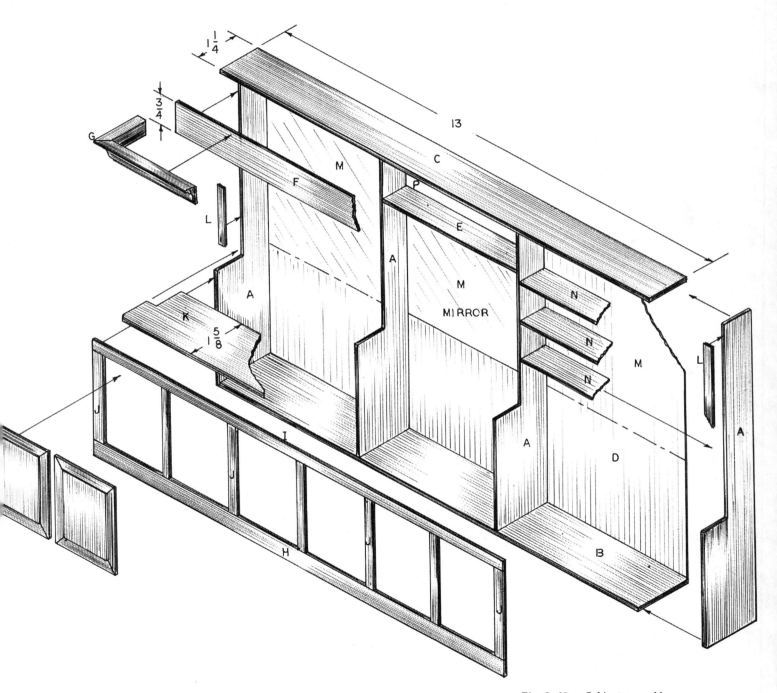

Fig. 2–65. Cabinet assembly

211

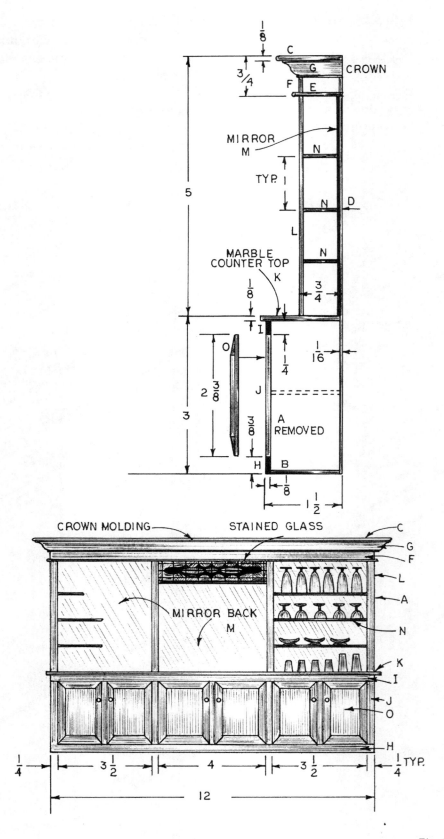

CROWN

MIRROR
M

TYP. 1

MARBLE
COUNTER TOP
K

A
REMOVED

CROWN MOLDING

STAINED GLASS

MIRROR BACK
M

TYP.

Fig. 2–66. Cabinet detail

3. Cut the counter top (K). The counter top should be simulated marble. The effect of marble can be achieved by using marble paper, and one source is the marble paper (model 811) from the J. Hermes Company.

4. Glue the counter to the seats on A. Cut the rails and stiles (I, J, and H) for the door openings. Glue the parts together and glue them to A, B, and K. Cut the top vertical stiles (L), and glue them between the counter top (K) and the bottom of the fascia (F).

5. Cut the crown molding (G) to size. Note the full side returns on the top. Glue this molding to F just under C. Make raised-panel doors to cover the openings. See the chapter on doors in Section one for construction detailing of cabinet doors. The doors can be operable or false units. Install the doors over the opening.

6. Sand the entire reproduction smooth. Remove all traces of glue. Stain the case to a

Fig. 2–67.   Miniature sodas, sundaes, and ice cream cones
(Courtesy It's a Small World)

color of your choice. Finish with several coats of lacquer or similar finish.

7. Make or purchase a small Tiffany-style window for the center section. AMSI Miniatures manufactures a suitable window (model

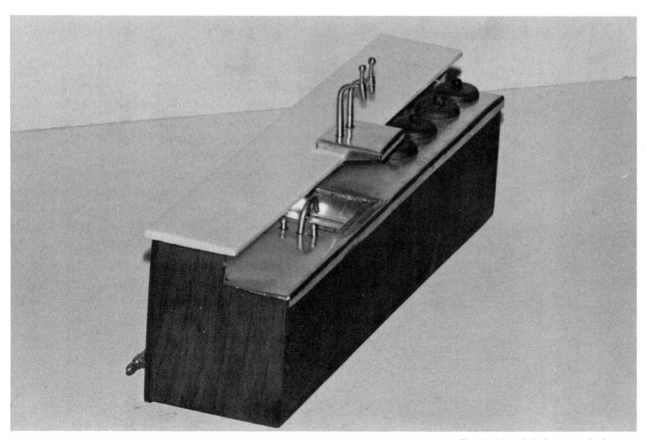

Fig. 2–68.   Miniature soda fountain

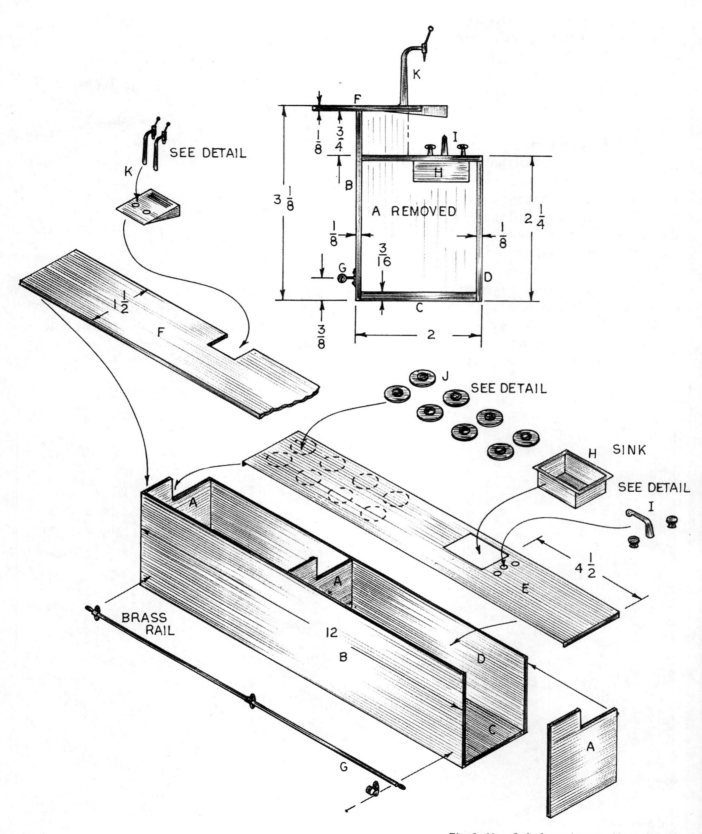

SEE DETAIL

K

F

$\frac{1}{2}$

F

SEE DETAIL

K

F

B

A REMOVED

$3\frac{1}{8}$

$\frac{1}{8}$

$\frac{3}{4}$

$\frac{1}{8}$

$\frac{3}{8}$

G

$\frac{3}{16}$

C

$\frac{1}{8}$

I

H

$2\frac{1}{4}$

D

2

J

SEE DETAIL

H   SINK

SEE DETAIL

I

A

$4\frac{1}{2}$

E

BRASS
RAIL

12

B

D

A

C

G

A

Fig. 2–69.   Soda fountain assembly and detail

214

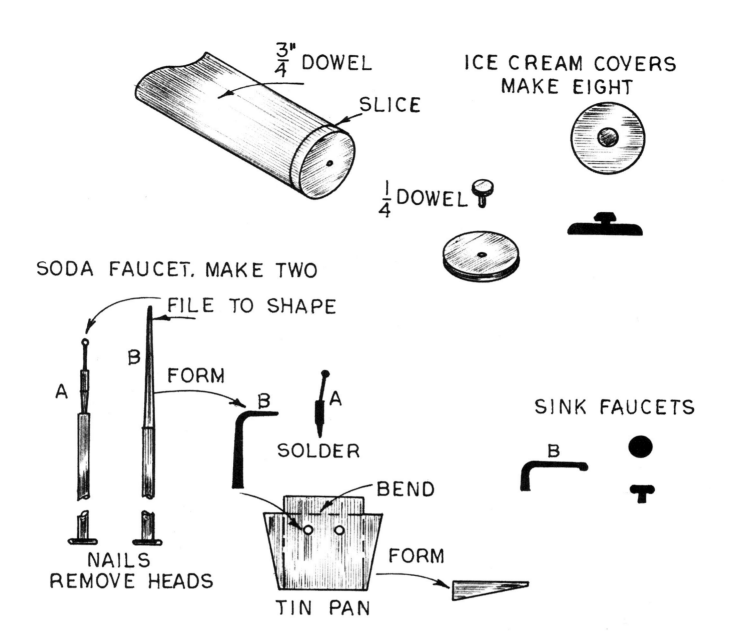

$\frac{3}{4}"$ DOWEL

SLICE

ICE CREAM COVERS
MAKE EIGHT

$\frac{1}{4}$ DOWEL

SODA FAUCET. MAKE TWO

FILE TO SHAPE

A

B

FORM

B

A

SOLDER

BEND

SINK FAUCETS

B

NAILS
REMOVE HEADS

TIN PAN

FORM

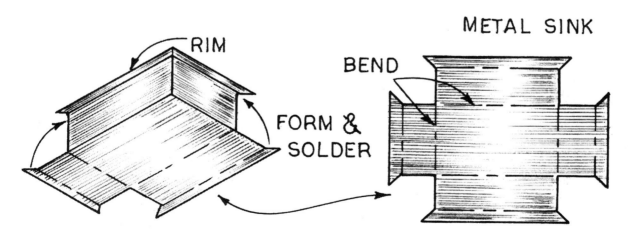

RIM

METAL SINK

BEND

FORM &
SOLDER

Fig. 2–70. Soda fountain patterns

215

Fig. 2–71. Miniature soda fountain table

SG 715). See figure 2–66. If you make the window, follow the steps given for the stained window used in the coat tree, which was discussed earlier in this chapter. Cut a piece of single-strength mirror to fit the back of this cabinet. Glue the mirror in place.

SODA FOUNTAIN

The soda fountain cabinet was the central furnishing of the ice cream parlor. It held a small sink, ice cream containers, and the twin fountains themselves. This reproduction has a simulated marble top, a brass rail in the front, and a stainless-steel work area.

Construction

Material List

Part	Amount	Size	Materials
A Sides	3	2″ x 3″ x ³/₁₆″	
B Front	1	3″ x 12″ x ⅛″	
C Base	1	1¾″ x 12″ x ³/₁₆″	
D Back	1	2⅛″ x 12″ x ⅛″	
E Drain counter	1	2″ x 12″	tin plate
F Counter	1	1½″ x 12½″ x ⅛″	marble
G Rail	1	⅛″ diameter x 12″	brass
H Sink	1	See pattern	tin plate
I Faucets	2	8d nails	
J Covers	8	See patterns	
K Faucet pan	1	See pattern	tin plate
L Soda faucets	2	8d nails, see pattern	

1. Lay out and cut the stock for A, B, C, and D. See detail in figure 2–70. Glue A to B, C, and D. Note the center part A is less thick than B and D, and less tall than C.

2. Lay out the tin plate stock and mark dimensions. Cut out the suggested sink well. Make a sheet-metal sink (H). See actual-size pattern in figure 2–70. Solder the finished sink into the metal drain counter. Make miniature-scale faucets and spout (I) from nails. See fig-

ure 2–70. Solder the finished faucets and spout to the metal counter.

3. Make eight ice cream covers (J). These covers are cut from a ¾-inch dowel. See detail in figure 2–70 top right. Attach a small handle to the center of each cover. Glue the covers to the sheet-metal drain counter. Glue the finished metal counter to the cabinet assembly.

4. Lay out and cut the counter top. This top can be hardwood or simulated marble. (Marble paper, such as the paper (model 811) from J. Hermes Company, can be used. Or, simulated marble can be purchased at plumbing outlets. Most often this stock is ¼-inch to ⅜-inch thick. This material, which is actually plastic, can be ripped thinner on a table saw.) Cut a notch ¾-inch wide and ½-inch deep where suggested in the counter top.

5. Make the soda faucet pan (K). An actual-size pattern is provided in figure 2–70. Turn two gooseneck faucets from 8d nails. See the center of figure 2–70 for procedure and patterns. Solder the faucets to the pan. Glue the finished pan into the notch in the counter top.

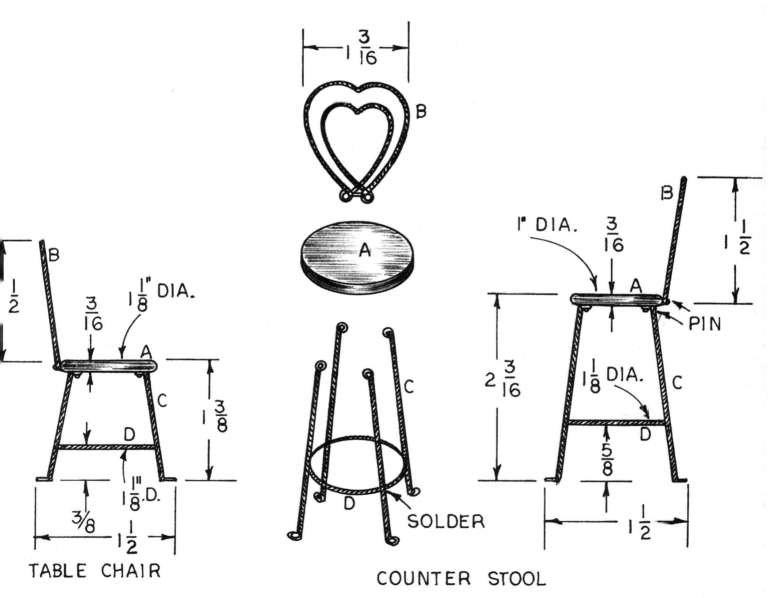

TABLE CHAIR

COUNTER STOOL

Fig. 2–72. Chair and stool detail

217

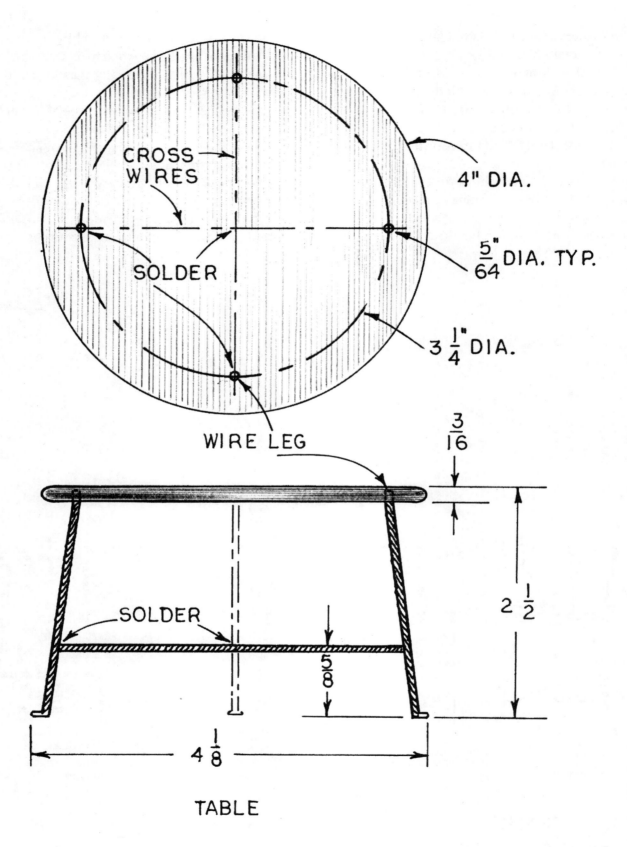

CROSS WIRES

4" DIA.

SOLDER

$\frac{5}{64}$" DIA. TYP.

$3\frac{1}{4}$" DIA.

WIRE LEG

$\frac{3}{16}$

SOLDER

$2\frac{1}{2}$

$\frac{5}{8}$

$4\frac{1}{8}$

TABLE

Fig. 2–73A.   Soda fountain table detail

Fig. 2–73B. Candy counter

Glue the counter top to the base assembly.

5. Turn the ends of a ⅛-inch brass rod for the foot rail (G). Make three sheet-metal brackets to go around this rod. Attach the rod via the brackets to (B).

6. Sand all wooden parts smooth and stain to a color of your choice. Finish with several coats of lacquer or similar covering. Install the completed fountain in front of the glass storage cabinet. Allow 3 inches between these two fixtures.

STOOLS AND CHAIRS

The wire stools and chairs have the same basic design, but they differ in seat height. The stools are meant to serve the three-foot soda fountain, while the chairs go with the tables.

Construction

These furnishings have twisted wire legs and backs. The best method to achieve uniform and tight wire twists is to insert two wire ends into the chuck of an egg-beater-type hand drill and the other wire ends into a vise or clamp. The turns of the drill handle twist the wires together. The twisted wire piece can then be cut to size and shaped. Number 18-gauge wire is suggested.

The seat of the stool (A) is a section of one-inch dowel. Twist the leg wire (C) and cut four legs to size. Drill four ⅛-inch-diameter holes into the bottom of the dowel seat. Using Krazy Glue, fasten the legs to the seat. Bend the legs out to achieve the suggested splay. Make a circle (D) from twisted wire and solder this circle between the four legs. See figure 2–72.

Make the stool back (B) from twisted wire. Form loops at the bottom ends of the design. Fasten the wire back to the seat with pins through these loops.

The chairs are made by the same methods outlined for the stools. The only difference is the seat is slightly larger and the legs are shorter. See figure 2–72. The fastening and back design are identical.

GLASS COUNTER

The following reproduction was designed as a candy display case for the ice cream parlor. However, this counter can be used in several different shops such as the millinery or general store.

Construction

Material List

Part	Amount	Size	Materials
A	1	1¼″ x 2″ x 6″	
B	2	⅛″ x 1½″ x 1¾″	
C	1	⅛″ x 1⅛″ x 5¼″	
D	2	⅛″ x ⅛″ x 5½″	
	3	⅛″ x ⅛″ x 1⅞″	
E	1	2″ x 6″	plastic sheet
F	1	³⁄₁₆″ x 1¼″ x 6½″	simulated marble

1. Lay out and cut the base stock (A). This is a solid piece with a routered, core-box design cut into the center edges. Lay out and cut the stock for B and C. Glue C to B as shown in figure 2–73–C top left. Glue this assembly to A.

2. Make the frame (D) using ship or half-lap corners. Sand the frame smooth and round the inside edges slightly. Glue a piece of heavy-gauge plastic sheet to the rear of the finished frame, and glue the assembly to A and B.

3. Glue the counter (F) on top of B. Simulated or actual marble is suggested; however, a wood counter can be used if preferred.

4. Sand and finish all wood parts. This counter can be stained and lacquered or painted.

5. If the display case is used for candy, small boxes of chocolates can be made by cutting the shapes from wood blocks. Paint the simulated boxes a suitable color and fasten a small ribbon bow to each box. You can purchase miniature candy and containers from several suppliers. See Section four for list.

TABLES

Twisted wire is used for the legs and stretchers. See previous notes on wire twisting. The table tops are made from simulated marble or hardwood covered with marble paper.

1. Cut a circle from simulated ³⁄₁₆-inch marble. Mark out the four leg locations on the bottom. Drill four ⁵⁄₁₆-inch-diameter blind holes at these locations. Make four legs from twisted wire. Using Krazy Glue, glue the finished legs into the table-top holes. Bend the legs to achieve the suggested splay.

2. Make two leg stretchers from twisted wire. Solder the stretchers to the table legs.

It is suggested that the ice cream parlor have three large tables with four chairs at each table. Two or more smaller tables, each with a 2½-inch-diameter top, and two chairs per table can be used along with the larger tables to complete the furnishings.

ICE CREAM PARLOR AND APARTMENTS

Most American cities have buildings that have stores or shops on the ground floor and apartments on the top floors. San Francisco has some of the finest examples of such Victorian architecture. Built around 1900, these buildings are often long and narrow with two or three floors above the street.

The following miniature construction was designed to go with the previous ice cream parlor building. The basic building length has been increased from 22 to 26 inches. The porch and rear stairs of the apartments extend over the ground-floor shop. The basic construction and furnishings for the shop itself remain the same as outlined in the previous drawings and outline.

In this construction, the ceiling of one level becomes the floor of the next level. All the fronts open as a large door and the two apartments have no rear wall to allow access to the interior. All of the walls are ½-inch or ⅜-inch stock. Plywood is suggested. Construction of this unit should be built as one continuous piece and not in sections.

1. Lay out and cut the stock for the walls. The side walls can be a single piece of ½-inch plywood measuring 26 inches by 36 inches. The front walls are cut by floors and hinged later to a side wall. The cut, or break lines, for the door openings should fall just under the fascia moldings on each floor.

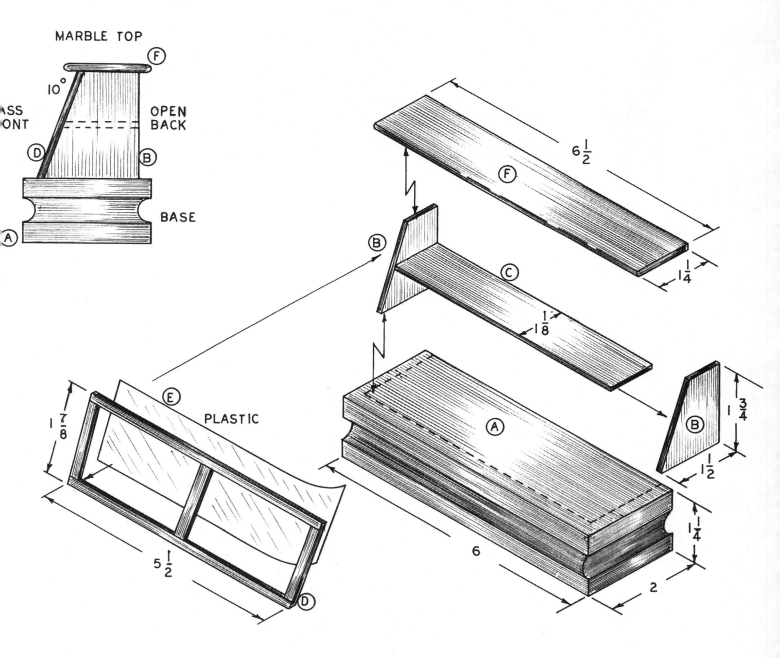

Fig. 2–73C. *Glass display case*

Fig. 2–74. Miniature ice cream parlor interior

2. Lay out and cut the suggested window and door openings. Install the millwork into these openings.

3. Install the fascia boards, moldings, and decorative lookouts as suggested in the previous drawings. Cut the stock for the flooring of the first, second, and third levels. These pieces should extend 6 inches beyond the building proper and become the rear porches. Cut the suggested stairwells in each floor piece. Score or cover these pieces to resemble flooring. The bedroom and living rooms should have parquet or regular flooring, while the kitchen and bath areas should have tile or linoleum floors. The porch area should have narrow flooring painted grey. Paint the ceiling side of these pieces glossy white. The floors are marked but not installed at this time.

4. Mark out the interior wall and room placement. Install any millwork trim required and decorate the various rooms at this time.

Figure 2–77 shows closets and a bathroom for each apartment. Both of these areas are blind; that is, they can only be seen through

doorways or a window opening. Some miniaturists may not want to put effort or fixtures into such remote areas; therefore their inclusion is optional. If the bath area is not furnished, it is recommended that the windows for this area have stained or frosted glass.

5. Mark out any electrical paths for wiring. It may be necessary to install any concealed wiring as work progresses. One of the apartment closets can be used to house a transformer, and the closet can also contain any feed wires, junction boxes, or connections.

5. Install the floor/ceiling boards in place and nail the side wall pieces to them. Make the interior walls of these apartments, install the millwork, and finish the interior decoration before installing them in the building itself. The interior walls should be installed as each succeeding floor piece is nailed in place.

6. Make the install the third-floor ceiling/roof board. This board is the same size as the floor pieces.

7. Make and install the exterior corner boards and casing where required. See Sec-

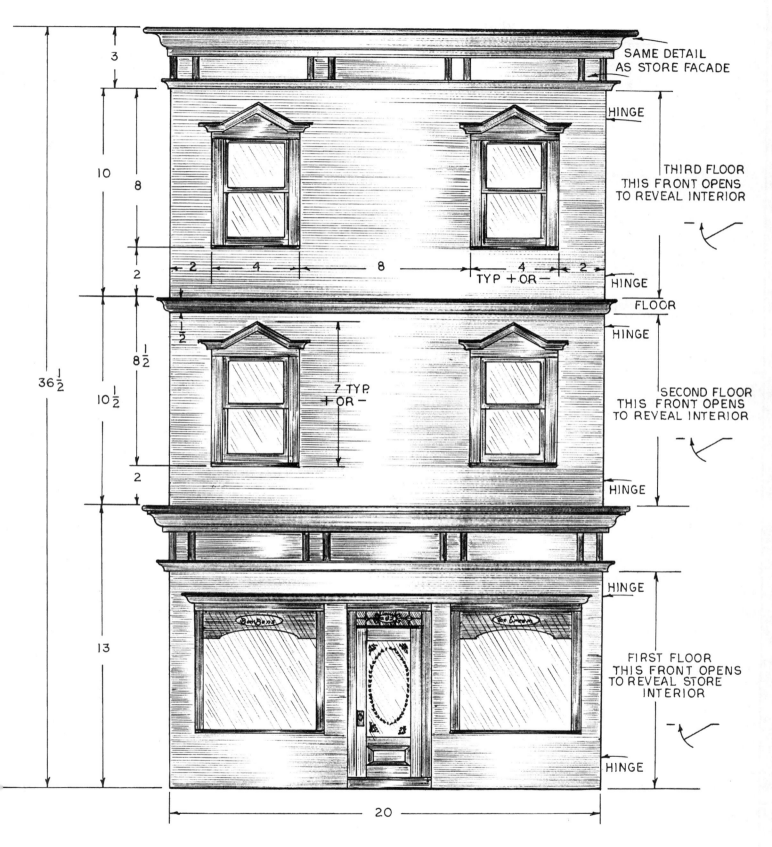

SAME DETAIL
AS STORE FACADE

HINGE

THIRD FLOOR
THIS FRONT OPENS
TO REVEAL INTERIOR

HINGE

FLOOR

HINGE

SECOND FLOOR
THIS FRONT OPENS
TO REVEAL INTERIOR

HINGE

HINGE

FIRST FLOOR
THIS FRONT OPENS
TO REVEAL STORE
INTERIOR

HINGE

3

10

8

2

$8\frac{1}{2}$

$10\frac{1}{2}$

2

13

$36\frac{1}{2}$

2   4   8   4   2
TYP + OR −

7 TYP.
+ OR −

20

Fig. 2–75. Store and apartment, front view

223

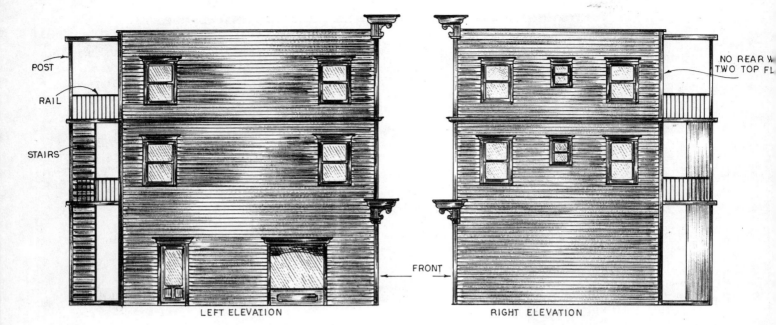

Labels on left elevation: POST, RAIL, STAIRS

LEFT ELEVATION

FRONT

Labels on right elevation: NO REAR W[ALL] TWO TOP FL[OORS]

RIGHT ELEVATION

Fig. 2–76. Store and apartment, side views

tion one and previous projects for procedure. Install the exterior clapboard to cover both sides. The fronts are solid wood. The store has a rear clapboard wall but the two apartments do not.

8. The rear porch and stairs require extensive work. Each floor and roof is supported by three ½-inch-square posts. The stairwells or openings are over each other.

Make and install the support poles. Cut the stair stringers for each floor. See pattern in figure 2–78. See Section one for stair construction detailing. Make and install the stair risers and treads. Install the completed stairways. These stair units require handrails and balusters on both sides. See detail figure 2–78 lower right.

9. Each porch circumference will require a 3-inch-high railing with balusters ½ inch to ⅝ inch on centers, except for the ground floor. The handrail is made from ⅛-inch by 3/16-inch stock. The balusters can be 1/16-inch (or smaller) dowels or square stock. The floor and handrail should be blind drilled to hold the balusters. Make the railing in sections, between posts or between post and building. Glue the balusters into the handrail. As a unit, glue the baluster ends into the porch floor.

10. Paint the exterior a color of your choice. A monochromatic selection is suggested. The roof top may be painted grey or black.

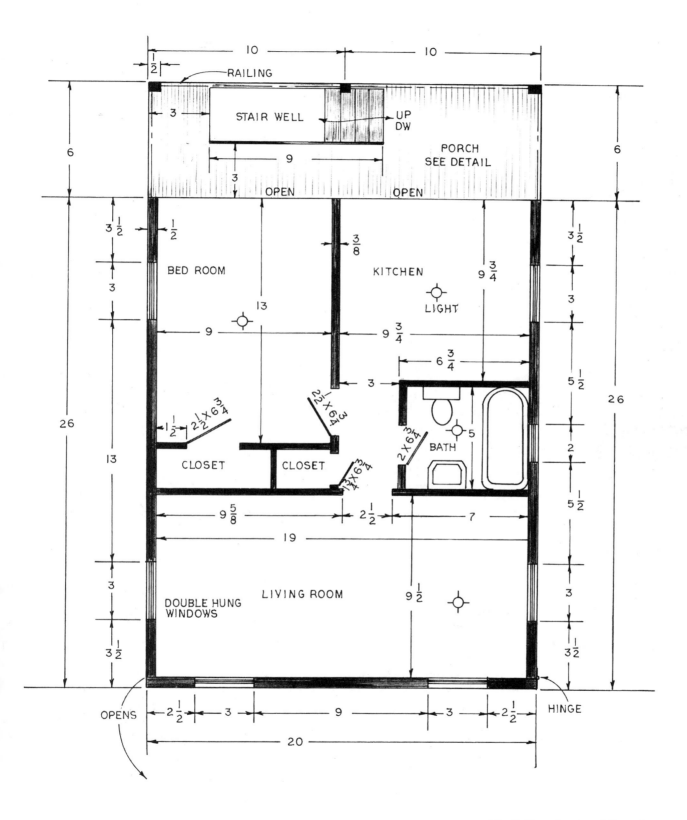

Fig. 2–77. Apartment floor plan

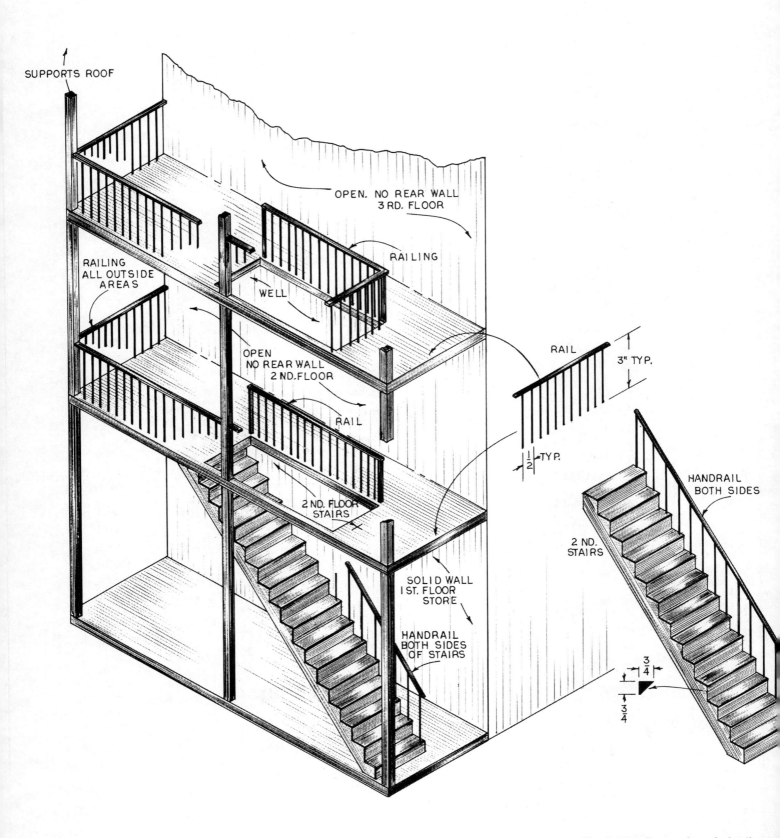

SUPPORTS ROOF

OPEN. NO REAR WALL
3 RD. FLOOR

RAILING
ALL OUTSIDE
AREAS

RAILING

WELL

OPEN
NO REAR WALL
2 ND. FLOOR

RAIL

RAIL

3" TYP.

$\frac{1}{2}$ TYP.

2 ND. FLOOR
STAIRS

HANDRAIL
BOTH SIDES

2 ND.
STAIRS

SOLID WALL
1 ST. FLOOR
STORE

HANDRAIL
BOTH SIDES
OF STAIRS

$\frac{3}{4}$

$\frac{3}{4}$

Fig. 2–78.   Rear and porch details

226

15. *General Store*

The general store is not restricted to any particular time period. Such stores were in operation before the 1800s, and some are still in operation today. The building design and shape may vary, but the general concept remains the same.

Many of these general stores were sectioned into areas. Farm tools, hardware, fabric and ready-made wear, household goods, fresh produce, patent medicines, and groceries each had a corner of their own. The local farmers either sold or bartered their produce to the store owner. Thus barrels of fruit or vegetables were placed in front of the counters or on the front porch. Large wheels of fresh cheese sat under a glass dome, and the cracker barrel was always available for a free sample.

In the miniature realm, the general store offers a means to display miscellaneous collec-

tions. Very few items, if any, will not fit realistically into a general store. The store in the following drawings was developed from the existing General Store behind Wiggins Tavern in Northampton, Mass. This museum is open everyday to the public with old-fashioned preserves, candy, and antiques for sale.

This miniature store is designed like the original one with a solid rear wall full of cabinets and stock. As a result, the storefront is designed to operate as a large door to allow interior exposure.

The interior furnishings are reproductions of the original store. After the basic building and cabinet work are completed, the readers can proceed to stock the shelves and bins with unlimited types of miniatures and create a treasure for generations to come.

Fig. 2–79.   General store, Wiggins Tavern, Northampton, MA

Construction

Material List

Part	Amount	Size
Floor	1	26" x 28" x ½"
Ceiling	1	25" x 27" x ½"
Sides	2	26" x 20" x ½"
Rear wall	1	11" x 28" x ½"
Front wall	1	11" x 28" x ½"
Roof	2	18" x 28" x ½"

Millwork

Windows, double-hung	4	2½" x 4"
fixed	2	4" x 5"
Entrance Doors	1	3" x 6¾"

Porch

Floor	1	6¾" x 29" x ½"
Roof	1	8" x 29" x ½"
Ceiling	1	6½" x 29" x ¼"
Posts	4	½" x ½" x 8"

Exterior trim

Corner boards	8	³/₁₆" x ⅓" x 11"
Fascia board		100" x ⅛" x ⅝"
Soffit		110" x ⅛" x ¾"
Rake trim		80" x ¼" x ⅝"
		80" x ⅛" x ³/₁₆"
Clapboard		2750" x ¹/₁₆" x ¾"
		(½" exposed)
Shingles	2200	¹/₁₆" x ¾" x 1½"

Interior trim

Casing		115" x ⅛" x ½"
Main beam		27" x 1" x 1"
Auxiliary beam		50" x ⅝" x ⅝"

Flooring and vertical sheathing are optional.

1. Lay out and cut the stock for the four walls and floor; ½-inch plywood is recommended. Lay out and cut out the rough window and door openings.

2. Two options are open for interior sheathing: (a) scoring the plywood itself into

random size boards, or (b) installing scale-size random-width boards to the plywood frame. See the chapter on wainscotting in Section one for such construction details.

Using either method, finish the interior. Install the windows and door units into the openings. Install the interior/exterior casing. Stain and finish the interior with lacquer or similar covering at this time.

Score the floor piece to resemble plank flooring or install scale-size planks. See the chapter on flooring in Section one for the details of this procedure. Stain and finish the floor at this time.

3. Nail the two side walls to the floor piece. Nail the rear wall to the floor and side walls. Cut the material for the interior beams. Make simulated hew marks on the beams. Install the beams as suggested in figure 2–84. Cut the stock for the ceiling. Paint the ceiling antique white. Install the ceiling board by nailing it into the beams. Nail the rear and side walls to the ceiling.

4. Cut the stock for the roof boards. Nail the roof boards to the pitched rakes on each side piece and to the rear wall. Note: If the attic space is to be used for electrical connections or a transformer housing, one roof board should be installed with hinges. The front wall is still open at this stage.

5. Cut the stock for the porch floor. Score into floor boards. Nail the front wall into the porch floor. Cut the stock for the porch ceiling/roof. Note that the porch ceiling follows the roof pitch line except at the point where the roof joins the front wall. See figure 2–81 for detail. The porch roof is built in a hip style. Measure the illustrations and dry fit the stock together to make the hip. Several fittings may be required before success is achieved.

6. Secure the hip roof/ceiling board to the front wall as suggested in figure 2–81. Cut the stock for the porch posts. Secure these posts to the ceiling and floor pieces.

7. Cut the stock for the fascia, soffit, and rake trim. Install this trim where required. See

Section one and Section three for this construction detailing. Cut the stock and install the corner boards on all four corners. Install the completed front wall or porch assembly to the building with a butt or continuous hinge. The break, or cut line, for the front wall should be just under the front cornice work.

8. Make a chimney as shown in figure 2–83. See note on the brick front building or Section one on masonry detailing. Attach the finished chimney to the building as shown in figure 2–83.

9. If any electrical work or feed lines are to be used, they should be installed at this time.

10. Cut the stock for the clapboard. See the chapter on miniature construction in Section three for details. Apply the clapboard to the completed dwelling exterior with ½-inch weather exposure suggested. It is recom-

Fig. 2–80. General store interior

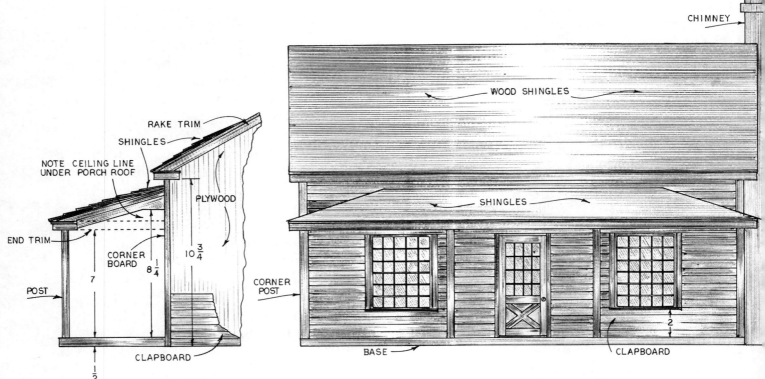

RAKE TRIM

SHINGLES

NOTE CEILING LINE
UNDER PORCH ROOF

PLYWOOD

END TRIM

CORNER
BOARD

$8\frac{1}{4}$

$10\frac{3}{4}$

POST

7

CLAPBOARD

$\frac{1}{2}$

CHIMNEY

WOOD SHINGLES

SHINGLES

CORNER
POST

BASE

CLAPBOARD

2

CLAPBOARD

Fig. 2–81. General store, front view

mended that each clapboard be glued in place, and pins or staples used on the top edge. Such fasteners will be covered by the succeeding clapboard.

11. Cut the stock for the wood shingles. See Section three for instructions on making shingles. Attach the shingles to the roof areas with ¾-inch weather exposure suggested. The shingles should be fastened with pins or staples about one inch up from the bottom. The succeeding row of shingles will cover the fastener heads. Stain the complete exterior except for the roof.

12. The choice of electrical fixtures depends upon the proposed time period for this building. Early American stores had oil lamps, therefore, install general lighting just under the front cornice or beam to illuminate the interior. If a later time period is desired, the interior electrical fixtures can be hung from the walls or beams. This work requires electrical paths and

circuits that should be completed during construction. The attic space can be used to house the equipment.

13. Now you are ready to install the stove. A 4-inch by 4-inch square is made from 3/16-inch by 5/8-inch simulated planks. Install this square in front of the chimney area. Fill the interior of this square with fine sand and install a potbelly stove in the pit. See figure 2–84.

COUNTERS

The sales counter miniature reproduction is a copy of the single-plank top counters found in the General Store at Wiggins Tavern. The front is slanted to allow room for the ever present produce, pickles, and cracker barrels. No set length is given in the following drawings, because any size counter can be made to fill individual requirements. There is no standard length.

Construction

Material List

Part	Amount	Size
A Side	2	2" x 2⅞" x ⅛"
divider	1	1⅞" x 2¾" x ⅛"
B Front	1	3" x any length x ⅛"
C Base	1	1½" x any length x ⅛"
D Shelf	2	1¾" x any length x ⅛"
E Counter	1	2½" x any length x ⅛"

1. Determine the length of the unit you prefer. Lay out and cut the stock for A, B, and C. Cut the required angles on B and C. Glue A to C. Glue and pin B to A and C.

2. Lay out and cut the divider(s) (A1). These dividers should be spaced 3 to 4 inches apart. If a counter is longer than 6 to 8 inches, it should have two interior dividers.

3. Glue the dividers to B and C. Lay out and cut the stock for the shelves (D). The shelves will have an angled face. Glue the shelves to A, A1, and B.

4. Lay out and cut the stock for the top (E). Glue the top to the lower assembly. Sand the entire reproduction smooth. Stain or paint to a color of your choice. Cover with several coats of lacquer or similar finish. Install one or more of these counters in the store. Mount produce barrels in front of the cabinets.

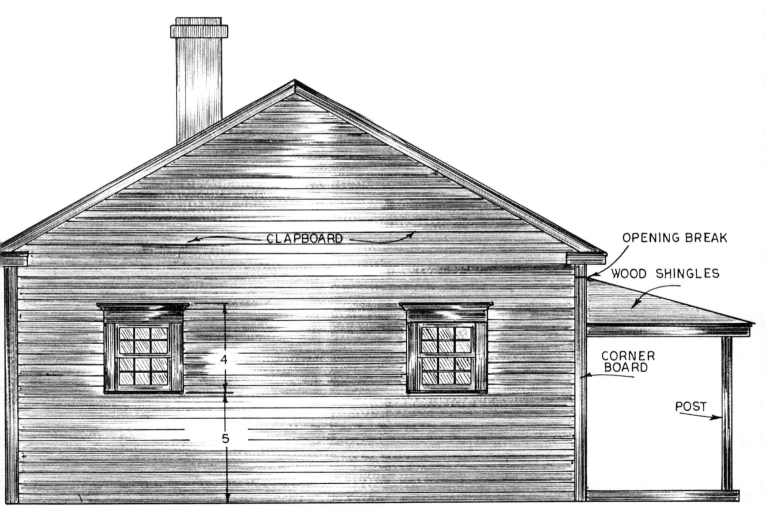

LEFT ELEVATION

Fig. 2-82. General store, left side view

SHINGLES

HINGE

⊢— 2 —⊣

5/8

RIGHT ELEVATION

Fig. 2–83.   General store, right side view

WALL CASES

Every store had walls lined with stocked shelves. Most often a store would start off with a few of these units and then add cases as the inventory and diversified stock increased. Many general stores became sectionalized with certain corners devoted to specialized items, such as patent medicines or hardware. This growth in inventory created a hodgepodge of wall cases sometimes with no two exactly alike.

The following miniatures are offered as a multiple-option unit. The top of the cases are identical, but the bottoms are designed to fit specific needs. The cases can be made with doors, drawers, hopper, or open shelves.

Because of the many options for construction, only the basic framing dimensions for the cases are given. The cases should be made in units of 3 to 3½ inches in width. The finish pieces can thus be grouped or stacked to cover complete walls. The wall itself becomes the case back.

Construction

Material List

Part	Amount	Size
A Side	2	1" x 6⅞" x ⅛"
Optional	2	1¾" x 6⅞" x ⅛"
B Bottom	1	1" x 3" x ⅛"

232

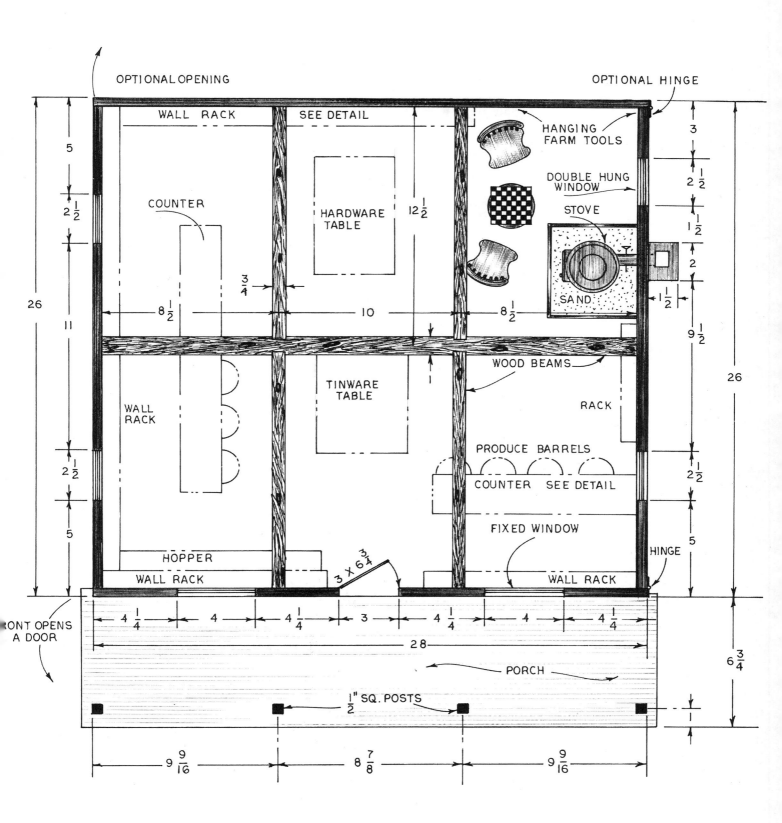

OPTIONAL OPENING

OPTIONAL HINGE

WALL RACK   SEE DETAIL

HANGING FARM TOOLS

COUNTER

HARDWARE TABLE

DOUBLE HUNG WINDOW

STOVE

SAND

5

2 1/2

26

11

8 1/2

3/4

10

8 1/2

12 1/2

WALL RACK

TINWARE TABLE

WOOD BEAMS

RACK

PRODUCE BARRELS

COUNTER   SEE DETAIL

2 1/2

5

HOPPER

WALL RACK

3 X 6 3/4

FIXED WINDOW

WALL RACK

HINGE

3

2 1/2

1 1/2

2

1 1/2

9 1/2

26

2 1/2

5

FRONT OPENS A DOOR

4 1/4   4   4 1/4   3   4 1/4   4   4 1/4

28

PORCH

6 3/4

1/2" SQ. POSTS

9 9/16   8 7/8   9 9/16

1

Fig. 2–84.   General store floor plan

233

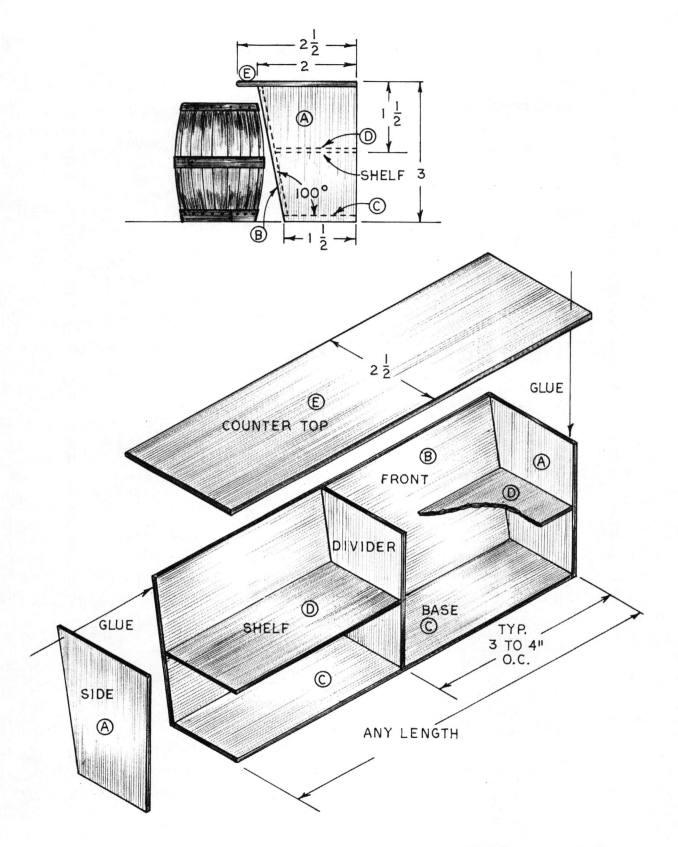

2 ½

2

E

A

D

1 ½

SHELF 3

100°

C

B

1 ½

2 ½

GLUE

E

COUNTER TOP

B

FRONT

A

D

GLUE

D

SHELF

DIVIDER

BASE

C

C

SIDE

A

TYP. 3 TO 4" O.C.

ANY LENGTH

Fig. 2–85.   Counter details and assembly

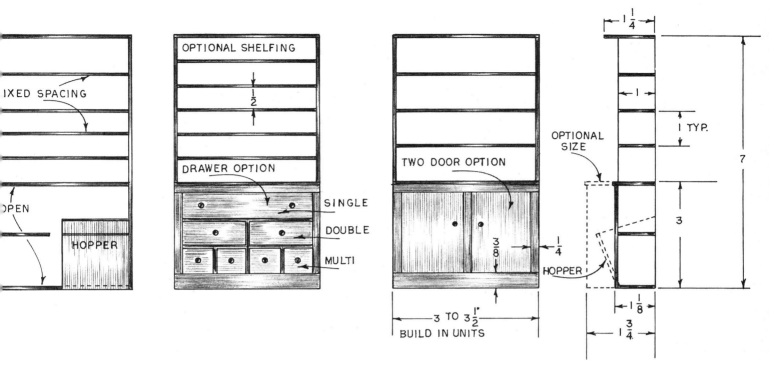

Fig. 2–86. *Wall display cases, details, and assembly*

Fig. 2–87. *General store accessories (Courtesy Scientific Models, Inc.)*

C Top	1	1¼" x 3" x ⅛"
D Shelf	4	1" x 2¾" x ⅛"
E Counter	1	1⅛" x 3" x ⅛"
Optional counter	1	1¾" x 3" x ⅛"

1. Determine the style unit you desire. See figure 2–86 left. Determine the size counter top desirable.

2. Lay out and cut the stock for A, B, and C. Glue A to B. Glue C to A. Lay out and cut the desired number of shelves (D) and the counter board (E). Glue the shelves between the sides A. Glue the counter to A. This makes the basic unit.

3. To construct the doors, lay out and cut rails and stiles to make two openings below the counter board. Glue these parts to A, B, and E. Make two doors and install these in the openings. See the two-door option, figure 2–86 right.

4. To construct the drawers, lay out and cut shelf-size material to make the desired drawer spacing. See option figure 2–86 center. One, two, or all three drawer designs can be used in one unit. Glue the spacing boards to A and to each other. Make the required drawer units to fit the openings.

5. For open shelves, lay out and cut the required shelf material. Glue these pieces to A.

6. Next construct the hopper. The hopper is tilted out and used to hold fruits and/or vegetables. The hopper face or front goes all the way across the base unit. The hopper is then divided into compartments. Lay out and cut the stock for the hopper front. Cut out any bin dividers, if required. Glue the angled cuts to A. Glue the hopper front to A. Cut dividers, and section the hopper unit into thirds or quarters.

Make wall cases of several different styles and install them along the building walls. See floor plan in figure 2–84.

The store is now ready to stock. Do not overlook the possibility of hanging tools or wares from the walls or from the overhead beams. The porch area can also be used for display. Barrels of produce or a table with items for sale can be placed against the front walls.

Miniature Houses

16. *Miniature House Construction*

The possible range of miniature houses is endless and depends only upon the builder's preference and intended usage. On one end of the continuum is the rustic, vaguely simulated dollhouse, while the precise, perfectly detailed replica is on the other end. The purpose of a miniature house, whether for a child's play or an adult's collection, determines its design.

Children, as a rule, do not play with miniature houses. Excess handling by inexperienced hands can ruin the fine construction detailing, the fragile furnishings, and often expensive millwork. The simpler dollhouse with its solid construction, oversized features, and simulated details is for children, and the material used for a dollhouse should withstand normal abuse.

Miniature houses, in contrast, are designed and built as exact replicas. Individual shingles, operable windows and doors, and scale-size trim or molding precisely duplicate full-size homes. Many times a miniature house will take as long to make as a full-size house, and some miniature buildings cost several thousand dollars.

This section was designed to offer readers a choice of miniature houses that can be made inexpensively from normal everyday lumber materials. While some items by necessity must be purchased, the expenditure required is minimal. Notes are given for each miniature house, and they offer possible options for millwork and specialized construction materials. In this respect the reader has the choice of making his own millwork by utilizing Section one of this book or purchasing such pieces from the list of suppliers listed in Section four.

In the following house plans, some compromise was necessary. Very often the methods and designs that work well for full-size

Fig. 3–1. *Miniature Fenno House built by the author*

Fig. 3–2. *Interior of Victorian-style miniature house (Courtesy H. L. Childs)*

239

Fig. 3–3. Victorian-style bathroom set (Courtesy Scientific Models, Inc.)

houses do not always lend themselves to miniature work because of normal interior blind spots or the fact that miniatures houses must have exterior walls that permit interior access. Such compromises were kept to a minimum, and every effort was made to retain the initial flavor of the original dwelling.

One of the main differences between dollhouses, full-size houses, and miniature houses is the width of the buildings. A majority of dollhouses are only one room wide; thus every room can be reached and viewed from the open back wall of the house. Miniature houses, being exact reproductions of normal homes, can be two, three or more rooms wide. Allowing for interior access becomes a governing criteria in planning and building miniatures.

ACCESS TO MINIATURE INTERIORS

Access to miniature interiors can be achieved by various means. Very often the entire rear wall of a miniature house is left open. This solves the viewing problem for the rear rooms. However, the problem still remains for the front of the house. One of the best ways to obtain access to the front interior areas is to build a removable front wall. There are several different construction methods for this wall.

A removable front wall can be made with a locking rabbet top and a hook and eye catch at the bottom. In this style of construction, a solid natural building member is chosen for the break or matching interlocking rabbets. In figure 3–5, the top cornice is selected for such a rabbet joint. The cornice piece offers a continuous straight horizontal line across the entire front wall. In the construction phase, a rabbet is cut into the top of the front wall. A matching rabbet is then cut into the solid cornice stock. The top rabbet of the front wall is then inserted into the cornice rabbet, and the wall bottom is pushed into place and locked on the bottom with a catch or a hook and eye.

The front wall and the cornice work should be installed at the same time. To insure proper alignment and continuity, the wall should be in place when all the exterior detailing is completed and installed. Any exterior corner boards should be split lengthwise with one part on the removable wall and the other part on the actual house side wall. When the wall is inserted and locked in place, the only visible sign that the wall is removable is a slight joint in the corner boards. The rabbet joint under the cornice work can be covered with scale-size moldings and will be unnoticeable.

Another construction possibility is to build a front wall that operates like a single door. Some buildings can have the whole front wall hinged to operate as an ordinary door. See figures 2–22 and 2–51. However, such an operation has its limits. Long buildings, with long front walls, become cumbersome with the

Fig. 3–4. Miniature house with hinged wall (Courtesy H. L. Childs)

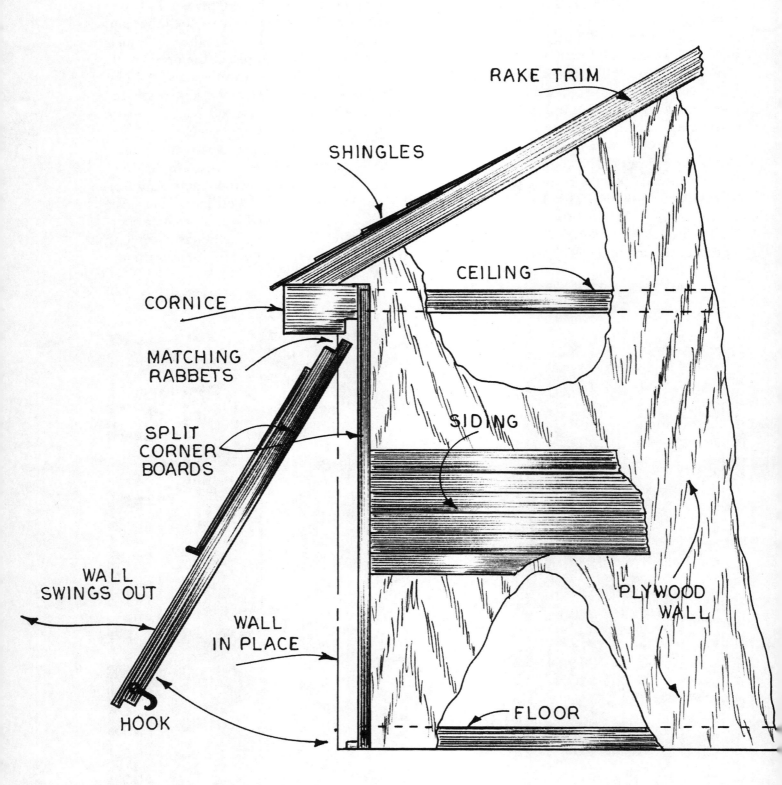

RAKE TRIM

SHINGLES

CEILING

CORNICE

MATCHING
RABBETS

SPLIT
CORNER
BOARDS

SIDING

PLYWOOD
WALL

WALL
SWINGS OUT

WALL
IN PLACE

HOOK

FLOOR

Fig. 3–5. Front wall rabbet lock

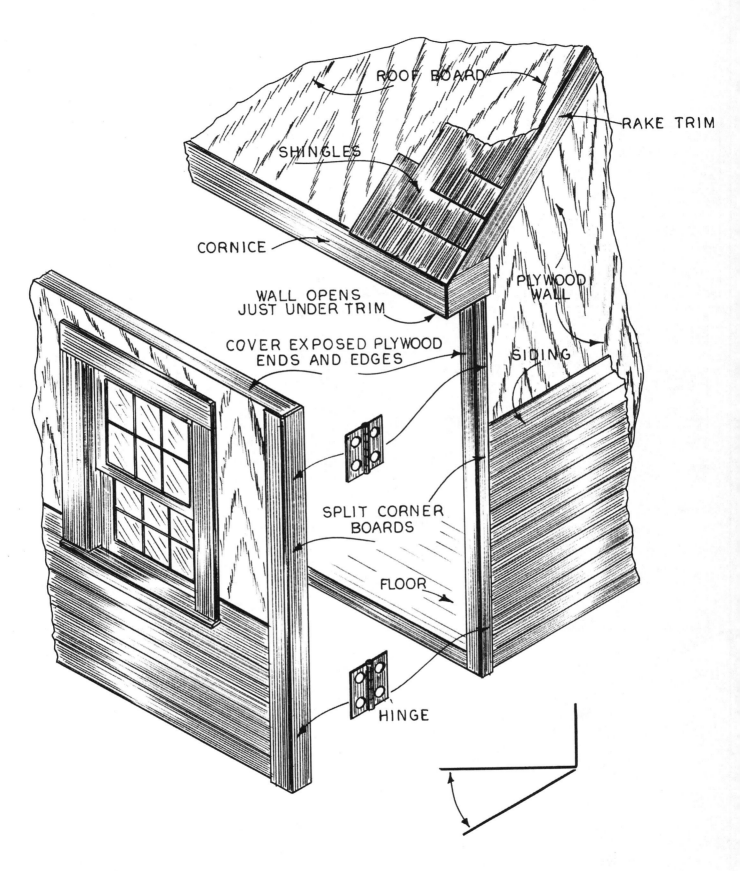

ROOF BOARD

RAKE TRIM

SHINGLES

PLYWOOD WALL

CORNICE

WALL OPENS JUST UNDER TRIM

COVER EXPOSED PLYWOOD ENDS AND EDGES

SIDING

SPLIT CORNER BOARDS

FLOOR

HINGE

Fig. 3–6. Hinging an exterior wall

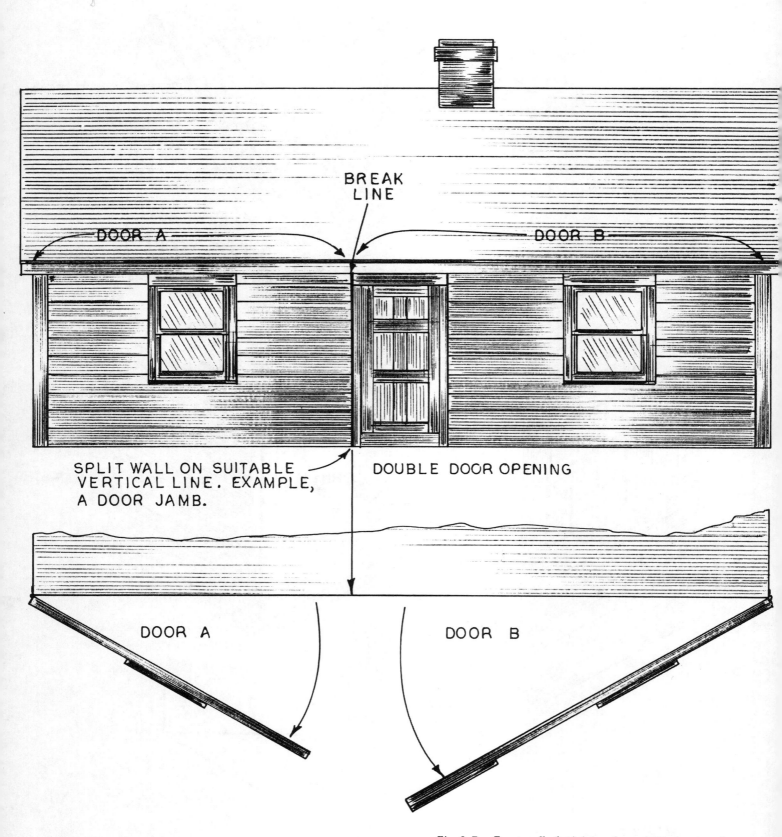

BREAK LINE

DOOR A

DOOR B

SPLIT WALL ON SUITABLE
VERTICAL LINE. EXAMPLE,
A DOOR JAMB.

DOUBLE DOOR OPENING

DOOR A

DOOR B

Fig. 3–7. Front wall of miniature house hinged as two doors

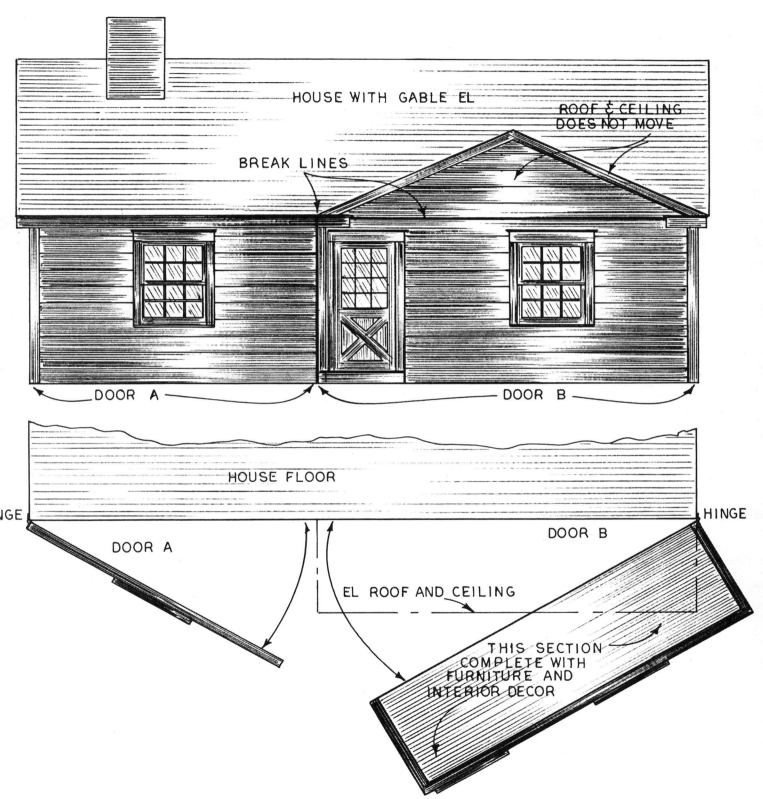

HOUSE WITH GABLE EL

ROOF & CEILING
DOES NOT MOVE

BREAK LINES

DOOR A

DOOR B

HOUSE FLOOR

HINGE

HINGE

DOOR A

DOOR B

EL ROOF AND CEILING

THIS SECTION
COMPLETE WITH
FURNITURE AND
INTERIOR DECOR

Fig. 3–8. Uneven house fronts with separate hinges

Fig. 3–9.   Victorian-style house with hinged wall (Courtesy H. L. Childs)

single door action. The large front area could upset the whole house when it is opened. The single door concept should not be employed for fronts over thirty inches long. Longer front walls should use the alternate means of interior access explained in the following paragraph.

Miniature houses with longer front or rear walls can be made accessible by splitting the wall section into a two-door operation. The two doors need not be equal in length. Figure 3–7 shows a sample house with its front wall split into two such doors. The split or break line was selected to occur on a suitable natural vertical line, in this case, the front door casing. The vertical door casing runs from floor to ceiling, and the break line is as indiscernible as possible. Such a break could just an easily occur at a bay window, molded facade, or any convenient floor to ceiling vertical line.

At times the house front or rear walls are unequal in design, such as when a projection of an L-shape is used. Figure 3–8 shows a sample house with an L-shape extension on the right side. The vertical plane line where the L-shape meets the house front is selected as the natural break line. Door A consists of just the house front section. However, door B contains not only the L front but the floor and ceiling of the L extension. This swing-out section is completed right down to the interior furnishings, which move in and out with the L. The roof over this L is built right to the house itself and remains stationary. The L door slides in and out just under the roof line.

All removable or operable walls are completely finished inside and outside. The interior is covered by wallpaper or paint, moldings, hanging pictures, and wall decorations.

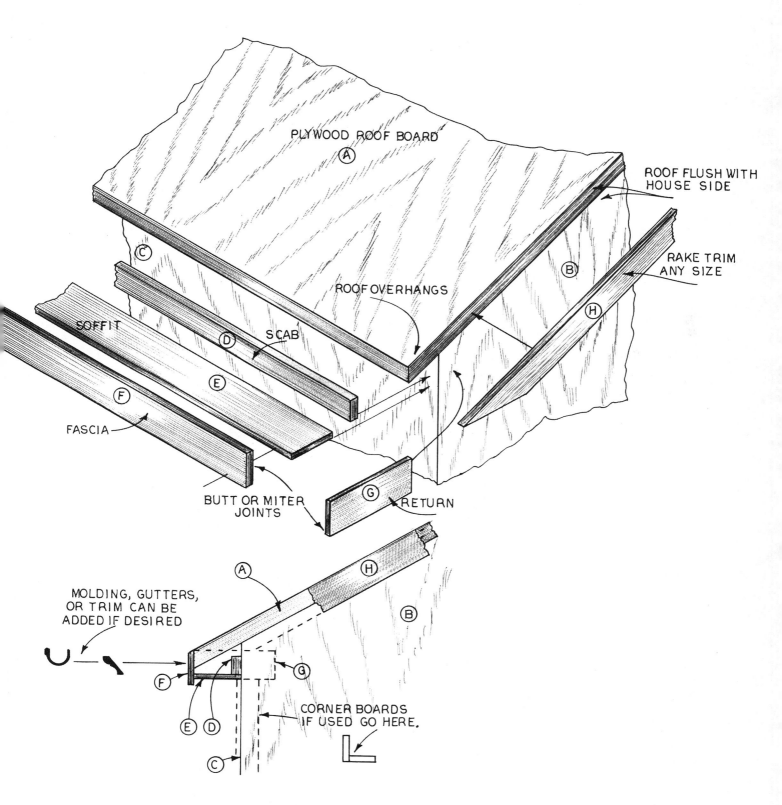

PLYWOOD ROOF BOARD
(A)

ROOF FLUSH WITH
HOUSE SIDE

(C)

(B)

RAKE TRIM
ANY SIZE

(H)

ROOF OVERHANGS

SOFFIT

SCAB
(D)

(E)

(F)

FASCIA

BUTT OR MITER
JOINTS

(G) RETURN

(A)

(H)

(B)

MOLDING, GUTTERS,
OR TRIM CAN BE
ADDED IF DESIRED

(F)

(G)

(E) (D)

CORNER BOARDS
IF USED GO HERE.

(C)

Fig. 3–10.   Separate board cornice

247

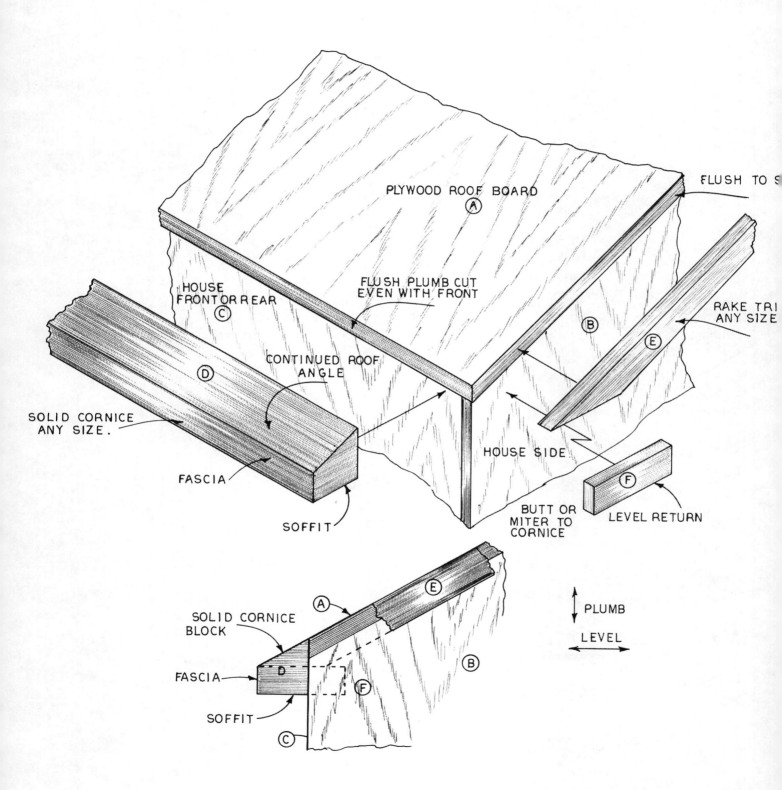

PLYWOOD ROOF BOARD
Ⓐ

FLUSH TO S

HOUSE
FRONT OR REAR
Ⓒ

FLUSH PLUMB CUT
EVEN WITH FRONT

Ⓑ

RAKE TRI
ANY SIZE

Ⓔ

CONTINUED ROOF
ANGLE

Ⓓ

SOLID CORNICE
ANY SIZE.

FASCIA

HOUSE SIDE

SOFFIT

BUTT OR
MITER TO
CORNICE

Ⓕ

LEVEL RETURN

Ⓔ

Ⓐ

SOLID CORNICE
BLOCK

PLUMB

LEVEL

FASCIA

Ⓓ

Ⓑ

Ⓕ

SOFFIT

Ⓒ

Fig. 3–11. Single-piece cornice construction

Fig. 3–12. Shake shingles, miniature Fenno House

The exterior contains the windows, doors, and any required siding. In the actual construction, secure any removable walls in place by whatever means selected, rabbets or hinges, and finish in the ordinary manner. When closed, the wall presents a finished room on the interior and a continuous appearance on the exterior. When open, interior access is achieved with little or no telltale interruption.

CORNICE WORK

The cornice contains all the finish trim between the roof edge and the house walls. This includes the soffit, the fascia, and any moldings, gutters, or decorations in the front or rear of the house. The cornice can be a very plain single board or a series of pieces of built-up decorations, as in the case of Victorian and gingerbread houses. The final size of the cornice depends upon the builder's choice, but most often a ¾-inch fascia and soffit is selected. Two different methods are offered for making cornice work. Cornice work is installed on the rear of the house either with or without a wall.

Separate Board Cornice

When separate soffit and fascia boards are used, the roof board must be allowed to over-

HAND SPLIT SHAKE SHINGLES

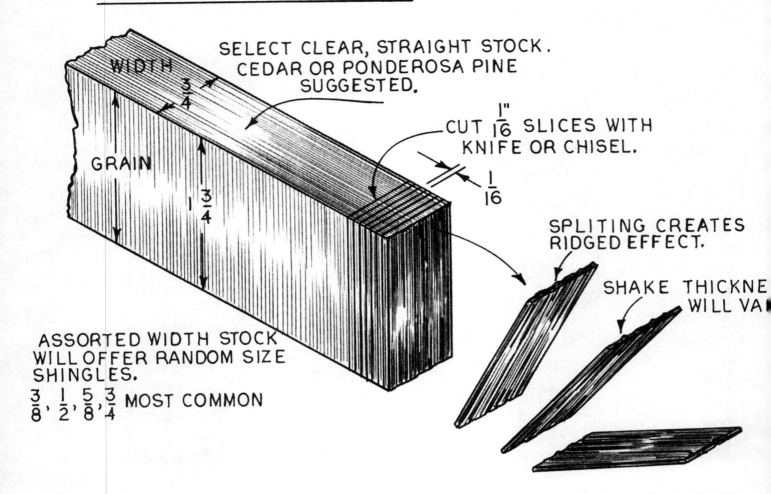

SELECT CLEAR, STRAIGHT STOCK.
CEDAR OR PONDEROSA PINE
SUGGESTED.

WIDTH

$\frac{3}{4}$

GRAIN

$1\frac{3}{4}$

CUT $\frac{1"}{16}$ SLICES WITH
KNIFE OR CHISEL.

$\frac{1}{16}$

SPLITING CREATES
RIDGED EFFECT.

SHAKE THICKNE
WILL VA

ASSORTED WIDTH STOCK
WILL OFFER RANDOM SIZE
SHINGLES.
$\frac{3}{8}$, $\frac{1}{2}$, $\frac{5}{8}$, $\frac{3}{4}$ MOST COMMON

Fig. 3–13. *Making hand-split shingles*

hang the required amount. See A in figure 3–10. The soffit (E) position is marked on the front or rear house wall. A scab (D) is fastened to the wall, and the soffit is secured to this scab. (See detail of D and E.) The width of this soffit board will determine the amount of roof board overhang. The fascia board (F) is fastened to E and to the overhanging edge of the roof board. If gutters or moldings are used, they are fastened in turn to the fascia piece.

All cornice work, regardless of size, requires some type of return or cornering that runs from the fascia to the house side wall. This member squares the cornice to the roof angles. If corner

boards are used for the siding, such boards are fastened under and butt to the return boards. (See detail in figure 3–10.)

The cornice trim that is fastened to the roof angles on the house sides is called the rake trim (H). Most often the roof boards are made even (cut flush) with the house side walls. The rake trim is then applied directly to the roof board edges, so that it overlaps onto the house side piece. The bottom edge of the rake trim cuts on a level angle right on top of the cornice return board (G). The rake trim can be any size suitable although ¾-inch by ¼-inch or ⅜-inch stock is typical.

Solid Cornice Work

In this type of construction, the soffit, fascia, and part of the roof slope are all one piece. See (D). The roof board (A) is made flush with the house front or rear. The solid cornice stock is cut so that the top edge is a continuation of the roof slope. This piece is fastened to the house front or rear (C), and the roof board edges (A).

The returns (F) are installed on all four corners. The rake trim (E) is fastened to the roof board ends and the house side walls. If moldings, gutters, or decorations are used, they are fastened in turn to the fascia part of the solid cornice board.

In all cornice construction, solid or separate boards, the top edges must be even with the top edges of the roof boards. When the roof shingles are installed, they are fastened to both the roof board and assorted trim pieces.

ROOF SHINGLES

Roof shingles are available in several different materials: asphalt, wood, slate, or tile. Many commercial companies produce these shingles for the miniature builder. See Section four for listings. The most common and realistic shingle used for miniature houses or shops is the cedarwood shingle. Such shingles can be made from normal lumberyard stock. Two different styles of wood shingles can be made from ordinary lumber: the hand-split shake shingle or the resawed, resquared wood shingle. Either one can be made inexpensively in the home workshop in volume.

Hand-split shakes are rough, highly ridged shingles that often vary in thickness. Such shingles, when used on a roof, are not uniform in height and the rows are wavy. Shake shingles were used in early colonial homes, such as

Fig. 3–14. Resawed shingles, detail from carpenter's shop

251

the Paul Revere house, and are today used on contemporary-style ranch homes.

Hand-split shakes are easy to make from normal stock. Select a piece of clear, straight-grained redwood or cedar. Any width and thickness will serve the purpose. Crosscut the board into 1¾-inch blocks, with the grain running vertical. With a sharp knife or wood chisel, slice ¹⁄₁₆-inch chips from the blocks. The slicing along the vertical grain lines creates the ridged effect.

The smoother uniform wood shingles are made on a table saw. Select a piece of clear, straight-grained cedar or redwood stock. On a table saw, rip the board into ¹⁄₁₆-inch strips. Stack several of these strips together and cut them off in 1¾-inch groups. This creates ¾-inch by 1¾-inch shingles. See figure 3–17.

Installing Wood Shingles

The roof installation is the same regardless of shingle style used. Most often a triple-lap installation is used. With a triple-lap installation the exposed area is ⅓ (or less) than the total shingle length. If a 1¾-inch-long shingle is

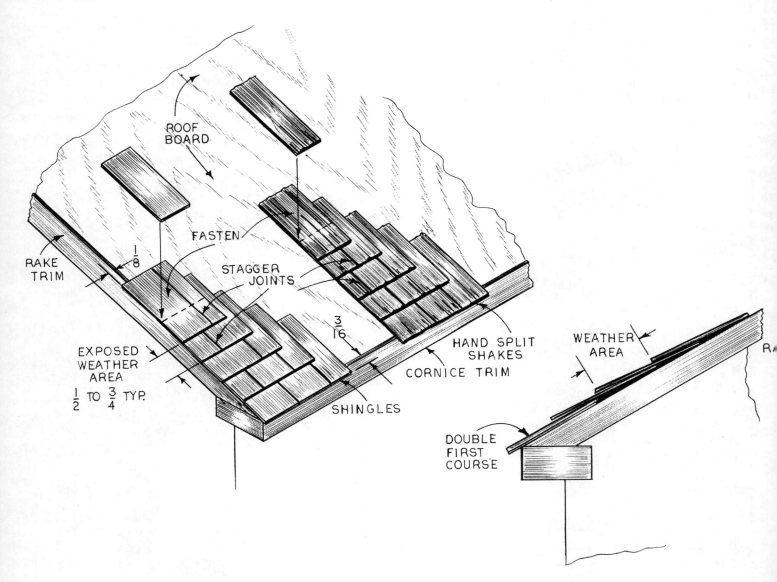

Fig. 3–15.   Installing wood shingles

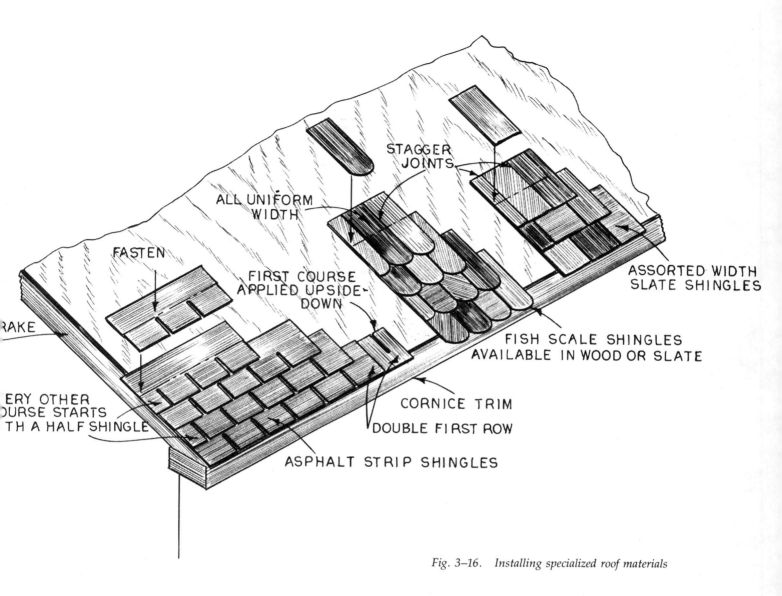

RAKE

FASTEN

ALL UNIFORM WIDTH

STAGGER JOINTS

FIRST COURSE APPLIED UPSIDE-DOWN

ASSORTED WIDTH SLATE SHINGLES

ERY OTHER URSE STARTS TH A HALF SHINGLE

FISH SCALE SHINGLES AVAILABLE IN WOOD OR SLATE

CORNICE TRIM

DOUBLE FIRST ROW

ASPHALT STRIP SHINGLES

Fig. 3–16. Installing specialized roof materials

used, the weather area should be around ½ inch.

All edge butt joints must be staggered, so that no three succeeding joints are in line with each other. Shingles are secured above the weather area so that succeeding shingles will cover any fastening heads. A regular paper stapler works very well to fasten shingles. Make sure the staple legs are spaced so that they enter two different shingles and thereby overlap the side butt joint.

The roof shingles are designed to extend beyond the cornice. Shingles should extend the rake trim by ⅛ inch and the fascia trim by ³⁄₁₆ inch. See detail in figure 3–15.

SPECIALIZED ROOFING MATERIALS

Several companies retail specialized roofing materials. Asphalt, fish scale, and slate shingles are available. The asphalt and slate materials are offered in assorted colors.

Asphalt Shingles

Scale-size asphalt shingles duplicate the full-size coverings. They are designed in three shingle strips with each shingle representing a scale width of 12 inches. When this style of shingle is applied, every other row starts with a half shingle or a scale of 6 inches. This application staggers the tab, or slot, line-up.

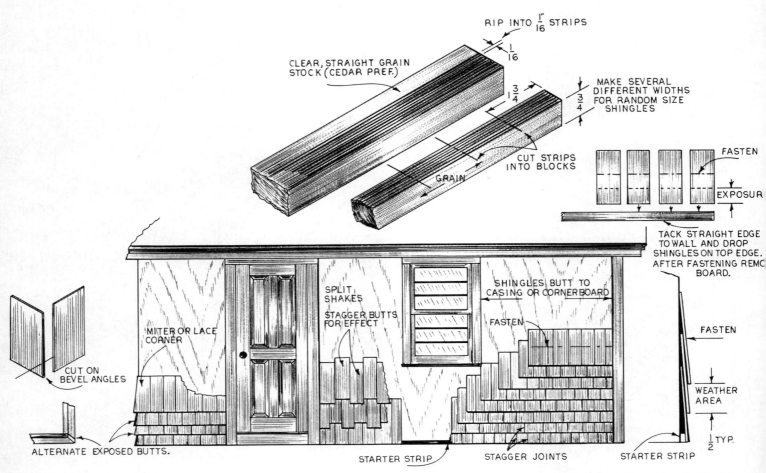

Fig. 3–17. *Installing sidewall shingles*

The first course of asphalt shingles is applied upside down, and a second row is installed over this upside-down row. This beginning application insures that the first row of tabs has roof material under it. The following rows of shingles are applied in a normal manner. Most manufacturing companies include directions with their products.

Fish-Scale Shingles

These decorative shingles were used very often for roofs and wide walls on Victorian houses. The fish-scale shingles are all uniform widths with rounded bottoms. The shingles are applied in the same manner as regular wood shingles. Every other row starts with a half shingle in order to stagger the edge joints.

Slate Shingles

Slate shingles are applied just like wood shingles, except they require an adhesive for fastening. The slate width varies, and any side joints must be staggered. The color selection should be random, just about the way they are picked out of the package. Retail companies include directions with their products.

INSTALLING SHINGLES ON A HOUSE WALL

Wood shingles or shakes can be installed on house walls as well as roofs. The fastening and the amount of exposed weather area is about the same as those laid out for roofing. In order to start the bevel effect of side wall shingles, a

254

¹/₁₆-inch-thick starter strip must be used. This strip is used under the first shingle course *only*. See detail in figure 3–17 right. A ¹/₁₆-inch by ³/₁₆-inch strip is applied to the very bottom edge of the exterior house walls. The first row of shingles is applied over this strip, so that the strip strikes the bottom of the shingle only. Once the first row of shingles assumes the bevel angle, all subsequent rows continue the slanted effect.

In order to keep the bottom edges of the shingle rows even during installation, a straight edge is used. Temporarily fasten the top of a straight board edge to the desired exposure marks. Drop the shingle bottoms on the top of the straight edge, and fasten the shingles in place. Remove the straight edge and continue this operation until the complete area is covered. Sidewall shingles must also have staggered edge joints. See notes in figure 3–17.

Hand-split shakes can be used on side walls in even or staggered bottom rows. Some early colonial homes had even-rowed shakes. The staggered or drop-edge rows were used on some Victorian and contemporary ranch houses.

CORNERS

Two methods are used to complete house exterior corners: the self-edge or corner boards. Of the two methods, the corner board installation lends itself best to miniature construction.

In the self-edge or mitered corners, the shingle edges are cut on the normal installation angle. Alternate the exposed edges with one edge exposed one way and the succeeding edge exposed the other way. See figure 3–18 left.

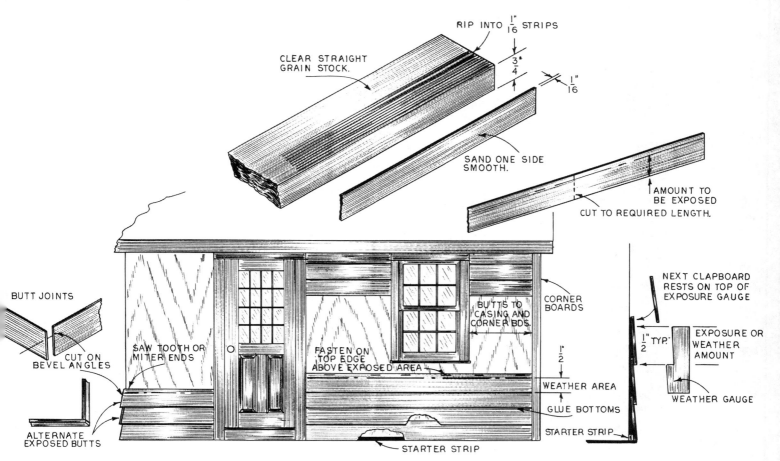

Fig. 3–18. House corner construction options

255

Corner boards are installed at every corner of the house. Most often these boards are ½-inch (or more) wide by ³/₁₆-inch or ¼-inch thick. The row of shingles or clapboards is then butted to the corner boards. See figure 3–18 right side. This cornering method offers greater strength and protection, plus it allows the walls to be removed for interior access.

CLAPBOARD

Bevel siding, or clapboard, is the most common exterior covering used. Several commercial companies supply ready-made miniature clapboards in different widths or exposure.

The miniaturist can make his own from normal lumberyard stock. The strips need not be beveled but will assume the slanted effect when properly installed with a starter strip. See figure 3–18. Select clear, straight-grained stock. Cedar, redwood, C-Select pine, or

Fig. 3–20. *Commercial vertical siding (Courtesy Midwest Products Co.)*

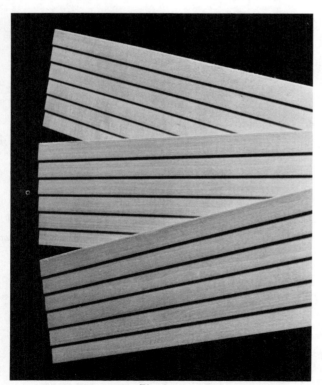

Fig. 3–19. *Commercial clapboard (Courtesy Midwest Products Co.)*

basswood is suggested. Rip the selected boards into ¹/₁₆-inch-thick strips on a table saw. This will make a ¹/₁₆-inch-thick by ¾-inch-wide clapboard. If available, a planer saw blade makes smoother cuts that require less sanding.

Installation

Clapboards are cut between any door or window trim and the corner boards. A thin ¹/₁₆-inch by ⅛-inch starter strip is fastened to the bottom of the house walls under the first clapboard *only*. See detail of cut in figure 3–18. Measure and cut the first clapboard to desired length. Glue the back side of this board and fasten it to the house wall over the starter strip. The bottom of the first clapboard covers the starter strip, which provides the first clapboard

256

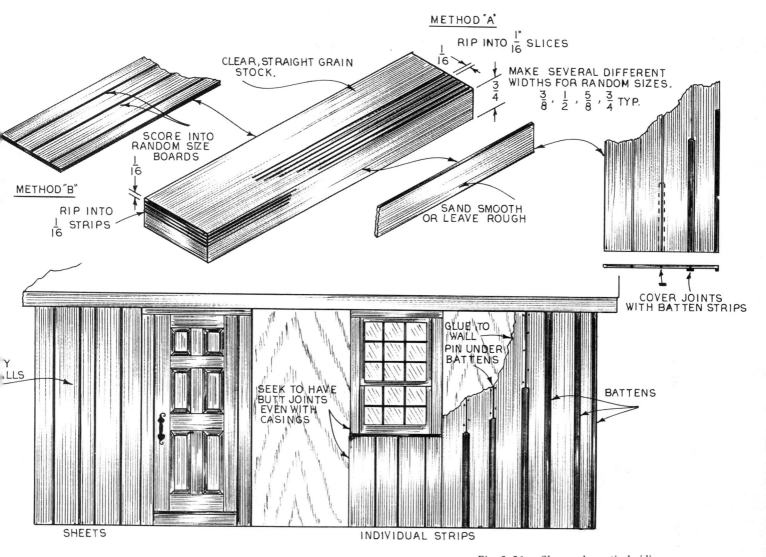

METHOD "A"

RIP INTO $\frac{1}{16}$" SLICES

$\frac{1}{16}$

$\frac{3}{4}$

MAKE SEVERAL DIFFERENT
WIDTHS FOR RANDOM SIZES.
$\frac{3}{8}$, $\frac{1}{2}$, $\frac{5}{8}$, $\frac{3}{4}$ TYP.

CLEAR, STRAIGHT GRAIN
STOCK.

SCORE INTO
RANDOM SIZE
BOARDS

$\frac{1}{16}$

METHOD "B"

RIP INTO
$\frac{1}{16}$ STRIPS

SAND SMOOTH
OR LEAVE ROUGH

COVER JOINTS
WITH BATTEN STRIPS

Y
LLS

SEEK TO HAVE
BUTT JOINTS
EVEN WITH
CASINGS

GLUE TO
WALL
PIN UNDER
BATTENS

BATTENS

SHEETS

INDIVIDUAL STRIPS

Fig. 3–21. Shopmade vertical siding

with the desired bevel. Succeeding clapboards continue this angle.

Weather Gauge

A weather gauge is made from scrap wood with the predetermined exposure amount built into it. Such a gauge negates the need to measure each row of siding. Most often the exposure will be ½ inch (6 inches in life-size) for all of the houses and shops given. See detail on right side of figure 3–18.

The weather gauge should have the angle and exposure amounts cut out in a step fash-

ion. The gauge notch or step is placed on the already installed siding strip, and the next clapboard to be installed is dropped onto the top of the gauge and fastened in place. The gauge is moved across the length of the siding several times to insure uniform exposure.

Fastening

Clapboards are fastened on the top edge above the prescribed weather exposure area. The succeeding clapboard covers any fastening heads used. Glue the clapboard bottoms in place. An ordinary paper stapler works very well for attaching clapboards. However, bank pins (sequin pins) can be used if preferred.

VERTICAL SIDING

Vertical siding can be made by two different methods: in sheet form or in individual strips, with or without battens.

For sheet-type siding, select clear, straight-grained stock. Cedar, redwood, basswood, or C-Select pine is suggested. Rip the selected board to a 3-inch or 4-inch width. On a table saw, cut this board into $1/16$-inch sheets. See method B in figure 3–21. These sheets can be sanded smooth or left rough. Score the sheets to resemble random or equal-size boards. Glue the sheets to the house walls. See figure 3–21, left side. The sheet stock will have to be cut to fit around door and window openings.

To make individual vertical boards, rip the selected stock into $1/16$-inch strips. See method A in figure 3–21. Several different widths of boards can be used to achieve random-size strips. The strips can be sanded or left rough. Apply the strips to the house wall with plain butt joints. Cover the joints with thin $1/16$-inch by $1/8$-inch battens. See detail in figure 3–21, right side.

HOUSE WALL ASSEMBLY

Before a miniature house is assembled, com-

Fig. 3–22. *Miniature house with interior papered before floors and ceilings are installed*

plete as much interior work as possible. After the various wall parts are cut out of the plywood sheets, install the windows and doors in the openings. Such millwork should be painted before installation. The windows and doors have premade exterior casing, and these parts are used to fasten the units in place.

Individual wall pieces can then be marked for any interior wall junctions, thereby dividing the walls into possible room sections. The interior of such pieces can be painted or papered for individual decor or design. Note in figure 3–22 that the second-floor room on the left has red wallpaper, the center hall is painted, and the right-side bedroom has blue wallpaper. The junction of interior walls will cover the joints made by paper or paint coming together. The walls butting these exterior walls will be finished with the same materials and designs.

While the miniature house is still in an open or half-assembled state, the interior window and door trim can be painted and installed.

Such action reduces the need of fine, precise fitting or painting within cramped quarters.

Whenever possible, finish interior walls before installing them. Many times such walls can be finished on a workbench and installed as a unit. The walls could have operable doors, baseboards, fireplaces, or moldings completely finished before the walls are secured in place. This requires some preplanning, but the effort expended is well worth the time.

The directions for the following miniature houses follow the concept that most of the interior finishing work will be completed before installation. The suggested directions reverse the normal order for building houses; these miniature homes are worked from the inside, out. First floors are completed before the second floor or ceiling is installed. The exterior of the house is one of the last operations completed on miniature homes. Keep this concept in mind and complete as much detail and finish work as possible before installing interior pieces.

17. *Early American Houses*

EARLY AMERICAN SALTBOX

Some authorities claim that the saltbox-style roof developed in part from room additions made on existing houses. In colonial times, some homes were two stories high but only one room wide. Such a building could have a plain gable or gambrel roof. As the family grew, additional rooms were added to the rear on the ground floor. When the existing roof line was extended to cover the new addition, a long sloping rear roof was created, which resembled the shape of old saltboxes.

The following miniature was developed from the house known as the Parsonage in Sturbridge Village, Mass.

Construction

Material List

Part	Amount	Size
Exterior		
Double-hung window with jambs	20	2½" x 5"
Double-hung windows with jambs	2	2" x 5"
Exterior doors with jambs	3	3" x 7"
Clapboard		30' x $^1/_{16}$" x ¾"
Shake shingles	2200	$^1/_{16}$" x ¾" x 1¾"
Rake trim		90" x $^3/_{16}$" x ⅝"
Corner boards		120" x $^3/_{16}$" x 1"
Cornice material		80" x ¾" x ¾"
A.C. Plywood	2 sheets	48" x 96" x ⅜"

Fig. 3–23. Richardson House, Old Sturbridge Village, Sturbridge, MA

Interior

Interior doors with jambs	2	3" x 7"
Interior doors with jambs	6	2½" x 7"
Interior doors with jambs	1	2" x 7"
Flooring		1840 square inches x ⅛"
Wainscotting material		1000 square inches x 1/16"
Clear stock for wainscotting		5 square feet
Window and door casing		350" x 1/16" x 5/16"
Baseboard (optional)		400" x 1/16" x ½"

1. Study figures 3–27 through 3–30 before starting work. Two different options are given for the rear wall construction: the rear wall is often open for access or viewing (A), or the rear wall is hinged to open as a door(s) with the break line occurring on the door jamb (B).

2. Lay out the exterior walls, floors, and ceiling outlines on the selected plywood sheets. Cut out the required parts. See figure 3–30 for suggestions. Roughly cut out the window and door openings in the plywood pieces. Mark out the interior wall placement on the floor pieces. Lay out any hearth locations on

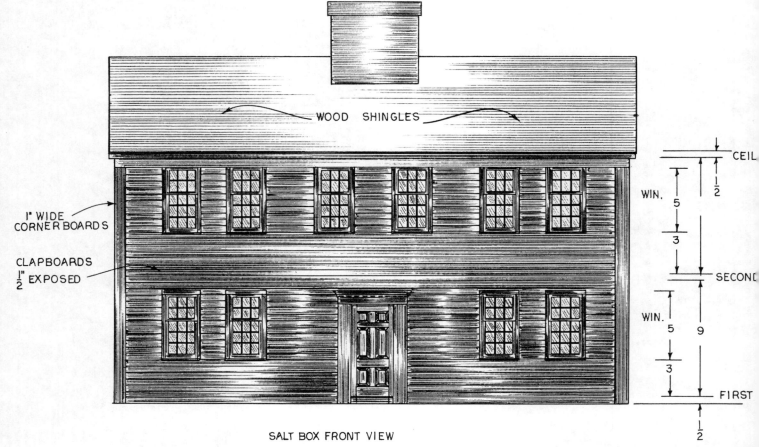

WOOD SHINGLES

1" WIDE
CORNER BOARDS

CLAPBOARDS
$\frac{1}{2}$" EXPOSED

CEIL

WIN.

5

3

SECOND

WIN.

5

9

3

FIRST

$\frac{1}{2}$

$\frac{1}{2}$

SALT BOX FRONT VIEW

Fig. 3–24. Front elevations

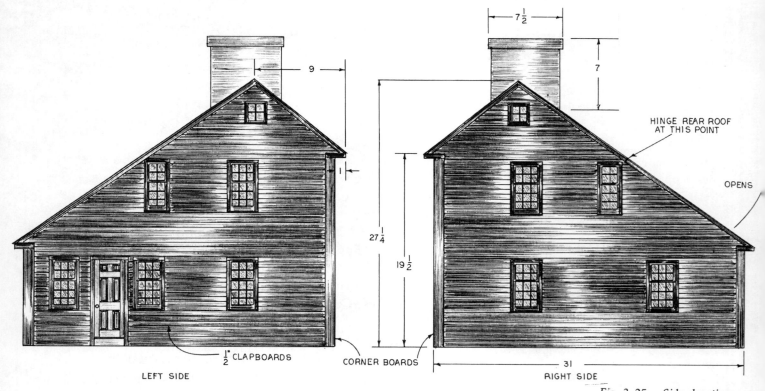

9

7$\frac{1}{2}$

7

HINGE REAR ROOF
AT THIS POINT

1

OPENS

27$\frac{1}{4}$

19$\frac{1}{2}$

$\frac{1}{2}$" CLAPBOARDS

CORNER BOARDS

31

LEFT SIDE

RIGHT SIDE

Fig. 3–25. Side elevations

the plywood floor pieces. Install the hearths in a material or your choice. See Section one for details on making hearths. Apply the finished flooring to the first and second-floor plywood pieces. Finish the bottom of the second-floor plywood piece to resemble a ceiling.

3. Screw the side walls into the finished first-floor piece. Make and finish the first-floor interior walls. If wainscotting or paneling is to be used, install it on the interior and exterior side walls at this time. Install any windows or doors required for the two side walls. Finish the interior of these walls complete with paper, paint, or paneling. The front and back wall areas are still open at this time. Glue and nail or screw the first-floor walls (A, B, C, D, and F) to the first-floor board.

4. Install the second-floor piece by nailing it into the first-floor interior walls. Nail the side walls into the second-floor stock. Make, finish, and install the second-floor interior walls (G, H, I, and J). Note: wall I contains the fireplaces; these should be completed before installation. Install the second-floor ceiling board by nailing

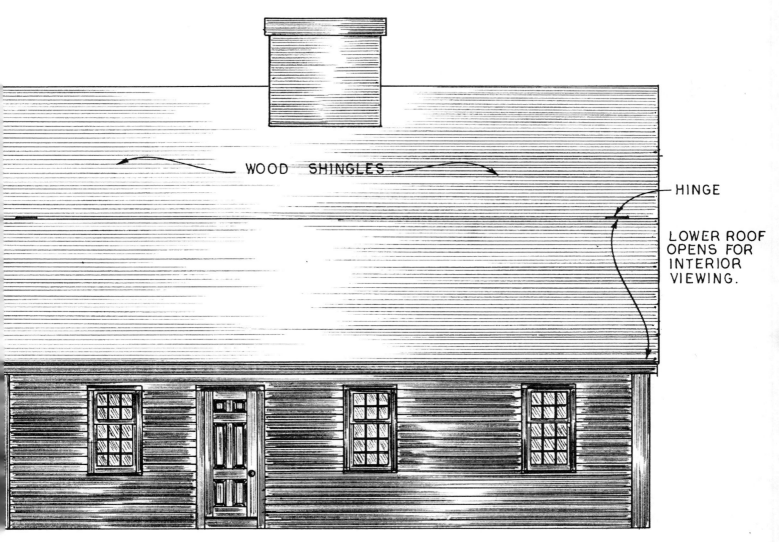

OPTIONAL REAR WALL

Fig. 3–26. Optional rear wall

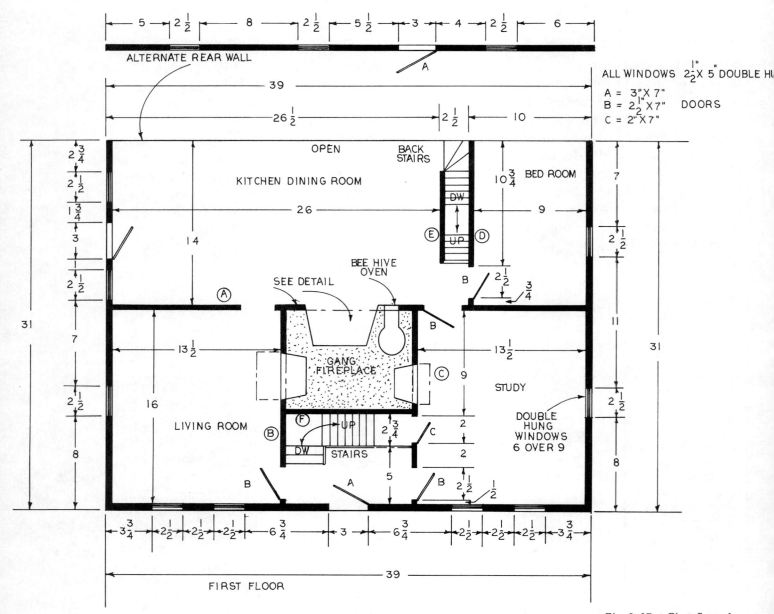

ALTERNATE REAR WALL

ALL WINDOWS $2\frac{1}{2}$X 5" DOUBLE HU
A = 3"X 7"
B = $2\frac{1}{2}$X7"   DOORS
C = 2"X 7"

OPEN   BACK
         STAIRS

KITCHEN DINING ROOM

BED ROOM

DW

UP

SEE DETAIL

BEE HIVE
OVEN

GANG
FIREPLACE

LIVING ROOM

STUDY

DOUBLE
HUNG
WINDOWS
6 OVER 9

UP

DW   STAIRS

FIRST FLOOR

Fig. 3–27.   First-floor plan

it into the interior walls. Nail the house side walls into the ceiling stock. Note that the second-floor ceiling piece runs from the front of the house to the G wall only. Finish the second-floor interior side walls at this time. Install any casing or trim to windows and doors, and install finished baseboard, if used.

5. Lay out and cut the roof boards. The rear roof board is split and hinged to open as a door.

See figure 3–25. Secure the roof boards to the peaked cuts on the side walls. If the roof sags, use a peaked center support on the second-floor ceiling. The peaked center support should be the same size and shape as the house side wall peaks. Hinge the rear roof boards together. Lay out and cut the cornice stock. See figures 3–10 and 3–11 for possible construction options.

It is recommended that the house front wall be rabbeted for removal, while the rear wall, if used, be constructed as a double door with the door break occurring at the back door's vertical trim. See figures 3–7 and 3–8 for reference. Install the cornice, returns, and rake trim.

6. Make and fit the front and rear walls. Fasten the walls temporarily in place. Install any windows or doors required. Cut and fit the corner boards. These corner boards should be split so that part covers the end grain of the front or rear wall pieces and part is secured to the house side walls. Secure the corner boards in place. Make and install the exterior chimney.

7. Secure the selected roof materials to the roof boards. Shakes or wood shingles are suggested. See figures 3–13 and 3–15 for procedures. Install the suggested clapboards to the complete house exterior. Half-inch weather exposure amounts are recommended. Stain or paint the exterior at this time. The Sturbridge Village original is painted barn red with white casing and trim.

8. Remove the front and rear walls from the

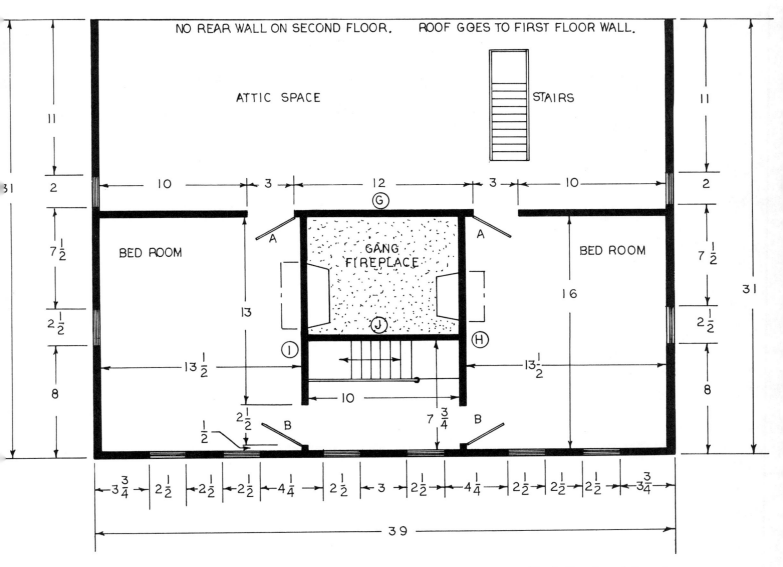

Fig. 3–28.   Second-floor plan

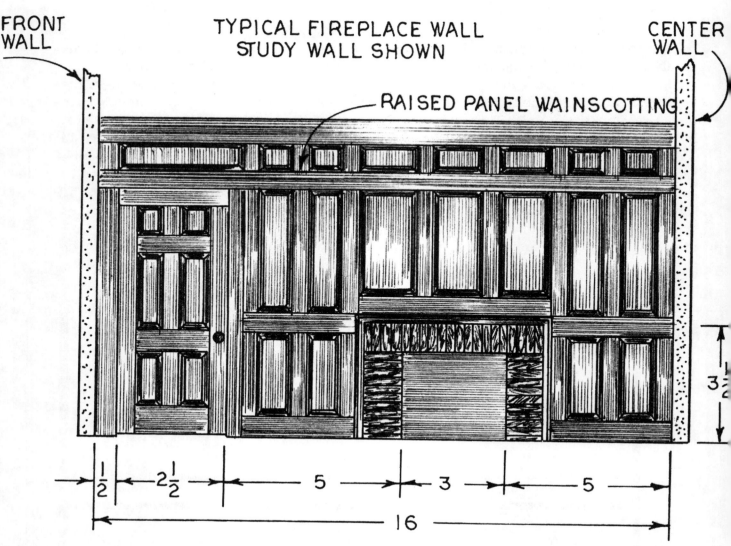

TYPICAL FIREPLACE WALL
STUDY WALL SHOWN

FRONT WALL

CENTER WALL

RAISED PANEL WAINSCOTTING

Fig. 3–29.   *Typical fireplace wall section*

house. Finish the interior areas of these walls to match the rooms they abut. Note figure 3–29 for suggested detailing. When the walls are closed, the rooms should be complete.

It is suggested that the study and living room have floor-to-ceiling raised paneling. See sample wall section, figure 3–29. Raised panels can be made (see Section one) or purchased (see Section four).

The kitchen area has floor-to-ceiling, random-width wainscotting. See Section one or four for sources. The small downstairs bedroom has partial wainscotting with paint or wallpaper above it. See figure 3–32. The

second-floor bedrooms are wallpapered with baseboard trim. Ceiling moldings are optional.

PAUL REVERE HOUSE

Paul Revere's House, which is still standing in Boston, is a garrison-style house. It has the unique feature of an overhanging second floor. This characteristic developed from the need to defend the house from possible outside forces. On the frontier, the second-floor, overhang flooring boards could be lifted up to reveal a bird's-eye view of anyone trying to gain entry through the ground-floor windows or doors.

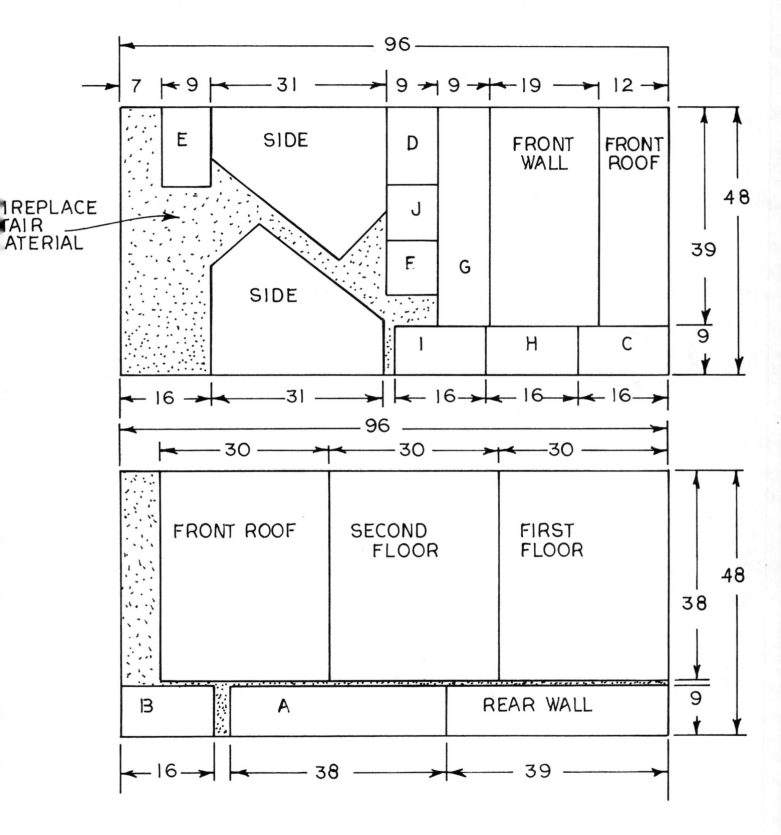

Fig. 3-30. Plywood wall lay-out.

Scalding water, boiling oil, or pike poles manned from the floor above proved a formidable defense. Long after the need for house protection was over, the colonial builder realized such a building added living space without additional cost, and retained the charm of this particular design. The garrison overhang has remained in use ever since.

Construction

Material List

Part	Amount	Size
Plywood framing	1¾ sheets	⅜″ or ½″
Casement windows with trim	7	3″ x 3″ x ½″
Casement windows with trim	3	1½″ x 3½″
Double hung windows with trim	3	2½″ x 4½″
Exterior doors with jamb and trim	2	3″ x 7″
Exterior door with jamb and trim	1	2½″ x 7″

Fig. 3–31. Fireplace and paneled wall, Richardson House

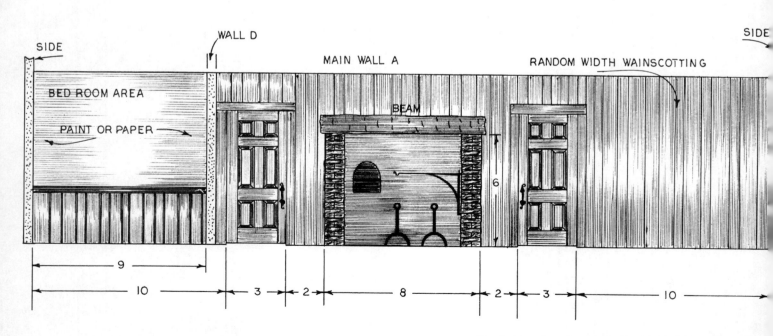

Fig. 3–32. Sample main wall with kitchen fireplace

Fig. 3–33.   *Ceiling and corner beams, Richardson House*

Fig. 3–34.   *Paul Revere House, Boston, MA*

Fig. 3–35.   Overhang detail

Fig. 3–36.   Window detail

Interior doors with jamb and trim	2	3″ x 7″
Interior doors with jamb and trim	4	2″ x 7″
Cedar clapboard	420 linear feet	¹/₁₆″ x ¾″
Clear stock, cornice and trim	1	¾″ x 6″ x 36″
Cedar shingles	1600	¹/₁₆″ x ¾″ x 1¾″
Clear stock, interior beams	1	¾″ x 4″ x 36″
Wainscotting, interior trim	1	¾″ x 6″ x 48″
Hardwood flooring	1568 square inches	¹/₁₆″ x random width
Stock for chimney and fireplaces	1	¾″ x 6″ x 36″

270

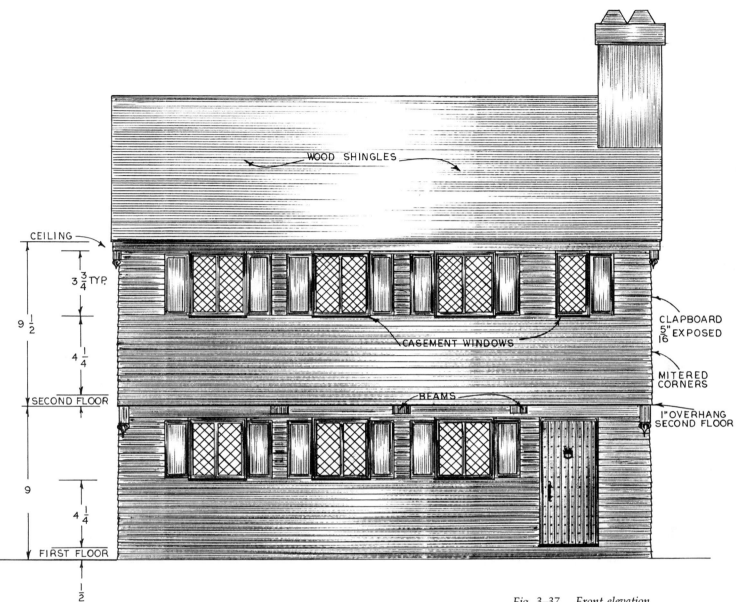

CEILING

$3\frac{3}{4}$ TYP.

$9\frac{1}{2}$

$4\frac{1}{4}$

SECOND FLOOR

9

$4\frac{1}{4}$

FIRST FLOOR

$\frac{1}{2}$

WOOD SHINGLES

CLAPBOARD $\frac{5}{16}$" EXPOSED

CASEMENT WINDOWS

MITERED CORNERS

BEAMS

1" OVERHANG SECOND FLOOR

Fig. 3–37. Front elevation

1. Review the house plans in figures 3–37 through 3–44 before starting. Note that the kitchen area has a slanted side wall. The second floor does not have this wall angle. The right side wall is cut, and it contains the kitchen and study side walls as one unit. The design shows that the house is open at the rear. Because the dwelling is only one room wide, the front wall is fixed in place and does not move. This allows you to miter the clapboard corners.

However, clapboard corner boards can be used if preferred.

2. Lay out the various house parts on the plywood sheets. See figure 3–44 for suggestions. Cut out the parts. Roughly cut out the window and door openings. Apply the hardwood flooring to the first and second-floor pieces; be sure to allow for the fireplace hearths. Construct the fireplace hearths in the correct locations. Stain and finish the two floor

pieces at this time. See Section one for details.

3. Fasten the side walls to the first-floor piece. Make the first-floor interior walls. Construct and finish the required fireplaces. See details in figures 3–47 and 3–48. Walls A, B, C, D, and E can be made as one unit and installed in place. Install any wainscotting or paneling before installing. Finish painting or staining before installing the walls. Secure the wall unit to the first-floor piece. Make and install the kitchen-fireplace wall. Cut the stock for the primary and secondary beams. See detail in figures 3–45 and 3–46. Install the first-floor beams as suggested. A half-beam is installed

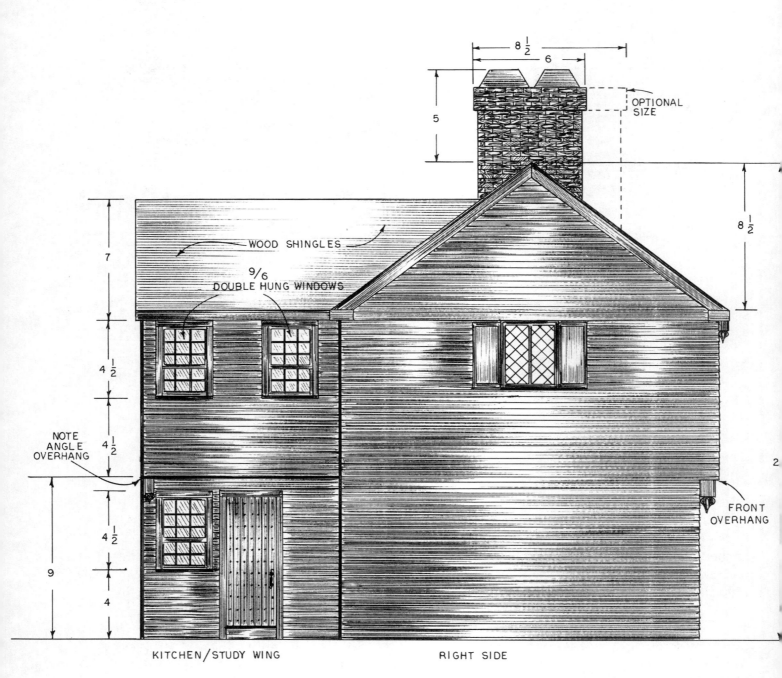

KITCHEN/STUDY WING   RIGHT SIDE

Fig. 3–38.   Right-side elevation

272

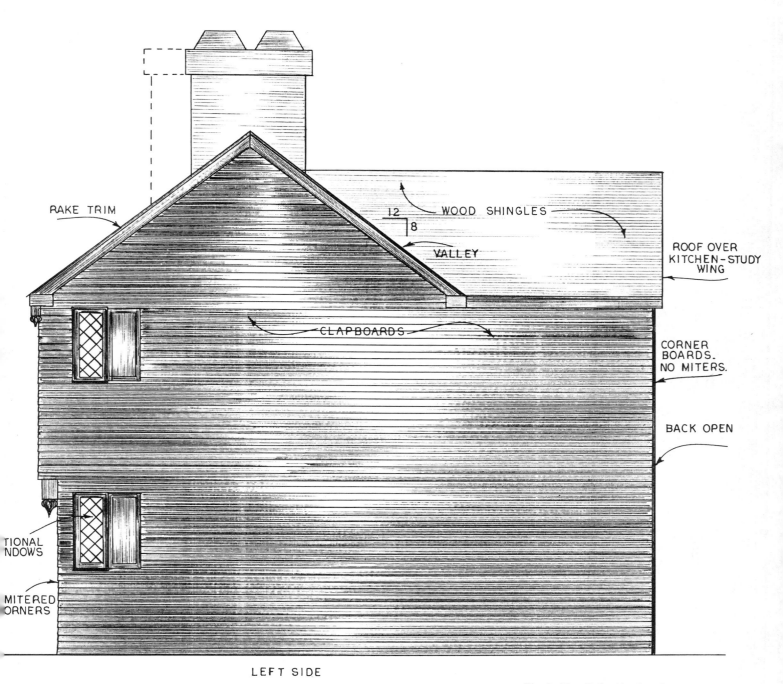

RAKE TRIM

WOOD SHINGLES

12
8

VALLEY

ROOF OVER
KITCHEN-STUDY
WING

CLAPBOARDS

CORNER
BOARDS.
NO MITERS.

BACK OPEN

...TIONAL
...NDOWS

MITERED
...ORNERS

LEFT SIDE

Fig. 3–39.   Left-side elevation

all around the house perimeter including the rear wall. The beams should be hewed and finished before installation.

4. Paint the underside of the second floor to resemble a ceiling. Fasten the second-floor piece in place by nailing it into the first-floor beams and walls. Nail the side walls into the

floor piece. Make the required second-floor wall assembly with walls G, H, I, J, K, and L. Form the suggested fireplaces. See figures 3–47 and 3–48.

Finish the wall assembly with suggested wainscotting or trim and paint. Install the second-floor walls in place. Cut out and install

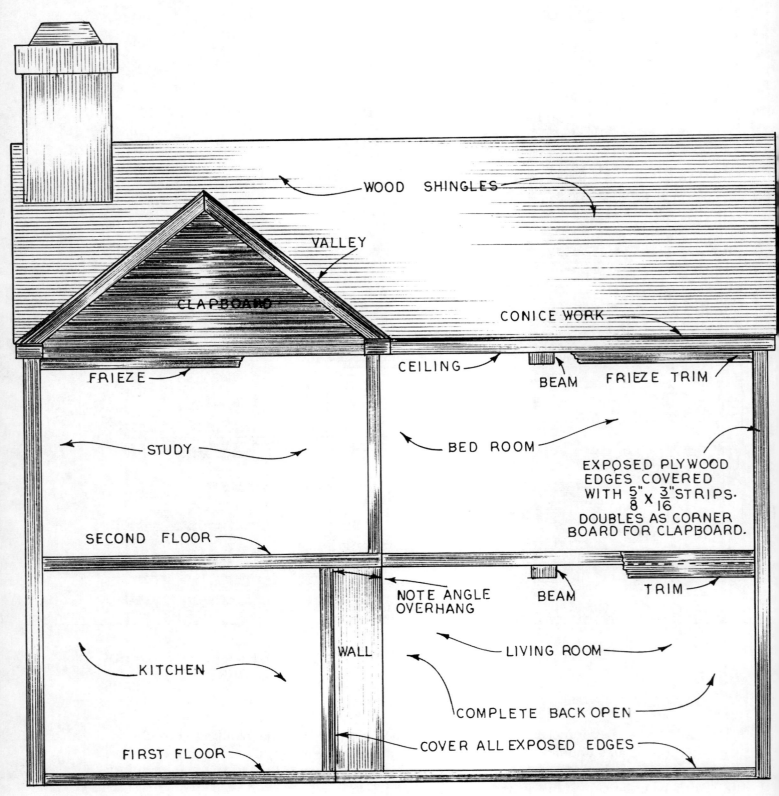

REAR VIEW

Fig. 3–40. Rear elevation

274

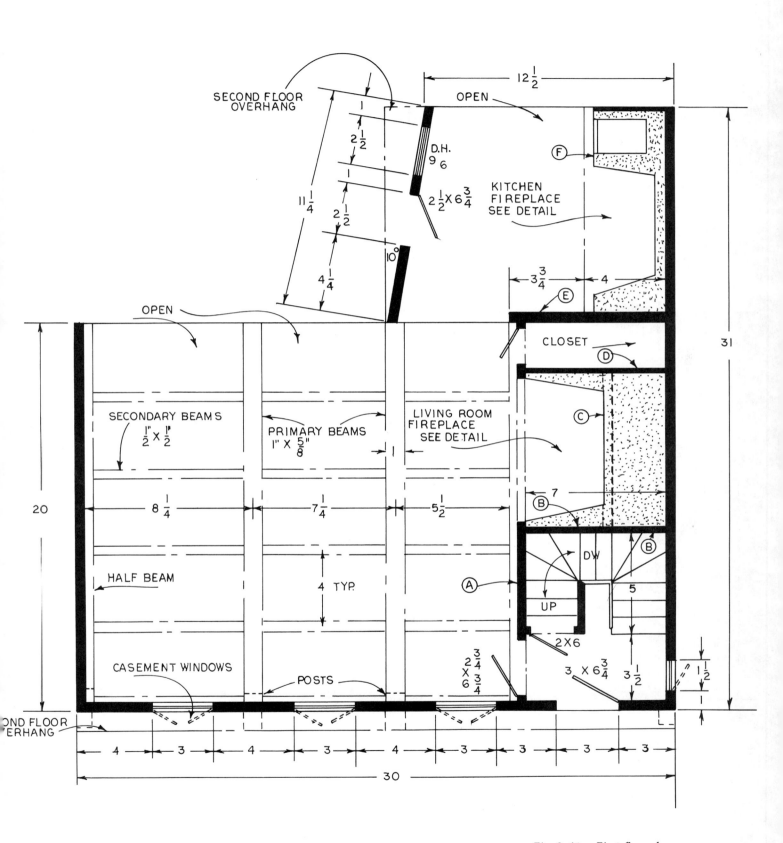

SECOND FLOOR OVERHANG

2 $\frac{1}{2}$

2 $\frac{1}{2}$

11 $\frac{1}{4}$

4 $\frac{1}{4}$

10°

D.H.
9 6

2 $\frac{1}{2}$ X 6 $\frac{3}{4}$

12 $\frac{1}{2}$

OPEN

KITCHEN
FIREPLACE
SEE DETAIL

F

3 $\frac{3}{4}$

4

E

31

CLOSET

D

OPEN

SECONDARY BEAMS
$\frac{1}{2}$" X $\frac{1}{2}$"

PRIMARY BEAMS
1" X $\frac{5}{8}$"

LIVING ROOM
FIREPLACE
SEE DETAIL

C

1

20

8 $\frac{1}{4}$

7 $\frac{1}{4}$

5 $\frac{1}{2}$

7

B

HALF BEAM

4 TYP.

DW

B

A

UP

5

CASEMENT WINDOWS

POSTS

2 $\frac{3}{4}$ X 6 $\frac{3}{4}$

2X6

3 X 6 $\frac{3}{4}$

3 $\frac{1}{2}$

1 $\frac{1}{2}$

OND FLOOR
ERHANG

4

3

4

3

4

3

3

3

3

30

Fig. 3–41. First-floor plan

275

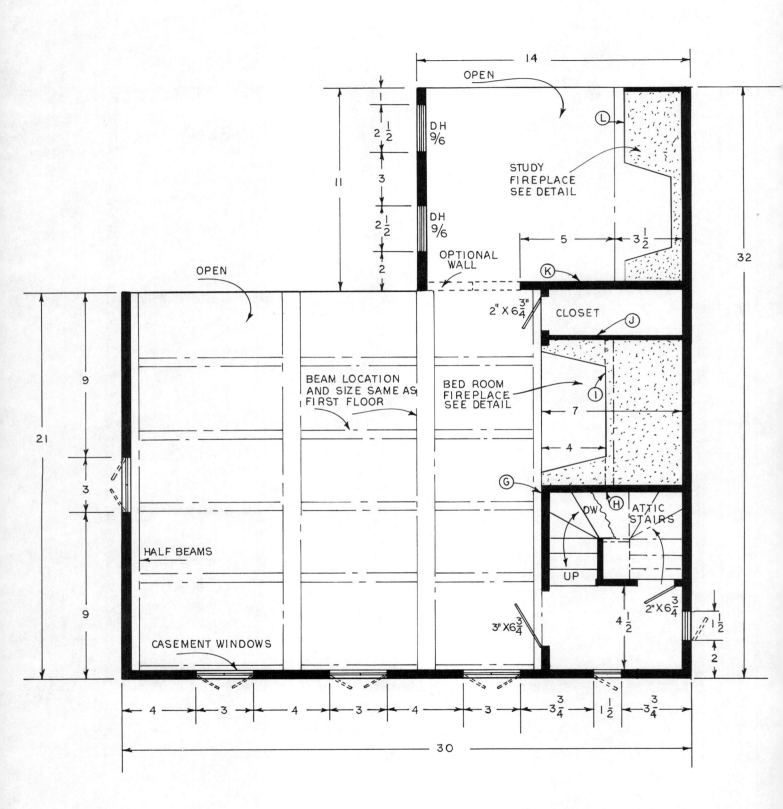

Fig. 3–42. Second-floor plan

276

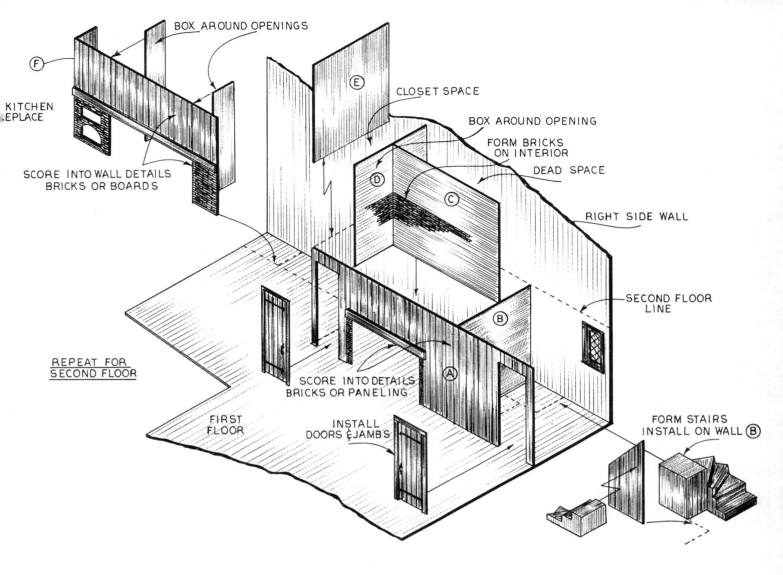

Fig. 3–43. Assembly plan

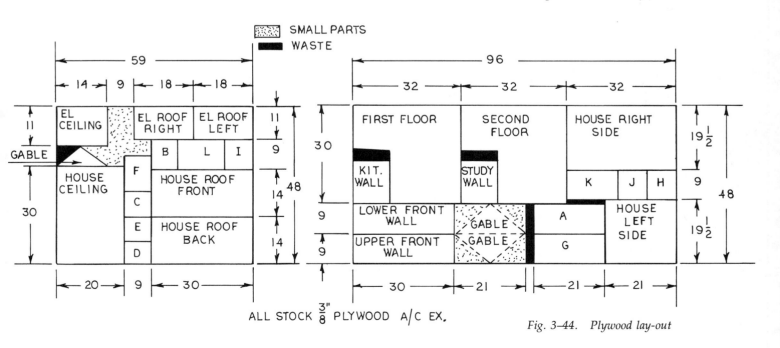

Fig. 3–44. Plywood lay-out

In the assembly plan (Fig. 3–43), the following labels appear:

- BOX AROUND OPENINGS
- F
- KITCHEN FIREPLACE
- SCORE INTO WALL DETAILS BRICKS OR BOARDS
- E
- CLOSET SPACE
- BOX AROUND OPENING
- FORM BRICKS ON INTERIOR
- DEAD SPACE
- RIGHT SIDE WALL
- D
- C
- B
- SECOND FLOOR LINE
- REPEAT FOR SECOND FLOOR
- A
- FIRST FLOOR
- SCORE INTO DETAILS BRICKS OR PANELING
- INSTALL DOORS & JAMBS
- FORM STAIRS INSTALL ON WALL B

In the plywood lay-out (Fig. 3–44):

Left panel (59 × 48):
- 14, 9, 18, 18
- EL CEILING
- SMALL PARTS
- EL ROOF RIGHT
- EL ROOF LEFT — 11
- GABLE
- B, L, I — 9
- HOUSE CEILING
- F
- HOUSE ROOF FRONT — 14
- 48
- C
- 30
- E
- HOUSE ROOF BACK — 14
- D
- 20, 9, 30

Right panel (96 × 48):
- 32, 32, 32
- FIRST FLOOR
- SECOND FLOOR
- HOUSE RIGHT SIDE — 19½
- KIT. WALL
- STUDY WALL
- K, J, H — 9
- LOWER FRONT WALL
- GABLE
- A
- HOUSE LEFT SIDE — 19½
- 30
- 9
- UPPER FRONT WALL
- GABLE
- G
- 9
- 30, 21, 21, 21
- 48

SMALL PARTS

WASTE

ALL STOCK ⅜" PLYWOOD A/C EX.

277

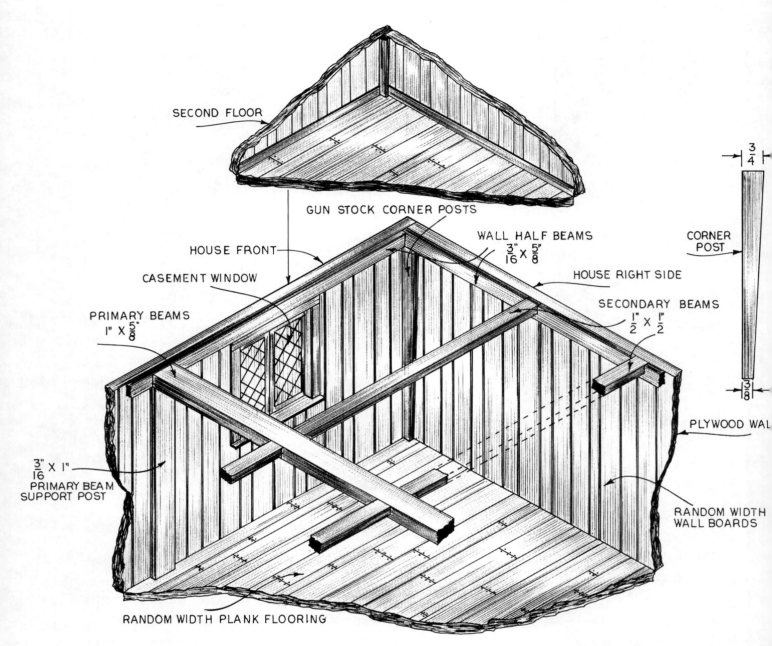

SECOND FLOOR

GUN STOCK CORNER POSTS

HOUSE FRONT

WALL HALF BEAMS
$\frac{3}{16}" \times \frac{5}{8}"$

CASEMENT WINDOW

HOUSE RIGHT SIDE

PRIMARY BEAMS
$1" \times \frac{5}{8}"$

SECONDARY BEAMS
$\frac{1}{2}" \times \frac{1}{2}"$

CORNER POST

$\frac{3}{4}$

$\frac{3}{8}$

PLYWOOD WALL

$\frac{3}{16}" \times 1"$
PRIMARY BEAM
SUPPORT POST

RANDOM WIDTH
WALL BOARDS

RANDOM WIDTH PLANK FLOORING

Fig. 3–45. First-floor construction

the second-floor primary and secondary beams. Note that a half-beam is installed around the house perimeter including the rear walls.

5. While the front wall is still removed, make and install the suggested stairs and landing. The attic stairs are optional. A solid door can be used at this point, if preferred.

Install the front wall windows to the

plywood stock. Finish the interior of the front walls to match the various rooms they abut. Install any interior trim or moldings. Nail the front walls into the floors and the house side pieces.

6. If fireplace lights are to be used, the feed wires should be run through the chimney area. The lights should be installed at this time. Either the attic space or one of these side closets

can be used to store a transformer. Run any household voltage feed wires at this time. See Section one for wiring details.

7. Paint the lower side of the second-floor ceiling board. Install the ceiling piece by nailing it into the second-floor beams and interior walls. Nail the house side walls into the ceiling piece. Cut and install the roof boards. The rear roof boards can be hinged at the peak. The roof boards may require a center support. An angle brace made the same size as the house roof peaks can be installed in the center of the house attic. Nail the roof boards in place. Note that the room over the study area is made in a valley. If the rear roof board is hinged, this will include the valley.

8. Cut and install the cornice and rake trim. See figures 3–10 and 3–11 for suggestions and options. Install hand-split cedar shakes to the roof boards. A ½-inch to ¾-inch weather exposure is suggested. See figures 3–13 and 3–49 for procedure.

9. Cut and install the clapboard. A ½-inch weather exposure is suggested. The clapboards have mitered or laced corners. Use a ¹⁄₁₆-inch by ⅛-inch starter strip under the first

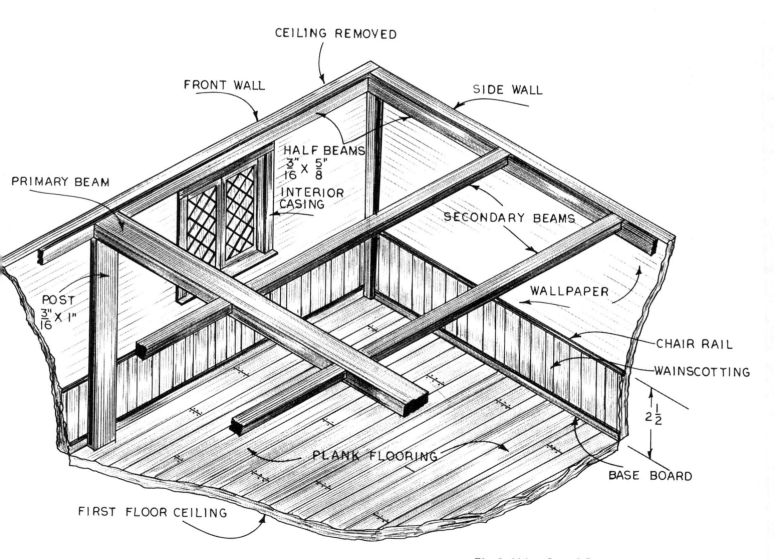

Fig. 3–46A. *Second-floor construction*

279

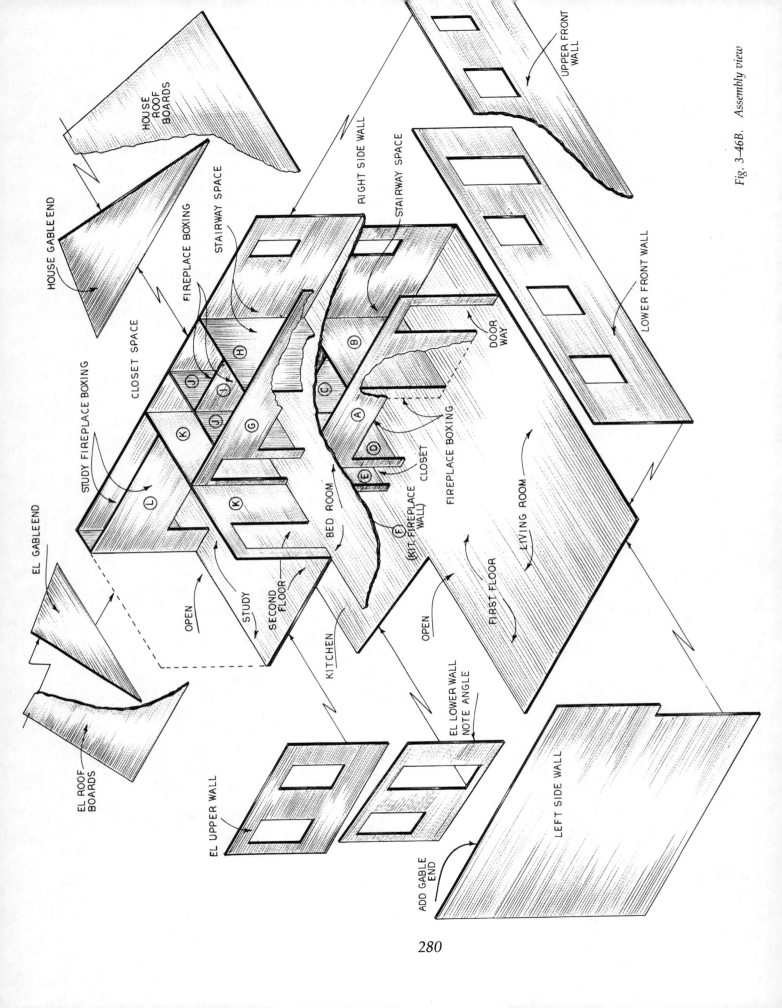

UPPER FRONT WALL

LOWER FRONT WALL

HOUSE ROOF BOARDS

HOUSE GABLE END

RIGHT SIDE WALL

STAIRWAY SPACE

FIREPLACE BOXING

STAIRWAY SPACE

CLOSET SPACE

STUDY FIREPLACE BOXING

HOUSE GABLE END

EL GABLE END

EL ROOF BOARDS

DOOR WAY

CLOSET

FIREPLACE BOXING

LIVING ROOM

FIRST FLOOR

OPEN

(KIT. FIREPLACE WALL)

BED ROOM

SECOND FLOOR

STUDY

OPEN

KITCHEN

EL LOWER WALL NOTE ANGLE

EL UPPER WALL

ADD GABLE END

LEFT SIDE WALL

Ⓐ Ⓑ Ⓒ Ⓓ Ⓔ Ⓕ Ⓖ Ⓗ Ⓘ Ⓙ Ⓚ Ⓛ

Fig. 3-46B. Assembly view

280

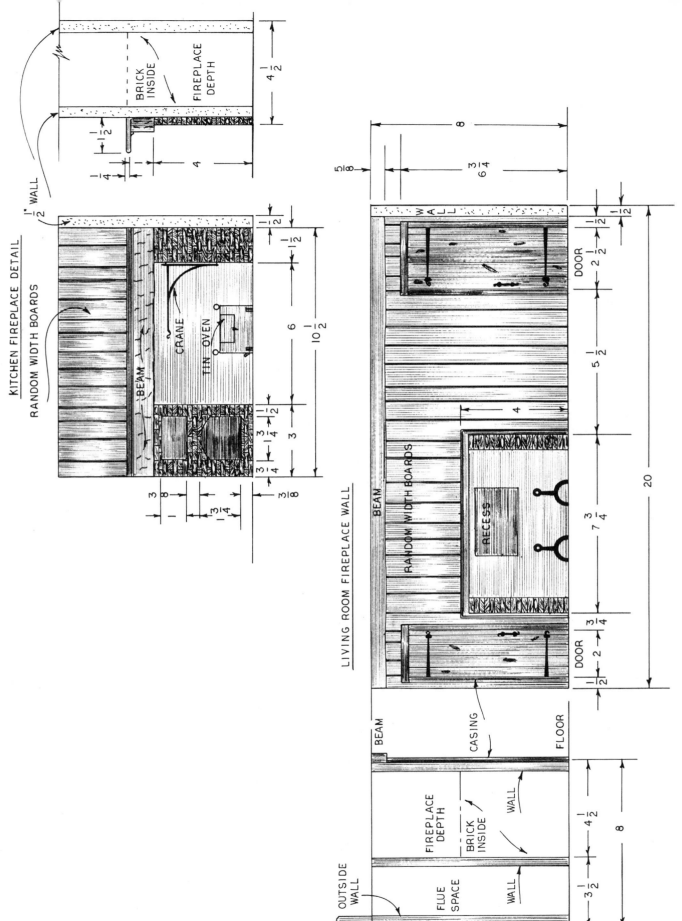

KITCHEN FIREPLACE DETAIL

RANDOM WIDTH BOARDS

BRICK INSIDE

FIREPLACE DEPTH

1" WALL

BEAM

CRANE

TIN OVEN

LIVING ROOM FIREPLACE WALL

WALL

BEAM

RANDOM WIDTH BOARDS

ACCESS

DOOR

DOOR

BEAM

CASING

FLOOR

OUTSIDE WALL

FIREPLACE DEPTH

BRICK INSIDE

WALL

WALL

FLUE SPACE

Fig. 3-47. Living room, kitchen wall, and fireplace details

281

clapboard. This strip provides the suitable board angle. Install the first clapboard to the right-side piece allowing the board end to extend beyond the house front. When the front clapboard is put in place, it forms an angle with the side clapboard. Mark this angle, and cut the side clapboard at this angle. The front clapboard is then installed, overhanging the side cut. This front clapboard is marked on the angle and cut. When installed, the two clapboards will form a butt joint but on the normal tilted angle. Reverse the procedure for the next row of clapboards so that only every other end joint will show from one particular side.

Once the entire house is covered with clapboard, stain all exposed wooden areas includ-

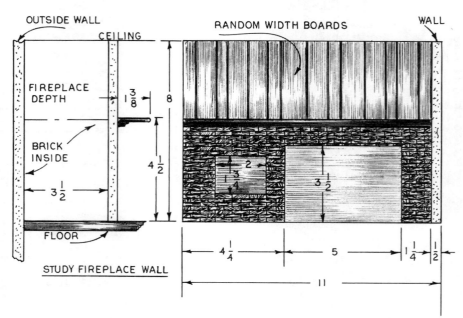

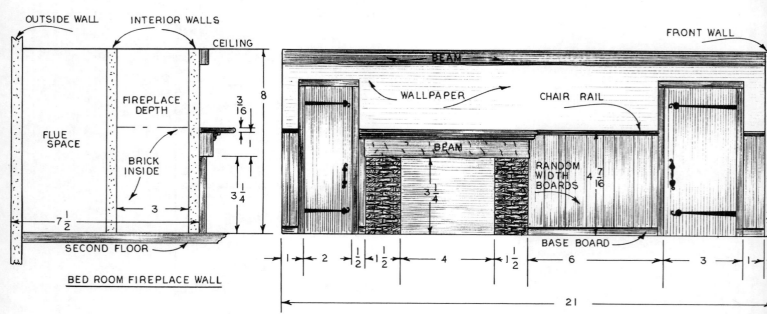

Fig. 3–48.   Bedroom, study wall, and fireplace details

282

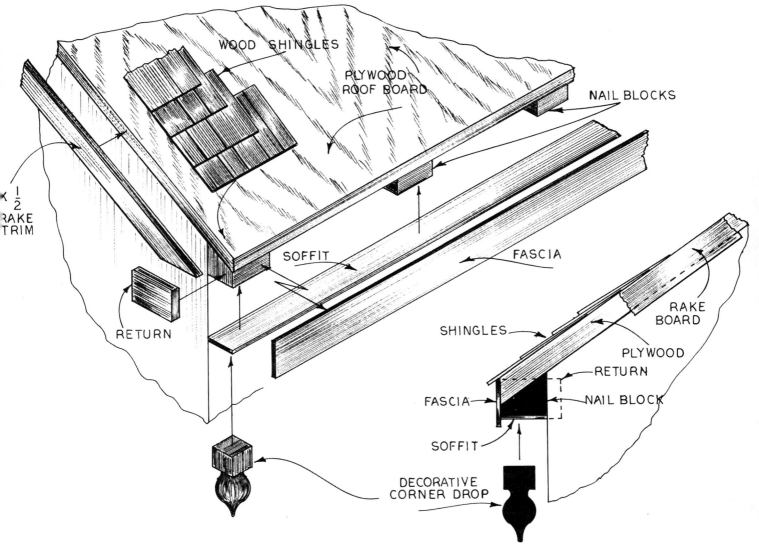

WOOD SHINGLES

PLYWOOD ROOF BOARD

NAIL BLOCKS

1/2 RAKE TRIM

SOFFIT

FASCIA

RETURN

SHINGLES

RAKE BOARD

PLYWOOD

RETURN

FASCIA

NAIL BLOCK

SOFFIT

DECORATIVE CORNER DROP

Fig. 3–49. Cornice and shingle details

ing the windows and doors. Do not stain the roof. Make a simulated brick chimney and install it on the roof.

The interiors of the saltbox house and the Revere house should be furnished with period-style furniture. Check museums and books for such construction. *Building Early American Furniture* and *Building Colonial Furnishings, Miniatures, & Folk Art* are excellent reference books for this period and style.

18. *Contemporary House in Two Styles*

The following miniature house was developed from several contemporary New England homes. It is offered in two different styles: as a story and a half colonial, and as a single-story low ranch. The basic floor plan is the same for both houses, except that the ranch style does not have a second floor.

This design was included to illustrate that almost any house, historical or contemporary, can be made in miniature. This design also presents the option of constructing a small miniature house to builders who do not desire a large period dwelling. Such a miniature can be furnished with almost any type of furniture desired.

Both styles of this miniature house have the option of an open rear wall or a rear wall operated as two large doors. The following material lists include a full rear wall.

Construction: Colonial Gambrel-Roof House

Material List

Part	Amount	Size
Exterior		
A.C. plywood	2 sheets	48″ x 96″ x ½″ (⅜″)
Double hung windows with jambs	11	3″ x 5″
Double hung window with jambs	1	3″ x 3″
Double hung window with jambs	1	2½″ x 3″
Exterior doors with jambs	2	3″ x 7″
Clapboard	220 linear feet	¹⁄₁₆″ x ¾″
Shingles	1300	¹⁄₁₆″ x ¾″ x 1¾″
Cornice and chimney trim stock	1	¾″ x 6″ x 40″

284

Fig. 3–50. *Contemporary colonial-style house, East Longmeadow, MA*

Interior

Hardwood flooring	1600 square inches	1/16" x random width
Interior door with jambs	1	3" x 7"
Interior door with jambs	6	2½" x 7"
Interior door with jambs	4	2" x 7"
Window casing		200" x 1/16" x 1/4"
Door casing		210" x 1/16" x 5/16"
Baseboard		360" x 1/16" x 5/16"
Stair and fireplace stock	1	¾" x 3" x 36"
Bathroom fixtures	2 sets	
Kitchen cabinets	1 set	

Construction: Single-Story Ranch House with Gable Roof

Material List:

Part	Amount	Size
Exterior		
Plywood	1½ sheets	48" x 96" x ½" (⅜")
Double hung windows with jambs	8	3" x 5"
Double hung windows with jambs	2	3" x 3"
Exterior door with jamb	1	3" x 7"

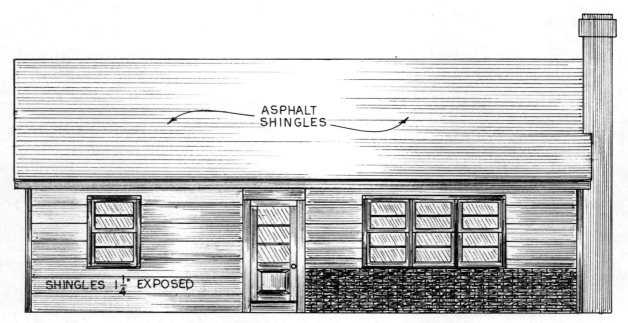

ASPHALT
SHINGLES

SHINGLES 1¼" EXPOSED

SINGLE STORY RANCH STYLE — GABLE ROOF

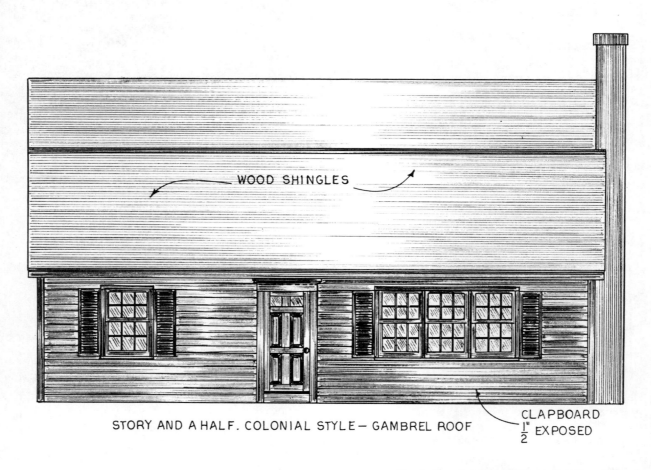

WOOD SHINGLES

STORY AND A HALF. COLONIAL STYLE — GAMBREL ROOF

CLAPBOARD
1½" EXPOSED

Fig. 3–51. Front elevations, colonial-style house

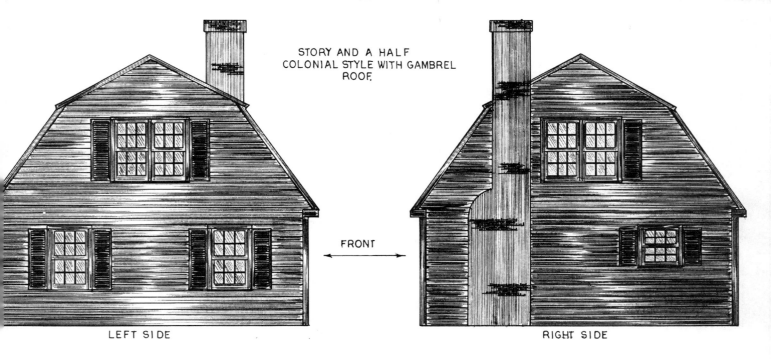

STORY AND A HALF
COLONIAL STYLE WITH GAMBREL
ROOF.

FRONT

LEFT SIDE

RIGHT SIDE

Fig. 3–52.   Side elevations, colonial-style house

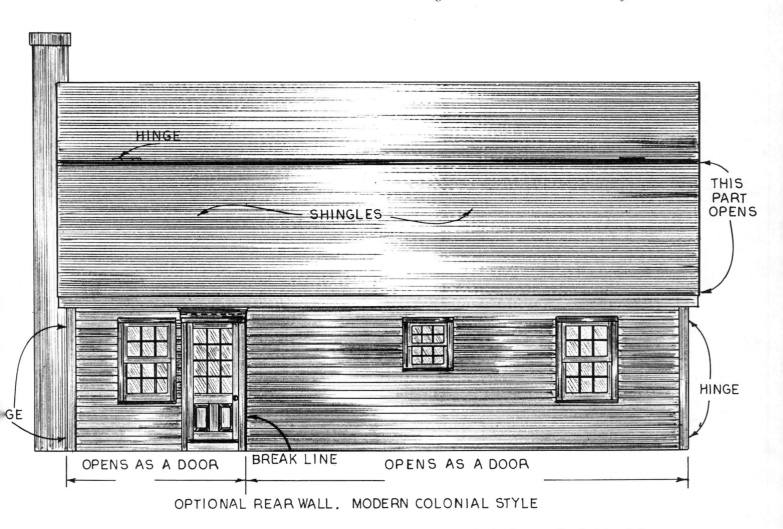

HINGE

THIS
PART
OPENS

SHINGLES

HINGE

GE

OPENS AS A DOOR   BREAK LINE   OPENS AS A DOOR

OPTIONAL REAR WALL. MODERN COLONIAL STYLE

Fig. 3–53.   Optional rear wall, colonial-style house

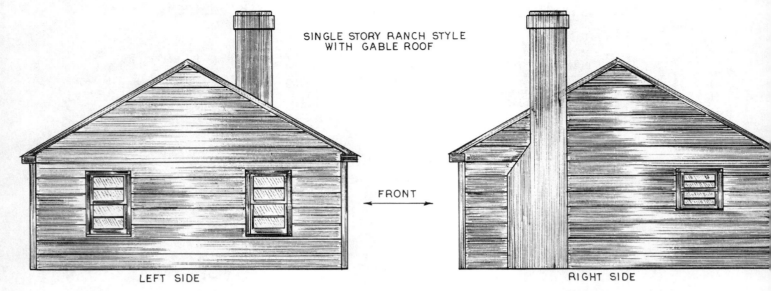

SINGLE STORY RANCH STYLE
WITH GABLE ROOF

FRONT

LEFT SIDE

RIGHT SIDE

Fig. 3–54. Side elevations, ranch-style house

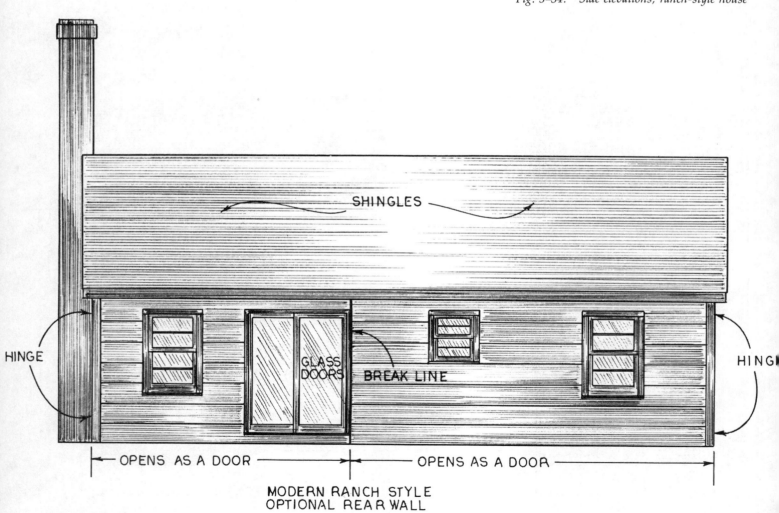

SHINGLES

HINGE

GLASS
DOORS

BREAK LINE

HINGE

OPENS AS A DOOR

OPENS AS A DOOR

MODERN RANCH STYLE
OPTIONAL REAR WALL

Fig. 3–55. Optional rear wall, ranch-style house

288

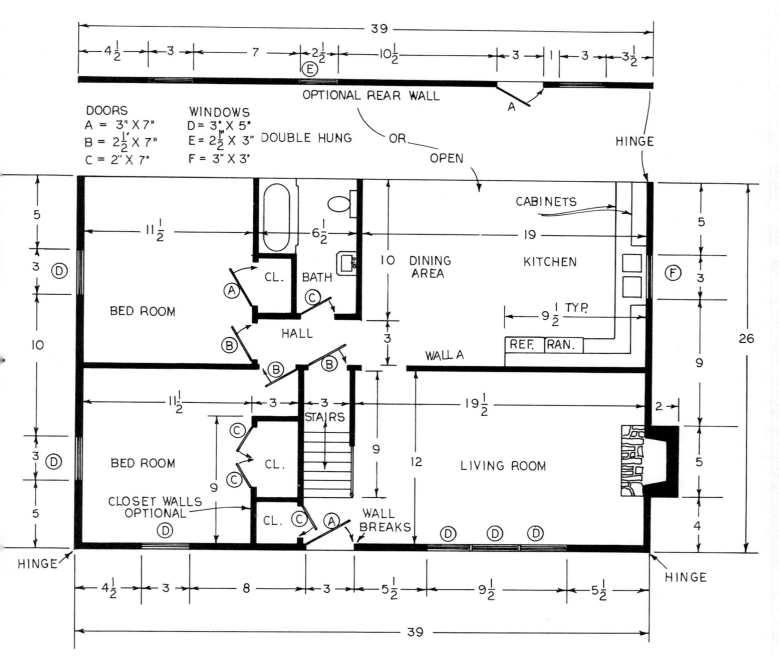

Fig. 3–56. Floor plan, colonial or ranch-style house

DOORS
A = 3" X 7"
B = 2½' X 7"
C = 2" X 7"

WINDOWS
D= 3" X 5"
E= 2½" X 3" DOUBLE HUNG
F= 3" X 3'

OPTIONAL REAR WALL

OR

OPEN

HINGE

CABINETS

BED ROOM

11½

6½

10   DINING AREA

19   KITCHEN

5

CL.

BATH

A

C

9½ TYP.

F

3

HALL

B

REF. RAN.

9

WALL A

11½

3

3

B

B

19½

2

STAIRS

C

9

CL.

9

12   LIVING ROOM

5

CLOSET WALLS OPTIONAL

BED ROOM

C

D

CL. C

A

WALL BREAKS

D   D   D

4

HINGE

HINGE

5   10   3   3   5

26   5   3   9   5   4

4½   3   8   3   5½   9½   5½

39

39   4½   3   7   2½   10½   3   1   3   3½

Sliding glass doors with jambs	1	6" x 7"
Asphalt roof shingles	1300 square inches	
Cedar shake shingles	1500	1/16" x 3/4" x 1 3/4"
Cornice/trim fireplace stock	1	3/4" x 6" x 40"

Interior

Hardwood flooring stock	1000 square inches	1/16" x random width
Interior door with jamb	1	3" x 7"
Interior doors with jambs	3	2½" x 7"

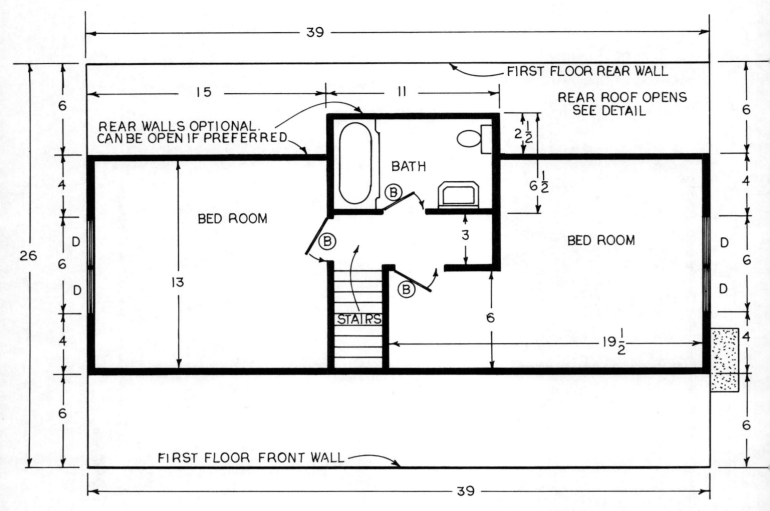

Fig. 3–57. Second-floor plan, colonial-style house

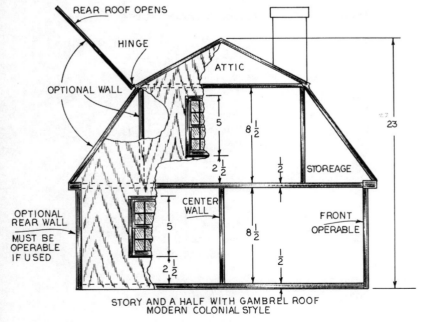

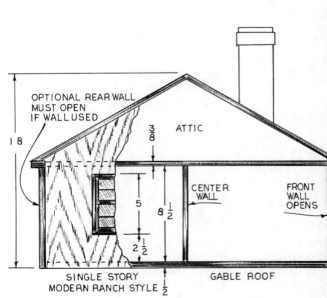

Fig. 3–58. Construction views, colonial or ranch-style house

PLYWOOD LAYOUT, MODERN COLONIAL HOUSE - GAMBREL ROOF

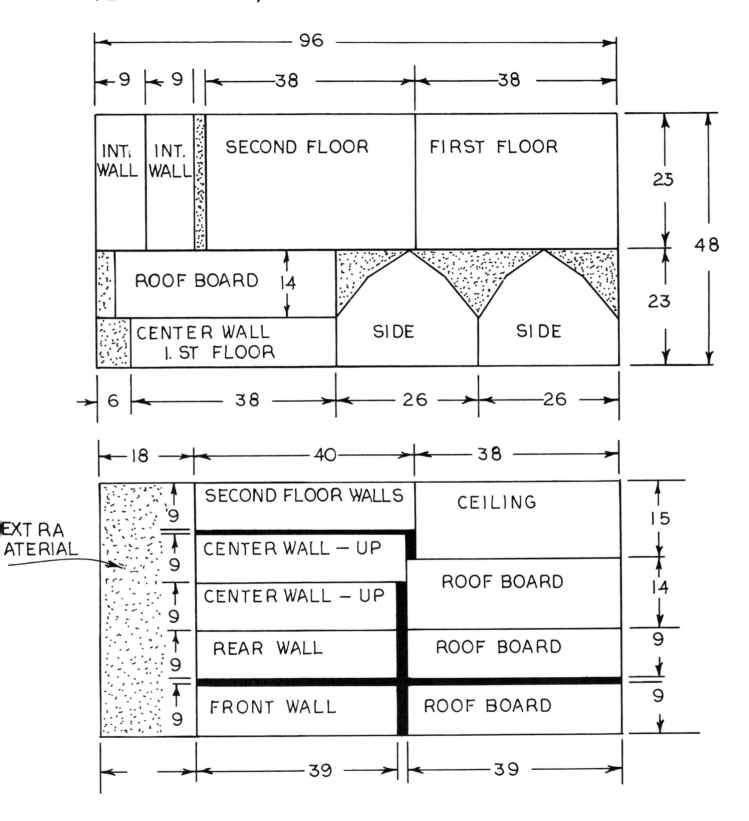

Fig. 3–59. Plywood lay-out, colonial-style house

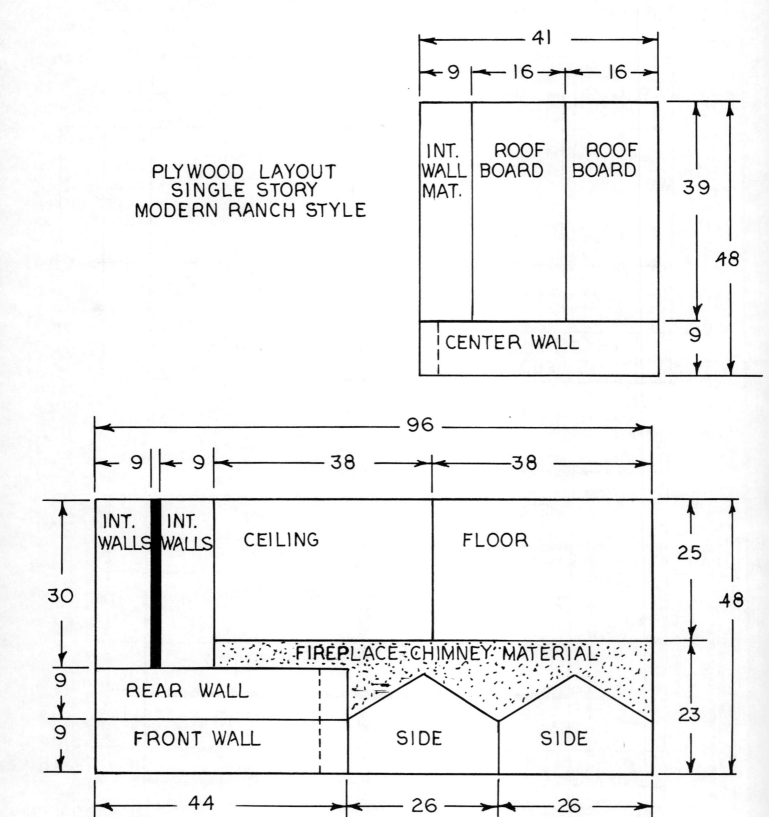

PLYWOOD LAYOUT
SINGLE STORY
MODERN RANCH STYLE

Fig. 3–60.   *Plywood lay-out, ranch-style house*

Interior doors with jambs	4	2" x 7"
Baseboard	250 lin. in.	250" x ¹/₁₆" x ⁵/₁₆"
Window casing	160 lin. in.	160" x ¹/₁₆" x ¼"
Door casing	160 lin. in.	160' x ¹/₁₆" x ⁵/₁₆"
Bathroom fixtures	1 set	
Kitchen cabinets	1 set	

Note that all the interior rooms are painted or wallpapered. The bathrooms can have scale-size wall tiles, and the kitchen and bathroom can have scale-size linoleum flooring.

Construction

The construction notes are given for the colonial-style house. The ranch-style house is exactly the same except the second floor is eliminated.

1. Study figures 3–56 through 3–60 carefully before starting. Lay out the various house walls and parts on the plywood sheets, and cut the parts to size. Roughly cut out the window and door openings in the exterior walls.

2. Lay out the interior wall locations on the floor pieces. If linoleum or tile is to be used in the bathrooms or kitchen, apply it to butt to the hardwood flooring where the interior room walls will cover the joints. Apply the hardwood flooring to the two floor pieces. Lay out and make the fireplace hearth where suggested. Stain and finish all hardwood floors at this time.

3. Install the windows and doors into the various exterior walls. Mark the exterior walls where the interior walls will join. Apply wallpaper or paint to the interior side walls to match the various rooms they will form. Nail the two side walls into the first-floor piece.

4. Install any required doors into the interior walls. If interior electrical wiring is to be used, run the various feed wires before any interior decorating. See the chapter on electrical wiring in Section one for details. Paint or paper the interior wall sections. Install the required interior walls by nailing the first floor into the walls. Paint the bottom of the second floor piece to resemble a ceiling. Nail the second-floor piece into the first-floor interior walls. Nail the side walls into the second-floor piece. Note that the front and rear walls are still open at this time.

Fig. 3–61. *Miniature kitchen cabinet set (Courtesy Scientific Models, Inc.)*

5. Make the interior fireplace unit and mantel. See figure 3–87. Install this unit in the living room. Make the open stairway and install it in place. Apply all interior casing and baseboard to all walls. The trim should be cut to size, and stained or painted before installation.

6. Make the second-floor interior walls and install any required doors into the openings. Paint or paper the various room walls. Install the second-floor interior walls in place. The rear upstairs wall is optional and can be eliminated for rear viewing and access. If a rear wall is used, it must be removable. See detail in figure 3–58.

Apply any trim or casing to the second-floor room walls. Paint the ceiling board and install it by nailing it into the second-floor interior walls. Nail the side walls into the ceiling piece.

7. Make the front and rear walls. Both walls should be hinged to operate as doors for easy access. A convenient break line would be the vertical door trim members. Paint or paper the interior side of these walls. Install any required interior trim or casing. Install the walls to the house side walls.

8. Nail the roof boards to the peaks on the side walls. Use a compatible angle support in the center of the attic area. Make and install the cornice and rake trims. See figures 3–10 and 3–11 for options. Install the exterior corner boards.

9. Apply the shingles to the roof boards. Make and install the exterior fireplace/chimney. Install the exterior siding shingles or clapboards. See figures 3–17 and 3–18 for options and application procedure. Paint or stain the exterior a color of your choice.

10. Install the interior bathroom and kitchen fixtures. Furnish the house with furniture compatible with the style selected.

19. *Victorian House*

The Victorian style was once defined as "everything overdone." Woodwork of that style featured ornate turns, scrolls, cutouts, and decorative drops. One highlight of Victorian style is simulated structural strength. In reality, the average house cornice does not require the decorative lookout supports; nor do the windows demand the heavy build-up of several tiers of thick moldings. However, without such embellishments, the style would not be Victorian.

There is no set rule or defined standard for Victorian styling. Some Victorian houses could even be called simple, such as the house described in this chapter, or it could contain the thousands of board feet of gingerbread decorations seen in figure 2. In a broad sense, Victorian styling can be applied to a small, four-room, suburban house; or it can be used on a fifty-room California mansion. Its application has been endless and examples are found all over American landscapes.

The Victorian interiors were perhaps more ornate than the exteriors. Strings of glass or wooden beads hung in doorways, while elaborate drapes covered windows. Both etched and stained glass, once confined to religious structures, were used extensively in Victorian interiors. Ferns, peacock feathers, and ostrich plumes sprang from large Greek urns, and every furnishing was an overindulgence.

If one tool could describe the Victorian period, it would be the jigsaw. But time and economy dictate change. The severe cost of Victorian styling helped hasten its demise. Today these stately, solid, baroque homes are a reminder of the late 1800s and early 1900s when times were slower, and workers could create artistry in wood and give full play to their imagination.

295

The following miniature house incorporates many features found in pure Victorian styling. It was selected because it represented a happy medium between the gingerbread extreme and the classic Gothic styling. This house retains the formal exterior balance found in early American designs, yet it offers a means to incorporate the particular features that have come to symbolize the Victorian era.

Construction

Material List

Part Exterior	Amount	Size
A.C. plywood	1³/₅ sheets	¹/₂″ or ³/₈″
Double-hung windows*	10	2⁹/₁₆″ x 5″

Stained-glass window and jamb	1	2½″ x 2″	Cornice crown molding	6	½″ x 30″
Bay window	1	5″ x 7″	Cornice cove molding	6	5/16″ x 30″
Exterior door, etched glass	1	3″ x 7″	Copper foil, porch roof	1	8″ x 33″
Interior doors with jambs	7	3″ x 7″	Porch floor, ceiling	2	¾″ x 8″ x 30″
Clapboard	250 linear feet	1/16″ x ¾″	Chimney stock	1	¾″ x 8″ x 30″
Wood shingles	3000	1/16″ x ¾″ x 1¾″			
Cornice/trim stock	1	¾″ x 8″ x 48″			

Stained-glass window and jamb — 1 — 2½″ x 2″
Bay window — 1 — 5″ x 7″
Exterior door, etched glass — 1 — 3″ x 7″
Interior doors with jambs — 7 — 3″ x 7″
Clapboard — 250 linear feet — 1/16″ x ¾″
Wood shingles — 3000 — 1/16″ x ¾″ x 1¾″
Cornice/trim stock — 1 — ¾″ x 8″ x 48″

Cornice crown molding — 6 — ½″ x 30″
Cornice cove molding — 6 — 5/16″ x 30″
Copper foil, porch roof — 1 — 8″ x 33″
Porch floor, ceiling — 2 — ¾″ x 8″ x 30″
Chimney stock — 1 — ¾″ x 8″ x 30″

*Window sizes can be larger or smaller, if preferred. If a change in size is made, a similar change must be made in the placement and rough openings in the house walls.

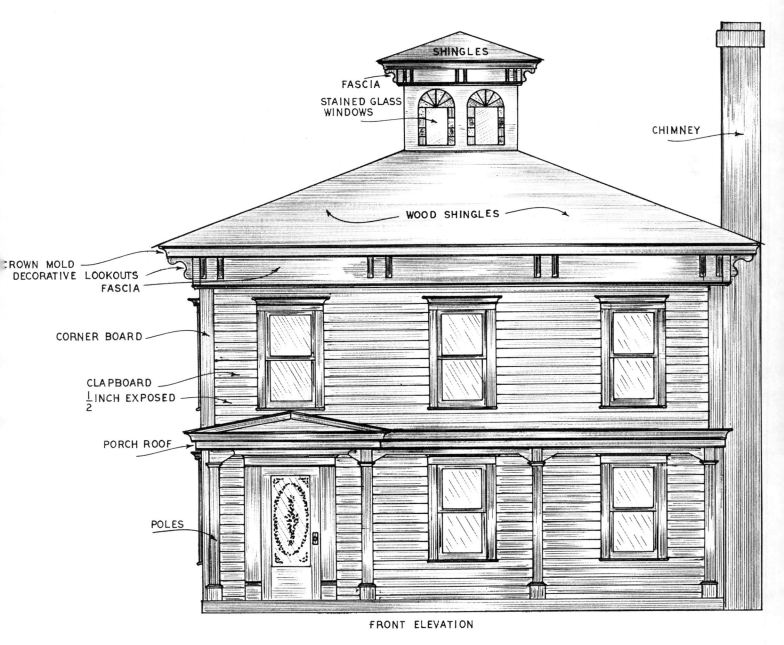

FRONT ELEVATION

Fig. 3–63. Front elevation

297

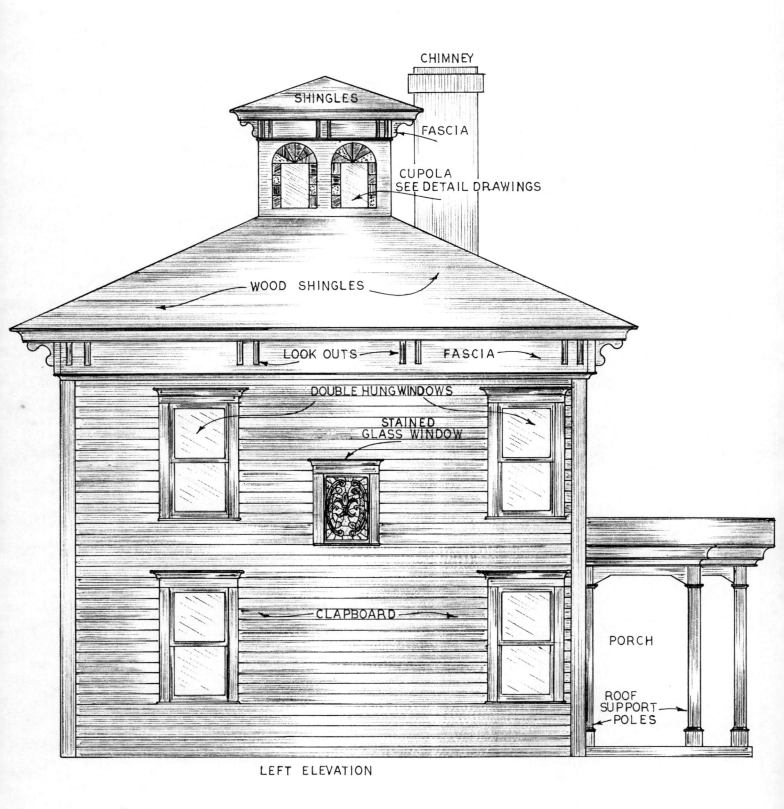

CHIMNEY

SHINGLES

FASCIA

CUPOLA
SEE DETAIL DRAWINGS

WOOD SHINGLES

LOOK OUTS   FASCIA

DOUBLE HUNG WINDOWS

STAINED
GLASS WINDOW

CLAPBOARD

PORCH

ROOF
SUPPORT
POLES

LEFT ELEVATION

Fig. 3–64. Left elevation

298

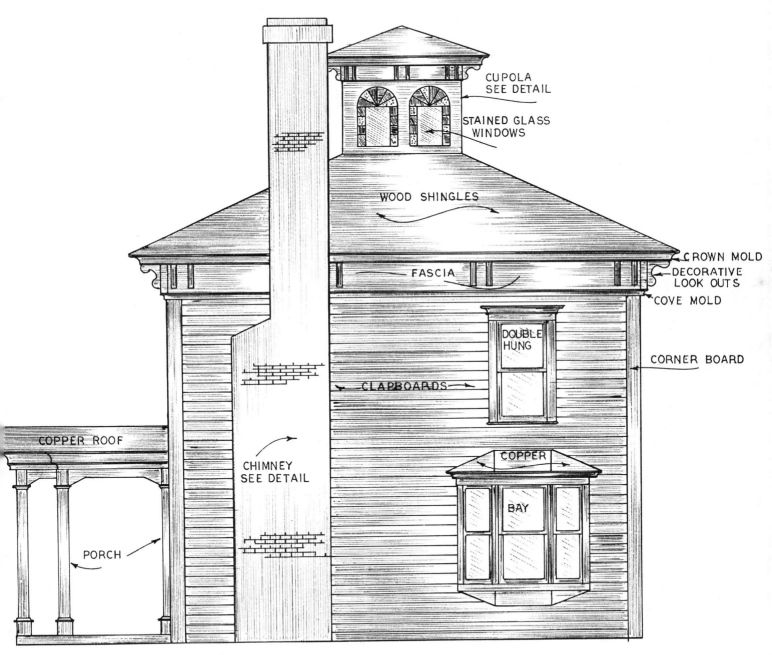

CUPOLA
SEE DETAIL

STAINED GLASS
WINDOWS

WOOD SHINGLES

CROWN MOLD

DECORATIVE
LOOK OUTS

FASCIA

COVE MOLD

DOUBLE
HUNG

CORNER BOARD

CLAPBOARDS

COPPER ROOF

COPPER

CHIMNEY
SEE DETAIL

BAY

PORCH

RIGHT ELEVATION

Fig. 3–65. Right elevation

299

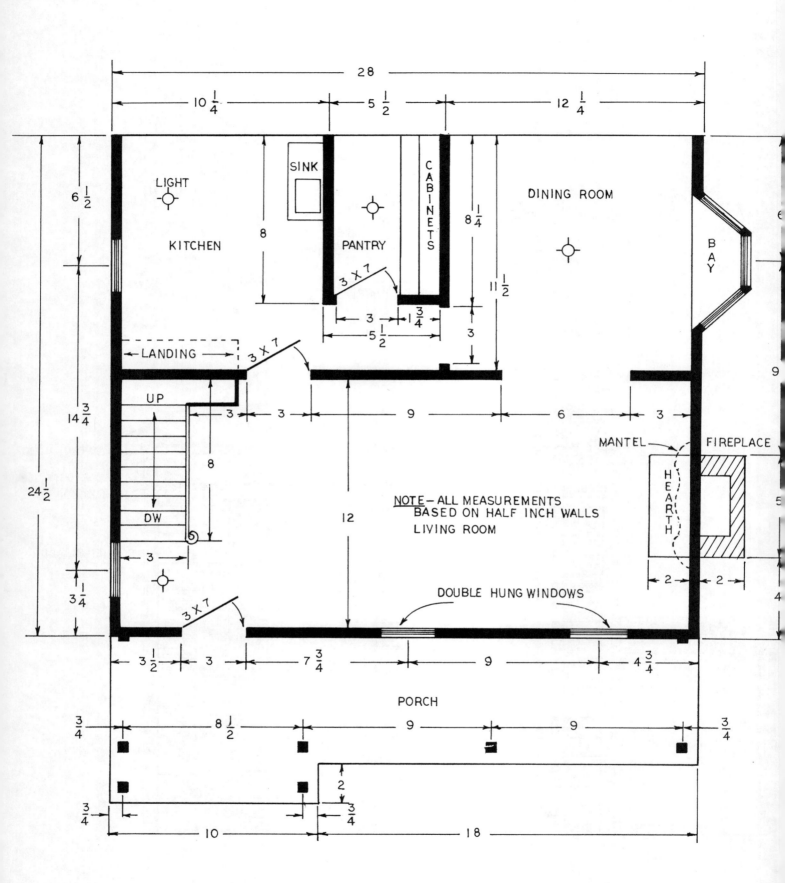

Fig. 3–66.   First-floor plan

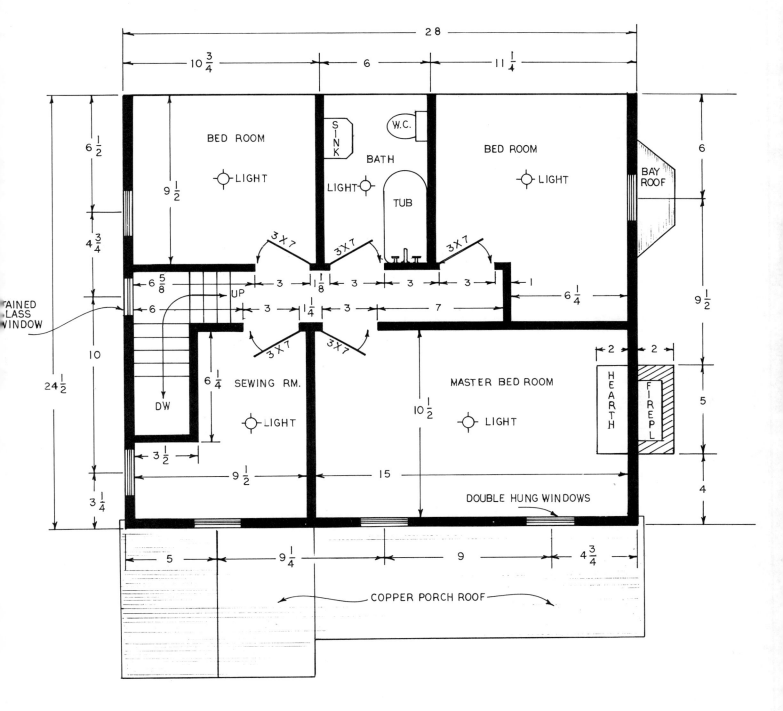

Fig. 3-67. Second-floor plan

301

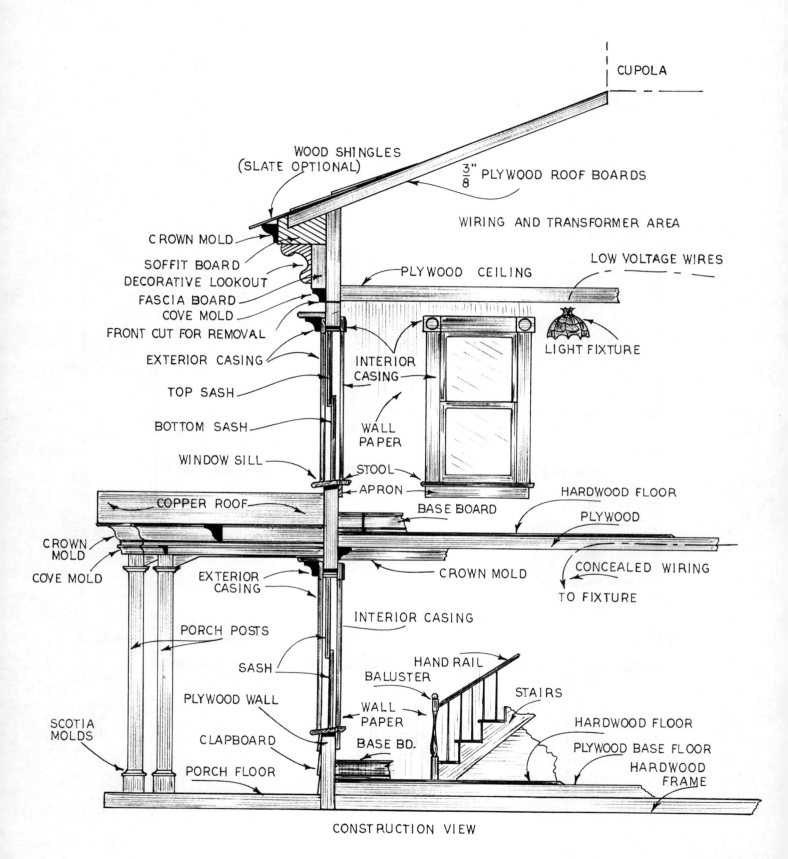

CUPOLA

WOOD SHINGLES
(SLATE OPTIONAL)

$\frac{3}{8}$" PLYWOOD ROOF BOARDS

WIRING AND TRANSFORMER AREA

CROWN MOLD

PLYWOOD CEILING

LOW VOLTAGE WIRES

SOFFIT BOARD

DECORATIVE LOOKOUT

FASCIA BOARD

COVE MOLD

FRONT CUT FOR REMOVAL

EXTERIOR CASING

INTERIOR
CASING

LIGHT FIXTURE

TOP SASH

BOTTOM SASH

WALL
PAPER

WINDOW SILL

STOOL

APRON

HARDWOOD FLOOR

PLYWOOD

BASE BOARD

COPPER ROOF

CROWN
MOLD

COVE MOLD

CROWN MOLD

CONCEALED WIRING

EXTERIOR
CASING

TO FIXTURE

INTERIOR CASING

PORCH POSTS

SASH

HAND RAIL

BALUSTER

STAIRS

SCOTIA
MOLDS

PLYWOOD WALL

WALL
PAPER

HARDWOOD FLOOR

CLAPBOARD

BASE BD.

PLYWOOD BASE FLOOR

PORCH FLOOR

HARDWOOD
FRAME

CONSTRUCTION VIEW

Fig. 3–68. Construction plan

302

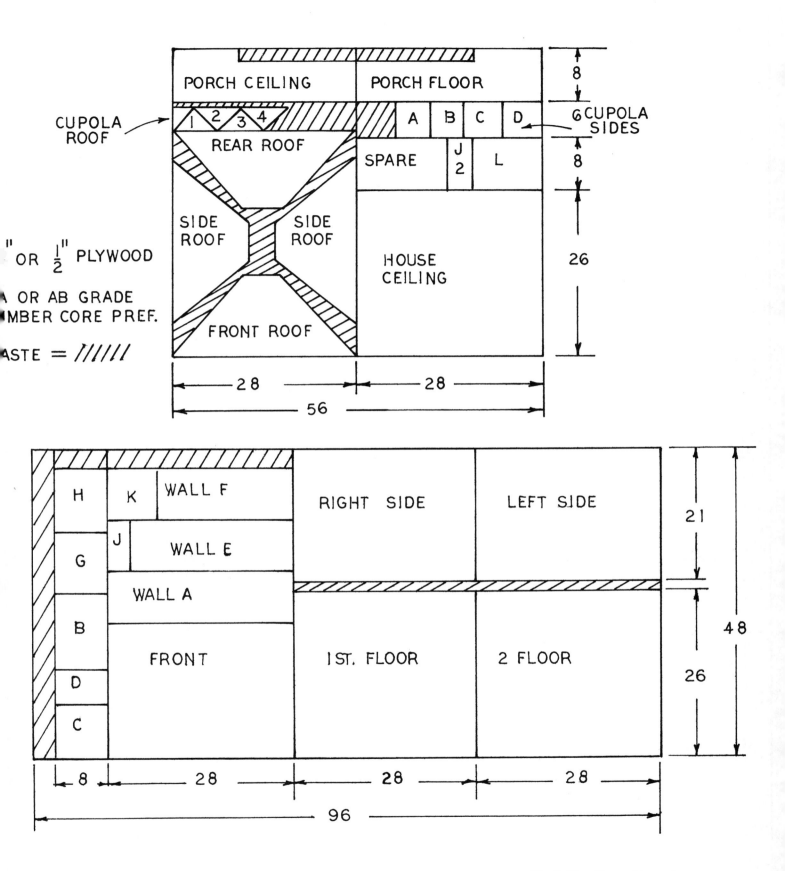

Fig. 3–69. Plywood lay-out

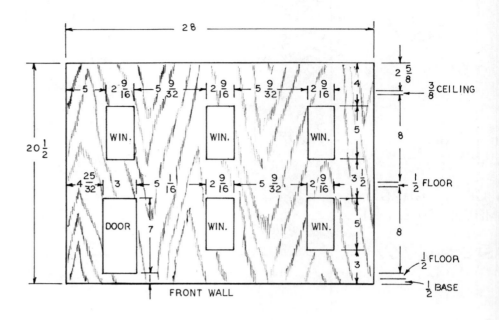

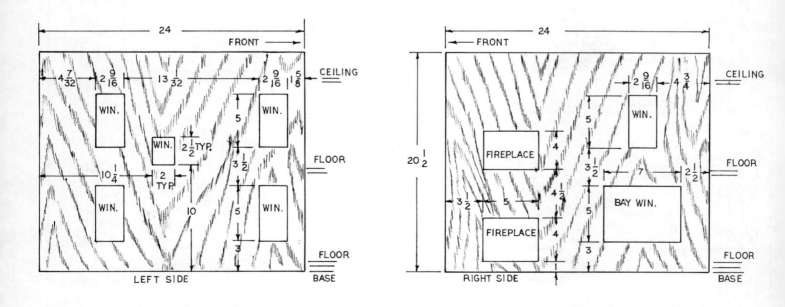

Fig. 3–70.   Lay-out of exterior wall opening

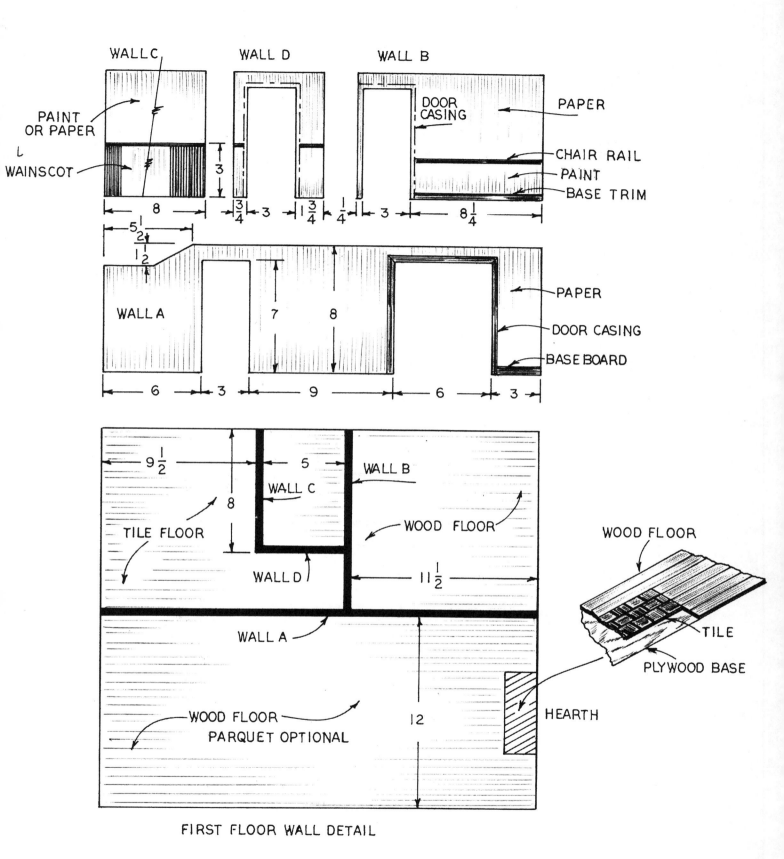

WALL C

PAINT OR PAPER

L WAINSCOT

3

8

WALL D

3/4 — 3 — 1 3/4 — 1/4 — 3

WALL B

DOOR CASING

PAPER

CHAIR RAIL

PAINT

BASE TRIM

8 1/4

5 1/2

1 1/2

WALL A

7

8

PAPER

DOOR CASING

BASEBOARD

6 — 3 — 9 — 6 — 3

9 1/2

8

5

WALL C

WALL B

WALL D

WALL A

TILE FLOOR

WOOD FLOOR

11 1/2

12

WOOD FLOOR PARQUET OPTIONAL

HEARTH

WOOD FLOOR

TILE

PLYWOOD BASE

FIRST FLOOR WALL DETAIL

Fig. 3–71. First-floor interior wall lay-out

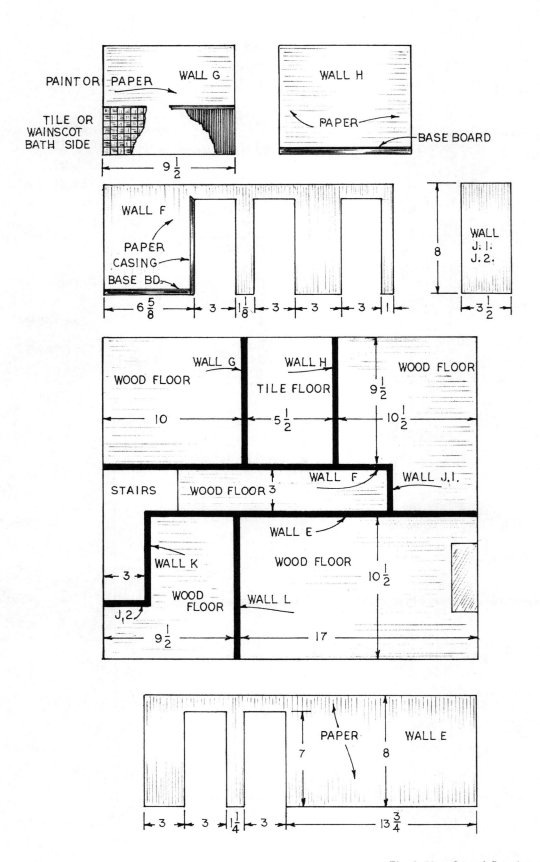

PAINT OR PAPER — WALL G

TILE OR
WAINSCOT
BATH SIDE

$9\frac{1}{2}$

WALL H

PAPER

BASE BOARD

WALL F

PAPER
CASING
BASE BD.

$6\frac{5}{8}$ 3 $1\frac{1}{8}$ 3   3   3   1

WALL
J. I.
J. 2.

8

$3\frac{1}{2}$

WOOD FLOOR   WALL G   WALL H   WOOD FLOOR

TILE FLOOR $9\frac{1}{2}$

10   $5\frac{1}{2}$ $10\frac{1}{2}$

STAIRS   WOOD FLOOR 3   WALL F   WALL J.I.

WALL E

WALL K

3   WALL L   WOOD FLOOR $10\frac{1}{2}$

J, 2.   WOOD
FLOOR

$9\frac{1}{2}$ 17

PAPER   WALL E

7   8

3   3 $1\frac{1}{4}$ 3 $13\frac{3}{4}$

Fig. 3–72.   Second-floor interior wall lay-out

306

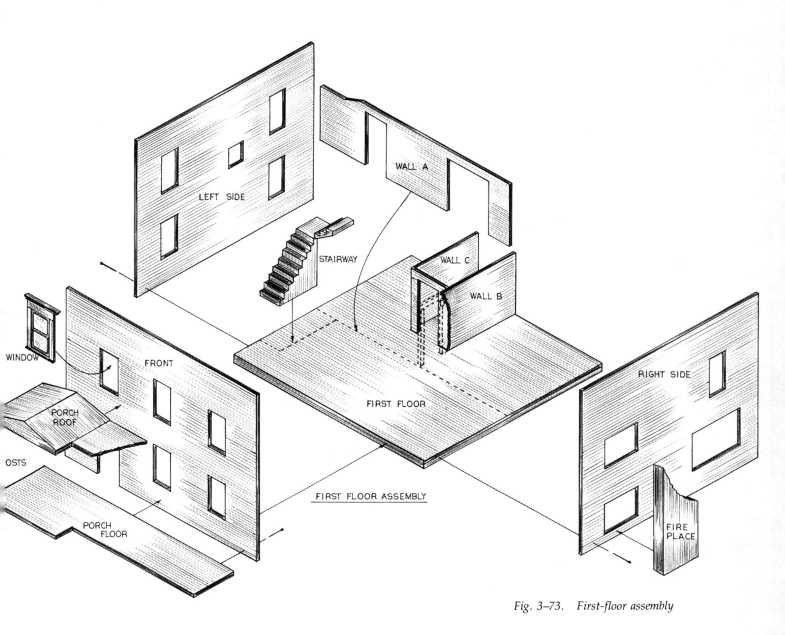

Fig. 3–73. First-floor assembly

Interior		
Baseboard		350″ x ¹/₁₆″ x ⅝″
Window casing		200″ x ¹/₁₆″ x ½″
Door casing		150″ x ¹/₁₆″ x ½″
Ceiling crown		
molding		350″ x ⅜″ x 30″
Scale-size		
kitchen floor		
linoleum	80 square inches	
Hardwood	1275 square	¹/₁₆″ x random
flooring	inches	width
Stairway stock	1	¾″ x 4″ x 24″
Stair balusters	18	¹/₁₆″ x 3″
Newel post	1	³/₁₆″ x 3″

Fireplace fronts
and mantels
(see Fig. 3–89.)
Victorian
bathroom
fixtures   1
Victorian kitchen
sink/cabinet   1
Victorian pantry
cabinets   1

Notes on Interior Finish

The living room, bedrooms, and the dining

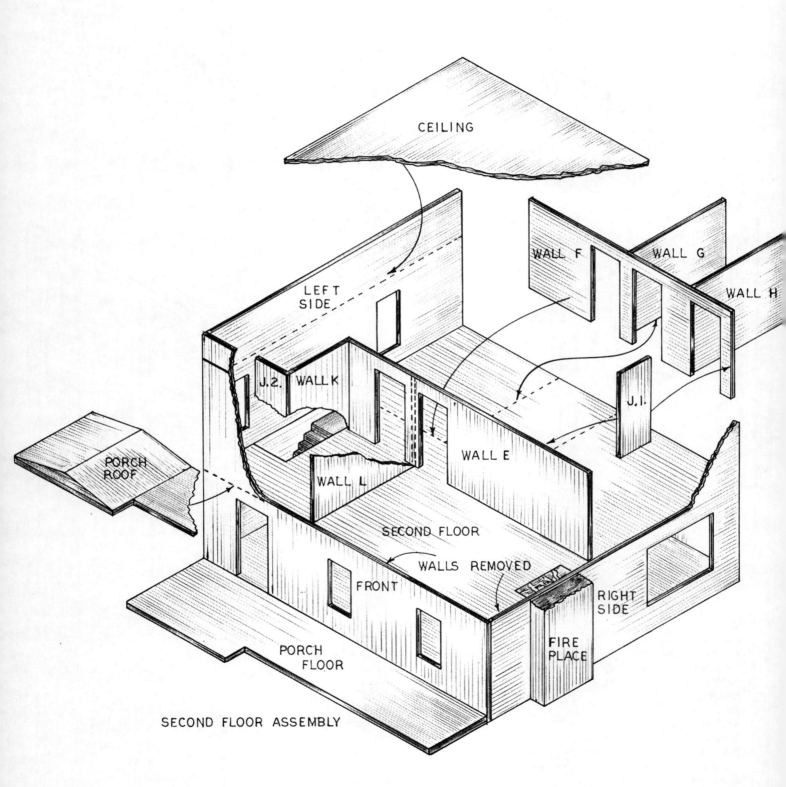

CEILING

WALL F

WALL G

WALL H

LEFT
SIDE

J.2. WALL K

J.1.

PORCH
ROOF

WALL E

WALL L

SECOND FLOOR

WALLS REMOVED

FRONT

RIGHT
SIDE

FIRE
PLACE

PORCH
FLOOR

SECOND FLOOR ASSEMBLY

Fig. 3–74. Second-floor assembly

Fig. 3–75.   *First floor completed and marked (Note tiled hearth and linoleum in kitchen)*

Fig. 3–76.   *Electrical feed wires in second-floor piece (Note exit wires at fireplace openings)*

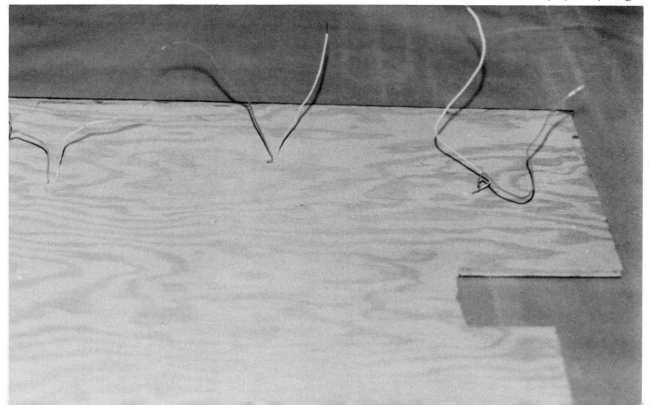

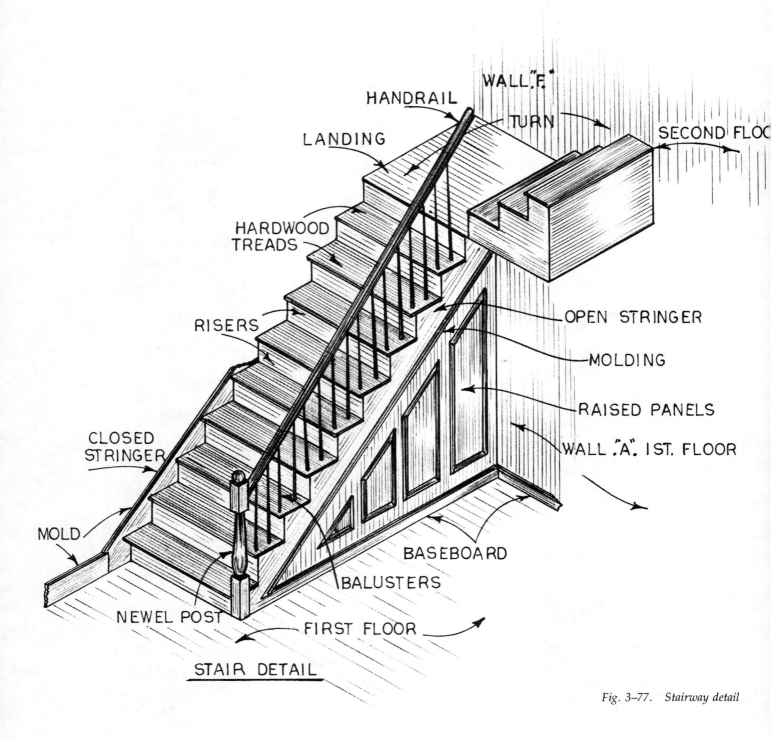

HANDRAIL

WALL "F."

LANDING

TURN

SECOND FLOO

HARDWOOD
TREADS

RISERS

OPEN STRINGER

MOLDING

RAISED PANELS

CLOSED
STRINGER

WALL "A". IST. FLOOR

MOLD

BASEBOARD

BALUSTERS

NEWEL POST

FIRST FLOOR

STAIR DETAIL

Fig. 3–77. Stairway detail

rooms are wallpapered. The bathroom has 4-inch-high tile walls and wallpaper above the tile line. Tile can also be used for the bathroom floor. The kitchen and pantry have wainscotting 3 inches high and painted walls above. Each room has an overhead light fixture with feed wires in the second floor and ceiling pieces. Wiring connections are made in the chimney void. A transformer can be placed in

the attic area under the cupola for ventilation. Ceilings are painted white. All woodwork is painted glossy white. Wainscotting can be stained to a color of your choice.

1. Study figures 3–63 through 3–74 before starting work. The windows and door sizes are suggestions only. Larger or smaller units can be used. However, adjust your rough opening cuts to accommodate any change in sizes. Be-

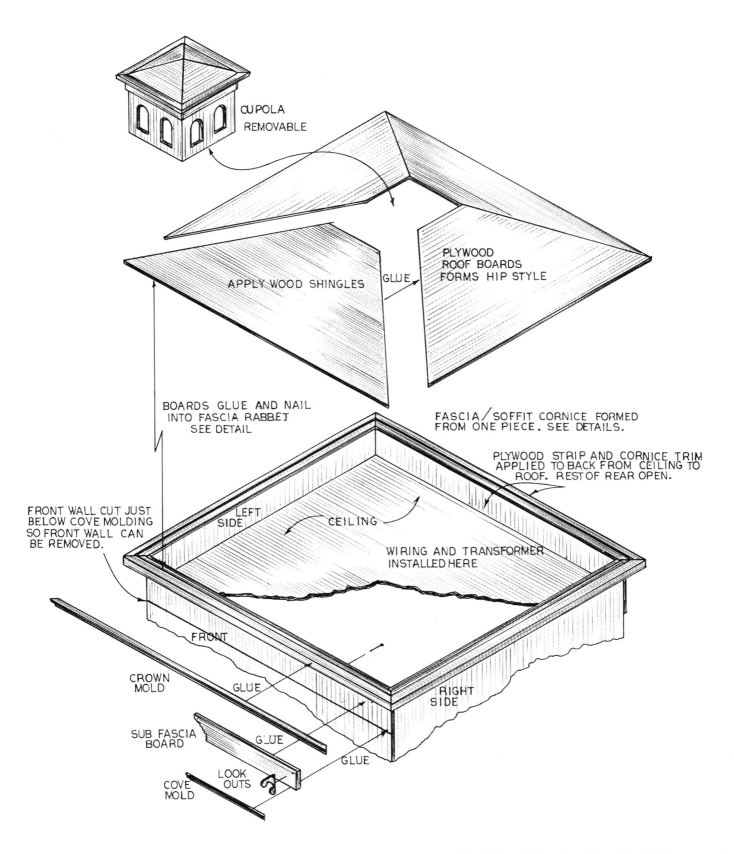

CUPOLA REMOVABLE

PLYWOOD ROOF BOARDS FORMS HIP STYLE

APPLY WOOD SHINGLES

GLUE

BOARDS GLUE AND NAIL INTO FASCIA RABBET SEE DETAIL

FASCIA/SOFFIT CORNICE FORMED FROM ONE PIECE. SEE DETAILS.

PLYWOOD STRIP AND CORNICE TRIM APPLIED TO BACK FROM CEILING TO ROOF. REST OF REAR OPEN.

FRONT WALL CUT JUST BELOW COVE MOLDING SO FRONT WALL CAN BE REMOVED.

LEFT SIDE

CEILING

WIRING AND TRANSFORMER INSTALLED HERE

FRONT

RIGHT SIDE

CROWN MOLD

GLUE

SUB FASCIA BOARD

GLUE

GLUE

COVE MOLD

LOOK OUTS

Fig. 3–78. Attic and roof assembly detail

311

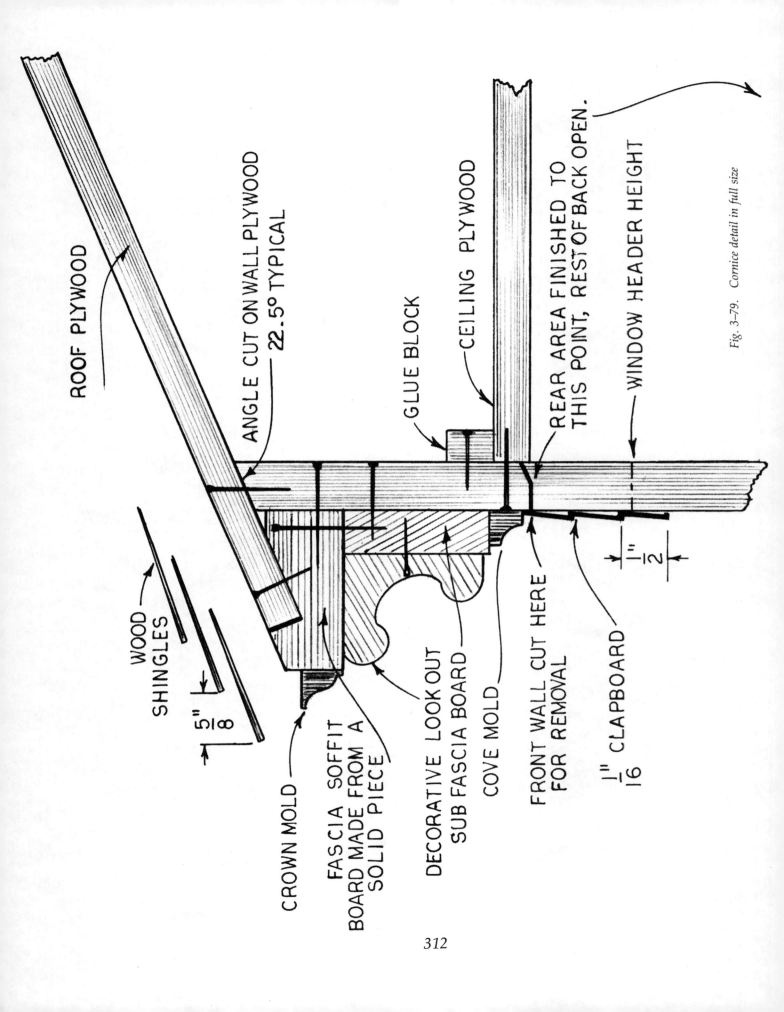

ROOF PLYWOOD

WOOD SHINGLES

$\frac{5"}{8}$

CROWN MOLD

FASCIA SOFFIT BOARD MADE FROM A SOLID PIECE

ANGLE CUT ON WALL PLYWOOD 22.5° TYPICAL

GLUE BLOCK

CEILING PLYWOOD

DECORATIVE LOOK OUT SUB FASCIA BOARD

COVE MOLD

FRONT WALL CUT HERE FOR REMOVAL

REAR AREA FINISHED TO THIS POINT, REST OF BACK OPEN.

WINDOW HEADER HEIGHT

$\frac{1"}{2}$

$\frac{1"}{16}$ CLAPBOARD

Fig. 3-79. Cornice detail in full size

312

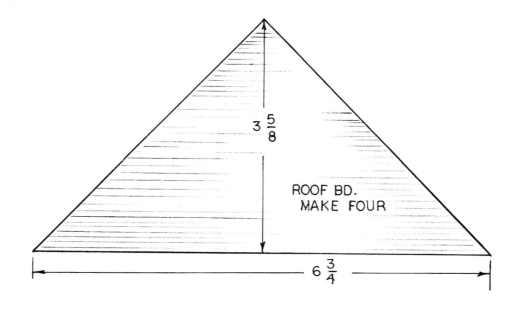

ROOF BD.
MAKE FOUR

$3\frac{5}{8}$

$6\frac{3}{4}$

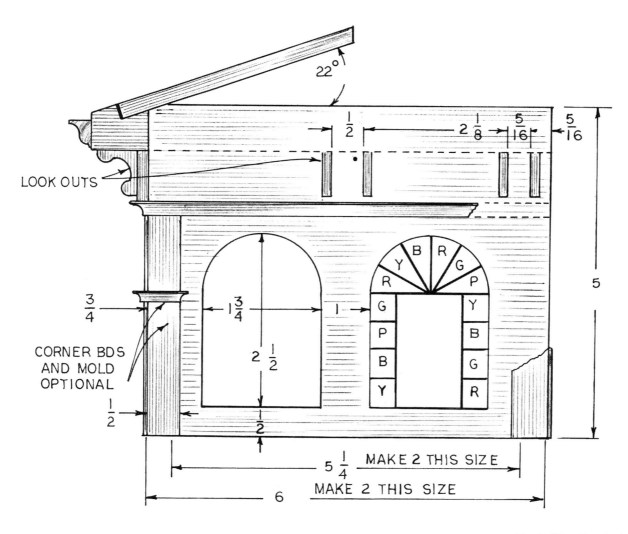

22°

LOOK OUTS

$\frac{1}{2}$ $2\frac{1}{8}$ $\frac{5}{16}$ $\frac{5}{16}$

$\frac{3}{4}$

CORNER BDS
AND MOLD
OPTIONAL

$\frac{1}{2}$

$1\frac{3}{4}$ 1

$2\frac{1}{2}$

$\frac{1}{2}$

5

Y B R G
R P
G Y
P B
B G
Y R

$5\frac{1}{4}$ MAKE 2 THIS SIZE

MAKE 2 THIS SIZE

6

Fig. 3–80.   Cupola detail

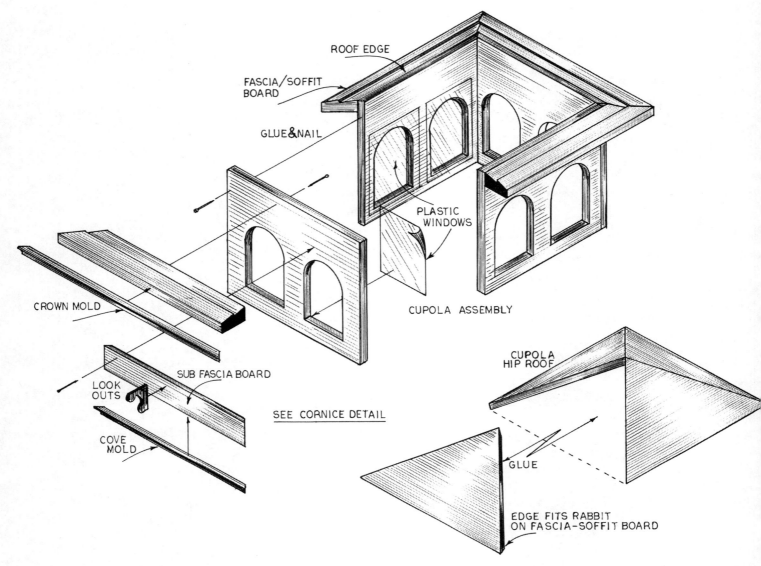

ROOF EDGE

FASCIA/SOFFIT
BOARD

GLUE&NAIL

PLASTIC
WINDOWS

CROWN MOLD

CUPOLA ASSEMBLY

LOOK
OUTS

SUB FASCIA BOARD

SEE CORNICE DETAIL

COVE
MOLD

CUPOLA
HIP ROOF

GLUE

EDGE FITS RABBIT
ON FASCIA–SOFFIT BOARD

Fig. 3–81. Cupola assembly

fore construction begins, have your window and door units made or purchased. If adjustments have to be made due to manufacturer's variances, they can be so marked on the plywood stock.

Lay out the various parts on the plywood sheets. Check all layouts for squareness. Cut out the suggested parts and mark each section. Roughly cut out the required openings in the exterior and interior walls.

2. Mark out on the first-floor and second-floor pieces where the walls of the various room will go. Mark the second-floor piece for

the location of the first-floor overhead lights. With a router, plow out the wire-feed troughs to supply the overhead lights. Make the feed wires exit at the chimney openings; the electrical connections can be made within the fireplace chimneys. The second-floor hardwood flooring will cover the low-voltage feed wire troughs.

3. Install the hardwood floors for the various rooms. See Section one for details. Make and install the required fireplace hearths. Install linoleum and tile in the kitchen, pantry, and bathroom floor areas. See figure 3–75.

Stain and finish the hardwood floors. Paint the bottom of the second-floor piece to resemble a ceiling.

4. Install the door and window units into the exterior wall pieces. Mark the place on the exterior walls where the interior walls and the second floor and ceiling will join. Paint or paper these wall units for the various rooms they will form. For example, the right-side wall will be divided into the living room on one lower end, and the dining room on the other lower end. This same piece will have two different bedroom wallpapers on the top half. See figure 3–66.

5. Install the interior window casings where required. Paint this trim before installation with a final coat given after assembly. Install the optional crown ceiling moldings at the second floor and ceiling lines. See construction view, figure 3–68. Nail the side wall pieces into the first-floor piece.

6. Make the first-floor interior walls. See figure 3–71. Install any doors. Paint or paper these walls to resemble the rooms they will form. For example: wall A will have living-room paper on the front side and kitchen wainscotting and dining-room paper on the back side. See figure 3–66. Once completed, install the finished interior walls in place. Nail the first-floor piece into the wall units. Install the finished second-floor piece into place. Nail the second-floor piece into the first-floor interior walls, and nail the side walls into the second-floor stock. At this stage, the front and rear walls are still open.

7. Make and install the open stairway. See

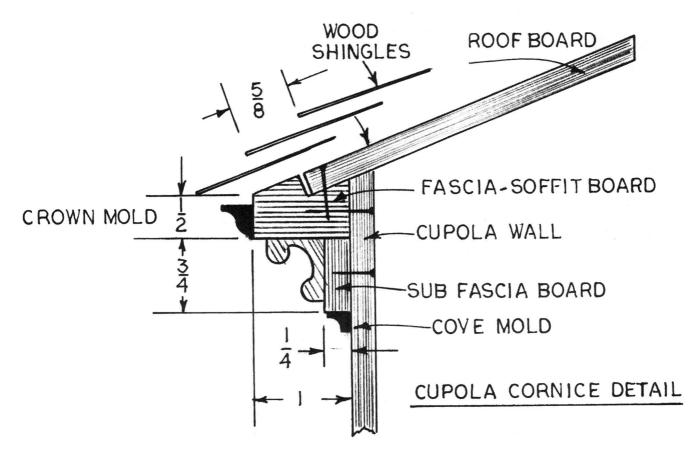

Fig. 3–82. *Cupola cornice and roof detail in full size*

Fig. 3–83. Finished scale-size cupola

Section one for shopmade units and Section four for commercial stairs. See figure 3–66 for location.

8. Make the second-floor interior walls. Paper these walls to resemble the rooms they will form. Install any doors required. Install the second-floor interior walls by nailing the side walls into the interior pieces. Install the interior baseboards in all rooms formed on both the first and second floors. Paint the ceiling piece and install it by nailing it into the second-floor interior walls. Nail the house side walls into the ceiling board. Finish all interior trim at this point. The front wall will be finished as a separate unit, and there is no rear wall except a small head piece over the second-floor ceiling.

9. Add a strip of wood long enough to run from the bottom of the ceiling board up to the top of the side wall pieces in both the house front and rear. See figure 3–68 for detail and placement. Note that the complete cornice work is secured to these strips, and the front wall butts under this strip. Figure 3–78 shows where the front and rear attic strips are added. This strip is the only enclosure on the rear wall and also serves as the break line for the removable front wall.

10. Cut the solid cornice boards. See figure 3–79 for suggested size and shape. Note that the cornice board is rabbeted to receive the roof board ends. Attach the finished cornice boards to the front and rear strips and to the side walls with miter joints on the exterior corners. Cut the four hip-roof boards. Make the meeting angles compatible with the hip-style joints that occur on all four pieces. (Note that the roof top

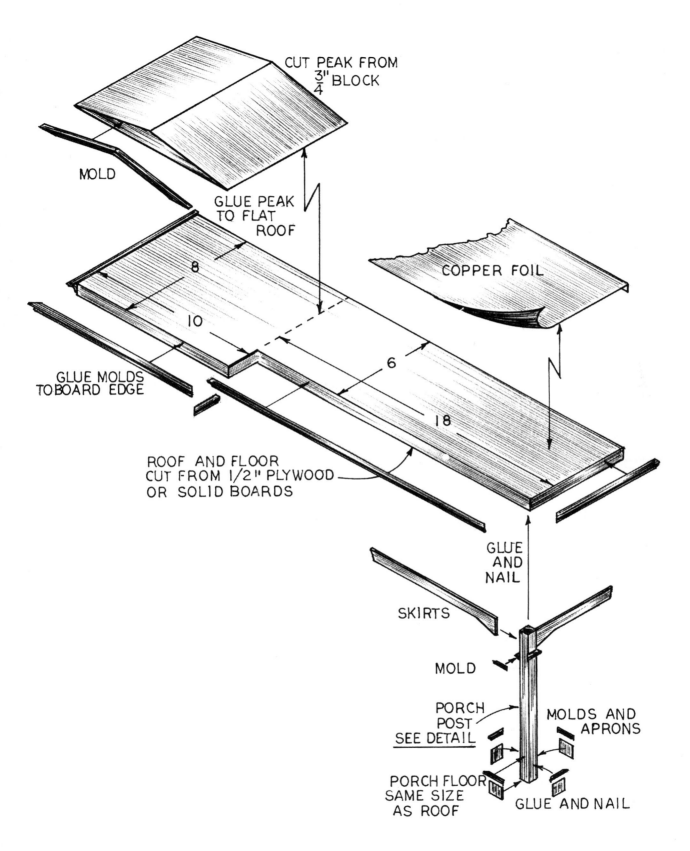

CUT PEAK FROM
$\frac{3}{4}$" BLOCK

MOLD

GLUE PEAK
TO FLAT
ROOF

COPPER FOIL

8

10

6

18

GLUE MOLDS
TO BOARD EDGE

ROOF AND FLOOR
CUT FROM 1/2" PLYWOOD
OR SOLID BOARDS

GLUE
AND
NAIL

SKIRTS

MOLD

PORCH
POST
SEE DETAIL

MOLDS AND
APRONS

PORCH FLOOR
SAME SIZE
AS ROOF

GLUE AND NAIL

Fig. 3–84.   Porch assembly detail

317

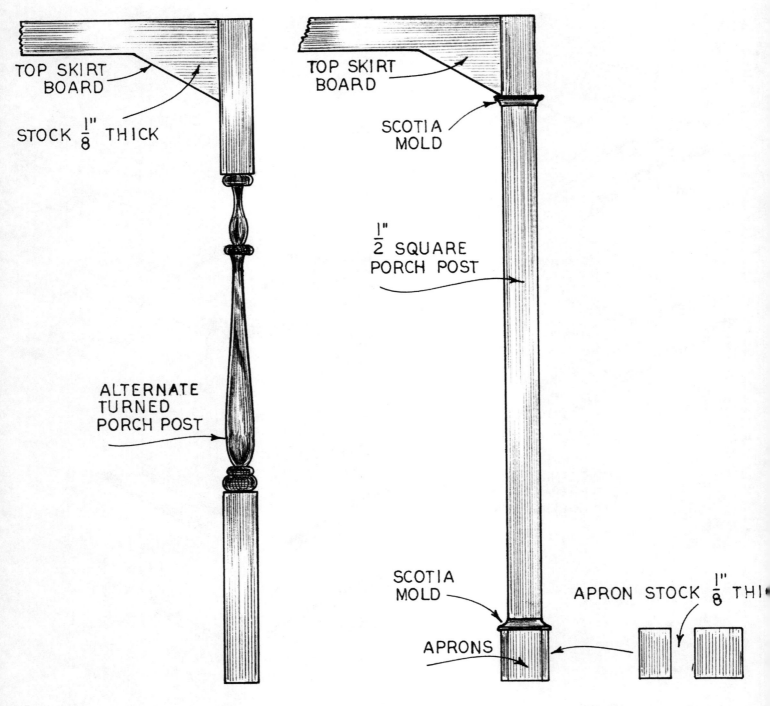

TOP SKIRT BOARD

STOCK $\frac{1}{8}$" THICK

ALTERNATE TURNED PORCH POST

TOP SKIRT BOARD

SCOTIA MOLD

$\frac{1}{2}$" SQUARE PORCH POST

SCOTIA MOLD

APRONS

APRON STOCK $\frac{1}{8}$" THI

Fig. 3–85. Porch post options

is truncated in order to receive the removable cupola.) Glue and nail the finished roof boards into the premade rabbets on the cornice boards and to each other. See assembly details in figure 3–78.

11. Make and install a ½-inch by 1½-inch sub-fascia board just under the solid cornice stock. Make and install the decorative lookouts between the cornice board and the sub-fascia board. See figure 3–79 for shape and size. See figures 3–63 through 3–65 for spacing and locations.

12. Install a crown molding to the front of the solid cornice board. The top edge of this molding must be in line with the roof slope so that the roof shingles will attach in a straight continuous line.

13. Make and install the wooden roof shingles. The shingles should be flush with the cupola seat on the top of the main roof. Install a cove molding under the sub-fascia board. See details in figure 3–79.

14. Cut out the cupola parts and make the suggested cupola. Cut out the window openings. Make exterior casing to frame these windows. (Palladian-type commercial windows can be used in the cupola, if preferred. See Section four for sources.) Cover the window openings with heavy plastic sheet stock or single-strength window glass. Draw or paint in the stained-glass pane lines in flat black. Paint the various window panes in stained-glass colors. Commercial staining-glass paints are available in most hobby outlets. Install the finished stained-glass window sheets over the premade openings. Install the casing frames over the window areas.

15. Cut and install the solid cornice board as shown in figure 3–82 on the cupola sides. The cornice boards will have a rabbet to receive the plywood roof board ends. Miter the exterior corners. Cut out and install the cupola roof boards into the cornice rabbets. Install a ¼-inch by ¾-inch sub-fascia board under the cornice board. Cut out and install the decorative lookouts between the two pieces. See figure 3–80 for locations and figure 3–82 for suggested shape and size.

16. Install a crown molding to the cornice stock and a cove molding between the sub-

Fig. 3–86. Porch unit

fascia bottom and the cupola sides. Install wood or fish-scale shingles to the roof boards. Install corner boards to the cupola sides. See figure 3–80 for suggested size.

17. Paint the entire cupola bright white. Or, the cupola's side walls can be covered with clapboard or fish-scale shingles. If the cupola is finished with clapboard or shingles, the corners of such finishing can be mitered, or corner boards can be used. Also, a weather vane can be made for the cupola top from paper clip wire.

18. The finished cupola sits upon the main roof. Install the cupola with dowel tenons on the bottom; in this way, the cupola can be removed easily in order to gain access to the low-voltage transformer and the wire connections in the attic space.

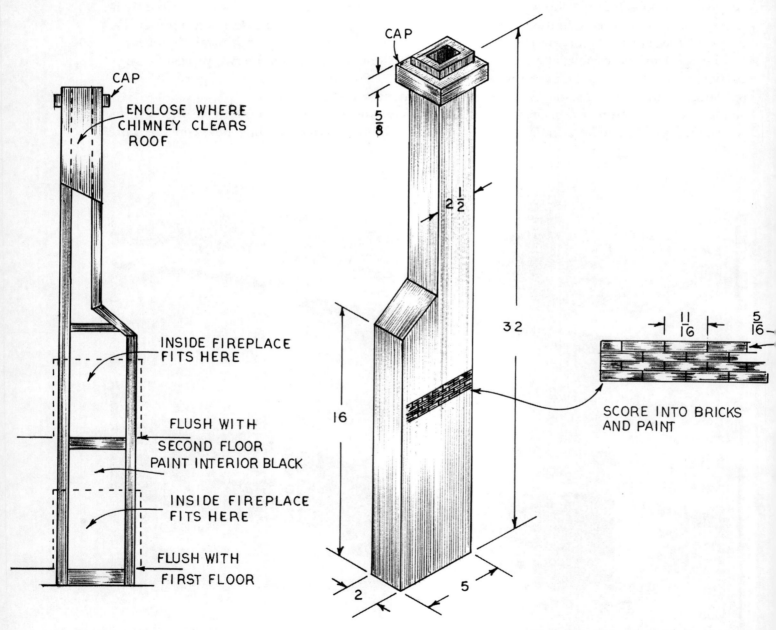

Fig. 3–87. Chimney construction details

320

19. Now you are ready to construct the porch. The porch runs completely across the house front. Cut out the stock for the porch floor and roof. The floor piece is scored to resemble flooring boards or covered with hardwood scale-size floor material. Mark the location of the porch posts. See figures 3–66 and 3–67 for locations.

The porch roof is made from two boards. A small peaked board is glued to the main ceiling board to create the roof line desired. A crown molding is secured to the fascia and rake trim edges of this assembly. Paint the complete ceiling, moldings, and cornice bright white. Mark the porch ceiling for the post-top locations. See figure 3–66.

20. Make the required number of porch posts. Figure 3–85 gives possible options for these parts. Secure the porch floor and ceiling to the posts. This makes the porch a complete assembly, which is then attached to the house front wall as a unit. Cover the porch roof with copper foil. Line up the porch to the front wall piece, and nail the front piece into both the floor and ceiling stock before finishing the interior of this wall.

21. The exterior chimney is made from clear, knot-free, solid stock. See figure 3–87 for size and design. Cut out and make the chimney as suggested. Score the boards to resemble bricks. Paint the entire unit battleship grey and allow it to dry. With a rubber-sponge paintbrush, paint the chimney brick red. The rubber-sponge brush is so stiff that it will not paint in the scoring lines. The lines remain grey to resemble mortar lines.

22. Line up the chimney with the right-side wall location. This chimney must be in line with the rough openings made in the side wall for the fireplaces. Note that the house cornice and sub-fascia boards require cutting in order for the chimney to fit flush to the side wall.

23. The fireplace and mantels are the next task. The living-room fireplace has a simulated marble face. This marble style can be achieved by several means: scale-size marble contact

Fig. 3–88. Miniature chimney ready for installation

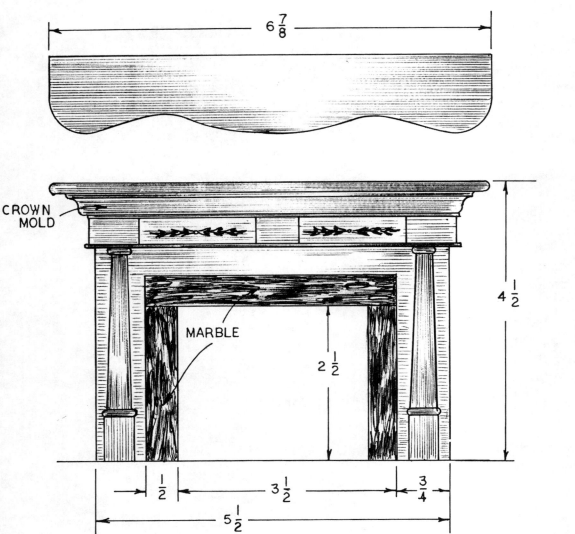

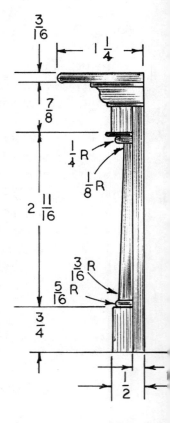

Fig. 3–89. First-floor fireplace

paper can be purchased from suppliers; color advertisements with marble motifs can be cut out and glued to the fireplace; samples of Formica or similar plastic counter top material can be cut and glued to the fireplace; actual marble cut to scale-sizes can be purchased from miniature suppliers or local stonecutters; or simulated plastic marble can be obtained from local bathroom or plumbing supply outlets.

Make the first-floor fireplace as suggested in figure 3–89. Install the finished fireplace over the interior rough opening in the side wall of the living room.

24. Make the bedroom mantel and fireplace as shown in figure 3–90. The whole fireplace is made of wood painted a color compatible with the bedroom wallpaper or a plain glossy white. The corner half-columns and rosette can be shopmade or purchased from miniature suppliers. Glue the finished fireplace over the rough opening in the second-floor, front-bedroom side wall.

25. Fit the front wall (complete with attached porch) in place. The top of the front wall will rabbet fit the front strip containing the cornice and sub-fascia pieces. Install the corner

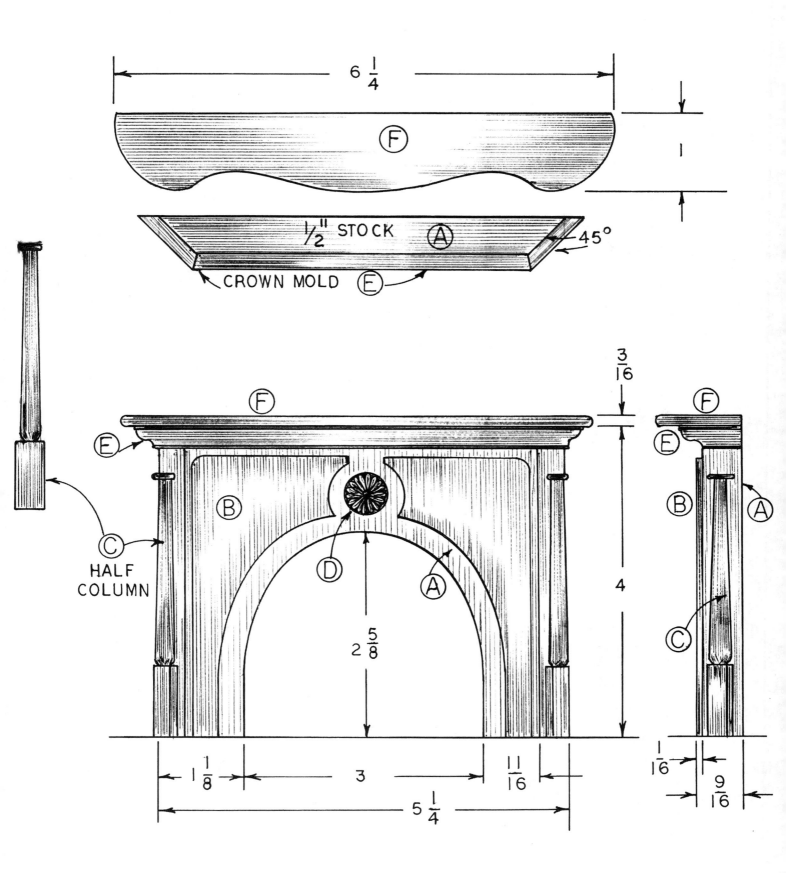

Fig. 3–90. Bedroom fireplace and mantel

323

Fig. 3–91.   Miniature fireplace

Fig. 3–92.   Side and floor units in place

Fig. 3–93. Cornice boards installed

Fig. 3–94. Roof completed

Fig. 3–95. Interior completed

Fig. 3–96. Exterior framed

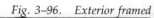

Fig. 3–97.   Front view

boards as suggested in figures 3–63 through 3–65. These corner boards will cover the plywood end-grains and the edges of the back piece. Fasten the bottom of the front wall piece to the side wall pieces with hooks and eyes or other suitable catches. Or, the front wall can be hinged as a large door.

26. If specific interior electrical lamps or fixtures are to be used in various rooms, wires must be run to feed such intentions. For example, the table lamps in the living room or bedrooms need wiring. Exterior feeding of such electrical fixtures does not allow much leeway for rearrangement of furniture; therefore extra care should be taken in selection of fixture placement.

The low-voltage feed wires are run into troughs cut into the house exterior walls with a router. The external clapboards will cover the pathways and the wires. The wire ends should exit in the attic space or in the chimney for connections with the low-voltage transformer. Test all connections before concealing the feed wires.

Fig. 3–98. Right-side view

27. Fasten all the exterior clapboards to the entire house walls. See figure 3–18 for detailing of this operation.

28. Remove the house front wall and finish the interior design work such as trim, wallpaper, and paint. There will be a small space created where the second-floor piece meets the front wall. This space will not have any wallpaper or paint, so cover it with a thin piece of clear stock or molding. Paint this piece plain white. When the front wall is in place, the piece will not show. When the front wall is removed or swung open, the white strip will not distract from the overall appearance. Paint the entire exterior white.

29. Install the bathroom fixtures and the kitchen and pantry cabinets. These units can be shopmade or purchased. The open rear wall gives ample access to these rooms. A full rear wall can also be used, if so desired. Such a wall will match the instructions given for the construction of the front wall. A window placed in the center of each room and a rear door in the kitchen area will be required.

30. Furnish the finished house with Victorian period furniture. Several suppliers offer such furnishings in a wide price range.

31. Install a 110-volt electrical feed line up the chimney to exit into the attic space. Connect a 12-volt transformer to this line and make all the low-voltage connections. See the chapter in Section one on electrical work.

Suppliers, Organizations, and Publications

20. *Miniature Supplies and Their Suppliers*

There are very few items of the past or present that are not produced by someone in miniature. Very often the problem is not that a special item is not made in $1/12$th scale, but rather finding who makes and sells the merchandise. Special hardware, electrical fixtures, complete building materials, period furnishings, silverware, wallpaper, and Tiffany glass are only a few of the products sold in miniature outlets. Thousands of businesses, both large and small, are devoted to miniature production. Some major outlets supply hundreds of different items, while smaller concerns specialize in a few choice offerings.

The following list of suppliers was developed to help readers obtain the supplies, tools, materials, and information required for their construction hobby. It is suggested that readers exhaust their local hobby, craft, or miniature outlets before turning to mail-order

purchases. With the growing popularity of miniature making, more and more local stores carry a complete line of building materials.

Some of the following companies listed are wholesale outlets. In this respect, they cannot honor individual retail requests. The X-acto, Houseworks, and Carlson companies fall into this wholesale category. Local craft outlets most often carry or can obtain the products of these companies for retail sales. Several of the mail-order concerns listed also carry a similar line of merchandise for retailing.

It is recommended that the reader have on hand any specialized building material or millwork before commencing work. Sizes will vary from manufacturer to manufacturer, and the miniature lay-out work should be based upon the peculiarities and dimensions of such materials.

Many of the following suppliers, both

Fig. 4–1. Miniature furnishings
(Courtesy DeShane Miniature Galleries)

cerns may not be listed only because their existence is unknown to me at this time.

MINIATURE MAKING SUPPLIES

(Check local concerns first for availability.)

Scale-Size Lumber

AMSI Miniatures
Bits and Pieces
Carlson's Miniatures
Childs, H. L.
Craftsman Wood Service Company
Midwest Products Company
Miniature House
Northeastern Scale Models Inc.
Rev-Model Products

Scale-Size Brick and Stone

AMSI Miniatures
Binghamton Brick Company
Childs, H. L.
Craft Products Company
Houseworks Ltd.
Holgate and Reynolds

wholesale and retail, offer catalogs of their wares at a nominal fee. These catalogs are an immense aid to the miniature builder. They offer a visual concept of the actual piece, and they list the overall and special sizes or dimensions required. Serious builders build up a library of such catalogs and have a wealth of information at their fingertips. Many local or regionalized miniature clubs and organizations have acquired a similar library of both retail and wholesale catalogs for their membership.

The following listings are not to be regarded as the final word on miniature making or suppliers nor as an unqualified endorsement of such company products. I do feel every concern listed is an honest, well-organized, reliable outlet. I have dealt with most of these merchants and found them to be most helpful. In the same respect, many worthwhile con-

Fig. 4–2. Miniature kitchen pieces
(Courtesy It's a Small World)

Fig. 4–3.   Wood shingles (Courtesy Midwest Products Co.)

J. Hermes Company
Mini Brick and Stone Company

Exterior Siding: Clapboard

AMSI Miniatures
Midwest Products Company
Northeastern Scale Models Inc.
S/W Crafts Inc.

Wood Shingles

Green Door Studio
Houseworks Ltd.
Midwest Products Company
Miniature Architectural Design
Northeastern Scale Models Inc.
S/W Crafts Inc.

Asphalt/Slate Shingles

AMSI Miniatures

Fantasy House Construction Co., Inc.
Mini Brick and Stone Company
What's Next? Inc.

Windows and Doors

AMSI Miniatures
Carlson's Miniatures
Chestnut Hill Studio Ltd.
Fantasy House Construction Co., Inc.
Favorites from the Past
Houseworks Ltd.
Northeastern Scale Models Inc.
X-acto House of Miniatures

Stained Glass: Tiffany Style

AMSI Miniatures
Carlson's Miniatures
Coachlight Studio
The Dollhouse Factory
Kummerow

Scale-Size Moldings

AMSI Miniatures
Carlson's Miniatures
Fantasy House Construction Co., Inc.
Favorites from the Past

Flooring

AMSI Miniatures
Carlson's Miniatures
Houseworks Ltd.
Midwest Products Company
Mini Brick and Stone Company
Northeastern Scale Models Inc.
Unique Miniatures
X-acto House of Miniatures

Fireplace Mantels

AMSI Miniatures

Bits and Pieces

Carlson's Miniatures
Colonial Craftsmen, Pewter Workshop Inc.
Houseworks Ltd.
It's a Small World
Mini Brick and Stone Company
The Miniature Mart
Unique Miniatures
X-acto House of Miniatures

Stairs (stringers, treads, risers, balusters, handrails)

AMSI Miniatures
The Calico Dollhouse
Carlson's Miniatures
Fantasy House Construction Co., Inc.
Houseworks Ltd.
Miniature Architectural Design
Northeastern Scale Models Inc.

Fig. 4–4.   Millwork and molding (Courtesy Houseworks Ltd.)

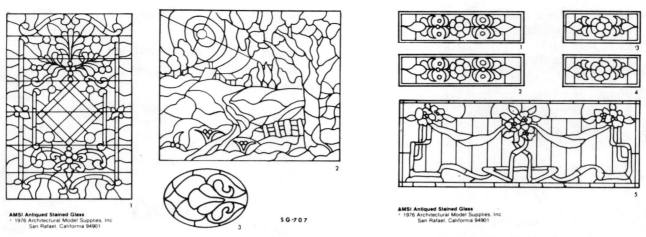

SG-707

Fig. 4–5. Stained glass (Courtesy AMSI Miniatures)

Fig. 4–6. Fireplace (Courtesy X-acto Co.)

Interior Millwork (casing, baseboard, moldings)

AMSI Miniatures
Carlson's Miniatures
Houseworks Ltd.
Northeastern Scale Models Inc.
Unique Miniatures

Wainscotting Panels

AMSI Miniatures
Carlson's Miniatures
Houseworks Ltd.
Northeastern Scale Models Inc.
Unique Miniatures

Lighting/Electrical Supplies

AMSI Miniatures
Cir-Kit Concepts Inc.
Clare-Bell Brass Works
Craft Products Company
The Dollhouse Factory
E-Z Lectric
Houseworks Ltd.
Illinois Hobbycraft Inc.
It's a Small World
Sonia Messer Imports
The Village Smithy

Wallpapers

AMSI Miniatures
Andrews Miniatures
Craft Publications Inc.
Favorites From The Past
J. Hermes Company
X-acto House of Miniatures

Hardware/Hinges

Aaron Supply Company
AMSI Miniatures
Colonial Craftsmen, Pewter Workshop Inc.

Craft Products Company
Houseworks Ltd.
Northeastern Scale Models Inc.
X-acto House of Miniatures

Specialized Supplies: China, Brass, Copper

Andrews Miniatures
AMSI Miniatures
Cards Etcetera
Childs, H. L.
Clare-Bell Brass Works
The Copper Corner
Kummerow
The Miniature Greenhouse

Tools

(Check local discount, craft, hobby, or hardware outlets first.)
AMSI Miniatures
Dramel Mfg. Company
Emco Lux Corporation
Illinois Hobbycraft Inc.
Sears. Stores or catalog.
X-acto House of Miniatures

Furnishings, Store Fixtures, Small Products

AMSI Miniatures
Andrews Miniatures
Bits and Pieces
Cards Etcetera
Carlson's Miniatures
Chestnut Hill Studio Ltd.
Childs, H. L.
Colonial Craftsmen, Pewter Workshop Inc.
The Copper Corner
Country Store Miniatures
The Enchanted Doll house
Favorites from the Past
Glass Blowers Workshop
Grandmother Stover's Inc.
Green Door Studio
Houseworks Ltd.

Fig. 4–7. Miniature table and chairs (Courtesy It's a Small World)

Illinois Hobbycraft Inc.
It's a Small World
Kummerow
Maxwell House Miniatures
Metal Miniatures
Mini Haus
The Miniature Mart
Miniatures By Elnora
Scientific Models Inc. (Realife Miniatures)
B. Shackman and Company
Tom Thumb Miniatures
Village Smithy
X-acto House of Miniatures

MINIATURE FIRM LISTINGS

Aaron Supply Company. 435 Benefit Street, Pawtucket, RI 02861

AMSI Miniatures, Architectural Model Supplies, Inc. P.O. Box 3497, 115-B Bellam Boulevard, San Rafael, CA 94902

Andrews Miniatures. Patrick Street, Ashland, VA 23005

Architectual Scale Models. 910 North 24th Street, Phoenix AZ 85008

The Beehive Studio, Inc. 826 Deerfield Road, Deerfield, IL 60015

Binghamton Brick Company. P.O. Box 1256, Upper Broad Avenue, Binghamton, NY 13902

Bits and Pieces. 6343 Goodman Drive, Merrian, KS 66202

The Calico Dollhouse. Route 130 and Quarry Lane, North Brunswick, NJ 08902

Calico Miniatures. 83 North Post Road, RD#1, Lawrenceville, NJ 08648

Cards Etcetera. 10 North Union Ave., Cranford, NJ 07016

Carlson's Miniatures. Route 1, Box 306, Delavan, WI 53115

Chestnut Hill Studio Ltd. Box 907, Taylors, SC 29687

Childs, H. L. 25 State Street, Northampton, MA 01060

Chrysnbon, 6553 Warren Drive, Norcross, GA 30093

Cir-Kit Concepts Inc. 612 North Broadway, Rochester, NM 55901

Clare-Bell Brass Works. P.O. Box 369, Southington, CT 06489

Coachlight Studio. P.O. Box 459, Hazelwood, MO 63042

Collector Miniatures Inc. RD #1, Quakertown, PA 18951

Colonial Craftsmen, Pewter Workshop Inc. 800 Wyman Park, Baltimore, MD 21211

The Copper Corner. 3904-52 Street, West Bradenton, FL 33505

Country Store. 111 Sandstone Drive, Rochester, NY 14626

Craft Incorporated. 1930 Country Street, South Attleboro, MA 02703

Craft Products Company. 2200 Dean Street, St. Charles, IL 60174

Craftsman Wood Service Company. 2729 South Mary Street, Chicago, IL 60608

William Dixon Company. 750 Washington Avenue, Carlstadt, NJ 07072

The Doll House, Inc. 375 Pharr Road NE, Suite 117, Atlanta, GA 30305

The Dollhouse Factory. 157 Main Street, Lebanon, NJ 08833

The Enchanted Doll House. Route 7, Manchester Center, VT 05255

Fantasy House Construction Company. 160 East Hawthorne Avenue, Valley Stream, NY 11580

Favorites From The Past. 2951 Harris Street, Kennesaw, GA 30144.

Glass Blowers Workshop. 1212 South Coast Highway, Laguna Beach, CA 92651

Grandmother Stover's Inc. 1331 King Avenue, Columbus, OH 43212

Green Door Studio. 517 East Annapolis Street, St. Paul, MI 55118

Holgate and Reynolds. 601 Davis Street, Evanston, IL 60201

Houseworks Ltd. 3937 Oakcliff Industrial Center, Atlanta, GA 30304

Illinois Hobbycraft Inc. 605 Broadway, Aurora, IL 60505

It's a Small World. 555 Lincoln Avenue, Winnetka, IL 60093

J. Hermes Company. Box 4023, El Monte, CA 92506

Kummerow. 16460 Wagonwheel Drive, Riverside CA 92506

Fig. 4–8. Miniature highboy (Courtesy X-acto Co.)

Maxwell House Miniatures. 310 Hillcrest Drive, Edinboro, PA 16412

Midwest Products Company. 400 South Indian Street, Hobart, IN 40342

Mini Brick and Stone Company. 343 Route 46, Fairfield, NJ 07006

Mini Haus. P.O. Box 43352, Cincinnati, OH 45243

Miniatures Architectural Design. P.O. Box 955, Lakewood, NJ 08701

Miniatures by Elnora. 205 Elizabeth Drive, Berrien Springs, MI 49103

Northeastern Scale Models Inc. P.O. Box 425, Methuen, MA 01844

S/W Crafts Inc. 600 East Western Avenue, Lombard, IL 60148

Scientific Models Inc. 340 Snyder Avenue, Berkeley Heights, NJ 07922

Shackman and Company. 85 Fifth Avenue, New York, NY 10003

Sonia Messer Imports. 527 West 7th Street, Los Angeles, CA 90014

Tom Thumb Miniatures. 1 Oak Ledge Circle, South Norwalk, CT 06854

Unique Miniatures. 6968 North Crawford Avenue, Lincolnwood, IL 60646

The Village Smithy. RD#5, Hemlock Trail, Carmel, NY 10512

What's Next? Inc. 1000 Cedar Avenue, Scranton, PA 18505

X-acto House of Miniatures. 43-35 Van Dam Street, Long Island City, NY 11101

21. *Organizations and Publications*

Miniature clubs and organizations have developed and grown as the hobby has grown. Some of these clubs are local, while others are national in scope. Many of these clubs send out newsletters or publications to aid miniature makers. The affiliated publications offer a fine listing of advertisers who have retail mail-order sales, plus they offer assistance in specialized craftwork. In addition to the national headquarters, these organizations have regional workshops, shows, or houseparties where enthusiasts can assist each other, as well as compare notes and work.

A listing of such organizations, plus the regional offices, are listed in this section.

As the miniature hobby has developed, so too have the requests for specialized information. Several bi-monthly, monthly, or yearly publications devoted to miniature making are now available. These publications are listed with their subscription offices. However, don't overlook regular specialized magazines such as *Yankee* or *Early American Life*. These publications can give readers period styles and information can be converted to a $1/12$th scale. Such publications carry full-size project patterns that can be the basis for perfect miniature reproductions.

PUBLICATIONS

Creative Crafts. Carsten's Publications, P.O. Box 306, Delavan, WI 53115

Miniature Gazette. National Association of Miniature Enthusiasts. Box 2621, Anaheim, CA 92804

Miniature Makers Journal. Miniature Publications. 409 First Street, Evansville, WI 53536

The Miniature Magazine. Carsten's Publications. P.O. Box 306, Delavan, WI 53115

Miniature Reflections. Miniature Publications, 409 First Street, Evansville, WI 53536

Mouse Squeaks. Elsie J. Snyder. 205 Elizabeth Drive, Berrien Springs, MI 49103

Nutshell News. Catherine B. MacLaren, P.O. Box 1144, La Jolla, CA 92038

The Scale Cabinetmaker. Dorsett Miniatures. P.O. Box 87, Pembroke, VA 24136

Small Talk Monthly. Joann Jones. Box 334, Laguna Beach, CA 92651

The Miniature Catalog. Boynton and Associates. Clifton House, Clifton, VA 22024.

MINIATURE ASSOCIATIONS

Many local areas have clubs and/or organizations devoted to miniature making and collecting. Such associations have many advantages, including magazines, workshops, houseparties, and possible adult miniature making classes.

Many worthwhile organizations sponsor miniature shows, displays, or exhibits. In these events, several hundred retailers maintain booths for general sales. Such exhibits are a storehouse of miniature building information. The shows are regional; therefore, dates and places are listed in many miniature publications for public information. The National Association of Miniature Enthusiasts (N.A.M.E.) has its main office at Box 2621, Anaheim, CA 92804. They offer individual or group membership. *Miniature Gazette* magazine is issued quarterly to members.

Glossary

Apron: a piece of horizontal trim or molding installed just under the window sill against the house wall. Also, a section of horizontal stock used to join furniture legs and support table tops.

Balusters: the smaller vertical decorative pieces installed on stairways to support the handrail. Most often installed two per stair tread.

Bank pin: a small ½-inch straight pin. Often called "sequin pin."

Batten door: a house door made up of individual vertical boards held together with horizontal and angle cleats called "Z" battens.

Bevel: see chamfer.

Blind hole: a hole drilled only part way through the stock.

Blind drill: to drill only part way through the stock.

Butt: a plain simple edge or right-angle joint where boards come together. Also, a term used for door hinges, i.e., butt-hinge.

Casing: the trim around a door or window, either interior or exterior; and/or the finish covering of a post or beam if boxed in.

Chamfer: to cut away the edge of a board on an angle.

Chuck: the end member of a drill that holds the cutting bit, usually with three jaws that open and close with a chuck-key. Also, a unit on a lathe that contains the turning stock, and/or a drill bit.

Circle template: a plastic sheet containing several circles of a given size. Example: 1/16-inch diameter up to 1½-inch diameter in units of 1/16 inch.

Copper flashing: sheet metal used to cover window or door jamb tops to prevent rain or water from entering. Also used to seal fireplace or chimney to a roof.

Corner boards: vertical boards secured to exterior house corners to make right angles. Very often used with clapboard that butts to the corner stock.

Cornice: exterior trim of a building at the meeting of the roof and walls. Contains the soffit, fascia, and any moldings or gutters.

Counterbore: where a larger hole is drilled over a smaller hole in order to fit a screw or bolt head below the surface.

Countersink: to cut the edges of a hole so as to fit the natural slope of a flathead screw and enable the screw head to fit flush or below the surface. Most often cut at a 60-degree angle.

Cyma curve: a profile made from part concave and part convex curves. Most often found in crown moldings.

Dado: a recess or U-shaped groove cut into one board so as to receive and support another board at a right angle.

Dado, blind: a recess or U-shaped groove cut into a board that stops short of the board's edge.

Dadosaw: a combination of two circular saw blades and

assorted cutter/spacers used to plough out various width dadoes.

Dentil (molding): a molding resembling small wooden blocks that project like a row of teeth.

Dowel: sized hardwood round stock. Example: ⅜-inch dowel would be ⅜ inch in diameter.

Escutcheon pin: a nail or pin with a round or decorative head.

Fascia arch: the horizontal top facing board on cabinet work that is cut into an arch.

Fascia, cornice work: the horizontal, outside face board. In cabinet work: the horizontal top face or trim board.

Finish nail: a series of nails that have a small head that can be driven in below the surface of the wood with any resulting surface indentation filled in.

Half-lap (brickwork): where one horizontal brick end joint meets halfway over the the adjoining brick courses.

Half-lap joint: where one half of a board's thickness is removed from the stock to be joined so that when the right angle is formed, each piece will contribute one-half the thickness allowing a larger surface for fastening.

Hip roof: a type of roof that rises from all four sides of a building with no gable end.

Jamb: the top and two sides of a door or window unit that comes in contact with the sash and/or door.

Jig: the construction of a pattern or frame used to hold stock in a fixed position during assembly. Most often used when several units of the same size and style are required.

Kerf: the slot or cut made by the saw teeth.

Lathe: a machine containing a head and tail stock used to support and turn material between these centers. Used to turn (cut) circular shapes or turnings. Very often contains a chuck or live center that turns the work, and a dead center that supports the stock at the other end.

Lathe chisel: a series of cutting chisels used to create turnings on a lathe.

Lathe turning: the stock cut on a lathe.

Millwork: the term used to describe products made in lumber mills or woodworking plants (moldings, door frames, window units, stairwork, fireplace mantels, and cabinets).

Miter: a right angle made up of two 45-degree angle cuts.

Miter joint: an angle cut joint where two members join each other, most often at a 45-degree angle. Used to join two irregular shapes such as moldings.

Molding, bed: a molding commonly used for right-angle meetings such as wall and ceilings.

Molding, cove: a molding with a concave profile.

Molding, crown: a series of moldings with part concave and part convex profiles.

Mortise: a hole or recess made to receive a tenon.

Mullions: the wood members or bars forming the division between window units.

Muntin: the vertical and horizontal members dividing a window sash into various size panes of glass. In a six-over-six window sash unit, the muntins divide the sash into six individual panes of glass.

Nail block: an extra block of stock installed in order to reinforce a joint.

Newel post: the main post at the start of a stairs holding the end of the handrail. Also used at landings or where the handrail starts or finishes without a supporting wall.

Pegged: where hardwood dowels are used to join wooden members together. Filling screw-head holes with pieces of hardwood dowels to resemble pegged effect.

Plumb: exactly perpendicular or vertical.

Rabbet: a recess or L-shaped groove cut into one board so as to join another board at a right angle.

Rake: the trim that runs parallel to the roof slope which forms the finish between the roof and the house side walls. Also, the peak angles of the roof.

Rake trim: the lumber making up the rake fascia and moldings used along the gable or peaked ends of a dwelling.

Rail: horizontal pieces of a door, window, or cabinet.

Re-sawed: where normal lumberyard stock is re-cut in order to achieve thin widths and/or thicknesses.

Ring-casing: a turned round ring installed at the top joints of door or window casing as a Victorian-style decoration.

Rip fence: a table saw fixture attached to the table top that allows ripping to a given size.

Router: small hand-held electrical tool that turns at a high rate of speed, using assorted bits and cutters to make molded edges, rabbets, or mortises.

Sash: the framework containing the window pane(s) and any muntins. Each double-hung window will have two sash units, top and bottom.

Self-edge corners: where house exterior corners are made with the actual siding materials, applied with overlapping butt or miter joints.

Side rake angles: the pitch of the dwelling roof peak.

Soffit (cornice): the flat, underside, horizontal trim members that fit between the house wall and the fascia boards.

Soldier course (brickwork): where bricks are laid on end in a vertical position.

Splay: to spread out, increase angle. The angle of a chair leg as it descends from the seat to the floor.

Stack (brickwork): to lay the bricks directly over each other without any normal bond or half-lap joints. The mortar lines will be straight horizontal and vertical.

Stringer (stair): The rough framing members that contain the basic cut-outs for the risers and treads. With an open stringer, the risers and treads are visable. With a closed stringer, the risers and treads are against a wall.

Stile: vertical side pieces of a door, window, or cabinet.

Stretchers: wooden members used to reinforce and hold legs at a proper distance from each other.

T-square: a tool used in drafting to create straight horizontal lines.

Tenon: in joinery, a male projection on the end of a wood member that fits into a female mortise.

Trammel: adjustable pot hook used to hold cookware from a fireplace crane.

Tri-angle: plastic tri-angles of any size. Used to make vertical lines in drafting. Most common, 45-degree and 60/30-degree angles.

Tri-square: A small square used in woodworking.

Whitesmith: a colonial or early American sheetmetal worker. One who works with brass, tin, copper, zinc.

Wainscotting: woodwork installed in dwellings on the interior walls in a vertical, horizontal, or raised panel construction. Most often installed only part way up a wall, to chair-rail height (30 to 36 inches).

Weather Gauge (Gage): a measurement cut into a scrap board to constantly measure siding exposure. Used mostly with clapboard to insure constant measurement across the length of the siding.

White glue: polyvinyl or white liquid glue.

Window glass: single-strength, clear glass.

Wobble blade: A saw blade mounted with adjustable slanted bushing to offset the blade angle so as to cut a pre-determined, wider than normal cut. Used for dadoes.

Index

Page numbers in italics refer to illustrations.

JOSEPH DANIELE has extensive experience in the field of woodworking. In addition to his popular and successful books, *Building Early American Furniture* (Stackpole Books, 1974) and *Building Colonial Furnishings, Miniatures, & Folk Art* (Stackpole Books, 1976), Daniele is the director of industrial arts at a large New England high school and teaches adult classes in miniature-making. Prior to his career as a teacher, he was a carpenter, cabinetmaker, and general contractor. Daniele is a frequent contributor to woodworking magazines.